COFFEE PLANTERS, WORKERS AND WIVES

Coffee Planters, Workers and Wives

Class Conflict and Gender Relations on São Paulo Plantations, 1850–1980

Verena Stolcke
Professor of Social Anthropology
Universidad Autónoma de Barcelona

St. Martin's Press   New York

First published in the United States of America in 1988

Printed in Hong Kong

ISBN 0-312-01693-X

Library of Congress Cataloging-in-Publication Data
Stolcke, Verena.
Coffee planters, workers, and wives: class conflict and gender
relations on São Paulo plantations, 1850–1980/by Verena
Stolcke.
p. cm.
Bibliography: p.
Includes index.
ISBN 0-312-01693-X : $30.00 (est.)
1. Coffee plantation workers—Brazil—São Paulo (State)—History.
2. Women coffee plantation workers—Brazil—Sã Paulo (State-
-History. 3. Coffee plantation workers' wives—Brazil—Sã Paulo
(State)—History. 4. Métayer system—Brazil—São Paulo (State)-
-History. I. Title.
HD8039.C6382B67 1988
305.5'63—19—dc19   87-30767
                                              CIP

To Da Cida, Da Alzira, Da Maria,
Da Antonia, Da Ditinha...and to
Isabel and Nuria

Contents

List of Figures

List of Tables

Preface

Coffee is the second commodity after oil in terms of pecuniary value in world trade. About half of the world's population are people who work in agriculture and over half are women. This book is about those people, both women and men, who with their work made Brazil the first coffee producer for the world market and provided the enormous wealth that allowed the country's industrialisation.

Coffee was introduced into Brazil in the early part of the eighteenth century. Initially it was consumed mainly domestically and in the coffee houses of major European cities. But as coffee consumption expanded rapidly with the Industrial Revolution so did production in Brazil. By the mid-nineteenth century coffee had become the country's principal export crop. Until 1880 the bulk of Brazil's coffee was grown by slave labour in the north, northeast and west of Rio de Janeiro, the Imperial capital. As the good lands in the Paraíba Valley became exhausted, coffee shifted south to São Paulo and large coffee estates progressively expanded westward in the province. By the 1890s São Paulo had become the world's main coffee export centre. By then also, São Paulo coffee was produced by free labourers hired in family units by the estates. These labourers worked under a distinctive task-and piece-rate system, the *colonato*, which combined work in coffee with self-provisioning and which persisted until the early 1960s when casual wage labour took its place.

This book is an anthropological history of changing productive relations on São Paulo coffee plantations. My aim is to rescue the dynamic element in this process, namely its subjects – planters and workers, women and men – who through their interaction, informed by specific goals and values, shaped the history of São Paulo coffee. History has often been written as a succession of events without people. Anthropology frequently tells about people without history. As I will show, only by investigating the complex interaction between class interests and cultural values which are shaped by and in turn themselves shape social relations is it possible to account for this history.

The historical meaning of the *colonato* system and the circumstances which gave rise to it on São Paulo coffee plantations and its extinction in the 1960s have been the object of much controversy. No history of São Paulo coffee existed until now, however, which traced the varying fortunes of the state's coffee bourgeoisie and the forms of labour exploitation they adopted under changing domestic and international conditions from the 1850s when São Paulo planters made the first experiments with free labour to the 1970s when the coffee sector at last lost its economic and political hegemony and wage labour became dominant on coffee plantations.

Historical studies of the *colonato* system generally end before or around 1929 under the assumption that coffee, and with it São Paulo's coffee bourgeoisie, lost out to industry thereafter. Coffee, however, remained Brazil's main foreign exchange earner until the late 1950s. Only when the country's exports became more diversified in the 1960s did the São Paulo coffee sector enter into political decline. Until then, official coffee policy coupled with unrestricted exploitation of labour under the *colonato* system ensured profitable coffee production despite recurrent crises and attest to coffee planters' lasting political influence. It is precisely by investigating the moments of change (both when the *colonato* system was introduced and later when wage labour took its place) and the politico-economic and ideological forces at play that an explanation for these transformations becomes possible.

Analyses of the transition to wage labour have focused mainly on the economic processes which are thought to have eventually succeeded in overcoming 'non-capitalist' productive relations. With the single, prominent, exception of Caio Prado Jr, the *colonato* system, like sharecropping, was seen as a stage in the transition to wage labour. Little attention was, however, devoted to the political conditions under which particular systems of labour use operated or the ways in which workers resisted their exploitation. By contrast, my aim in this book is to highlight the contradictions which I see as having been responsible for the constitution of the *colonato* system in the first place and for its substitution by wage and in particular casual wage labour more recently. Instead of interpreting the spread of wage labour as an almost necessary consequence of the 'capitalisation' of agriculture understood as an interaction between the nature of labour supply and progressive technification of production I inquire into the politics – that is the forms of domination of labour and the workers' resistance to it – which characterised productive relations at specific points in time, and I investigate the way in which these conditioned labour exploitation and changes in the production process.

This book, then, like a number of recent studies on the coffee economies in other Latin American countries,[1] is also set in the context of the debate on the dynamics of capitalist development in Latin American agriculture, firmly integrated into the world market. These studies have gone a long way in illuminating the class relations and conflicts that emerged as the moving forces in the formation of the coffee economies in the respective countries. What remains to explore further, however, are the historically specific reasons *why* the 'capitalisation' of agriculture took the forms it did in each case.

The Russian author, Bogdanov (1873–1928), was certainly not the only marxist to dispute the view of sharecropping as a stage in the transition to wage labour, though he was perhaps the first one. Many years later, in the 1960s, Caio Prado Jr and André Gunder Frank in Brazil and Martinez-Alier in Spain, questioned the idea of sharecropping as a 'semi-feudal' or 'non-capitalist' institution. Still some years later, in Paris and also in England, the investigation of systems of land tenure and of labour use began to be dominated by a concern with the 'articulation' of different forms of productive relations and with the 'formal' and 'informal subsumption' of labour to capital. As the debate grew in conceptual sophistication, the attention paid to the empirical study of exploitation diminished and a substantial point was lost – namely that the study of concrete forms of labour exploitation is useful to predict and take sides in the forms that class struggle in practice assumes. This book shows how the confrontation between the power of São Paulo coffee growers and the different modes of worker resistance to exploitation – at times individual, at other times collective and organised – provided the force that transformed productive relations on São Paulo coffee plantations.

However, neither the women or the men who produced São Paulo's coffee confronted or confront as individuals standing alone the planters who hire their labour. The generic 'worker' as a formally free individual is a particular, masculine category. Beside their class position the women and men are also part of family relations and responsibilities which shape their respective identities as workers.

In effect, one feature of the *colonato* system which has received hardly any attention is the exploitation of family labour. The *colonato* system, like sharecropping, is typically a family labour system. I do not share the simplistic view that interprets the institution of the family as a preconceived strategy of capital designed to reduce the cost of reproduction of labour. In this particular instance, São Paulo coffee growers were able to adopt a family labour system because of a pre-existing family structure and a set of moral values. Under the *colonato* system coffee growers exploited these moral values – only to threaten them later, when, as their control over labour was challenged, they opted for individual wage labour. A proper understanding of the *colonato* system and its replacement by wage labour requires an analysis of the links that exist between the larger politicoeconomic processes and the workers' family structure and ideals as well as their gender consciousness.

The unpaid and paid work of women plays as crucial a role in family reproduction now as it did then. But women's and men's status and behaviour in the workplace take specific forms which are related with their socially constructed gender roles. A man's social identity rests essentially on his ability to work, but women never cease to be first and foremost wives. Although labour has become individualised, even men's individuality as workers continues to be constrained by their commitments as family heads and breadwinners. Precisely because women and men, even when they work as individuals for a wage, do not cease to be part of a family – being thus part of a set of social relationships which entail specific roles and values – their class consciousness as workers is mediated by a gender consciousness. For this reason women and men experienced changing conditions of life and work in specific ways and gender relations with their meanings were challenged and new conflicts arose.

I began research for this book in the early 1970s at a time when the controversy over the spread of wage labour in Brazilian agriculture was reaching its peak. Typically for an anthropologist, I began with a field study of a gang of casual wage labourers who worked on a large coffee plantation. Most of these workers were women. My intention was to understand, through the workers' own life stories, the processes which had turned them into wage labourers as they perceived them themselves. Sider has recently suggested that if economic trends and political processes are made by people who conduct their lives in ways that create and invoke knowledge, then we need to investigate this knowledge which is socially based in its origin and in its effects.[2] Historical memory is then a social construct rather than a source of hard historical 'facts'. Present experiences inform the memory of the past as much as past experiences inform present perceptions, actions and reactions. However, it also soon became clear that the particular historical perceptions of these workers grounded in their experience as a class needed to be placed in the context of the larger economic and political processes fully to comprehend the contradictions which lent them force. At this point the collaboration of my friend and colleague, the historian Michael Hall, was invaluable. Nonetheless, it would not have been possible to understand the historical evidence on systems of labour exploitation without the insights the workers themselves provided. The way the workers perceived the surplus labour exploitation typical of the *colonato* system helped to explain why this system of labour use had persisted for so long. To the workers it was obvious, if not to many of those who have studied it, that an incentive wage system like the *colonato* was a more efficient way of labour use than wage labour. But despite the greater labour intensity it entailed, workers themselves preferred this system because the alternative, namely straight wage labour (by precluding self-provisioning and thus depriving them of the relative autonomy as regards the provision of their subsistence they enjoyed before) made them entirely dependent on the vagaries of the market. But if, as I suggest, the *colonato* system can be shown to be a particularly efficient form of labour use, then the replacement of *colonos* by wage workers in the early 1960s seemed to be an economic paradox. The dialogue between historical evidence and the workers' political memory and perceptions again provided the beginning of an explanation. However, the workers' memory served not only as a source of unrecorded evidence of past experiences. It also became an analytical tool with which to comprehend the class consciousness of today's workers which is not just a reflection of present material conditions but is also informed by their class-specific memories. Class consciousness is a historical phenomenon not only because it is subject to change but also because memories of forms of exploitation, grievances and hopes in the past form an inextricable part of today's sense of self-worth, class consciousness and struggles.

V.S.

Acknowledgements

This book has been in the making for a decade. Many people have helped and encouraged me in this task. My greatest debt is, however, with the women and men whose willingness to share their experience and knowledge of life and work in coffee made this book at all possible.

Throughout my research I taught anthropology at the Universidade Estadual de Campinas in São Paulo. The encouragement and support I received from my colleagues at the university provided a constant stimulus. I am especially grateful to Michael Hall, whose acquaintance with the early history of labour and coffee in the state enabled me to give the book its historical depth. Mariza Correa's concern for women contributed greatly to my appreciation of the true stature of the women in the gang. With Peter Fry I shared the experience of getting acquainted with as large and complex a country as Brazil. My students, in particular Armando Boito Jr, provided a critical audience for my initial attempts to make sense of my findings.

But a book must also be written. I found the tranquillity this requires at St Antony's College, Oxford. Malcolm Deas, Rosemary Thorp, Judith Heyer, Maria Antonieta Leopoldi and Jane Guyer read part of the manuscript offering very helpful advice and Jane Corbitt taught me some statistics to set my impressions on a more solid basis. The writing of this book was financed by the Wenner-Gren Foundation for Anthropological Research with some additional help from St Antony's College and the Gasparian Fund. My special thanks go to Selina Cohen for her editorial assistance.

Finally, the family is, indeed, a basic social fact. My two daughters, Isabel and Nuria, who shared part of my research experience, made a proper woman of me in the eyes of the workers thus facilitating communication with them. My mother helped me in gathering documentary evidence in the Swiss Archives. And Juan Martinez-Alier's knowledge of the political economy of rural labour provided one of the starting points for this book. I am grateful to them all.

V.S.

1 The Introduction of Free Labour on Saõ Paulo Coffee Plantations, 1850–90[1]

'The division of land among peasants after the abolition of serfdom [in Russia in 1861 was a] ... concealed form of selling labour power. The large landowner lets out his land in small plots in preference to conducting large scale cultivation himself, because in this way he obtains a larger quantity of work. It is easy to imagine how difficult the stage of transition of the peasant into wage labourer must be.' A. Bogdanov, *Short Course of Economic Science* (London, 1923) p. 297

As a country with abundant land and a relatively scarce population, Brazil confronted special problems in the creation of a labour force. Until the 1850s, slaves made up the bulk of the workforce needed by large-scale export agriculture. By the mid-nineteenth century, as slavery came under increasing attack, some São Paulo coffee planters began experimenting with free labour. The abolition of the slave trade in 1850 coincided with the expansion of coffee in western São Paulo, due to the decline of the other main coffee-growing region – the Paraíba Valley – and in response to the growing international demand for coffee. The introduction of free labour in São Paulo agriculture is an instance of the creation of a free labour force in a situation of extensive agricultural development under conditions of potentially scarce labour supply. 'Our soil offers unlimited wealth, but we lack labour' – this was the crucial obstacle which São Paulo planters faced in the second half of the nineteenth century.[2] The most forward-looking coffee planters clearly saw that a way of replacing slave labour, or at least supplementing it, would have to be found in order to provide the workers required for this very labour-intensive crop. Slavery continued until 1888, but it was precisely the increasing debate over the labour question, and the experimentation by São Paulo planters, which eventually made possible a relatively smooth transition to free labour.

1

In the absence of a readily-available local reserve of labour, São Paulo planters resorted to the use of immigrant workers. However, their experience with slaves had made them acutely aware of the need for effective forms of labour control. The issue planters faced throughout the second half of the nineteenth century was thus not only that of finding a new source of labour to replace the slaves, but also of how to organise and control free labour efficiently. This was both an economic and a political process, arising from the planters' pursuit of profit and from the bargaining power available to labourers to resist the planters' impositions.

In São Paulo, the absence of an established labour market decisively influenced the planters' choices of labour systems and their evolution. The early difficulties with free labour have been attributed to the relative unprofitability of immigrant workers in comparison to slaves,[3] yet what induced planters to introduce free labour in the first place was their increasing awareness that slavery was doomed. The more interesting initial question, then, is why planters first chose sharecropping as the labour system under which free labour was to be introduced, rather than a straight wage system or some other arrangement. The success of the labour systems chosen was not only determined by cost factors (in the narrow sense of the cost of obtaining immigrant labour), or even by the planters' ideology (their supposed 'backwardness' or, alternatively, their exemplary entrepreneurial spirit), but importantly by the confrontation of planters' actions and workers' responses which challenged labour discipline. The interaction between mechanisms of labour exploitation and patterns of labour resistance accounts for the transformations of the forms of labour contracting adopted.

SHARECROPPING

In 1847, Senator Vergueiro, the owner of a large estate near the town of Limeira, in the province of São Paulo, became the first planter to introduce immigrant labour for work in coffee production.[4] Vergueiro had foreseen that the end of slavery was only a matter of time.[5] Initially the immigrants seem to have been offered two kinds of contract: a sharecropping and a labour leasing (*locação de serviços*) contract, but they opted for the former.[6]

According to the sharecropping contract, the planter financed the immigrants' transportation from their country of origin to the port of

Santos, advanced the cost of transportation from Santos to the plantation as well as the foodstuffs and tools the immigrants needed until they could pay for them with the proceeds from their first crops. The workers would take care of an unspecified number of coffee trees and the planter granted them a self-provisioning plot in addition to a house, free of charge. Their pay consisted of half the net revenue from coffee and from the food crops. The labourers were obliged to repay the expenses incurred by the planter on their behalf with at least half of their yearly returns from coffee. The initial contract did not specify its length, but stated the amount of the debt owed by the immigrant on account of his transportation costs and other advances. For any amount outstanding after two years, the labourer was to be charged interest, which was to be the case with other advances after one year. Finally, the immigrants could not legally move off the plantation until they had repaid their debts. Should they do so, they incurred a substantial fine. Work was organised and supervised by the planter or his administrator.[7] The planters thus transferred all the expenses of obtaining immigrant labour to the labourers themselves, who started out already burdened by a substantial debt. It was generally expected that a diligent labourer with his family would take an average of four years to pay off his debt.[8]

In the early 1850s, a number of planters, impressed by the apparent success of the Vergueiro experiment and concerned with the effects of the recent termination of the slave trade, approached Vergueiro and Co. to obtain immigrant labourers for themselves. Contracts became more onerous for the immigrants. Not only did Vergueiro and Co. begin to charge a sizeable commission, to be debted to the labourers, but interest on debts was now charged from the date of arrival, sometimes at a rate of 12 per cent rather than the previous 6 per cent.[9] Moreover, the whole immigrant family was held liable for the debt, which was the way found by planters to protect themselves against losses in the case of the death of the family head.[10] Finally, while free labourers had initially been expected to process the coffee they harvested, by 1856 they were gradually relieved of this task, and instead were charged a fixed fee per unit of coffee harvested.[11]

By 1855 there were about 3500 immigrant labourers working on 30 plantations in the province of São Paulo. In most cases free labour existed side by side with slavery. All tasks beyond coffee cultivation and harvesting, and which were said to require constant supervision, or were inappropriate for sharecropping, continued to be executed by slaves. Such tasks included preparing the soil for various crops, sowing yearly crops for the plantation's consumption, planting new coffee, and the processing of coffee.[13]

Almost simultaneously, a further measure was introduced. In 1850 a Land Law was passed which consolidated private property rights and was intended to prevent immigrants from becoming landowners by settling on public lands.[14] The existence of vast expanses of unoccupied territory posed a serious obstacle to employing the scattered national population of free workers, who never formed a significant part of the plantation work force in the nineteenth century.[15]

The recruitment of immigrant labour required an initial investment by the planters and one of their concerns was to guarantee this capital investment.[16] For the immigrants, however, the initial debt weighed heavily on their income. Their returns from coffee cultivation turned out to be markedly lower than the stipulated 50 per cent. The consequences were far reaching.

The first serious sign of discontent among immigrant labourers came in mid–1856, when a group of Swiss workers revolted on the Nova Olinda plantation near Ubatuba. The trouble apparently started when cattle invaded their food plots, and disagreement over compensation led to the intervention of the police. Eventually, when the Swiss consul visited the plantation, the central issue became the general conditions of the immigrants: quality of food plots, fulfilment of contracts, housing, etc. Planters typically attributed the events to instigation by subversive elements. The conflict was finally resolved when the consul promised the immigrants that they would be transferred to a government colony, that part of their debts would be forgiven, and that no interest would have to be paid.[17] This conflict reveals the crucial points of contention between planters and workers.

The most important revolt, however, began in December 1856, among Swiss and German labourers on Senator Vergueiro's model plantation, Ibicaba. The presence of a Swiss school teacher, Thomas Davatz, contributed to converting the resentment of the immigrants into a movement of protest against what they felt were grave irregularities in the fulfilment of their contracts. They did not question the terms of the contract as such but protested against:

the calculation of returns from coffee produced, the charging of the commission, the unfavourable exchange rate used to convert their debts into local currency, the charging of transport from Santos to the plantation, and the strange division of profits from the sale of coffee.[18]

The revolt was sparked off by disillusionment with the previous harvest which, contrary to their hopes, did not allow the workers to reduce their debts. As Davatz later wrote, what he and his compatriots demanded was no more than just treatment.[19] The revolt ended when Davatz was expelled and some of the other leaders left the plantation. Many planters were terrified that the revolt would not only spread to free labourers on other plantations (a link with the earlier Ubatuba conflict was repeatedly suggested),[20] but worst of all might incite the slaves. One measure of the apprehension which the revolt produced was the accusation levelled against Davatz that not only was he in alliance with extraneous elements, but that he harboured communist and other terrible plots.[21]

This revolt and the frauds committed by planters which supposedly triggered it off are generally deemed to explain the failure of the sharecropping system under which the first immigrants were hired, and the alleged decline of interest among planters in the use of free labour.[22] But these irregularities (fraudulent measures, dishonest calculation of profits, etc.) only added to the growing disillusionment of immigrants with their living and working conditions. The planters, for their part, had not counted on the resources available to the immigrants in resisting what they considered unjust contractual conditions and impositions. The main difficulty was not the threat of possible reprisals from the immigrants' national governments, since protection was reluctant and limited at best.[23] Rather, the introduction of free labour required a capital outlay whose amortisation demanded a level of exploitation which the planters were unable to enforce. Under these circumstances the sharecropping contract proved inadequate for creating a reliable labour force.

Why then did São Paulo planters adopt the sharecropping system? It has long been maintained that sharecropping is less efficient than wage labour. Since sharecroppers receive only a part of the product they will allegedly stop work earlier than a wage labourer does.[24] More recently, the option for sharecropping has been attributed to its greater efficiency in risk dispersion.[25] In the case of São Paulo, Holloway suggested that uncertain conditions of coffee production and marketing induced planters to forgo some of the potential income which was exclusively theirs under slavery for it prevented the frightening possibility that wages might absorb more than the income from the crop.[26] But this interpretation conceals an important trait of sharecropping, namely the distinctive incentive features this system of labour exploitation contains. Sharecropping in a situation of expensive and scarce labour is in fact more efficient than wage labour, provided the employer has the political power to enforce a profitable share.[27] It is a form of labour use similar to a carefully negotiated piecework system, a way of securing extra effort from labour, of making labourers work harder and better for only a small increase in total pay over that of wage labourers. Remuneration in the form of a proportion of the product constitutes an incentive for the labourers to intensify their effort since it is on the amount produced that their returns will depend. They will cultivate with greater care, again because part of the result will accrue to themselves. In addition, the supervision required will be negligible, since control of work is exercised by the labourers themselves.[28]

Because of the absence of a local supply of workers, labour costs in São Paulo were, at least initially, high. Moreover, coffee is a very labour-intensive crop. Because of the incentive element characteristic of sharecropping it could be expected that sharecroppers would tend more coffee trees per worker than would wage labourers. Consequently, fewer workers would be required, and initial investment would be lower. Sharecroppers are usually hired in family units. Planters had always opposed recruiting single men since, they argued, immigrant families were less prone to abandon the plantation. This may be so but equally important was surely the fact that the immigrants' families constituted a cheap labour reserve.[29] A share-cropper will usually accept a division of the product that will not fully cover the potential market price of family labour, which would otherwise remain under- or unemployed. Planters, in fact, sometimes prohibited immigrants and their families from working outside the plantation.[30] The planter obtained this additional labour at a cost below that which he would have had to pay had he hired them on the market as wage labour. Since labour needs during the harvest were about one-fifth greater than during cultivation,[31] the workers' wives and children could satisfactorily cover this additional demand.

Labourers were also allotted a food plot on which they were expected to produce strictly what they needed for their subsistence and of which they had no effective possession. These plots were

usually located on marginal lands inappropriate for, or on virgin
land later planted in, coffee. Self-provisioning constituted a further
source of surplus labour appropriation also diminishing unit
labour costs.[32]

Because their unit labour costs in comparison with wage labour
were lower, sharecroppers must have initially appeared to the
planters as a very appropriate replacement for slave labour. The
incentive element must have seemed a satisfactory substitute for the
coercion which made slaves work. The question was not merely to
fill the potential gap in labour supply, but to do so in a profitable
way. Immigrants, however, were free workers. As sharecroppers, they
were in principle free to decide on labour intensity and the allocation of
labour. Their diligence and productivity in coffee, in fact, depended
on their own appraisal of returns. Planters and immigration agents
sought to create the illusion that immigrants would quickly be able
to repay their debts and acquire their own land. In practice, however,
immigrants usually had to wait for at least two years before receiving
significant returns for their efforts. The share to which they were
entitled from the first harvest took almost another year to be paid
because of delays in the marketing of coffee; but since the contracts
stipulated that half of the workers' annual earnings from coffee were
to be withheld to cover their debts, and in the meantime they had
accumulated new debts from further advances, only in the third year
could they expect to receive much cash.[33] It is hardly surprising that
the immigrants grew increasingly discontented.

The 1856 revolt remained an isolated event.[34] The majority of the
immigrants reacted in a less dramatic, but at the same time more
insidious, manner by systematically restricting output in coffee
cultivation. Planters soon grew concerned about the immigrants'
low productivity in coffee. As late as 1860, a government official
noted that:

> most plantations are not yet in a condition to receive free labour
> even under the sharecropping system, mainly when workers
> already start out burdened with a debt ... The transportation
> costs are excessive and consequently the labourers' share is
> insignificant ... The delay in the sale of coffee forces the workers
> to wait over eight months for payment ... As a consequence, the
> workers generally tend a reduced number of coffee trees, preferring
> to plant food crops to supply their homes and cover their needs, in
> addition to obtaining immediate benefit. Yet it is evident that this

system cannot be advantageous for the planter, whose main interest is coffee.[35]

The initial debt, even without arbitrary additional difficulties, discouraged any effort by the workers in coffee cultivation beyond what was strictly necessary. As another observer remarked:

> They [the labourers] abandon the coffee trees, which as a result do not produce but deteriorate, and the planter is deprived not only of his share in the product but also of that of the immigrant which is the only source of amortisation [of the debt] he has.[36]

The contract said nothing about the number of coffee trees a family had to tend. The size of the food plot was initially left to the decision of the labourers themselves. As immigrants lost hope in being able to repay their debts within the expected time, they were able to divert their labour to food crops, the returns of which accrued to them directly and immediately. Many observers remarked on the alleged laziness and lack of interest of the immigrants.[37] What happened in reality was an alternative allocation of labour to food crops, rather than the absolute underuse of labour capacity.[38]

Most of the immigrants in the early 1850s were rural or urban poor who were driven by the economic crisis in Central Europe to abandon their home country, in many cases as a matter of sheer survival. What they probably initially hoped for was to make a secure living.[39] Since the conditions they encountered in São Paulo made it almost impossible for them to obtain a profit from work in coffee, they preferred to dedicate a significant part of their efforts to food crops. As a result, productivity in coffee was low. As Carvalho de Moraes quite appropriately observed, 'the planters were at the mercy of the *colonos*'.[40]

The planters' power to control labour and to enforce a satisfactory level of productivity in coffee cultivation was limited by the absence of a local reserve of labour. Planters presumably thought that the incentive element contained in sharecropping would effectively replace market forces in reducing wage costs. However, the debt which resulted from the employers holding the immigrants responsible for paying the costs of passage and settlement cancelled out the incentive element, and the planters lacked any effective means of forcing their workers to produce coffee. The threat of dismissal, which is the usual form of persuasion used by employers to enforce labour contracts, was hardly practical since it would have meant the partial or total loss of the planters' investment. The immigrants could not legally abandon the plantation until they had paid off their debts, but neither could the planters make them work beyond what the labourers themselves were willing to do. Even the use of state power, as in the case of the Ibicaba revolt, was of little avail. The leaders of the revolt were expelled, but those who remained did not work any harder. The use of extra-contractual means to amortise their investments had backfired:

> it is incontestable that the planters, when the labourers would not work, could not enforce the fulfilment of their obligations and thus suffered harm from the mistreatment of their coffee trees, the reduction of the harvest, and the total or partial loss of their advances.[41]

THE LABOUR-LEASING CONTRACT

After 1857 the sharecropping system was gradually abandoned in São Paulo. The number of immigrants engaged in coffee cultivation during the next two decades declined only slowly. Reports reaching Europe on the immigrants' hardships eventually persuaded both the Swiss and Prussian governments to take severe measures which practically halted emigration from the two countries to São Paulo.[42] Nevertheless, in 1870 it was estimated that approximately 3000 free labourers – some of them Brazilians – still worked on the plantations, a decline of about 500 since 1860, and the debate over possible solutions to the labour problem had not abated.[43]

Many planters continued to explore alternative labour systems and to devise institutional safeguards which they hoped would allow for a more effective enforcement of contracts. In order to deal with the related problems of control of productivity and amortisation of debt, sharecropping was gradually replaced by a labour-leasing contract. Instead of a share of the value of production, labourers were paid a pre-established rate for each measure of coffee produced. By reducing uncertainty over income and eliminating long delays in payment, it was argued, labourers would feel encouraged to apply themselves with greater diligence to coffee cultivation.[44] In addition, the size of the food plot was fixed and/or let against a rent in an attempt to discourage immigrants from diverting labour to food crops.[45] Free labourers also ceased to participate in coffee processing, either directly or through a fee. This task reverted to slaves until the 1880s, when it was then carried out by wage labour. Significantly, it was this stage in coffee production, as well as transportation, which were rapidly mechanised in the early 1870s as slave labour became increasingly problematic.

Labour-saving innovations were not, however, introduced in coffee cultivation. Mechanisation of the harvest was technically infeasible, and the mechanisation of weeding by the use of a cultivator would have more severely seasonalised labour demand, either producing excess labour during the cultivation period, or a shortage for the harvest in a situation of scarcity of free labour.[46]

The labour-leasing contract continued to provide payment by results, but it still could not assure an adequate level of productivity because it did not resolve the basic problem of debt as a disincentive. Planters, in fact, felt they lacked legal powers to protect themselves against the non-fulfilment of contracts and specifically the non-payment of the debt.[47] The law regulating sharecropping was largely ineffective. It allowed planters only to rescind the contract or to demand compensation for damages; the former implied loss of the immigrants' debt, and the latter increased the debt without, however, providing the means to oblige labourers to work to pay for it.[48]

Occasionally, planters also tried to apply to sharecropping a law of 1837 regulating labour-leasing contracts. According to this law, any labourer who, having been dismissed, did not pay his outstanding debt, could be jailed and condemned to public works until he had paid up. In cases of abandonment of the plantation, he was to be arrested immediately and not released until his debts had been paid.[49] The applicability of this law to sharecropping had proved uncertain.[50] A further reason for planters to prefer the labour-leasing contract was surely their desire to avail themselves of the more severe penal sanctions contained in the 1837 labour-leasing law.

However, there is little evidence that even the 1837 law was ever widely applied. The contracts had not usually stipulated a fixed period for the amortisation of debt and, in any case, the use of the law to press for repayment did not secure the planters' primary objective, which was to achieve greater productivity of labour in coffee. As long as the immigrants were willing to remain on the plantation, there was little the planters could do to make them work, short of outright coercion, which they knew could produce untoward results.

Productivity in coffee continued to be low.[51] Carvalho de Moraes published a survey of families resident on the plantation Martyrios in 1869, the property of Senator Francisco Antonio de Souza. Labourers were hired under the labour-leasing system. The survey contains data on the size and composition of the families and on the number of coffee trees tended by each. It is thus possible to calculate the number of trees cultivated per family and per labourer by the consumer/worker (c/w) ratio of the family (see Table 1.1).

Table 1.1 Number of coffee trees tended per family and individual labourer by consumer/worker ratio of the family, Plantation Martyrios, 1869

c/w ratio	1.0–1.4		1.5–1.9		2.0 and over	
	Per family	*Per worker*	*Per family*	*Per worker*	*Per family*	*Per worker*
Trees tended	2109	566	2071	709	1940	813
Number of families	11		7		5	

Source: Carvalho de Moraes, *Relatório apresentado*, Appendix 17. That with increasingly more favourable consumer/worker ratios (1.0–1.4) the number of trees tended per family should rise is because those families generally contained a larger absolute number of workers.

The average number of coffee trees a labourer cultivated varied from 566 to 813 trees. The larger the productive capacity of the family (families with a c/w ratio between 1.0 and 1.4) the smaller the number of trees tended by each worker in it. The overall production intensity per labourer was low, especially when compared to the usual average of 2000 to 3000 trees tended from the 1890s onward by workers who were also producing food crops at the same time. Moreover, families that had the comparatively largest productive capacity exerted themselves least in coffee cultivation. And the quality of work appears to have deteriorated under the labour-leasing contract. In general, piecework is not used for many agricultural tasks because the quality of work suffers. Under the labour-leasing contract, while the immigrants were keen on harvesting as much coffee as possible, they tended to be negligent in weeding.[52]

ABUNDANT LABOUR, CHEAP LABOUR

The decade of the 1870s had begun amid predictions of an impending labour crisis, both in terms of future supply and of labour control. Planters attempted to deal with the situation in several ways. Many continued to introduce free labour on a limited scale, though privately sponsored schemes had lost most of their appeal.[53] Moreover, planters' faith in this system of immigration was further shaken by a new outbreak of labour conflict on some plantations run with free labour.[54] At the same time abolitionist agitation was growing, especially after the 1868 Manifesto of the Liberal Party which called for an end to slavery. Pressure thus mounted for a comprehensive solution to the labour problem.

Nevertheless, coffee production during the 1870s expanded to almost twice what it had been in the previous decade.[55] In fact, planters were still able to postpone until 1888 the effective end of slavery. They temporarily solved the anticipated labour shortage by generally rationalising coffee production. They managed to disarm the abolitionists with a limited concession: the Rio Branco law of 1871 which declared that children born of slave mothers were to be free.[56] Planters also continued to purchase substantial numbers of slaves from the Rio de Janeiro region and from northern Brazil.[57] The great expansion of railroads in the coffee-growing areas which took place in the 1870s also helped postpone an acute labour shortage. It allowed planters to reassign to other tasks the slaves they had previously had to use in transporting their crop to market.[58] Moreover, by lowering the cost of transportation and reducing the damage the crop suffered in transit, the railroad helped compensate the planters for rises in the cost of slave labour.

The introduction of labour-saving machinery in the coffee industry was another important element in forestalling the crisis.[59] José Vergueiro, Senator Vergueiro's son, perhaps best exemplified the spirit shown by the more astute planters when he remarked in 1874 that 'saving labour is the principal objective which we must always have in mind since, if time is money, the saving of labour is also'.[60] Coffee production on the plantations run by slave labour, still the large majority, became generally more rational. As one São Paulo official put it, not only had the introduction of machinery 'profitably replaced a good part of the work force', but 'the direction of the workers has become more intelligent, and the division of labour has been put into practice'.[61]

Although São Paulo planters managed to cope with their labour needs quite successfully during the period, the issue of negotiating the transition from slavery to free labour became increasingly urgent.[62] It was the old problem: Brazil 'possesses the best climate in the world, almost all the precious metals and a prodigiously fertile soil, but lacks population and for that reason is poor'.[63]

At the 1878 Agricultural Congress, called by the government to evaluate the general state of agriculture, one group of planters opposed large-scale immigration as a solution to the labour problem because of its costs to themselves or to the country. They demanded, instead, laws to combat the alleged aversion of the local population to work. They sought means of disciplining *agregados* and of forcing work from *ingénuos*, as well as provisions to tighten the 1837 law regulating labour-leasing contracts.[64] In the end this position was to be overruled by those planters who believed that reliance on former slaves after abolition, or on the available local population, would be highly problematic, and who saw in subsidised mass immigration the only solution.

Similarly unsuccessful were also those who from the start, when a replacement for slavery was being sought, had warned of the perils of mass immigration and had advocated the establishment of government or privately sponsored settlements of smallholders. They saw in smallholder colonisation not only a way of solving the labour problem, as some planters did, but also through the creation of a peasantry a solution to the country's social and political ills. The Central Society for Immigration (*Sociedade Central de Imigração*) founded in 1883 mainly by non-planters, European merchants and intellectuals, condemned the large 'latifundia' which they felt must inevitably come to be replaced by small farms. The short-sightedness and boundless ambitions of the planters were causing economic backwardness and social polarisation. As José Vergueiro, whose own high hopes for the recruitment of European labourers directly for the plantations had been sadly disappointed, argued in defence of what he called 'spontaneous immigration', a policy of government sponsored settlements would not only increase the population, provide labour for agriculture, raise the value of land

and lead to the proliferation of smallholdings and the expansion of crops, it would, in addition, benefit 'national virility by crossing of the races so necessary to the nation'.[65] A few government sponsored colonies were eventually created and planters occasionally paid lip service to the establishment of smallholdings, but for the most part, they were sceptical about the efficacy of a peasantry as a labour reserve for the plantations.[66]

Before those planters who demanded subsidised immigration finally succeeded in forcing the state to assume full responsibility for mass immigration, the government made a last attempt to relegate this task to the planters themselves by granting them some additional legal powers to discipline the increasingly unruly free labourers. In 1879, the 1837 labour-leasing law was replaced by a new regulation covering both labour-leasing and sharecropping contracts and providing prison sentences not only for abandoning the plantation without just cause but also for strikes and incitement of others to strike through threats or the use of violence.[67] This law was surely not least the result of renewed outbreaks of labour unrest on some plantations. Almost simultaneously with the Agricultural Congress, the Tyrolean labourers on the plantation Salto Grande in Amparo, owned by Joaquim Bonifacio do Amaral, went on a much publicised strike [68] at the onset of the coffee harvest in protest over a number of abuses and omissions of which they felt they had been the victims.[69] It was feared that the strike might spread to other estates. Although the planter raised the piece-rate from 500 reis per *alqueire* of coffee harvested to 600 reis, and agreed to charge interest on outstanding debt only after two years, the labourers could not be persuaded to resume work. The owner then stopped providing foodstuffs, a well-known means of forcing labourers back to work, and at the same time had the leaders prosecuted and condemned to prison sentences for non-fulfilment of contract under the 1837 law.[70] These events seem to have convinced even such a staunch defender of privately sponsored immigration as Amaral of the urgent need for subsidised mass immigration, although he still insisted that more severe laws to enforce contracts were equally necessary.[71]

Other São Paulo planters, in contrast, emphatically demanded that labour contracts be liberalised and legal reforms introduced as prerequisites for a successful programme of government sponsored immigration, which they regarded as the only solution to the labour problem. The relatively low coffee prices of the early 1880s, and the difficulties planters faced in securing credit, acted as further deterrents to privately sponsored immigration, since they left many planters unable or unwilling to advance passage money to immigrants.[72] On the other hand, the 1879 law was largely ineffective and even counter-productive. As Antonio Prado, one of the most prominent São Paulo planters, noted, immigrants in jail were neither repaying the planters' loans nor harvesting their coffee, and in addition the law only served to discredit Brazilian colonisation in Europe. Prado further observed that the law would soon become unnecessary in any case, at least in São Paulo, since the Assembly of that province had approved a measure in 1884 providing free passage for immigrants who went into agriculture.[73]

Planters became generally aware that 'it is impossible to have low salaries, without violence, if there are few workers and many people who wish to employ them'.[74] The way out of this dilemma and the essence of the São Paulo immigration system, was explained by another member of the Chamber of Deputies shortly after abolition: 'it is evident', he said, 'that we need labourers . . . in order to increase the competition among them and in that way salaries will be lowered by means of the law of supply and demand'.[75]

By the early 1880s abolition had become unavoidable. A comprehensive solution had to be found. The São Paulo planters, whose power in the government had been increasing steadily, finally succeeded in imposing their solution to the labour problem. Although more than two years and several important modifications of the law providing for subsidised immigration were required before the system functioned satisfactorily, Prado was essentially correct in affirming that the problem had been solved by the mid-1880s. After 1884, the state sought to obtain cheap and obedient labour for the plantations by flooding the labour market with subsidised immigrants. By 1886 the provincial government had found an effective way of providing complete subsidies for immigrants, and the result was almost immediate. By May 1887, some 60 000 to 70 000 immigrants, by now predominantly Italian, had already been placed in the agricultural establishments of São Paulo.[76] This figure exceeds the estimated 50 000 slaves who were being used on São Paulo coffee plantations in 1885.[77] Immigration policy remained essentially unchanged until the First World War. Between 1884 and 1914, some 900 000 immigrants arrived in São Paulo, mostly as cheap labour for the coffee plantations. The immigration programme allowed São Paulo planters not only to abolish slavery with only moderate inconvenience, but the scheme – aided by initially high coffee prices – also created the conditions for sustained expansion of coffee production. Between 1888 and 1902 the number of coffee trees in São Paulo increased from 221 million to 685 million.[78]

Planters had previously encountered two difficulties with free labour – the debt and labour discipline. Since planters no longer had to advance passage money to immigrants and were assured of an abundance of fieldhands by the state, the 'shameful' 1879 law fell into disuse and was finally repealed in 1890 because 'among the economic measures most strongly demanded by the present state of the country is the need to populate it, since public wealth develops in direct proportion to the increase in population'. Contracts henceforth should be 'acts of pure convention based on mutual agreement, which elevate the labourer to the category of partner in the contract'.[79] The 1879 law, however, had not only served to enforce debt repayment, but also prohibited strike action. Among other liberal reforms of the period was one replacing the 1879 provisions with a decree on so-called 'crimes against the freedom of work' which penalised the inciting of either labourers or employers to increase or reduce work or wages through the use of threats of violence.[80] Planters did indeed employ coercion and violence to keep labourers on the plantations and to extract profit, but in general they came to deal with the problem of keeping down labour costs by increasing supply. Extra-economic coercion, which was at times substantial, served essentially to improve the planters' bargaining position in the labour market.

Even after the 1880s, planters regularly claimed that there was a shortage of agricultural labour in São Paulo. There are, however, indications that these laments were debating points to press for continued mass immigration so as to assure the low wages the planters wanted to pay. For one thing the two alternative sources of labour (the freedmen and so-called national labour) were never tapped in any substantial way before the First World War, when subsidised European immigration became impractical. Both these groups were largely ignored by the planters even during alleged labour shortages.[81] Moreover, agricultural wages varied little between 1884 and 1914,[82] even at times when complaints over labour shortages became particularly vehement.[83]

THE *COLONATO*

Those planters who still worked their plantations with free labourers by the late 1860s had gradually introduced further adjustments in the labour contract. Some planters had begun to apply a new form of remuneration, a mixed task and piece-rate system, the *colonato*. Coffee weeding was now paid for at a fixed annual rate per thousand trees tended, and the harvest at a piece-rate.[84] By paying a separate set rate for weeding, a sort of fixed minimum wage[85] which assured the labourers a stable income independent of coffee yields, it was hoped that workers would cease to neglect the coffee groves during the off season. In addition, since part of the labourer's pay under the new contract depended directly on the number of trees tended it could be assumed that they would feel encouraged to cultivate a larger number of trees. By maintaining the piece-rate system for the harvest, however, labour costs could still be adapted to annual fluctuations in yields.

Food plots were now allocated in proportion to the number of trees tended by the family. In this way, the aim of extracting a labour rent in addition to the surplus produced in coffee cultivation was achieved without the peril of jeopardising work in coffee.[86] Bonardelli in 1916 estimated that food crops grown by labourers made up one third of their income.[87] The combination of cash crops with self-provisioning by the labourers could pose problems for the planters – as late as 1922 planters stressed the need to restrict food crops since 'the landowner cannot permit that labourers plant extensively cereals when labour is lacking for coffee cultivation'.[88] However, if effectively controlled the arrangement was very advantageous. Since food crops were grown during the coffee cultivation season when labour demands were comparatively lower, the planters could make full use of the immigrants' family labour throughout the year.

A final way the planters devised to reduce unit labour costs was their declared preference, not only for families, but for large families, i.e. units containing at least three workers.[89] The more workers per consumers there were in a family, the lower the cost of reproduction of each individual worker and consequently the lower the task-rate could be.[90]

Subsidised mass immigration reduced initial labour costs drastically. Advances for food and agricultural tools were now minor. On the other hand, without the burden of the initial debt and with the enforcement (owing to the abundant labour supply) of stricter regulation of work and of fines for non-execution of tasks which began to be applied already in the 1860s, labour productivity in coffee increased markedly. By the late 1880s the average number of coffee trees tended by an adult man ranged between 2000 and 3000, while women usually cultivated half that number.[91]

Planters continued hiring immigrant labour under the mixed task and piece-rate system coupled with subsistence production which was to prevail until the 1960s. Food prices were persistently high at the time since foodstuffs were to a large extent imported as a consequence of the planters' almost exclusive interest in coffee.[92] As the President of the province noted in 1887: 'Coffee gives the best returns . . . it would be an error to disdain it in order to cultivate something else'.[93] Even with an abundant labour supply, the *colonato* system continued to be more profitable than straight wage labour.

The obstacles to more than sporadic individual resistance to growing exploitation were immense, and planters did what they could to suppress any expression of discontent. Observers sometimes remarked on the *colonos* 'submissiveness, respectful and docile' behaviour, although this was often more apparent than real.[94] All societies or associations of labourers were prohibited.[95] Yet, despite severe control, individual labourers were often turbulent and sometimes violent, and strikes occurred with some frequency.[96] From the beginning the relations between planters and free labourers were fraught with rather explicit tensions. Even had the planters desired to establish paternalistic relations of personal dependence – and the point is arguable – a number of factors limited the ready use of such mechanisms. Not only were São Paulo plantations large, but the work force was both new and foreign born, thus depriving the planters of many of the traditional sanctions – religious and otherwise – which rural ruling classes have often enjoyed.

As long as sharecropping prevailed, struggle between labourers and planters centred around the share in net revenue from coffee. Exceptionally, labourers revolted, but more generally they resisted by withdrawing labour from coffee cultivation. As long as food growing was not subject to systematic restraints, the labourers were able, without jeopardising their own survival, to deprive the planters of part of their labour power, diverting a significant part of their productive capacity to food growing, beyond what they required for subsistence. Though essentially individual, these actions were decisive in determining the readjustment of the labour system.

The transition from sharecropping to the mixed task and piece-rate system, the *colonato*, was a process of increasingly systematic exploitation of labour, aided after the mid-1880s by the massive importation of immigrants. Once a capitalist labour market had been created, planting rights restricted to the basic minimum, and increasingly severe labour discipline instituted, conditions effectively disappeared for individual struggle at the level of work against what were considered unsatisfactory returns. By the turn of the century immigrant labourers constituted a homogeneous mass, subject to more or less uniformly harsh conditions. Under normal circumstances they had the possibility of moving to the coffee frontier or of abandoning agriculture altogether either for work in Brazilian cities or in Argentina. Labour mobility among plantations and outright departures were considerable. But for those who remained in agriculture, low wages or any additional exactions by planters, such as the non-payment of wages, the prohibition of food growing, or a reduction in wages, could trigger off collective action in the form of strikes. By increasing labour discipline, planters had contradictorily created the conditions for collective – and thus potentially much more damaging – action by the immigrants.

CONCLUSION

Most of the analyses which centre around the failure of the sharecropping system argue that in the last instance it was the planters' own backwardness that condemned the early sharecropping experiments – that planters resorted to forms of coercion that were unacceptable to the free labourers who, in turn, reacted by rebelling. The implicit conclusion is that planters did not know where their true interests lay. They revealed themselves incapable of appreciating the requirements of a contractual relationship, an incapacity derived from their long tradition as slaveholders.[97] By using coercion rather than economic incentives, they undermined the labour system they themselves had chosen as a replacement for slavery.

These interpretations contain a mixture of elements from both the 'feudal' and capitalist theses. The early sharecropping system is implicitly interpreted as capitalist, but its failure is generally attributed to the planters' traditional ideology which led them to treat free labourers as if they were slaves.

I have argued that São Paulo planters introduced free labour to replace or add to their slave force because the most forward-looking of them were aware by the middle of the century that some substitute for slave labour eventually had to be found. Under these cirumstances, they were willing to experiment with new forms of labour, the productivity of which they initially did not know. However, only a minority of São Paulo planters opted for free labour at the time, and the end of slavery was not immediate. Thus there was no acute shortage of slaves, and planters could continue to staff their plantations with slave labour, whose productivity was familiar to them, in case free labour did not respond to their expectations. Not only those who have studied the early experiments with free labour, but also the planters themselves, repeatedly attributed the difficulties with free labour to its relatively low productivity in comparison to slavery. It may be true that slaves were more profitable than free labourers, but to go back to slavery was no permanent solution. Thus to explain the failure of the sharecropping system by its comparatively lower productivity would be reasonable only if it were not for the impending abolition of slavery. The spectre of abolition left planters with, in fact, only two alternatives: either to find a satisfactory substitute form of free labour, or to abandon coffee cultivation altogether.

The planters who initially took it upon themselves to find some replacement for slave labour were the first of a remarkable group of agricultural and commercial entrepreneurs. They viewed labour as a cost and adopted a labour system – sharecropping – which they thought would assure them a cost per unit of output lower than that of straight wage labour, rather than comparing this with slave labour. That some of them became disenchanted with the experiment and temporarily returned to slave labour was due fundamentally to the absence of one essential prerequisite, a surplus population of free labour which would have kept their workers intimidated and subjected to exploitation. But under the circumstances, neither economic incentives contained in the sharecropping contract, nor fraud and occasional coercion, succeeded in assuring a profitable and reliable labour force. The immigrants either systematically restricted the output of coffee and/or they rebelled, which led some planters to conclude that 'at the cost of any sacrifice the work of a slave is preferable to that of a free man'.[98] Others attempted to resolve their labour problems by introducing contract changes and more effective labour laws, yet with scarcely greater success. The permanent problem of labour productivity and discipline was resolved only in the 1880s when the state began to subsidise mass immigration and thus lay the foundations for an effective capitalist labour market.

The vast and growing literature on the history of Brazilian agriculture[99] has tended to apply macro-models to the plantation labour systems examined in this chapter rather than posing the crucial question of why planters opted for the various arrangements in the first place. Insufficient attention has thus been paid to the conditions under which free labour was introduced, to the dynamics of the labour systems themselves, and to the reasons for their transformation.

In part, recent debates have continued the long dispute about the supposed feudal, or at least non-capitalist, nature of Brazilian agriculture.[100] The implicit point of reference for both the 'feudal' and 'capitalist' interpretations is straight wage labour as the characteristically capitalist form of surplus labour appropriation. Those who endorsed the feudal thesis emphasised the distinctive features of the plantation labour systems as proof of the non-capitalist nature of Brazilian agriculture.[101] Those who supported the capitalist thesis generally took as their point of reference the larger economic system into which Brazilian agriculture was integrated and argued for the underlying identity between the specific labour systems used and wage labour. While such authors explained the prevalence of these systems by their greater productivity in contrast to wage labour, they still did not account for their transformations.

More recently, yet other interpretations have been proposed to account for the productive relations which have for so long characterised Brazilian agriculture. One position has argued that from the perspective of capital accumulation, these productive relations in agriculture were functional for the economy because they benefited capital accumulation in industry through relatively low prices for agricultural commodities.[102] This view has been contested with the argument that low agricultural productivity, on the contrary, set distinct limits to accumulation: in reality, the relatively low prices of agricultural products imply high 'social costs' and relatively low 'social productivity'.[103] From this perspective, the articulation of the the two sectors of the economy is seen as contradictory, a contradiction produced by the relatively low level of productivity in agriculture on account of what are interpreted as predominantly pre-capitalist or backward productive relations. Productivity in agriculture is indeed lower, in money terms, than in industry. But again, why planters should have for so long opted for low productivity rather than adopting more productive innovations is not explained. It seems reasonable that planters should prefer cheap labour-intensive methods of production rather than increasing fixed capital. But this posits the question of why the cost of labour was so low for so long. Low agricultural wages imply a restriction in the consumption of wage goods, but then why should planters be concerned with that, rather than with their own levels of profit? Such an attitude has important political consequences for it generates social tensions, but then capitalist development is hardly a harmonious process.

An analysis of the particular form taken by productive relations under concrete historical circumstances is relevant for historical understanding in so far as it helps to throw light on the nature of the contradictions which generate change. The advance of capitalism is not determined by the logic of capital accumulation as a kind of *deus ex machina* but, as has been shown in the specific case of São Paulo coffee plantations, by the specific form of class struggle it entailed. Resistance by labourers to the rate of surplus labour appropriation imposed by planters, produced readjustments in the form of labour exploitation which, in turn, created new forms of struggle.

2 The Symbiosis of Coffee and Food Crops

'If monoculture is an evil, this was not so with coffee. Coffee was autarkic; it demanded for its cultivation the simultaneous production of the most varied crops, even cattle raising. These were subsidiary crops, no doubt, but their total production was voluminous. It was cheap production, because it was an accessory that offered the people abundant and healthy food.' Bento A. Sampaio Vidal, Federal Deputy for the Democratic Party of São Paulo, and President in 1935 of the *Sociedade Rural Brasileira*, *Revista da Sociedade Rural Brasileira* (September 1940) p. 13

'I must say that together with my sons we produce one hundred thousand bags of coffee per year and hand over twenty thousand to the 'sacrifice quota' for incineration... This is my profit, to reduce the coffee available and to sell the remaining 80 per cent at a better price... To retain coffee is always a ghost on the market and its expenses absorb the value of coffee. To leave coffee unharvested is impracticable. To get rid of a good tree is a crime, because this is the only patrimony Brazil possesses. To get rid of a tree that does not yield does not reduce production.' Bento A. Sampaio Vidal, *Folha da Manhã* (22 June 1935)

The distinctive labour system the planters devised as a substitute for slave labour, the *colonato*, provided expanding coffee plantations with cheap and disciplined labour. The extraordinary spread of coffee, whose production increased fivefold between 1890 and 1907, is proof of their success.[1] São Paulo coffee soon became the main foreign exchange earner for the country while Brazil became the main coffee supplier for the world market, a position both were to maintain until the 1950s.[2]

At the turn of the century approximately 80 per cent of the agricultural labour force of the state of São Paulo was engaged in coffee production under the *colonato* system, the final outcome of the planters' patient and shrewd experimentation in search of a profitable form of labour exploitation.[3] A Prussian agronomist who had

23

Table 2.1   São Paulo coffee production as percentage of Brazilian and world coffee production, 1886–1920 (yearly averages)

Period	São Paulo production (million bags/60 kg)	São Paulo production		Brazilian production as % of world production
		As % of Brazilian production	As % of world production	
1886	259	42	25	59
1910/11–				
1919/20	941	70	47	67

Source: 'Café no Estado de São Paulo: Situação e Perspectivas da Produção', *Agricultura em Sao Paulo*, VIII (8) (August 1961) p. 21.

worked on a government sponsored settlement in the 1880s was able fully to appreciate the planters' feat:

> One fact in relation to this labour system [the *colonato*] ... is of outstanding importance: it educates workers for intensive work ... I have only mentioned this point here as evidence for my assertion that the labour system predominating now on the plantations of São Paulo deserves to be regarded as an almost ideal one. Let us honour the untiring ambition and intelligence of São Paulo planters who by introducing this labour system ... have made an outstanding contribution to solving the social question.[4]

But, as I will argue in this chapter, the *colonato* system offered yet another advantage to coffee planters. It endowed them with a special flexibility to adjust to price fluctuations which proved decisive for them to resist successive over-production crises relatively unscathed. Because coffee was combined with food crops grown by the labourers, planters could compress money wages when coffee prices declined without jeopardising labour supply, and they did.

In effect, under the *colonato* system coffee was not a monoculture in the strict sense, as some contemporaries and later analysts maintained. On the contrary, as coffee expanded, so did food crops. Coffee and other cash crops for export threatened food production for the domestic market only from the 1960s on when wage labour spread. The difficulties that arose for the country's economy as coffee became its main export crop were due, instead, to the growing dependence on one single crop which made the economy very vulnerable to price fluctuations on the world market.

THE FIRST COFFEE CRISIS AND STATE INTERVENTION

In the mid-1890s domestic and world coffee prices began to decline presaging a prolonged crisis produced by over-production that was to end only in 1910.[5]

Save for their common interest in protecting the economy and the coffee sector from the effects of the price slump, there was initially little clarity among planters or within the government on how best to respond to the crisis. As the crisis developed, however, a number of measures were undertaken on either side to stave off the slump. Pressed as much by planters as by the importance of coffee for the Brazilian economy, the government eventually decided upon a two-pronged market intervention approach in the form of a prohibition on new planting followed by successive price support schemes through withdrawal of coffee from the market.[6] But of equal if not more importance for the survival of coffee production were the successful endeavours the planters themselves made to compress production and in particular labour costs.

Government intervention in coffee marketing was proposed for the first time in the 1890s. Murtinho, the Finance Minister in 1898 was convinced, however, that 'official intervention could only augment our troubles, [but if] the government allowed for the reduction of coffee [production] through natural selection, [this would determine] the elimination of those who had no conditions for survival. Production [would thus remain] in the hands of those who were strongest and better organised for the struggle'.[7] But those who preferred to rely on market forces were eventually overruled by those who sought a corporatist policy that would benefit the coffee sector as a whole and would demand no special sacrifice of any planter.

The coffee sector itself was divided over what had caused the price slump. Latent antagonisms existed between São Paulo coffee planters and foreign coffee merchants. Some planters even blamed the crisis on foreign coffee dealers for artificially depressing purchasing prices to increase their own profit margins.[8] But coffee growers by the turn of the century were also divided amongst themselves with regard to solutions to the crises.

São Paulo owed its extraordinary expansion of coffee as much to the continuous search for virgin soil offering higher coffee yields as to the exceedingly favourable world market prices. As a consequence, by the turn of the century the state had three distinct coffee regions: the frontier in which coffee was being newly introduced, an established region in which the groves were fully productive, and a region in decline.[9] The virgin frontier lands promised high coffee yields at comparatively lower labour costs. New coffee groves were planted by labour hired on four-year contracts. They were entitled, throughout the four years, to grow as much food as they wanted among the young trees and received at the end a fixed amount for each tree they had planted. Working on new plantations on the frontier was attractive to the labourers because they could obtain higher food yields with less effort compared with the older plantations where they usually were granted separate food plots.[10] On new plantations they tended their food crops while they weeded the coffee. Regional differences in soil fertility and the age of trees, therefore, generated potentially conflicting interests among planters because they had a bearing on the supply and cost of labour. Indeed, the 'nomadism' of the *colonos* was a constant source of concern for coffee growers in the older regions.[11]

As the crisis deepened a first unsuccessful attempt was made to do something about the volume of production. The rate at which new coffee was being planted had begun to decline in the late 1890s, but because coffee trees take so long to mature, the effects of this slow down were delayed.[12] In 1902, a tax was introduced on all new trees planted for the next five years, which was subsequently renewed for a further five years.[13] This measure was of doubtful efficacy in reducing coffee production.[14] Planters, especially those opening up new plantations on the frontier, were less than enthusiastic about a tax that virtually prohibited further planting. The prominent planter, exporter and banker, Antonio Prado, expressed the feelings of many of his more powerful fellow planters when he described the prohibition as both 'anti-economic' and 'anti-liberal'. In a similar vein he also opposed coffee valorisation somewhat later. As the owner of a business empire that covered all spheres of coffee from planting to trading and export, the reduction of coffee trading jeopardised his interests as a merchant and exporter.[15] The tax was welcomed, however, by planters in the established coffee regions because they feared the competition from new high-yielding plantations; as one of its advocates argued:

> The limitation of new plantings would not produce the abandoning of old groves. If the measure were general nobody would have new groves to awaken the greed of the *colono*; he, the *colono*, would no longer be attracted by this and would have no interest in changing his employer. If new plantings were limited, the introduction of new immigrants would have the great advantage of reducing wages more and more through the competition that would then arise among them. Without this limitation, the introduction of new immigrants will only contribute to the increase of new plantations and increase the affliction of the afflicted.[16]

The first price-support scheme, negotiated at the Taubaté Convention between the main coffee-producing states of São Paulo, Rio de Janeiro and Minas Gerais, was adopted in 1906 in view of the limited effect that tax had had and the expected large size of the coming harvest. Under the agreement, with the aid of an issue of money backed by a foreign loan guaranteed by an export tax on each bag of coffee, the São Paulo state government agreed to buy coffee surpluses to stabilise prices. The expectation was that accumulated stocks would be sold off in years when production was low.[17]

Coffee valorisation was successful in the short run. By 1910 it had contributed to the recovery of coffee prices. But because it stabilised prices at a level high enough to make coffee profitable for even the high-cost producers, in the long run it stimulated domestic and foreign production which eventually led to a repeat over-production followed by a renewed decline in prices. Brazil, in addition, bore the burden of market regulation which often benefited competing coffee producing countries as, for instance, Colombia.[18]

A second coffee valorisation programme was introduced in 1917–18 to offset the possible effects of the First World War on demand and prices. This time the scheme was financed by the Federal government. The end of the war, and a severe frost in São Paulo in 1918, doubled coffee prices in 1918 and 1919 valorising accumulated stocks and at the same time stimulating new planting followed by a renewed drop in prices between 1920 and 1923. A policy of sustained market regulation was adopted in 1921 (initiated by the Federal government and transferred to the São Paulo state government in

1924) which produced an early price recovery which once again found expression in new planting. By 1929 the number of coffee trees planted in the state of São Paulo was double that of 1902. Coffee prices were consistently high from 1924 to 1929 when a new and prolonged slump set in, the compounded effect of a new high in oversupply and the world depression.[19]

Finance Minister Murtinho may have been right in his predictions that price support by withholding coffee from the market was no effective solution to the over-supply crisis. But market intervention alone did not account for São Paulo planters' ability to withstand crises and expand coffee production. Besides bringing their weight to bear on the state and Federal governments, São Paulo coffee growers used a variety of methods at the point of production to reduce labour costs to protect profit levels.

The Cost Flexibility of the *Colonato* System

By the 1890s coffee plantations were large and complex organisations, with *colonos* making up about 50 per cent of a plantation's labour force who had by then become a fairly homogeneous group living in special separate settlements on the plantations called *colonias*.[20] A well-staffed plantation would ideally have all tasks related to coffee cultivation and harvesting executed by resident *colono* families. But plantations were sometimes unable to attract enough *colonos*; harvests may have been exceptionally large, or as happened during the crisis at the turn of the century some plantations reduced their labour force to cut down costs, especially in the older, declining region. Under such circumstances, planters would reluctantly resort to *avulsos*, i.e. single men hired for a daily wage to work as labourers in gangs harvesting coffee or carrying out other odd jobs on the estate. This was never seen as anything more than a temporary solution which was regarded with some distaste: 'the wage labourer is for agriculture a bleeding that must be stopped before it exhausts the patient'.[21]

Besides the *colono* families a plantation always had a group of *camaradas*, single men or young families who lived on the estate and were paid a monthly wage. Tasks such as transporting the coffee within the plantation, drying and processing coffee, preparing pastures, building and mending fences, maintaining the roads within the estate and other manual jobs were usually carried out by these workers.[22] *Colonos* could also be employed for odd jobs for a daily wage which constituted an additional source of income for the *colono* families. And finally, estates employed a number of skilled workers.[23]

Labour, particularly of *colono* families, constituted a substantial proportion of a coffee plantation's production costs. Mechanising coffee cultivation to reduce costs in view of declining returns was still deemed infeasable, at least so long as coffee had to be picked by hand.[24] Coffee planters resorted instead to generally increasing exploitation of labour in a variety of ways. Most of the Italian observers who inspected the working and living conditions of immigrant labourers at the turn of the century commented on the arbitrary methods planters used to reduce labour costs, such as company stores, confiscation of produce, fraudulent measures to weigh coffee, withholding of wages and inordinate fines. But most important was the more conventional practice of compressing wages.[25] Planters responded to their critics by claiming that 'the crisis' had forced them to treat their labourers in this way, although indications are that even after the mid-1890s reasonably well-run plantations were still returning a profit.[26]

Wage levels depend on labour supply and on the degree of coercion employers are able to impose.[27] Planters by the beginning of the century were again complaining about alleged labour shortages.

In 1902, it seemed that the planters' fears of a labour shortage were vindicated after all when Italy declared a ban on all subsidised immigration to São Paulo, and the Spanish government followed suit in 1911. Both bans were reactions to reports reaching Europe of deplorable conditions on São Paulo coffee plantations.[28] Nonetheless, they were only partially effective. It is revealing in itself that, despite the publicity given by foreign government officials to the hardships the immigrants encountered in São Paulo, it should have needed an official ban to stop immigration. Potential immigrants may well have heard conditions in São Paulo described in sombre terms, but coffee plantations at least promised the certainty of work and food. Moreover, Brazilian labour recruiting agents in Europe did much to counteract the denunciations by government officials. It is difficult, in retrospect, to assess what expectations and aspirations emigrants cherished when they decided to come to São Paulo, for there is always an element of hope in any decision to emigrate.[29] Subsidised emigration may in itself have provided too strong an incentive to resist. Moreover, after 1902 Spanish and Portuguese labourers supplemented the Italians and, from 1908, the Japanese as well, all of whom had the added advantage of being less 'nomadic' than the Italians.[30]

Table 2.2 Percentage of immigrants landed at Santos employed in agriculture and coefficient of permanent settlement, 1908–33

Nationality	No. of immigrants	No. of agricultural workers	% in agriculture	Coefficient of permanence of agricultural workers in %
Japanese	139 199	137 584	98.84	96.3
Spanish	207 326	164 306	79.25	91.3
Italian	199 201	100 553	50.48	41.3
Portuguese	265 751	129 027	48.5	93.1

Source: F. Maurette, *Some Social Aspects of Present and Future Economic Development in Brazil*, ILO, Studies and Reports, Series B, 25 (Geneva, 1937) pp. 88 and 90.

Even during the first ten years of this century, foreign immigration never came to a standstill and, in fact, picked up quite markedly in the three years preceding the First World War. Some immigrants were dissuaded from coming in the first place. And although a significant number who had already come to São Paulo returned to Italy, or left the plantations either for Argentina or (to a lesser degree) for the cities which, after all, were also affected by the depression, these departures were probably as much due to lack of work. The first year in which statistics of emigration revealed an excess over arrivals was 1900.[31] Merrick and Graham calculated the rate of return migration among Italian immigrants at 65 per cent between 1902 and 1913. But against the high natural rate of increase of the Italian immigrant population in Brazil, the effect of these departures on the total foreign-born population base was inconsequential.[32] They merely slowed down its rate of growth. Overall the planters' complaints were thus again largely rhetorical.

Despite the obvious drain the departures of subsidised immigrants meant also for the state finances and the difficulties high labour mobility created for coffee production, alternative forms of colonisation again did not attract more than passing and largely symbolic attention from the planters. Botelho, the São Paulo Secretary of Agriculture, for example, early in the century called for the granting of land ownership to immigrants: 'We must settle the immigrants on the soil ... but this must be effected so that they will be at the disposal of the large proprietors when the latter have need of their labour', for, as he emphasised somewhat later, 'having at hand in the colonies a reserve of labour for the harvest would enable us to transform and industrialize the cultivation of coffee, and to reduce the expenses of production by doing away with the necessity of supporting throughout the whole year the number of labourers required at harvest time'.[33]

But planters continued to be sceptical as to whether they could rely on smallholders being available for work on the plantations when they needed them. The smallholders were very reluctant to harvest coffee on the plantations preferring to work their own land.[34]

Moreover, the *colonato* system had proved an extraordinary success not only because it constituted a very efficient form of surplus labour appropriation but also because it allowed flexibility when the market deteriorated and prices declined. The *colonato* system, in effect, by combining a cash crop with self-provisioning by the labourers not only permitted planters all manners of fraud without jeopardising the workers' basic livelihood. It also enabled them, by offering more favourable self-provisioning conditions to the labourers, to compress money wages when coffee prices dropped. High food prices during the first decade of this century, moreover, may well have stepped up the *colonos*' own interest in more favourable food-growing rights.[35]

Some planters from Avaré in the established coffee region noted in 1904, 'low coffee prices which have reduced the labour force and disorganised work have persuaded many planters to allow inter-cropping of maize in mature groves which has produced great damage to the coffee trees and a reduction in yields'.[36] The effect of intercropping maize and also beans on coffee yields is a disputed issue. But then, as Ramos noted, the planters' decision to allow the cultivation of food crops among mature coffee trees was based on an economic calculation:

That the intercropping of maize among coffee trees does diminish the size of the harvest is a fact of observation. But on the other hand, maize growing constitutes an income supplement. These are already two elements in opposition – one reducing and the other increasing returns. If the price of coffee is high and that of maize low, coffee as against the intercropping of maize gains the cause. If coffee prices are low, the return from maize attenuates the reduction of income from coffee. But there are other aspects to the question as well. It is well known that in Brazil and especially in São Paulo it is unlikely that a *colono* will remain on a plantation that does not allow him to intercrop maize among the coffee trees he is in charge of. Here the planter encounters another dilemma; either he intercrops maize, reduces the cost of labour and retains the *colono* or he loses him. If he needs the *colono* and cannot find a substitute, the problem will become worse because it will affect the following harvest.[37]

Early in the century two distinct food-producing sectors had emerged, namely the *colonos* within the plantation system who grew their own provisions and sold some surplus at markets nearby or to the planters, and an expanding sector of independent smallholders, probably predominantly national at the time, who produced food crops outside the plantation complex for urban consumption.[38]

Sitios, i.e. small and medium farms, coexisted with large coffee estates. In 1904–5 the Secretary of Agriculture estimated that of the total area of the state, 12 per cent was cropped and another 28.9 per cent was under pasture. Of the total cropped land, 60 per cent was planted in coffee and the remaining 40 per cent in a variety of crops such as sugar cane, cotton, rice, beans, tobacco.[39] The food-production boom that followed the tariff on foodstuffs of 1905 seems to have taken place mainly in the old region of the state, where some large plantations had sold off land. The average size of properties as well as of the largest estates had become smaller. São Paulo agriculture thus experienced some diversification as a result of the first over-supply crisis at the turn of the century. The extent to which this happened prior to the 1929 recession is, however, still unclear.[40]

A further indication that there was no absolute shortage of labour is the evolution of wages. Agricultural wages, as Hall has shown, varied little between 1884 and 1914. There was a decline at the end of the century when coffee prices fell, followed by a moderate rise between 1902 and 1910 due to the departures and to the relatively small number of immigrants coming into the country. This was countered by increased immigration in 1912 and 1913 and by 1914 money wages were back where they had been in the mid-1880s. Over the same period the labourers' real incomes seem to have experienced a decline.[41]

As coffee prices plummeted, some contemporaries even proposed a return to sharecropping. Lacerda, a planter in S. Carlos do Pinhal in the expanding Mogiana region at the beginning of the century, was adamantly opposed to any new taxes and, with characteristic radical liberalism, argued that:

> the class of tax payers is exhausted, gentlemen [legislators]! What is the use of this extensive administration? It is necessary to reduce the army and likewise the civil service. The planters have no money to pay for this luxury, but they have the land to feed those who are willing to contribute with their labour.[42]

So, as he thought, rather than penalising planters with a new financial burden, what was needed was a way of producing cheaper coffee. This could be achieved by shifting to a cheaper system of production, namely sharecropping. The crucial issue in sharecropping is, however, determining the shares. Employers endeavour to introduce sharecropping in a situation of declining returns with the aim of inducing labour to work harder for only a slightly higher remuneration than under the preceding arrangement. But since the workers are usually aware of the heavier demands of sharecropping, they will expect to earn correspondingly more. Unlike other contemporary proponents of a return to sharecropping, Lacerda recognised that it was unrealistic to expect labourers willingly to agree to shares that would be attractive to the planters.[43] As he noted, when coffee prices drop 'the *colonos*, fearing a further fall in prices and having, as they have, work with fixed results, reject sharecropping'.[44] And he went on to argue that, in order to introduce sharecropping, it would first be necessary to reduce the existing number of coffee trees in the state by 20 to 30 per cent. By the law of supply and demand wages would then fall dramatically and, in addition, large tracts of land would become available to the labourers for growing staples. Finally, with declining wages the labour market would become unified and *colonos* would cease to object to sharecropping.[45]

But Lacerda's pleas to the planters to follow class interests rather than their own personal gain, fell on deaf ears. His proposal to reduce the number of coffee trees went unheeded and coffee never went unharvested for want of labour, a further indication that the planters' allegations of a labour shortage were groundless.[46] As Piza, the Director of the São Paulo Labour Office, argued in 1929, 'share-cropping... [is] a sign of decadence. When the landowner lacks resources, either because the soil is exhausted or because cultivation is no longer profitable, he will resort to labourers who are defeated, who are incapable of finding any other occupation, who in order not to perish accept sharecropping as a last resort before vegetating'.[47]

Labourers Resist

But the workers were not sufficiently defeated to warrant a return to sharecropping. Instead, as working conditions deteriorated, labour mobility increased and relations between planters and workers became more conflict ridden.[48]

The rate of renewal of *colono* families rose most at times when income was declining because of falling wages and/or low coffee yields. Under such circumstances opportunities in the new coffee region exerted a special attraction. The prohibition on new coffee planting temporarily undermined the *colonos'* chances of moving to the frontier region, but from 1907 onward planting resumed, even if at a slower rate.[49] Planters dreaded their labourers' restlessness because it meant that each year renewed efforts had to be made to recruit new families and renegotiate contracts. And labour rotation also affected labour productivity. New immigrants required training. The number of coffee trees tended by recent arrivals was usually somewhat lower than that of established *colono* families.[50] It was also not uncommon for *colonos* to flee from the plantation at night before their contracts had expired if they felt overburdened by heavy fines, debts, low wages or illness in the family that they saw no chance of breaking even by the end of the year. Most plantations by now had their own band of armed guards, *capangas*, to ensure that the planter's wishes were enforced, to protect him from the wrath of the labourers and to control the movements of workers to and from the estate.[51]

The most notorious case of outright violence occurred in 1900 when Francisco Augusto Almeida Prado, a member of the prominent Prado family, was careless enough to stroll through his coffee groves one day without the protection of his bodyguards. Several of his labourers took advantage of the situation and murdered him, covering his body with knife wounds and chopping it into pieces with their hatchets and hoes. This murder was apparently carried out in retaliation for a punishment Prado had inflicted on his workers for refusing to put out a fire on the estate of one of his relatives.[52] Another dramatic murder took place also in 1900 when Diogo Sales, the planter brother of the then President of the Republic, was assassinatd because his son had tried to seduce the sister of one of his *colonos*.[53]

Strike action was also fairly frequent. By 1913, the Italian-language newspaper, *Fanfulla*, had registered several dozen strikes. Between 1913 and 1930, the *Patronato Agrícola* (a state agency founded in 1911 to ease planter–worker tensions through mediation) as well as the labour press, cited over 100 strikes on the coffee plantations. Although most of these strikes were confined to a single plantation, there was a case in 1911 when about 1000 labourers from half a dozen plantations in the Bragança area went on strike for 20 days and as a result secured a slight increase in pay. The following year, labourers on more than a dozen plantations in the Riberão Preto area went on strike and also secured a small wage rise. The largest strike of the period took place in the same area in 1913, but although mobilising between 10 000 and 15 000 labourers, it ended in total defeat.

Strikes generally occurred over issues such as poor harvest piece-rates, non-payment of wages, attempts to reduce pay, arbitrary or unreasonable discipline and heavy fines, or restrictions on the right to grow food.[54] On this occasion, apart from a pay rise, the striking labourers were also demanding the lifting of a ban on intercropping and the end to certain malpractices depriving them of part of their earnings. This time the planters organised themselves to resist the spread of the strike movement, probably sparked off by the poor harvest,[55] and with police backing succeeded to break the strike by threatening the labourers with immediate eviction and by denying food supplies.[56]

During the three years of prosperity between 1910 and 1913, overall conditions for the *colonos* seem to have improved little, and in some instances even deteriorated,[57] one indication of this being that in 1913 quite a number of Italian *colonos* asked their Consulate for repatriation.[58]

Growing labour unrest, and an uneasy sense on the part of the planters that their labour supply might be in jeopardy, produced the beginnings of some sort of protective legislation for the *colonos*. A law giving preference to the debts owed to them by planters in the event of bankruptcy was enacted in 1906, and in 1911 the *Patronato Agrícola* was set up to arbitrate somewhat one-sidedly in disputes between planters and *colonos*. In 1913, for example, the *Patronato* refused to intervene when three *colonos* were arrested, allegedly for speaking back at a police officer, because they (the *colonos*) were said to have 'violated the "agricultural pact" by striking',[59] a 'pact' that was obviously regarded by the *colonos* as unfair. Also in 1913, a law was passed that provided for the expulsion of foreigners from the country. Although it was directed more towards controlling urban unrest, it also served to reduce the rural labourers' leverage *vis-à-vis* the planters. By the end of 1913 *colonos* had made literally thousands of claims for outstanding wages and, foreseeing further trouble from them, the *Patronato* declared all forms of protest outside the 'lawful' (i.e., bureaucratic) channels, as illegal.

On their part, the planters had learned to stand together against any threat from their labourers. They had successfully resisted the 1913 strikes. In 1914 the planters of S. José do Rio Pardo, for instance, reached an agreement to reduce wages and to boycott all labourers suspected of being in debt to their previous employer.[60]

The Social Mobility Debate

Contemporary critics denounced the extreme exploitation of *colonos* which left the labourers little room for improvement. The defenders of the *colonato* system emphasised the opportunities it offered immigrants to make good. Italian sources were mostly sceptical, pressing for improved working conditions for their nationals. The São Paulo Labour Department, for example, in its publications for the 1910s, in an effort to attract more immigrants, conveyed the impression that *colonos* were becoming smallholders *en masse*.[61]

The controversy persists. It has now moved, however, beyond the quantitative assessment of the proportion of immigrants among landowners, to an analysis of the dynamics of the *colonato* system as

a combined cash and food crop system and the specific opportunities for accumulation it may have offered labourers as coffee
prices fluctuated.

Critics and defenders now all seem to agree on one point, namely
that immigrants had one single aim, to move off the plantation.[62]
According to the critics, the income levels and general living conditions of *colono* families were poor and probably got worse in the
first decade of this century. For this reason, the labourers made every
conceivable effort (to the point of fleeing at night) to move away.
Since opportunities to accumulate were minimal, they tried to move
to the newer plantations on the frontier, or to leave the country
altogether. Few ever succeeded in becoming smallholders, though
many departed because it was easier to save the money needed to
repatriate than the larger amount required to buy a family farm.[63]
The optimists, by contrast, contend that working conditions were not
too bad. They did allow a significant proportion of *colonos* to save up
enough to acquire land of their own, so they could abandon the very
situation they were presumed to find rewarding.

Holloway attributed this desire to leave the plantations to an
unexplained 'dream of the peasant, to work his own farm'.[64] His disagreement with the critics is over what opportunities the *colonato*
system offered the labourers to fulfill this dream.

According to this author, in 1905 as many as 14 per cent of landed
properties were owned by Italians, a proportion that by 1920 had
risen to 15 per cent. By 1923 of the total number of coffee-producing
properties in the state of São Paulo, 32 per cent were in the hands of
Italians.[65] The average value of Italian-owned properties was,
however, much lower than those owned by Brazilians.[66]

Hence, a significant number of immigrants seem to have succeeded in acquiring at least a small plot of land. But then it turns out
that *at most* 8 per cent of *first generation* immigrants had achieved
landownership by the first decade of this century.[67]

Font has argued more recently that in the late 1920s an emerging
group of immigrant smallholders, who initially grew food but eventually moved into small-scale coffee cultivation, began to challenge
the São Paulo planters' control over the export sector.[68] According to
his estimates, by 1934 as many as 48 per cent of the properties in the
state of São Paulo were foreign owned. Even discounting second
generation immigrants, at least a quarter of all foreign-born
labourers may have come to own land.[69] In contrast to Holloway,

Font dates the origins of these ex-*colono* smallholdings to the 1910s
and 1920s rather than earlier. In the 1910s, *colonos* were able to
benefit from rising coffee prices in an expanding local economy. As
coffee expanded again in the 1920s, coffee planters offered *colonos*
more favourable self-provisioning conditions in order to ensure an
adequate supply of labour. Food surpluses sold on an expanding
market at rising prices constituted the *colonos'* main source of
accumulation.[70] In this sense, the *colonato* system contained the
seeds of its own destruction. Font's argument rests on the assumption that coffee planters improved self-provisioning conditions at
times of good coffee prices – which is, however, a misinterpretation.
It was precisely when coffee prices were low, as they were at the
turn of the century, that planters even in the old, established region
allowed their workers to intercrop foodstuffs. When prices were low
the adverse effect of intercropping on coffee yields became negligible.
As an agricultural inspector in the Riberão Preto region noted in
1902, foodstuffs grown by *colonos* were predominantly in the
coffee rows.[71]

Once coffee prices began to improve, particularly after 1910,
however, planters prohibited intercropping in order to protect coffee
yields. In some instances the *colonos* were compensated for this loss
with a slight wage increase. But this improvement in earnings was
largely illusory, for it rarely made up entirely for lost self-
provisioning and rising food prices further eroded these apparent
gains.[72] Planters offered the labourers plots outside the coffee groves,
but these were generally some distance away, required extra labour
and, in addition, often had poor soil. The *colonos* frequently had to
pay exhorbitant prices at company stores for the provisions they
could not provide themselves.[73] Only in the frontier region did the
colonos continue to benefit from intercropping among young trees
and from more fertile soil.

In the period between 1910 and 1913 the established coffee region
experienced its most extensive *colono* strikes, above all against the
prohibition of intercropping of foodstuffs. Hence it would seem that
from 1907 to the beginning of the First World War, *colonos* in the
established coffee region had fewer opportunities to produce surplus
food for sale than at the beginning of the century when planters used
intercropping to compress money wages.

Even on Holloway's and Font's reckoning, the number of
immigrants who had become smallholders by the pre-war years was
relatively small. The war put a temporary end to immigration and

closed the European markets for coffee. Coffee prices declined once more, there was pressure on wages, and food prices continued to rise; a combination of circumstances very similar to those obtaining at the turn of the century.

Planters' renewed lament about labour shortages again concealed their concern over the nomadic tendencies of their *colonos*, which became more intense as food prices continued to rise and coffee yields in the older region declined.[74] As I indicated earlier, in 1914 planters in the S. José do Rio Pardo region took concerted action to reduce wages, probably made possible also by the influx of urban workers into agriculture because of the short-term effects of the war in reducing industrial activity.[75] In 1917, 'the flight of the Italian workers from the West and the Northwest, valorising labour enormously, has already produced the consequences of attracting national labourers to the large estates'.[76]

The planters in the older region had several options to offset their comparative disadvantages in relation to the newer plantations. They abandoned the old estates,[77] parcelled them out and sold the land,[78] they moved to the frontier to open up new plantations on virgin land, or they continued to work the ageing plantations making concessions to the labourers to compensate for declining yields which affected earnings during the harvest. New coffee planting slowed down by comparison with the three-year period preceding the war and planters in the older region again used the well-tried method of giving more favourable planting rights to stop the exodus of the *colonos*.[79]

There is the second part to Font's thesis, namely that in the 1920s a significant sector of smallholders, in which immigrant landowners played a relevant role, began to challenge the traditional large planters – coffee traders alliance's control of the coffee market.[80] Font bases his case on an incomplete survey of São Paulo coffee farms for 1930 and a census for 1935-6.[81] It is not possible to distinguish the pre- from the post-1929 period with these data. Font also gives no figures on the proportion of coffee trees grown on small farms. Such an estimate is available, however, for 1927. Buesco calculated that by that year 18.4 per cent of São Paulo coffee trees were grown on 73.7 per cent of all coffee farms with less than 20 000 trees, 33.4 per cent of the trees were grown on 20.2 per cent of the farms having between 20 000 and 100 000 trees and the remaining 48.2 per cent of the trees were cultivated on 6.1 per cent of the estates with over 100 000 trees.[82] No figures are given on the proportion of

immigrants among the small coffee growers. Font gives only the percentage of foreign owned coffee farms in the total number of coffee
estates without distribution by size.[83] Buesco's figures, however,
indicate at least two things. Land distribution under coffee was very
unequal and the amount of coffee produced by smallholders was
small in 1927, so that it could hardly have constituted a serious
challenge for large planters at the time.

The immigrants' chances to acquire land of their own depended,
however, not only on the opportunities they had to accumulate but
also on the availability and prices of land.

Martins has maintained that the planters' monopoly over land
made it impossible for *colonos* to purchase land of their own.[84] Nonetheless, it appears that while government sponsored colonisation
schemes never accounted for much of the land owned by
smallholders, a degree of fragmentation of large estates and the
activities of large private settlement companies were gradually
making land available to potential buyers of modest means.

At the turn of the century some plantations went bankrupt and
estates were auctioned, probably belonging to planters who, availing
themselves of easy credit in the 1890s, had hoped to profit from the
extraordinary coffee boom that looked as if it would go on forever.
And some planters in financial difficulties sold off land unsuited to
coffee. The famous Ibicaba plantation lost part of its land to four
other estates and was finally sold at an auction.[85] In the late 1910s
some break-up of run-down plantations and their sale in smaller
units occurred when planters began to abandon the older region in
search of new land on the frontier.[86]

Private land-settlement companies contributed to an expanding
market for land.[87] Monbeig has suggested that land occupation
patterns on the frontier responded to a combination of factors such
as coffee prices, *colono* wage levels and the quality of communications. The predominance of small and medium-sized properties in the Alta Sorocabana region, in contrast with the Northwest,
where large estates existed alongside smallholdings, depended on
the different moments at which the railways penetrated each of the
two regions. In the Alta Sorocabana region, the railway opened
when coffee prices were rising and wages were relatively good. But
planters were discouraged from moving into the area by the greater
distance from the markets and by their distrust in the new state-
owned Sorocabana railway. In the Northwest, by contrast, where in

the 1920s smallholdings coexisted with large estates owned by planters who had moved to the frontier from the declining regions of Riberão Preto, Araraquara and Jaú, the railway opened earlier during a slump when *colono* wages were low.[88] By the 1920s more land was becoming available through the activities of private land-settlement companies on the frontier. On the other hand, for planters in the older region the decision to open up new lands on the frontier for coffee cultivation was no longer a matter of choice but of necessity. Between 1919 and 1930 almost 700 million new coffee trees were planted in the state of São Paulo, partly by planters who were abandoning the declining coffee regions.[89]

In the 1920s foreign workers arrived at over double the rate they had done during the late 1910s. Nonetheless, planters began hiring national labour in growing numbers. Between 1911–15 and the late 1920s the proportion of foreigners in the total number of immigrants entering the state of São Paulo declined from 95 to 60 per cent.[90]

The war years had seen the emergence of nationalist sentiment amongst the élite in Brazil. In their search for the roots of the native-born Brazilian's moral degeneracy which many had held responsible for Brazil's backwardness, the racialist interpretations of the native population's marginal existence were revised. Planters quickly forgot their prejudices towards nationals and now rejoiced in their strength, loyalty and perseverance as labourers: 'Immigration declined and national labour gained value. It gained value and was utilised. Wages had risen. It was then perceived that it was not only the lack of ambition that had marginalised the national labourers; it was also the insignificant wage'.[91]

Although there was no absolute shortage of labour on the coffee plantations in the 1920s, the money wages did improve during this period. With more favourable coffee prices and high profits already having stimulated new plantings in the first half of the decade, planters were willing to raise wages to ensure both a stable supply of labour and proper care of the trees. Also, competition for labour between the old and the new coffee regions was becoming more intense and, being unable to grant better self-provisioning conditions, planters in the old region were having difficulty keeping their *colonos*. With such high coffee prices, the owners of productive groves would have been ill-advised to permit the intercropping of food with coffee. On the old declining plantations this was even less advisable because of soil erosion.[92] On the other hand, to have given the *colonos* more extensive rights to self provisioning on separate plots would have reduced the labour time they had available for coffee. Under these circumstances and in view of high profits, stable prices and an abundance of cash, by 1928, planters were probably more disposed than before to making monetary wage concessions. High coffee prices had enabled the planters to finance the bumper crop of 1927–8 without having to dip into their cash reserves and they therefore had more money at their disposal than ever before this century.[93] They could now satisfy their *colonos'* demands for 'the high coffee price justified all these anomalies'.[94] This combination of circumstances increased the relative disadvantages of planters in the declining region.[95] An estimated 15 to 20 per cent of coffee trees in the state of São Paulo changed hands during 1928 and 1929. Part of these were presumably old estates being sold off by owners moving to the frontier to establish new ones.[96]

Colonos were able to get on and perhaps even accumulate some savings only under exceptionally favourable circumstances such as having a large and healthy family, no fines, a well-paying employer who was liberal with food-planting rights, the proximity of a market for food surpluses and no natural calamities. Early in the century such a combination of circumstances was becoming rare. If *colonos* in the established coffee region were able to accumulate at all in the 1920s, it would essentially have been because of higher money wages rather than of more favourable self-provisioning conditions. Their decision to invest in a plot of land seems to have repeated a typical pattern, whereby immigrant labourers moved off the plantations to set up independently if they could only after a period of prosperity. In the late 1920s, this decision was further justified by a sharp decline in wages in late 1929,[97] which marked one of the first signs of the impending disaster. At this point growing numbers of immigrants continued to leave the plantations, some of them to buy up land of their own. The private-settlement companies, on their part, were aware that their potential clientele were people of limited means. Relatively easy land purchasing terms were arranged,[98] probably making the late 1920s the most favourable period so far that the *colonos* had ever experienced. New coffee planting in the second half of the 1920s spread beyond large-scale capitalist operations without challenging their hegemony. *Colonos* who had managed to accumulate now bought land on the frontier which they cleared and planted in coffee. During the first years when the coffee trees were unproductive, they fed and supported themselves with the produce of intercropped foodstuffs.[99]

Contrary to all expectations and hopes, the 1927–8 bumper crop was followed, with the interval of only one year, by another very large crop in 1929–30. Unfortunately for coffee planters, this coincided with the onset of international depression. It was impossible to sell the huge accumulating coffee stocks but Brazil also failed to obtain the foreign financial assistance that would have been needed to withhold sufficient coffee to support prices. In October 1929 the collapse came. Coffee prices plummeted and by the end of the year they had fallen by about 35 per cent. By 1932 they had dropped by over 50 per cent.[100] Very much as during the first coffee crisis at the turn of the century, prices had been halved and money wages were compressed to a similar extent. The boom had come to a sudden end but, as before, this did not spell the end of São Paulo coffee.

THE CRASH OF 1929

The world depression in 1929 has for long been regarded as a watershed in Brazilian history on account of the far-reaching structural changes in the country's economy that are said to have resulted from it. The 1929 crash has been interpreted as initiating a process of slow but definitive economic and political decline of the coffee bourgeoisie, as striking a death blow at the coffee latifundia by forcing the break up of large estates as cropping patterns changed and the economy diversified. A careful analysis of the performance of the coffee sector in the 1930s, although it reveals important changes, offers a much less catastrophic picture instead. First of all, the decline in coffee prices between 1929 and 1930–1 was no greater than that which had occurred at the turn of the century and which had not spelled the demise of São Paulo coffee production then.[101] Furthermore, in the 1930s coffee production in the state continued to be consistently high and the volume of coffee produced regularly exceeded demand.[102] In effect, it took some 15 years of very low coffee prices and another world war to reduce Brazil's productive coffee capacity to about the level of demand. Only in the 1940s and after some 70 million bags of coffee had been destroyed by the government in an attempt to stabilise prices, did coffee production at last begin to diminish steadily until the 1950s, which saw yet another boom.

44

Table 2.3 Coffee production and prices, share in world coffee imports and incineration, Brazil, 1928-9 to 1945-6

Year	Production Brazil[a] São Paulo (million bags)		Coffee exports[b]	% of production exported	World Imports (million bags)	Coffee Destroyed (million bags)	Brazil's share in world imports	Average price/ bag in US $
1928–29	18.60	8.8	14.10	75.8	22.23	–	63	22.93
1929–30[c]	28.20	19.5	14.70	52.1	23.55	–	62	13.10
1930–31	16.60	10.1	16.50	99.3	25.15	–	65	9.29
1931–32	28.30	18.7	14.90	52.6	23.73	2.8	62	10.80
1932–33	19.90	15.0	13.80	69.3	22.85	9.3	60	10.46
1933–34	29.70	11.7	14.80	51.5	24.45	13.6	60	12.34
1934–35	18.20	–	14.70	80.7	22.68	8.2	64	10.58
1935–36	21.00	13.5	14.70	70.0	25.85	1.6	56	11.97
1936–37	26.40	17.7	13.20	50.0	24.89	3.7	53	13.80
1937–38	23.50	15.8	14.60	62.1	25.47	17.1	57	7.57
1938–39	23.20	15.6	17.00	73.2	26.73	8.0	63	8.01
1939–40	19.10	12.3	14.40	75.0	26.69	3.5	63	7.93
1940–41	16.50	10.2	11.60	70.3	–	2.8	–	11.06
1941–42	15.80	9.2	9.20	58.2	–	3.4	–	14.52
1942–43	13.60	8.5	8.70	63.9	–	2.3	–	14.94
1943–44	12.20	5.9	11.80	96.7	–	1.2	–	15.42
1944–45	9.10	4.7	13.90	152.7	–	1.0	–	16.18
1945–46	12.70	6.1	14.90	117.3	–	–	–	22.41

Source: Anuário Estadístico do Café, Coordenadoria de Estudos da Economia Cafeeira, 11 (Rio de Janeiro December 1977) pp. 52–4, 180.

[a] Refers to exportable coffee.

[b] W. Cano, Raízes da Concentração Industrial em São Paulo (São Paulo, 1977) p. 41, Table 2 for São Paulo coffee production until 1932–3.

[c] In 1930 the export of coffee below type 8 was prohibited, which reduced the share of coffee produced available for export.

I am not proposing that the society and economy were left unperturbed by the crash. As one observer noted somewhat dramatically at the time, in their despair many coffee planters had closed their lavish town houses in the city of São Paulo and had retired with their families to their plantations to live off the produce of the land so as to economise on very scarce cash.[103] It is true that after 1929 coffee was never to regain the extraordinary economic pre-eminence it had enjoyed in the mid-1920s. The crash did accelerate a process of structural change in the country's economy which eventually displaced the coffee sector from the dynamic centre of the economy, assigning to it a more subordinate yet important role. However, despite the shock produced by the sudden and largely unforeseen slump in coffee prices and the gloom that spread in the coffee sector, the depression did not entail the ruin of the coffee planters as a class.

The Umbrella of Official Price Support

Analysts have disagreed on the extent to which the price-support schemes adopted in 1931 did protect the coffee sector and the national economy from the full effects of the slump in coffee prices. Estimates vary over the degree to which a price-support policy softened the impact falling prices had in reducing aggregate income in the coffee sector. The contentious issue in this controversy is the extent to which the financing of coffee price support was born by the export sector and the effect it had on income levels. In his classical study of Brazilian economic development, Furtado argues that by guaranteeing a minimum buying price for coffee that was advantageous to the majority of coffee planters, employment levels in the export sector (as well as in sectors linked to it) were maintained. Price support, therefore, prevented a contraction in economic activity proportional to the price slump. Furtado estimated that, in effect, nominal income of the coffee sector had diminished only 25 to 30 per cent as compared to a price decline of over 50 per cent by 1932.[104] Peláez, a staunch critic of market intervention who was particularly sceptical about the beneficial effects of the 1931 price-support scheme on the country's economy, maintained more recently that the reduction in the coffee sector's income had amounted to as much as 41 per cent between 1928 and 1933.[105]

There are, however, two issues involved here. On the one hand, sustainedly high production until the late 1930s indicates that coffee was a profitable crop until the Second World War, but on the other this was due to a significant extent to a redistribution of income within the sector on account of the substantial cuts in nominal wages planters were able to impose on their labourers.

Three distinct moments can be detected in the price-support policy adopted by the Federal government in the 1930s. The year 1930 saw intense debate over what measures should be taken to contain the decline in prices. In 1931, a price-support scheme was adopted which entailed growing centralisation of coffee policy by the Federal government and the massive destruction of surplus stocks. And finally in the late 1937 the Federal government, in a drastic move, introduced free trade.

Immediately after the crash the coffee sector seemed united in its endeavours to salvage coffee production. In late 1929 the three agricultural associations, the *Liga Agrícola Brasileira* (the Brazilian Agrarian League), the *Sociedade Rural Brasileira* (SRB, the Brazilian Rural Society) and the *Sociedade Paulista de Agricultura* (the Agricultural Society of São Paulo) got together to plan a concerted strategy.[106] By 1931, yet another organisation was formed, the *Comissão de Organização da Lavoura* (the Commission for the Organisation of Agriculture) which pursued a strategy that was opposed to that of the older associations which by now had merged into an enlarged *Sociedade Rural Brasileira*. The *Comissão* was composed of regional coffee cooperatives set up in the interior of the state in defence of coffee interests and soon after was transformed into the *Federação das Associações da Lavoura Paulista* (FALP, the Federation of Rural Associations of São Paulo) which strongly opposed the *Sociedade Rural Brasileira* and constituted the backbone of the *Partido da Lavoura* (the Agrarian Party) founded in 1933 to contest the Constituent Assembly elections.[107]

As yet little is known of the political composition and precise economic interests of these opposed blocs. The *Sociedade Rural Brasileira* seems to have been dominated by old planter – exporter interests; it was closely connected with the *Partido Democrático de São Paulo* (the Democratic Party of São Paulo) founded in 1926 to combat political corruption and whose executive committee contained some of the most prominent representatives of the coffee sector.[108] The composition of the *Federação das Associações da Lavoura Paulista* is even less clear. In a manifesto of August 1931 the *Federação* protested strongly against the low prices paid by the Federal government for coffee surpluses and the export tax in gold demanding the gradual withdrawal of the tax and denouncing bankers and exporters whereas the *Sociedade Rural Brasileira*, by contrast, initially supported the Vargas government's coffee policy. This refusal to bear the burden of price support may indicate the *Federação* members' greater difficulty in absorbing the costs of market intervention on account of the smaller size of their estates and/or lower yields.[109]

During the critical stage of the crisis in 1930 and amidst heated debates, three alternative measures aimed at protecting coffee production and the national economy were proposed. First, it was suggested that a whole coffee crop not be harvested, though this would, however, damage the trees; second, that Brazil follow a policy of international dumping, but this was thought to be difficult because of the poor quality of much of the coffee in Brazil; and third, that coffee surpluses be withdrawn and/or destroyed.[110] This latter proposal won the day. With the creation of the National Coffee Council in 1931 in the first move to centralise coffee policy a price-support scheme was implemented which imposed a 10 shillings per bag tax on coffee exports (shortly afterwards raised to 15 shillings) to finance the withdrawal of coffee surpluses and the immediate destruction of part of the stocks. In 1932, new coffee planting was prohibited. In 1933, in response to a particularly large harvest, the Federal government divided the crop into three different quotas: 40 per cent to be compulsorily sold (at a price equivalent to the average cost of production) to the National Coffee Department for destruction, the so-called 'sacrifice quota'; 30 per cent could be shipped directly to the port; and the remaining 30 per cent was bought by the National Coffee Department for storage awaiting shipment and paid for at a set price.

The *Sociedade Rural Brasileira* had generally supported market intervention, at least until 1935. As long as prices were kept at a profitable level and the market situation showed a gradual improvement, export tax and even the Bank of Brazil's monopoly over all foreign exchange – its ability to force planters to sell their foreign exchange earnings from coffee to the bank at well below the market rate – were acceptable to planters who owned reasonably profitable plantations. The farm debt moratorium decreed in 1933, also helped alleviate their financial difficulties. Exporters, on their part, were not necessarily adverse to market intervention as long as price support allowed for continued trading but they never looked kindly on any direct control of trading, as for instance, the restriction on the shipment of low-grade coffees in 1930. The decline in coffee exports in 1932-3 had already caused some unease and the potential competition of the National Coffee Department's stocks was always a source of concern.

Paulo Prado, nominated first President of the National Coffee Council in 1931, in 1927, as a 'simple coffee producer, merchant and exporter' had already warned that heavy and innumerable taxes on coffee as well as the poor quality of the product were driving coffee 'to change the soil', i.e. move to other countries.[111] With increasing insistence, planters (along with the exporters) began to demand the withdrawal of this exchange confiscation as well as of the export tax and that debts from purchases of landed property be included under the farm mortgage moratorium.[112] Early in 1935 the *Sociedade Rural Brasileira* again called for a lifting of the fiscal burdens resting on coffee, arguing that an improvement of Brazil's competitiveness could no longer be achieved through a reduction in production costs because this would mean plunging *colonos* into utter misery.[113] Simultaneously, animosity toward the National Coffee Department grew for it was felt that the agency's policies had served only to spread distrust and instability in the market.[114] At the Congress of Coffee Growers of 1935 there were those who demanded progressive de-regulation of coffee trade, the lifting of direct and indirect levies on coffee and again the abolition of the Department itself.[115]

In 1936-7 Brazilian coffee exports fell by over 10 per cent at the same time as the country's share in world exports dropped to the lowest point in the century. Growing foreign competition from low-cost and high quality coffee countries such as Colombia emerged as a new and very serious threat to coffee producers as much as traders. Brazil sought to deal with this menace by persuading the governments of competing countries to restrict planting but failed in this endeavour not least because, for example, Colombia opposed such restrictions. In Colombia coffee was produced predominantly by small family farmers side-by-side with food crops entirely with family labour. They were able to withstand the declining returns on their labour and nonetheless to continue growing coffee.[116]

The eradication of coffee to reduce its productive capacity had temporarily fallen into oblivion and after 1930 some new planting had continued. By 1936-7, however, the compulsory or subsidised uprooting of trees was proposed once more. Nonetheless, despite large crops and declining exports, the attitude among planters continued to be consistently unsympathetic to such a drastic measure for it would ruin the coffee industry. In 1936 the *Sociedade Rural Brasileira's* President expressed the sentiments of many planters when he argued that:

> Each time the market in Santos is disturbed by the intempestive measures of the National Coffee Department, the idea of solving the crisis through the sale of old coffee trees for uprooting in order to re-establish the statistical equilibrium arises again. We have the spiritual strength and the courage needed to confront all situations and are not afraid to adopt radical measures. However, the more time passes and the more we reflect we regard this idea of uprooting coffee trees with horror for it would be our ruin and the final defeat of São Paulo's coffee production.[117]

Uprooting was ineffectual for several reasons. Partial eradication, it was argued, would only increase the yields of the remaining trees. Those who accepted subsidised eradication would use the resources from uprooting to plant new coffee in the neighbouring state of Paraná, where planting within certain limits was still allowed. And the resources used to finance subsidised uprooting of old trees would have to come from the funds of price support. What was urgently needed, instead, was the scrapping of taxes, the destruction of surpluses and freedom of trade. As a member of the *Sociedade Rural Brasileira* stressed in mid-1937, 'uprooting is no solution. The solution is to "sell coffee". To that end what is required is the confidence of the market and the elimination of the export tax which is the premium we give to our competitors, as well as all the restrictions and prohibitions that persecute coffee'.[118]

Regional differences in coffee yields again produced different responses among coffee producers to price support. Economically stronger coffee planters who owned well-run, high-yielding plantations, were better equipped to withstand falling prices and to bear the cost of price support. When, however, price support failed to ensure reasonable prices and continued trading, as was the case again in 1936–7, the coffee sector as a whole was able to unite at least temporarily to exert joint pressure on coffee policy.

By November 1937, the combination of pressures from the coffee sector and the realities of the coffee trade, at last forced the government into a drastic change of direction in its coffee policy. Price support had once more failed to achieve its goal, namely to achieve a price that would neither bring about the economic ruin of the producers nor raise the level of production too far in excess of demand. Price stabilisation had not only failed to discourage domestic coffee producers from remaining in the business of growing coffee. It had also stimulated coffee-growing abroad. And the costs of financing stabilisation and incineration were increasing while foreign exchange earnings were falling, with grave consequences for the national economy as well. The solution adopted was international coffee dumping. So as to lower international prices in order to increase Brazilian exports and to force foreign competitors into negotiating an international agreement on coffee, export duties were sharply reduced, the rate of exchange was freed and government intervention was discontinued.

Free trade produced a substantial recovery of Brazil's share in the world coffee market, but it also pushed coffee prices down to their lowest level this century. Free trade was allowed to operate without constraints for only about a year before European markets, which had been taking 40 per cent of world coffee supply by the onset of the Second World War, once more closed ushering in a new period of severe difficulty for coffee trading. Concern and discontent spread again among coffee planters, this time over the 'sacrifice quota'.[119]

The 1939 Coffee Agreement had set the 'sacrifice quota' at 15 and 30 per cent for preferential and common coffee respectively. Early that year the *Sociedade Rural Brasileira* denounced the 'low price policy'. If the 'sacrifice quota' did not serve to improve prices, it was considered unbearable, 'at this moment we are withholding coffee and selling below cost'.[120] If the withdrawal of coffee surpluses from the market failed to raise prices, then coffee planters as well as exporters rejected such a policy.[121]

The moratorium on farmers' debts renewed in 1941 was conceived partly to compensate planters for their difficulties.[122] In November 1940 the United States set up an agreement with 14 countries establishing quotas for import to that country and the following year, a ceiling price was set that was about double that of 1938–9. This system of price control continued in effect until 1946.[123]

The constraints imposed on coffee trading by the war were exceptional. Climatic conditions in the early 1940s accounted for part of the decline in São Paulo coffee production. Nonetheless, in 1941 new coffee planting had to again be prohibited, a restriction which was lifted in 1943. That same year the government was at last persuaded to definitely abandon the 'sacrifice quota' and in 1944–5, coffee incineration ceased. At the same time, planters were granted coffee financing for three years and the price in gold was raised.[124]

In 1944, for the first time some concern over under-production was voiced. By that time a large proportion of São Paulo's coffee trees were aging; an estimated 80 per cent of coffee trees in the state were either old or of intermediate age in 1940. Between 1926 and 1945 the tree population in São Paulo declined by about 220 million trees.[125]

Coffee Rebounds

In determining the performance of the coffee sector in the 1930s it is insufficient to assess only the effect official price support had on income of the sector as a whole. As important were changes that occurred in income distribution within the sector.

The reduction by over 50 per cent in the money wages paid to the *colonos* was probably the single most important factor, besides price support, in the coffee planters' remarkable resilience to the crisis also after the crash of 1929. Money wages were more than halved and intercropping of food with coffee rose to about 80 per cent of the total area planted in coffee. If one considers that labour costs accounted for about 70 to 80 per cent of production costs and that coffee prices had gone down by about 50 per cent, it is not surprising that even after the crash coffee production continued to be a profitable venture.[126]

It is doubtful, however, whether food concessions made up for the full loss in money income of the workers. In the same period, prices of basic staples such as black beans, rice and maize seem to have fallen, also by about 50 per cent.[127] The reduction in money wages thus entailed a decline in the agricultural workers' purchasing power with probable repercussions for industrial production as well.

The ability of São Paulo planters to adjust production costs to falling prices was noted by many contemporaries. The British Consular report for 1932 stressed the planters' continued strength:

> Brazil can produce and transport coffee to the chief consuming markets cheaper than any other country. Many planters can produce coffee at a profit at a lower level of price even than that ruling today, notwithstanding taxes and the relatively high

Table 2.4 Average nominal wages on São Paulo coffee plantations, 1929-31

Coffee zones	Average annual earnings (from weeding)			Average weeding task rate (1000 trees)			Average harvest piece rate (50 litre bag)		
	1929	1931	decline (%)	1929	1931	decline (%)	1929	1931	decline (%)
Paulista	450$	140$	68	80$	37.5$	37	1$500	550$	63
Mogiana	450$	185$	58	75$	37.5$	40	1$750	750$	57
Soracabana	450$	225$	50	80$	35.0$	56	1$600	650$	59
Araraquarense	450$	160$	64	48$	-	-	1$500	825$	45
Noroeste	425$	170$	60	73$	38.0$	48	1$850	800$	56

Source: Revista da Sociedade Rural Brasileira (December 1931) p. 556; average nominal wages have been calculated on the basis of maximum and minimum rates in each year. Annual earnings from weedings declined more than the weeding task-rate; this suggests that fewer weedings were carried out to cut costs.

exchange. With all that can be urged against the coffee plan, it should not be forgotten that the Coffee Institute is primarily a federation of planters: in essence its organisation may be compared with a co-operative marketing scheme on a vast scale in that its purpose is to ensure that the chief profits of the production shall reach the planter. Consequently there has been built up a body of planters whose resistance to unfavourable market conditions is much greater than is generally supposed, particularly in a country like Brazil, where, if the worst happens, the workers and the planters can support themselves in comparative comfort from the incidental production of their estates: vegetables and livestock, etc.[128]

It is unlikely that large coffee planters needed to live exclusively from the subsidiary produce of their coffee estates and the workers' comforts were modest, at most. Less diplomatic critics accused coffee planters of wasting their money on such extravagances as automobiles, perfumes and gambling at elegant clubs while 'exploiting human flesh' to continue planting coffee.[129] The São Paulo planters got away with such dramatic wage reductions not only by offsetting lost wages by more extensive self-provisioning rights, but also due to the rise in urban unemployment and by their ability to contain labour unrest (except for a few isolated strikes[130]) by getting together in an 'organisation of *fazendeiros* [landlords] for the purpose of setting wages'.[131]

The temporary, but serious, bout of urban unemployment caused by the reduction in industrial activity diminished the bargaining strength of agricultural labourers *vis-à-vis* the planters by swelling the agricultural labour force. When planters cut wages for the 1930 season, many *colono* families abandoned their plantations, sometimes to buy land with their savings, but more often in search of more favourable contractual conditions elsewhere. Variations in self-provisioning rights between coffee regions seemed to have virtually disappeared in the early 1930s. Unable to find alternative employment under better conditions, these labourers eventually had to return to be hired at much lower wages.[132] In addition, planters used other well-tried economy measures, such as delaying payment of wages.[133]

Unemployment, however, proved to be shortlived. Rapid industrial recovery after 1933, along with continued high coffee production and the notable expansion of cotton, raised employment levels to such an extent that by 1935 the São Paulo state government was obliged to re-establish subsidised immigration both for nationals from other states and for foreigners.[134]

Both the volume of production and the productive capacity of coffee continued to be consistently high in the 1930s.[135] New planting of coffee ceased completely in only 1937–8. In 1930–1 about 25 per cent new trees were added to the existing ones, and in the following two years a further 16 and 13 per cent respectively. The majority of these new trees were planted on the frontier. When new planting was once more prohibited in 1932, this was indeed justified. Nonetheless, the rise in coffee production was mainly due to the great number of trees planted in the late 1920s which were now reaching maturity. It would have been even higher had it not been for the accelerated decay of older trees through negligence, and for the general decline in yields due to extensive intercropping of food. Repeated proposals to get rid of a substantial number of old trees against some form of compensation, went unheeded.[136] Until 1935–6 an average 3 per cent of coffee trees were abandoned yearly. Only in 1937, when the export tax was removed in an attempt to improve Brazil's competitive position on the world market by pushing prices down, did the rate of abandonment of trees rise to 6 per cent.[137] For the most part, until the Second World War medium and high-cost coffee producers tended to get rid only of patches of low-yielding trees selectively to cut down costs. In the 1930s, giving up whole estates seems to have been rare, confined to the most run-down areas where some planters had already abandoned coffee before the 1929 crash.

Land Fragmentation and Crop Diversification

The coffee planters' notable resistance to the collapse in coffee prices, at least until the Second World War, stands in marked contrast to impressions conveyed by many contemporaries and later analysts. Much has been made of the 'democratising' effect of the 1929 crash in eroding the economic and political power of coffee planters as a class by causing the break up of latifundia and a proliferation of smallholders.[138] The spread of cotton in the state is interpreted as one symptom of the unprofitability of coffee and the transference of resources into more remunerative crops and welcomed by the critics of coffee monoculture as a sign of agricultural diversification.

Until recently, Milliet's was the only systematic assessment of changes in land-tenure structure in the early 1930s.[139] He believed that the 1929 crisis had, indeed, brought about an expansion of small properties to the detriment of latifundia. However, he detects significant regional differences in the incidence of smallholdings and in the break up of latifundia which do not allow one to establish a simple link between the two phenomena.

The fragmentation of large coffee plantations depended very much on the age and yields of coffee groves. In the older frontier region, large plantations resisted the price collapse quite successfully and there was no increase in smallholdings. On the frontier itself, latifundia still increased in number after 1929, in one region even at a quicker rate than smallholdings.

At the same time, however, the absolute number of small properties went up enormously. On the frontier, the evolutions of large estates and of smallholdings are two distinct processes. The expansion of smallholdings resulted essentially from the activities of the land-settlement companies and, as I mentioned before, was affected by the quality of communications and the distance to an urban centre. In the oldest coffee region in the North of the state, remote from any consumer market, coffee was replaced by extensive cattle farming. In the intermediary zone, however, two simultaneous but distinct developments took place. In areas close to an urban centre small properties spread, at the cost of medium and large plantations, which abandoned some of their coffee groves. In the more remote areas of the intermediary coffee region, however, the relative number of latifundia diminished markedly, to the benefit, however, of large holdings rather than small properties.

In short, the average size of coffee plantations tended to diminish in areas where coffee yields were declining, but this did not necessarily result in the proliferation of small properties. Instead, when latifundia broke up or shed part of their land because of low coffee yields, smallholdings sprang up and multiplied in the proximity of consumer markets. They tended, however, to occupy the less fertile land.[140] But the most substantial increase in the number of smallholdings occurred on the frontier, independently of the vicissitudes of the coffee latifundia which were increasing at the same time. Thus, for instance, in the Northwest of the state, the number of small properties rose over fourfold between 1930–1 and 1935–6,[141] a region which also experienced among the most intense demographic expansion between 1920 and 1940 in the whole state.

For lack of data Kageyama has analysed changes in patterns of land use by size of farm rather than in land tenure, on the assumption that the former reflected the latter. Despite the notable numerical increase in small producers between 1931-2 and 1937-8, as far as coffee farms were concerned, she discovered no profound changes in the land-tenure structure of São Paulo during that period.[142]

Table 2.5   Estimated distribution of coffee trees among coffee farms according to their size, São Paulo, 1931-2 and 1937-8

Farm size by no. of trees (1000)	1931-2		1937-8	
	% of farms	% of trees	% of farms	% of trees
under 5	42.2	6.0	39.3	5.6
5-10	23.1	9.1	24.8	9.8
10-20	17.3	13.6	18.6	14.6
20-50	10.8	18.6	11.1	19.2
50-100	3.7	14.5	3.7	14.5
100-250	2.2	18.2	2.0	16.2
over 250	0.6	20.0	0.5	20.1
Total	100.0	100.0	100.0	100.0

Source: A. A. Kageyama, 'Crise e Estrutura Agrária', p. 111, Table 31, p. 114, Table 33.

It appears then that the impact of the 1929 crash was felt truly only by coffee planters in the declining coffee region. They were the most likely to have to sell their estates either as a whole or in plots. In the intermediary coffee zone, by contrast, distinct efforts were made to rationalise coffee growing by getting rid of unproductive groves and/or marginal lands and by diversifying crops. The 1929 crisis only served to reinforce this trend.

Under adverse market conditions one could expect efforts to be made to increase productivity, especially if competition intensified.[143] In the early 1930s, various improvements in coffee harvesting were discussed among planters, such as more careful and selective picking of berries to produce a more uniform and better-quality coffee. Even some sort of coffee-harvesting machine was demonstrated at a meeting of the *Sociedade Rural Brasileira*. But, either because they were impracticable or because they would involve higher costs, and because price support constituted a disincentive to technical innovations in production, none of these new methods were adopted.[144] On the contrary, planters' endeavours to reduce labour costs probably led to a deterioration in coffee yields and in quality.[145]

Coffee Versus Cotton

Between 1930–1 and 1937–8 cotton production increased twenty fold.[146] The expansion of cotton in the state has often been attributed to the transfer of resources from coffee and seen as a further indication, besides the break up of coffee plantations, of coffee having virtually collapsed as a result of the crash.[147]

Table 2.6 Expansion of selected crops, São Paulo, 1901–39

Period	Sugar	Rice	Beans	Maize	Raw cotton	Coffee trees under production
		(volume of production)				
1901–3	100	100	100	100	100	100
1910–12	179	371	234	146	322	115
1919–21	230	954	510	238	1 705	139
1928–30	505	1 201	523	224	338	190
1937–9	1 150	1 390	427	307	13 411	257[a] 218[b]

Source: W. Cano, *Raízes da concentração industrial*, p. 41, Table 2 and p. 63, Table 6.
Notes:
[a] This index refers to 1935.
[b] A. A. Kageyama, 'Crise e Estrutura Agrária', p. 109 referring to 1937–8.

The slump in commodity prices in 1929 affected cotton relatively less than coffee. In 1932, the premium to cotton growers widened further when cotton prices began to go up again. The early recovery of São Paulo's textile industry gave cotton expansion an added impulse. Moreover, in a context of general economic uncertainty, cotton was an especially attractive crop because, as an annual plant, it could respond more easily than coffee to price fluctuations.

Initially it seems as if cotton attracted resources which, because of the ban on new coffee planting, could no longer be invested in coffee.[148] The investment immobilised in the coffee groves made it difficult for coffee planters to decide on a rapid change of land use. Moreover, it was widely recognised that the introduction of cotton along with coffee would entail potential labour problems, since cotton is a very labour-intensive crop and the coffee and cotton harvests coincide.

By the mid-1930s, however, a link can be detected, albeit an indirect one, between the expansion of cotton cultivation and the fate of coffee. By 1937-8, the bulk of São Paulo cotton was being grown in the intermediate and frontier coffee regions. Until 1935, coffee was the principal cash crop grown on the frontier, especially in the Northwest of the state. When cotton first penetrated this region, rather than replacing coffee, it was grown on newly-opened land. Export-crop diversification in the 1930s was most pronounced in the intermediate region where cotton substituted coffee and fruit production for the market also expanded markedly. But the penetration of cotton occurred in a selective manner. Low-yielding coffee trees were gradually uprooted. Between 1930-1 and 1937-8, the area planted in coffee was substantially reduced, whereas the number of coffee farms declined only slightly, the reduction in the area planted in coffee being only slightly less than the increase in that grown in cotton. The proportion of small landholdings in the region remained unaltered, but the average size of very large properties diminished.

In the old coffee region, by contrast, the decline in coffee cannot be attributed only to the expansion of cotton. The area in coffee was halved whereas cotton could have accounted for only one-fifth of this decline.[149]

In São Paulo, as elsewhere in the country, cotton was usually grown by small producers, either owner operators, sharecroppers or small tenants. By 1934, coffee planters were complaining about rising rural wages which some attributed to the competition of cotton for labour.[150] Under conditions of rising wages and favourable product prices, sharecropping or tenancy arrangements, rather than direct production, were profitable for landowners because they served to reduce labour costs for a very labour-intensive crop and such arrangements were also attractive for labourers because prices were high.[151]

The British (who purchased almost 60 per cent of the state's cotton exports) welcomed the low production costs of São Paulo cotton. Brazil had succeeded during the worst years of the depression in becoming one of the large suppliers of a highly-competitive world commodity.[152] This did not, however, produce a world of peasants.[153] The 'democratising' effect of the 1929 crisis was, at best, limited. Instead, 'Brazil's God number two', as cotton came to be known, contributed to the coffee planters' ability to withstand the slump in coffee prices. Cotton offered coffee planters the opportunity to transfer land planted in low-yielding coffee to this crop. In the 1930s, the bulk of cash crops for export continued to be produced on large estates.[154]

The development of food production was more differentiated. Sugar doubled between 1928–30 and 1937–9 but pig farming stagnated completely. Black beans decreased and rice and maize increased only slightly. None of the staples kept up with population growth in the state. Food production shifted from São Paulo, particularly to Minas Gerais and Rio Grande do Sul, setting in motion a trend towards the regionalisation of food crops.[155] There were a number of reasons for this. The 1929 crisis caused a sharp drop in food prices, cotton being planted on land formerly used for food crops and even intercropped with coffee.[156] Cotton sharecroppers and small tenants were allowed to intercrop food only when the soil was poor. In the case of coffee, although the decline in new planting meant that less food was produced, increased intercropping in the mature groves could have brought about an increase in food production, although in this case cotton would have competed with food for space in the coffee groves. Smallholders producing cotton combined the cash crop with food stuffs, but not for the market if prices were low. In all likelihood, the ban on new coffee planting and the extraordinary expansion of cotton, as well as the growth in sugar cane, accounted for the stagnation of basic staples at the time.

It is more difficult to assess whether (in addition to some land and capital) labour was also transferred to cotton because this, in part, depended on labour supply. Potentially cotton competed with coffee for labour. There were even those among São Paulo coffee interests who would have preferred to see other states assuming cotton

Table 2.7 Number of coffee farms, average number of trees per farm, coffee production and area planted in coffee and cotton by region, São Paulo, 1930–1 to 1937–8 (indices 1931–2 = 100)

Zones	1930–1 Index	1930–1 no.	1931–2 Index	1931–2 % of state	1934–5 Index	1935–6 Index	1937–8 Index	1937–8 % of state
Old								
Coffee farms	–	4 316	100	5.3	82	74	42	2.4
Average no. of productive trees/farm	–	9 242	100	–	97	76	102	–
Coffee production (tons)	79	19 636	100	1.7	59	50	29	0.6
Area (ha) in coffee	107	45 929	100	–	84	59	46	–
Area (ha) in cotton	–	19	100	–	1 489	23 321	18 763	–
Southern								
Coffee farms	–	5 657	100	6.9	96	108	62	4.7
Average no. of productive trees/farm	–	3 300	100	–	98	80	120	–
Coffee production (tons)	74	14 816	100	1.3	64	49	40	0.6
Area (ha) in coffee	95	28 118	100	–	81	72	57	–
Area (ha) in cotton	50	27 571	100	–	270	280	305	–
Intermediate in decline								
Coffee farms	–	4 790	100	5.8	125	115	84	5.3
Average no. of productive trees/farm	–	12 104	100	–	78	80	80	–
Coffee production (tons)	60	41 746	100	3.8	71	69	40	1.9
Area (ha) in coffee	83	79 330	100	–	95	83	60	–
Area (ha) in cotton	35	3 054	100	–	143	305	476	–

Zones	1930–1 Index	1930–1 no.	1931–2 Index	1931–2 % of state	1934–5 Index	1935–6 Index	1937–8 Index	1937–8 % of state
Intermediate								
Coffee farms	–	29 375	100	36.1	101	101	91	35.9
Average no. of productive trees/farm	–	24 218	100	–	94	90	78	–
Coffee production (tons)	76	526 215	100	48.0	64	62	63	37.7
Area (ha) in coffee	95	1 022 450	100	–	73	80	69	–
Area (ha) in cotton	48	27 898	100	–	644	852	1 222	–
New								
Coffee farms	–	37 113	100	45.6	113	117	104	51.5
Average no. of productive trees/farm	–	16 463	100	–	111	104	106	–
Coffee production (tons)	64	493 275	100	45.0	86	116	105	58.9
Area (ha) in coffee	90	1 075 712	100	–	106	90	78	–
Area (ha) in cotton	28	45 949	100	–	340	638	850	–
State of São Paulo								
Coffee farms	–	81 321	100	100.0	106	108	92	100.0
Average no. of productive trees/farm	–	17 684	100	–	101	95	99	–
Coffee production (tons)	70	1 095 688	100	100.0	74	86	80	100.0
Area (ha) in coffee	92	2 251 540	100	100.0	96	84	73	100.0
Area (ha) in cotton	39	104 471	100	100.0	397	622	919	100.0

Source: A. A. Kageyama, 'Crise e Estrutura Agrária'; these indices have been calculated on the basis of Tables 26, 27, 28 and 42 on pp. 103–6, 123.

cultivation, because coffee production was thought to be threatened by it.[157] By the mid-1930s, unemployment generated by the 1929 crisis in both industry and agriculture had diminished markedly, which was reflected in a rise in rural wages. At this point, for the first time, a rural exodus was watched with concern. New and expanding industries must have seemed to rural workers a very attractive alternative to the hardship of the countryside. Rural exodus increased the competition for labour in agriculture.[158] The extraordinary expansion of cotton without any significant decline in coffee cultivation now effectively threatened the supply of labour for the latter crop. Internal migration from other states, as well as the arrival of foreign immigrants in greater numbers, covered the increased demand to some extent. Nonetheless, particularly in the intermediate cotton zone where cotton partly replaced coffee, some transfer of labour occurred.

Conclusion

The history of coffee in Brazil is one of marked cyclical oscillations. As a tree crop of slow maturation, coffee is very unresponsive to sudden price fluctuations. Bi-annual variations in the harvest and climatic accidents caused sharp changes in levels of production. There is also a chronic tendency for coffee supply to exceed demand, resulting in recurrent over-production crises. Self-provisioning by the labourers (and in particular intercropping of food with coffee, coupled with successive price-support programmes) allowed planters, in the short run, to withstand the decline in prices quite successfully, even if in the long run both mechanisms served only to aggravate their problems by stimulating renewed over-supply and the consequent collapse in prices.

Through changes in self-provisioning conditions planters were able to adjust money wages and labour supply. Low coffee prices tended to produce a compression of money wages compensated for by more favourable self-provisioning conditions, especially intercropping of foodstuffs among mature trees. Simultaneously, however, new coffee planting slowed down, and with it overall food production with coffee. Conversely, when coffee prices were good, planters tended to forbid intercropping in mature groves granting separate plots and/or a rise in money wages instead, although self-provisioning was never entirely suppressed. At the same time, new coffee planting would expand greatly, intercropping of food on new plantations accounting for a growth in overall food production. On the frontier, however, planters had no need to offer their *colonos* more than the customary planting rights, because higher soil fertility in itself was enough of an attraction.

The frequent objection to export crops as imperialist products which subjugate especially food crops to their vagaries, needs qualifying in the case of São Paulo coffee.[159] Under the *colonato* system food crops formed part of coffee growing. The extent to which *colonos* sold food surpluses on the market is difficult to assess, but the large labour force working on coffee plantations fed itself, thus reducing potential demand. The plantation economy entailed a symbiotic relationship between coffee as the cash crop and foodstuffs.

The predominance of coffee in São Paulo agriculture did not preclude diversification, but diversification of agricultural production did not seriously challenge the state's land-tenure structure. As long as São Paulo had a frontier, there were no natural limits to the expansion of food production within as well as outside the coffee-producing sector. By the 1910s, food in the state was grown and in part consumed by the *colonos* and by an emerging sector of autonomous food producers operating completely outside the coffee sector. Rising food prices in the first decade of the century were produced initially by the tariffs on food imports rather than a shortage. Production, however, was quick to respond. By the late 1920s food prices rose, above all as a result of growing urban demand at a time of unprecedented prosperity.

This complementarity between coffee and food crops under the *colonato* system lent coffee planters special resilience to adjust to fluctuations in coffee yields and prices. Self-provisioning by the labourers operated as a sort of cushion that helped absorb part of the impact of adverse market conditions. A measure of the cost flexibility of the *colonato* system is the fact that even when prices were at their lowest point, nowhere until the late 1930s did crops go unharvested, or were coffee trees uprooted on a significant scale.

The extraordinary expansion of coffee in São Paulo threatened Brazil's economic stability in another way. In the 1920s this crop alone accounted for as much as 70 per cent on the country's foreign exchange earnings. It was this dependence on coffee for its export earnings, aggravated by the coffee sector's boundless ambitions, that made the Brazilian economy especially vulnerable to price fluctuations on the world market.

If the sustained high level of coffee production even after 1929 is any indication of the fortunes of coffee planters, then they showed remarkable resistance in a context in which profitable alternatives did exist as well in agriculture as in industry. This impression contrasts sharply with the sense of panic and dismay much of the writing of the period conveys. Ellis, a São Paulo Deputy to the Federal Chamber in the early 1930s, for example, described the 1929 crash in truly apocalyptic terms:

> The coffee drama which began in 1929 was like the bursting of a dam which as the water rushes across the wall floods and destroys everything in its way. Thus was also the coffee drama. In its suddenness, it produced such a transformation in São Paulo that all was flooded and changed with unbelievable speed ... The planters who were impoverished by the sudden price slump had to dispose of their estates endeavouring to make better use of what they had left, and resorting to other activities more rewarding for the effort made. With this the *colonos* of the plantations ... were becoming landowners.[160]

Even if coffee production in the 1930s was no longer a source of as enormous and rapidly-earned wealth as it had been in the 1920s, such descriptions of collapse, chaos, and the break up of properties should be regarded with caution. The crash of 1929 was felt to be so painful also because it came after a period of almost unprecedented boom. Even so, coffee planters were very slow and hesitant to move away from that crop, with the result that, rather than a sharp decline in production, there was stagnation in the late 1930s instead. As the elusiveness of market equilibrium indicates, planters were not discouraged from producing coffee at the low price to any significant degree. In this period coffee was only beginning to lose its economic pre-eminence. This was due, however, to the growth of other sectors of the economy rather than to an absolute decline in coffee production.

Neither was the coffee bourgeoisie destroyed or even politically marginalised by the crash. Coffee policy still favoured the majority of planters. The repeated moratoria of debts the government granted coffee growers in the 1930s, and the irritation of commerce and industry with what they felt were undue privileges, were indication enough that the planters as well as the exporters still wielded considerable influence, even though coffee policy was now formulated directly by the Federal government through the National Coffee Department.

As Paulo Prado wrote, with as much drama as lucidity, in 1933:

> Two years precisely, two years were enough for the catastrophe [he had foreseen in 1927] to take place ... The martyrdom of coffee has culminated. The storm, the levies have intensified. Even a bonfire like those of the Inquisition has been lit. The product of so much effort and energy has been dissipated in smoke and ashes. *Yet, coffee still believes in a miracle* [my emphasis].[161]

The coffee sector may have felt that it was burning at the stake, yet coffee growers were justified in believing in a miracle. In the 1930s, as before, the efforts and energies of the *colono* families were largely responsible for sustaining this belief.

3 The Transition: From *Colonos* to Wage Labour

'The patriarchal hoe is to give way once and for all to the modern tool, the primitive plough to the tractor.' UK Department of Overseas Trade, *Economic Conditions in Brazil* (December 1930) (London, 1931) p. 72

'Each worker drawn from the countryside and brought to town ceases to be a producer and has to transform himself into a consumer, whose demands grow in proportion to the improvement in his standard of living.' G. Vargas, 'Convocação a todos os Brasileiros para a batalha da produção agrária', 8 April 1952, in G. Vargas, *O Governo Trabalhista no Brasil* (Rio de Janeiro, 1954) II, p. 433

'One can no longer do anyone a good turn ... On one occasion I hired an unemployed and starving family on my estate. I gave a light job to the *cabolo* who was incapacitated. A few months later he and his wife took me to court demanding payment of the minimum wage, vacation and the annual bonus. I'll have to pay it all. But from now on I will only keep the indispensable workers. Otherwise I'll have to sell the land.' A landowner in Jaú, São Paulo, quoted in 'A Nova Face da Agricultura', *Coopercotia* (October 1968) p. 14

Until the Second World War the history of the São Paulo coffee planters was a story of remarkable success in withstanding recurrent market adversities. The unique form of labour exploitation, the *colonato* system, played a crucial role in this. But despite its proven efficiency, by the 1960s this labour system had virtually disappeared from São Paulo's coffee plantations. Between 1964 and 1975, the agricultural labour force of the state declined by 35 per cent while the number of workers resident on estates diminished by 52 per cent and the proportion of non-resident labour in the agricultural labour force rose from 15.8 to 35.8 per cent. As the *colono* families disappeared, a new figure, the *volante*, aptly called the 'new nomad', made its appearance on the São Paulo agricultural scene. He or she

earns his or her livelihood in agriculture but now lives in town.[1] By
1970, São Paulo had the largest proportion of casual wage labourers
in Brazil.

The disappearance of the *colonato* system from coffee plantations
and its replacement by casual wage labourers is only one instance of
a more general transformation of São Paulo's agricultural structure
beginning sometime in the 1950s. But because coffee played such a
prominent economic role and absorbed the largest proportion of the
agricultural labour force in the state at the time, it is exemplary of the
processes that produced the transition to casual wage labour.[2]

Table 3.1 Agricultural labour force by residence (rural or
urban) for selected states, Brazil, 1970

States	Urban residence	(%)	Rural residence	(%)	Total
Pernambuco	100 279	13.1	664 440	86.9	764 719
São Paulo	346 896	26.6	954 934	73.4	1 301 830
Paraná	105 780	7.4	1 333 058	92.6	1 438 838
Goiás	76 134	14.5	447 983	85.5	524 117

Source: E. N. Gonzalez and M. I. Bastos, 'O Trabalho Volante na
Agricultura Brasileira', Universidad Paulista, Botucatú, *A Mão-de-Obra
Volante na Agricultura* (São Paulo, 1982) p. 36.

Early studies attributed casualisation of rural labour primarily to
the effects of protective legislation made extensive to agricultural
workers in 1963.[3] Rural employers were said to have cut down their
permanent labour to a minimum and have hired casual wage labour
supplied by labour contractors instead to evade the new legal
obligations and the increase in labour costs they entailed.[4] In subsequent analyses, however, the politics of productive relations moved
very much into the background. Casual wage labour was now seen
both as a symptom and a consequence of the advance of capitalism
in Brazilian agriculture being alternatively attributed to technical
innovations in agriculture which affected labour demand,[5] to the
belated consitution of a labour market which now permitted landowners to release their resident labour force and recruit more efficient
casual wage labour,[6] to the rise in land value and the expansion of

commercial food production,[7] or to changing cropping patterns combined with more capital-intensive cultivation methods which again affected labour needs.[8]

Generally, these explanations for the spread of casual wage labour in São Paulo agriculture lack historical depth, resting on misconceptions regarding the specific character of the *colonato* system and fail to take into account the political context in which the transition occurred.[9]

Brant's study is exceptional in that he interprets casualisation of labour against the background of a systematic analysis of the *colonato* system which it superseded. In the absence of a labour market, in the 1920s in the region of Assis, hiring permanent labourers in family units entitled to self-provisioning became a way of securing scarce labour, diminishing the cost of its reproduction and, through payment by results, spreading the risk. But productivity was low implying an underuse of labour. When labour supply improved in the 1940s, planters adjusted labour use in accordance to the agricultural cycle. As a consequence family labour was liberated, small commercial food production was separated from the large estates and, in the 1960s, growing numbers of resident labourers were dismissed.[10] Brant is rightly sceptical of landowners' complaints about the economic burden protective legislation imposed on them in 1963. But his view that the *colonato* system was a way of securing scarce labour of low productivity is problematic. In effect, the *colonato* became prevalent on São Paulo coffee plantations precisely in the 1880s when subsidised mass immigration provided the labour reserve planters needed to expand coffee production. And it was a labour system which exploited the whole *colono* family most efficiently, being incompatible with mechanised cultivation because this would have made labour idle during part of the year.[11] Labour productivity was lower than it would have been had coffee cultivation been mechanised but not because the *colonato* system was a form of 'disguised unemployment'. On the contrary, labour exploitation was most intense.

D'Incão e Mello studied both the processes that gave rise to casual wage labour as well as the labourers' working conditions today in a region only slightly west to Brant's research, but her conclusions are quite different. The proliferation of casual wage labour was a necessary, yet contradictory, result of capital accumulation in agriculture in the form of land concentration, proletarianisation and social polarisation. In the region, the advance of capitalism meant the substitution of cotton grown by small tenants and sharecroppers for coffee and the expansion of extensive cattle raising. This latter process accelerated in the late 1950s and 1960s its victims being not only resident workers, be they *colonos*, small tenants or share-croppers, but also small owner operators who were driven to the towns where they now lead an increasingly 'marginalised' existance.[12] D'Incão e Mello's use of the concept of capital accumulation for extensive cattle raising and her treatment of sharecroppers and small tenants as proletarians is problematic.[13] Moreover, in contrast with Brant she attributes the limited extent of mechanisation in agriculture in the region to an abundance of labour.

Singer shares Brant's labour scarcity thesis but places his main emphasis on changes that occurred in food production. The capitalisation of food production is the dynamic factor in this scenario. Urbanisation increased the demand for food and raised food prices, in turn stimulating commercial food production and adding to the value of land. Productivity of food produced with industrial inputs improved by contrast with the *colonos'* subsistence crops. It was, therefore, cheaper for planters to employ wage labourers who bought their food on the market and who could be hired in accordance with seasonal needs, instead of having to be given time and land to grow their own food.[14]

Lastly, Graziano da Silva has recently focused attention on the technological modernisation of agriculture and the effect this had on the labour process and on productive relations. The late 1950s and early 1960s saw the mechanisation of São Paulo agriculture. A period of rapid economic expansion between 1956 and 1960 was followed by a period of stagnation which lasted until about 1967. It was during this time that a domestic industry of agricultural inputs (tractors, fertilisers, etc.) was established in the country which, coupled with government subsidised credit, particularly benefited large landowners. This, together with a rise in land values due to more intensive land use and to speculation, accelerated the technological development of agriculture in the late 1960s with far-reaching consequences for prevailing productive relations. In São Paulo, where mechanisation had advanced most, only part of the labour process in coffee was mechanised, which deepened the seasonality of labour on the estates. Planters consequently reduced their permanent labour force to a minimum, working their estates increasingly with casual wage labour hired in nearby towns. Contemporary events such as the passage of protective legislation for rural workers, changes in cropping pattern, massive uprooting of coffee trees in the early 1960s and their replacement by pastures and temporary crops such as soy beans and wheat and rising land values were subsidiary factors which only served to accelerate a process which Graziano da Silva attributes first and foremost to technological change.[15]

There is obviously little agreement on the factors which brought about the extinction of the *colonato* system and the spread of casual wage labour. Much of the debate focuses on the manner in which the advance of capitalism is thought to have eroded traditional forms of labour exploitation by introducing capital-intensive inputs which raise productivity. A fundamental shortcoming of all these analyses is that hardly any attention is paid to the important political developments and especially the mounting political tensions surrounding the agrarian question in the late 1950s and early 1960s, and which, as I will show, played *the* fundamental role. Changing production relations do not only involve the technical reorganisation of the labour process. Productive relations always entail specific forms of domination. At the time the whole structure of political domination in Brazilian agriculture came under attack. Coffee growers operated within a new set of relations both *vis-à-vis* labour and the State. It is this new political constellation which requires analysis.

THE DOCTRINE OF ECONOMIC DEVELOPMENT

Before the war, State intervention in the economy responded largely to particular conjunctures. In Brazil, systematic planning of the economy began in the early 1950s. At this point planning was inspired by a long-term development programme designed to achieve the country's economic independence from the developed countries through import-substitution industrialisation. Industry should lead economic development; the agricultural sector was assigned a supporting role. Coffee exports were to provide the foreign exchange required for accelerated industrialisation. Agricultural production for the domestic market was to furnish the raw materials and food needed by expanding domestic industry and to feed the growing urban population.

The development model of the early 1950s was informed above all by President Vargas's 'nationalist' project and by the development strategy formulated by the United Nations Economic Commission for Latin America (ECLA) whose goals were to increase the productivity of labour through technological innovation and to ensure the net inflow of foreign exchange earned, in the case of Brazil, mainly by coffee.[16]

Significantly, Brazil's economic development potential was the object of ECLA's first country case study which was prepared in 1953 at the request of Brazil's Economic Development Bank. And in 1958 ECLA, in collaboration with the United Nations Food and Agriculture Organization (FAO) prepared an extensive survey of the coffee production structure in São Paulo.[17] The ECLA reports as well as the Joint Brazil/United States Economic Development Commission studies provided both the Vargas and the Kubitschek governments with their data base for economic planning. President Vargas approved of the ECLA development theses because he shared their emphasis on the need for planning, and on industrialisation as the appropriate path for the country's social improvement and economic emancipation. He also agreed with the reformist approach of ECLA's development model which conceived of the possibility of economic growth without radical socioeconomic change.

By the late 1940s, two distinct sectors could be distinguished in Brazilian agriculture, one mainly supplying the domestic market, the other producing predominantly for export. The approach to agricultural development had to be double pronged. Productivity of agricultural production for the domestic market needed to be raised to improve the supply of food and of raw materials. Coffee policy, by contrast, was designed to regulate trade rather than transform the production structure, in order to maximise foreign exchange earnings from coffee for the industrialisation drive.

Agricultural Development or Structural Reforms

Already in the early 1950s the stagnation of agricultural production, especially for the domestic market, was diagnosed as a serious obstacle to sustained economic growth. All post-war analyses in some way or other dealt with the problem of food shortages for the growing urban population in a rapidly industrialising country. Attention focused on the causes for the lag in domestic food supply, its effects on foreign exchange expenditures and on industrial production costs as well as on social peace.

The distinguished economist Gouvêa de Bulhões offered a well-rounded vision of how the problem of lagging agricultural production was being perceived:

It is useless to discuss whether it is better to stimulate industrialisation or improve agricultural development. It is obvious that Brazil demands a greater development of her industries and also a substantial improvement in her agriculture. The interests of industry and agriculture need not be in opposition to each other, having to be, on the contrary, perfectly coordinated. By improving agriculture and turning it more productive, industrialisation will be made easier since in this way it will be possible to produce more economically and to obtain a larger quantity of raw materials to be processed by the national industries. In this way more labour will also be available for industry without the risk of a reduction in the supply of foodstuffs for the urban industrial population and without producing an increase in their cost. Moreover, a larger market would be created for industrial products in this way.[18]

Two economic reports of the early 1950s dealt with the problem of food supply, a study of the Brazilian economy prepared by the Joint Brazil/United States Economic Development Commission[19] and a special report requested in 1953 from an American consultancy firm by the Industrial Development Commission set up by the Vargas government.[20] Both reports focused on food prices, expressing the concern of many industrialists. The shortfalls in supply, which exerted pressure on prices, were attributed to market imperfections which needed eliminating rather than to inadequate production in relation to population growth. The ECLA report of 1956 (and more recently Edel) similarly argued that agricultural production for the domestic market had kept pace with rising urban demand in the 1940s and early 1950s.[21] Both reports, however, compare aggregate agricultural production, excepting export crops, with the rate of demographic growth but do not analyse the production structure or land-tenure pattern in the food producing sector. Precisely in the 1950s, the earlier trend towards an increase in the number of small producers also engaged in food production for urban markets, was being reversed.[22] As the market for export crops was improving, food production for the domestic market was probably contracting. And many of those who were migrating to the towns, because they were expelled by changes in land-tenure structure and/or were attracted by higher wages in industry, ceased to produce a marketable surplus and in addition stopped feeding themselves, which had a compounded effect on urban demand for food.[23]

In effect, as Baer has suggested, although poor transport and storage facilities which led to wastage of foodstuffs contributed to the inadequacy of food supply, rapid urban growth aggravated the problem. The annual rate of population growth between 1950 and 1960 was around 3 per cent, but whereas the urban population was rising at a yearly rate of 5.4 per cent, the rural population grew by only 1.6 per cent annually.[24]

President Vargas argued that rural exodus needed to be contained because it increased food demand without a corresponding increase in production.[25] Migration to the towns placed a heavy burden on urban services and 'created huge marginal populations, which are socially disorganised and receptive to subversive agitation'.[26] And rising inflation resulted in an increase in industrial action. As an industrialist and close associate of Vargas put it in 1953, the only way to prevent food shortages and to reduce prices was to intensify and rationalise agricultural production: 'In order to end social unrest in Brazil I propose a revolution for food. Nobody protests with a full stomach'.[27]

Vargas approached the food problem from two potentially conflicting perspectives combining the *trabalhismo* and *desenvolvimentismo* so characteristic of his political style which aimed at reconciling class interests. On the one hand he advocated the modernisation of agriculture but on the other he also argued for an improvement in working conditions for rural labour by making protective legislation extensive to them and for facilitating their access to land. An effective implementation of the labour laws in agriculture (a statutary minimum wage, job security, compensation for unjust dismissal, holiday pay, etc.) through which Vargas appealed to the rural workers, might well have induced landowners to mechanise production, which in turn would have raised productivity improving food supply and diminishing the inflationary pressure on wages, thus satisfying industrialists. But it would also have accelerated the displacement of rural workers to the towns, which the unification of the rural and urban labour markets was designed to contain.[28]

In the end President Vargas lacked the political support for effective reforms, but two initiatives in particular which were taken by his government to improve conditions of the rural poor were to have a profound if delayed effect for the structure of political domination in Brazilian agriculture. In September 1953, Vargas sent a bill to Congress which was designed to give the government ample powers to expropriate uncultivated land on latifundia to settle landless labourers.[29] Despite innumerable amendments, substitute bills and endless debates, however, all attempts at passing a land-reform law were blocked by Congress for the next decade. And Vargas's repeated pledge to extend protective legislation to rural workers in order to contain rural exodus in practice fared no better, although it was to have an important symbolic effect.

Upon his resignation as Labour Minister, in February 1954, Goulart submitted a draft of a law to Vargas which extended labour laws to agriculture.[30] In April of the same year Vargas endorsed the proposal in his Presidential message to Congress. In August 1954, however, driven by growing opposition to his social and economic policies, Vargas made a final political gesture of lasting effectiveness: the President committed suicide.

Vargas's other manifest goal was to modernise agriculture. Domestic capabilities to achieve this aim were very limited.[31] Domestic industry for agricultural inputs was very slow to take off despite the average price of a tractor, for instance, having almost trebled between 1948–52 and 1954.[32] Compared to potential demand, imports of farm equipment under Vargas's government were limited as well. Fertilisers had done somewhat better. After 1953, considerable import substitution of fertilisers occurred, in particular of phosphates, although imports remained high.[33] Nonethess, the average price of fertilisers rose comparatively less than that of tractors.[34]

On becoming President in 1956, Kubitschek took office already equipped with an extensive development plan. This Target Plan had as its explicit aim to consolidate the country's industrialisation effort by 'accelerating the accumulation process, increasing productivity of existing investments and applying new investments to productive activities'.[35] Agriculture was seen to deserve attention only in so far as distortions in that sector might jeopardise continuing industrialisation. As Kubitschek declared, the country was not a 'producer of primary goods by hereditary vocation'.[36] Deteriorating agricultural production for the domestic market demanded both infra-structural and pro-duction structure improvements. Nonetheless, only 3.2 per cent of the initial total planned investments under the Target Plan were assigned to ameliorating food production and supply.[37] The coffee sector was excluded from the Target Plan's development goals altogether, being dealt with through exchange policy.

The relegation of agriculture to second place was partly offset by subsidies to farm inputs and, equally important, by a tacit agreement by Kubitschek not to meddle with existing property and productive relations in agriculture. With regard to the agrarian question the continuity between the agricultural policies of Vargas and Kubitschek broke down. It is impossible to know, in view of his sudden death, whether Vargas's proposed transformations of property and productive relations were more than rhetoric, but he had kept these sensitive issues alive in his many public appearances. Landed interests obviously had felt threatened by his populist appeals. Under President Kubitschek the alliance with landed interests was once more consolidated.

The Target Plan gave priority to indirect investments in infrastructure (such as warehouses and silos, cold storage facilities and industrial slaughterhouses) and to the supply of farm equipment and fertilisers. But only these latter goals were totally accomplished. Between 1956 and 1961, over 7000 tractors were imported.[38] Domestic nitrogen production by Petrobrás and Economic Development Bank's financing of phosphates, along with authorised imports, permitted the fulfilment of the target for fertilisers.[39]

Nonetheless, Kubitschek's contributions to agricultural modernisation were only a drop in the ocean. The proportion of farms using only human labour, for instance, even rose betweeen 1950 and 1960 from 73 to 76 per cent of all farms. Despite the increase in the number of tractors in the country in the 1950s, in 1960 even in the four southern states (São Paulo, Rio Grande do Sul, Paraná and Santa Catarina) where the bulk of farm equipment was concentrated, there was still only one tractor for every 261 hectares of crop land, or one for every 22 farms. The increase in the absolute number of farms using mechanised power in 1960 did not accompany the rapid expansion of crop land and of the number of farms in the period.[40]

Moreover, agricultural credit from various sources constituted a minute proportion of the total credit given although it rose from 6 to 10 per cent in the 1950s. And the distribution of credit between crops was very uneven, São Paulo coffee production absorbing, for instance, 50 per cent of the credits given by the Office of Agricultural and Industrial Credit (*Carteira de Crédito Agrícola e Industrial*) to that state in the second half of the 1950s.[42]

The agrarian question under Kubitschek, on the other hand, was relegated to endless and totally ineffectual congressional debates against the background of growing demands by rural workers.

In 1955, Kubitschek had been elected on a coalition ticket drawn up between the PSD, representing large landed interests, and Vargas's PTB which had proposed Goulart as its candidate to the Vice-Presidency. Part of the minimum programme drafted by the PTB and accepted by Kubitschek was the 'extinction of latifundia' and the 'extension of the legal advantages of the labour laws and social security to rural workers'.[43] In his first presidential message to Congress, the new President had stressed that industrialisation required a 'solid basis in agriculture' as well as an 'expanding internal market'. The rural market was regrettably limited by the inadequate 'agrarian structure in terms of property relations' due to a 'disequilibrium between a reduced number of landowners and the very large number of those who worked on somebody else's land'.[44] No measures were taken, however, to right this imbalance during Kubitschek's government nor did Vice-President Goulart (who was at the time national President of the PTB and was repeatedly taken to task for his passivity by the progressive wing in his own party) do anything about diminishing the political influence of landed interests.[45] In effect, in the second half of the 1950s any attempt to obtain congressional approval for any measure that might challenge landed privileges was blocked.

Instead, agrarian representatives became more organised in Congress and were able to offer effective opposition to legal changes in social relations in agriculture. In December 1955, a Rural Lobby (the *Bloco Ruralista*) was formed in the Federal Chamber of Deputies, headed by the PTN Deputy for São Paulo, Miguel Leuzzi, and composed mainly of PSD deputies. It systematically obstructed any legal reforms of the agrarian structure.[46]

As the debate over land reform was gaining momentum, the agrarian oligarchy, through its own organisations, took the offensive. In 1956 the *Sociedade Rural Brasileira* made public its strong opposition to land reform, a position which was reiterated in 1959,[47] and sent a memorandum to Congress energetically rejecting the extension of labour laws to rural workers, a measure they denounced as sheer demagogy. Significantly, the association objected above all to job security for rural labour demanding an increase in productivity instead. This would, they felt, improve the position of workers and contribute at the same time to harmonious working relationships and the good of the whole community.[48]

Landed interests, however, and especially those engaged in export agriculture, not only exercised great political influence in both

Houses of Congress.[49] but the coffee sector in particular remained economically powerful as well.[50]

Coffee for Industrialisation

The realignment of economic forces in the country that began some time early in the century, was consolidated in the post-war years. Coffee lost its dynamic role in the Brazilian economy to industry. This does not mean, however, that coffee planters and exporters were deprived at one stroke of their economic and political pre-eminence. Import substitution industrialisation depended for its resources mainly on foreign exchange earnings from coffee.[51] As a contemporary put it, 'coffee, today is gold for us. It produces foreign exchange. It is wealth and credit. And, above all, it is economic survival'.[52] The renewed importance of coffee provided the coffee sector with political leverage which allowed planters and exporters to protect their interests from encroachment of the 'national' interest, at least until 1958-9, with considerable success.

Export agriculture in general, and coffee in particular, were subject to policies designed to maximise foreign exchange earnings. As distinct from the pre-war period, during the 1950s exchange policy in the form of what was disparagingly called 'exchange confiscation' assumed a central role. The coffee planters' and exporters' ability to offset the full effect the new coffee policy would otherwise have had in depressing their incomes raise two related questions, namely as to the political resources they had at their disposal to influence government policy and the extent to which they effectively succeeded in protecting their returns.

The net result of the 1929 depression and, in particular of the war years was a decline in world coffee production to the extent that remaining surplus stocks in Brazil were exhausted by 1949. Demand was expanding faster than supply; between 1946 and 1952 the volume of Brazilian coffee exports remained relatively stable, but prices trebled. Between 1950 and 1953, world market equilibrium was just maintained, but then reports of a severe frost in Brazil drove prices up to the unprecendented level of almost 1 dollar (for type Santos 4) a pound; for the whole of 1954 the price remained at 78.8 cents.[53]

This time, however, coffee growers, especially in São Paulo were initially more muted in their enthusiasm, and responded only slowly to the remarkable price recovery. At the end of the 1940s it was, above all, in the neighbouring state of Paraná that coffee expanded most,[54] whereas in São Paulo diversification of crops advanced. Crop land increased by 21 per cent between 1948 and 1958, but sugar cane and oranges for export accounted for a much larger share in this expansion than coffee. The area under cotton simultaneously diminished dramatically, while food crops increased.[55]

Existing coffee trees in São Paulo had aged and yields were low through years of neglect. Production was hence at first unresponsive to better cultivation once prices improved.[56] Moreover, by the early 1950s coffee in São Paulo had reached the frontier of the state, and a certain amount of new planting occurred in the old regions. By the mid-1950s, however, Brazilian coffee production was growing year by year and São Paulo's contribution was far from negligible. By 1957–8 a new over-production cycle gained momentum, and prices declined once more. By 1961 they had dropped by about 60 per cent;[57] coffee surpluses once again accumulated in Brazil, and market intervention was resumed by the government on a large scale.

Provided there was no market intervention, the country's exchange rate was closely linked to the international coffee price. High coffee prices meant a strengthening of the currency; inversely, depending also on market conditions, a devalued currency tended to depress international coffee prices. Any government intervention in the exchange market had repercussions for the coffee sector because it simultaneously affected international prices and internal value of coffee exports.

There had been earlier instances in which the government had regulated the coffee exchange rate, but nothing compared to the systematic control practised from 1953 onward.[58]

Immediately after the war the Brazilian government devalued the country's currency, adopting the 1937 parity with the dollar. But the currency remained overvalued. The coffee sector was, however, largely unaffected by this because growing world demand was driving up prices. They generally opposed currency devaluation even though their earnings in domestic currency would have improved, because after years of depression coffee planters were wary of any measure that might destabilise the market and lower international prices, and exporters were sceptical of the chances of a devaluation increasing exports.[59]

In May 1951, Congress received a bill from the Executive proposing the adoption of free exchange for exports and capital flows. The bill was approved in December 1952, to become effective in February of the following year.[60] Simultaneously, the currency was again devalued. A number of transactions were, however, excluded from the free exchange market most notably coffee. Imports were classified according to their degree of essentiality, the more essential ones being traded at the lower, official, rate, with agricultural equipment regarded as highly essential. Most exporters were entitled to sell part of their export earnings at the free market rate, which was more than double the official rate.[61] Coffee-export earnings, however, could be exchanged only at the official rate, which was roughly the same as the rate that had prevailed prior to the exchange reform. Consequently, coffee depreciated in comparison with other agricultural exports which had at least partial access to free exchange.

The aim of the new exchange policy was to stimulate exports of primary products in order to obtain much-needed foreign exchange to cover the mounting commercial arrears that had been accumulating during the Korean war boom and to finance raw material and capital goods imports for industrial development. This was to be done by transferring resources above all from coffee to essential imports through differential exchange rates.

Coffee planters felt that the new exchange system was highly unjust. Being obliged to sell all their foreign exchange earnings at an artificially high rate was doubly objectionable; not only did the government 'confiscate' about half their export earnings, but they were also denied preferential access to foreign exchange to pay for their imports.[62]

Planter associations protested vehemently over the government's 'exchange confiscation' which deprived coffee planters of the full benefits of their toil. Especially in the old coffee regions, it was argued, production was rapidly becoming a losing venture. With accelerating cost inflation, the new exchange system would inevitably drag coffee production into deficits irretrievably liquidating the best sources of foreign exchange the country possessed.[63]

When, in June 1953, the list of export commodities with access to free exchange was lengthened, but coffee was once again left out, coffee planters were adamant.[64] But in October, the entire scheme was replaced by a formal multiple exchange rate system, SUMOC Instruction No. 70. Differential bonuses were now granted to export commodities in accordance with market conditions. The Bank of Brazil regained its monopoly over foreign exchange transactions and paid the official rate plus a bonus of 5 *cruzeiros* per dollar for exchange earnings from coffee and of 10 *cruzeiros* for those from other agricultural commodities. In other words, coffee producers received an increase of 27.2 per cent in their *cruzeiro* earnings from coffee while other agricultural commodities got a rise in their *cruzeiro* returns of over 50 per cent.[65]

Throughout the 1950s, coffee producers were fairly successful in extracting successive readjustments of the bonus from the government, at times resorting to unprecedented methods of persuasion. In 1953, it appears, there was for the first time talk among coffee growers in São Paulo and Paraná of a march on the presidential palace in Rio de Janeiro to demand better earnings in domestic currency from the government.[66] The readjustment of the coffee exchange rate in October 1953 was certainly the result of this mounting protest. As one Federal Deputy stated at the time, 'either the government adjusts the exchange rate, or the hen of the golden eggs which is coffee production, will perish'.[67]

Under the new exchange system, direct quantitative controls on imports were abandoned for multiple exchange rates coupled with exchange auctions by the Bank of Brazil, which now provided resources for purchases abroad. Importers were able to buy foreign exchange at official auctions at a rate set by demand for foreign exchange. The difference between the official rate paid by the Bank of Brazil to coffee producers plus the bonus and the rate obtained by the government at the foreign exchange auctions from importers, constituted a continual loss of potential earnings by coffee producers.[68] Resources transferred to the government in the form of auction premiums in effect until 1959 are estimated to have contributed over 10 per cent of the government's total revenue during that period.[69]

The iniquities of 'exchange confiscation' became truly unacceptable only when prices fell. The turning point came in late 1954. In the middle of the year coffee prices had reached an all-time high, due partly to price support by the Brazilian authorities. The United States' government strongly objected to Brazil's high-price policy and US imports, which had accounted for about two-thirds of Brazilian exports, fell dramatically and permanently.[70] Soon after price support had to be abandoned and prices dropped.

Coffee growers were, therefore, only temporarily mollified by the exchange bonus they had obtained in 1953.[71] In effect, by 1955 they, this time allied with exporters, had succeeding in extracting two further readjustments to the coffee exchange rate from the authorities. These increases in *cruzeiro* receipts from coffee more than compensated growers for the decline in international prices.[72]

By interfering with trading, recurrent adjustments of coffee exchange and the 1954 export debacle had affected exporters very adversely as well. Hence, early in 1955, it was their turn to protest. The regrettable deterioration of the coffee market, they felt, more than ever demanded stability and constancy in coffee policy. They also objected to coffee's ommision in a recent raise of the bonuses for other agricultural commodities, and rejected the official justification that an increase in the coffee bonus would produce a decline in world prices. On the contrary, it was the authorities' constant meddling with the exchange rates that damaged the market.[73]

At times of declining demand, a depreciation of Brazilian coffee would indeed have depressed external prices. Coffee exporters knew this well, but they hoped that a devaluation would improve exports.[74] Exporters were free traders by profession; anything that stood in the way of exports, be it government price support by withholding surpluses or an exchange policy designed to maximise foreign exchange earnings at a time of shrinking demand, was a threat to exporters' interests. At this point, producers and exporters for once agreed over depreciation, even though for different reasons. Producers demanded higher bonuses because they would bring more *cruzeiros* for their exports. Exporters advocated depreciation of coffee because they hoped that this might stimulate lagging exports.

Coffee policy remained unaltered until mid-1957, when the authorities drew up a Coffee Defence Plan, which re-established a minimum price, extended a premium to high-quality coffee and assured the purchase of any surpluses by the government.[75] Early that year coffee producers had once more threatened to march on the presidential palace if exchange was not freed.[76] The Plan did not entirely satisfy them but the authorities argued that they had to protect the country's economy before attending to the coffee sector's just demands. Only with a strengthened economy and adequate foreign exchange earnings, could an internal price policy based on effective market intervention be successful.

Under adverse market conditions, it was probably too late anyway to manipulate coffee exchange without causing a further drop in international prices.[77] A guaranteed price and market stability, through withholding surpluses, may well have been preferable to through withholding surpluses, may well have been preferable to exchange readjustment. Especially when the government bought one-third of the 1957–8 crop at the market price, coffee planters appeared quite satisfied. General prosperity tended to temper conflicts of interest between planters and exporters, and among the different sectors of coffee production, but they resurfaced when the market deteriorated.

The premium on good-quality coffee constituted one sore point. It benefited those producers and exporters who held no remaining stocks from the previous harvest, but it created special marketing difficulties for those who, in the hope of the 'Producers' March' bringing about an exchange reform, had withheld stocks to sell at a better *cruzeiro* price. And the premium discriminated against producers of low-quality coffee. And finally, although export firms obviously denied this accusation, the large foreign exporters seemed to be reaping the premium to the detriment of the medium and small coffee producers by persuading them to sell their new crop at lower prices through alleging that the government lacked the resources to purchase excess coffee[78] Be this as it may, exporters themselves objected strongly to the premium because it had created two parallel coffee markets, to the disadvantage of old coffee stocks.

In 1958, the financial situation of the country (and with it that of coffee) became dramatic. Price support, which entailed printing money, stimulated inflation, was costly, and had not succeeded in restoring prices and exports. Some coffee growers came out in defence of price support, but they now faced strong opposition which blamed the withholding of extensive stocks of coffee for the country's desperate financial situation.[79]

As part of a new stabilisation plan, the recently appointed Finance Minister cut down the support price for export coffee and for surplus purchases. To improve subsidies, he argued, would only encourage growers to produce more coffee at a time when production was already over-abundant.[80] But the coffee sector reacted with unity and strength. For the first time, the repeatedly threatened march on the presidential palace in Rio de Janeiro went beyond a mere gesture. The Finance Minister was forced into calling out the army to block roads to prevent the irate coffee growers from reaching the capital in a motorcade of 2000 vehicles. The drastic reaction dissuaded the organisers from proceeding with the march and, for the meantime, the movement (if not their anger) was contained.

It is difficult to know what upset the coffee planters most, their momentary defeat or, as the Paraná Coffee Producers' Association lamented, 'the lack of understanding on the part of the authorities [which] should have led the glorious and respected National Army to fulfill a role incompatible with its tradition. . . [namely of defending] the healthy principles of democracy and freedom'.[81] There was a rush of declarations of democratic sentiment elicited by the army's intervention from members of a class which only a few years later was to support a military coup.[82]

Coffee planters may have been indignant about this affront, but they did not accept their defeat as definitive: although 'the Producers' March has been prevented, the old and invincible General Coffee has not however been killed. Victors, beware!'.[83]

The government had succeeded in fending off pressure from the planters for better coffee returns, but not for long. In the years that followed, among mounting rumours that the exchange system would be totally reformed, and largely to appease exasperated planters and exporters, the coffee bonus was readjusted no less than three times. And in March 1961, the entire multiple exchange rate system was abolished at last.[84] As Clemente Mariani Bittencourt, Finance Minister in the newly-elected Quadros government proudly proclaimed, he was now able to impose 'true exchange'[85]. As a consequence, the currency was devalued by 100 per cent. All imports and exports were henceforth to be effected through one market at a single exchange rate, but coffee and cocoa, along with a few essential imports, were exempted. These two commodities were also to be negotiated through the free market, but SUMOC Instruction No. 205 of May that year established an export tax ranging from 24 to 26 US dollars per 60 kg bag to be paid into a coffee defence fund.

Coffee producers were still denied the full benefit of their exchange earnings, but on account of the massive devaluation, earnings from coffee in *cruzeiros* had risen substantially above the previously fixed dollar rate.[86] The export tax was designed to reduce government expenditure on surplus buying which, at the IMF's insistence, was from then on to be financed by the coffee sector.[87]

On this occasion, 'national' and coffee interests coincided. Even at times in the 1950s, however, when they were at odds, planters and exporters were far from uninfluential in the formulation of coffee policy. The sector's constant complaints about diminishing returns were, in fact, mainly responsible for the concessions obtained from the government. Until the mid-1950s, coffee producers were unlikely to have been negatively affected by over-valued exchange because international prices were extraordinarily high.[88] When world coffee prices thereafter gradually declined, successive exchange readjustments more than compensated coffee producers, until 1958, for this fall.

Baer has calculated the effect of government exchange policy on coffee producers' purchasing power in the 1950s. He notes that only in 1959 did returns to planters from their exports fall by more than the decline in world coffee prices. And coffee producers' incomes only fell by more than the country's foreign exchange earnings from coffee from 1958 onward.[89]

But the vagaries of coffee exchange policy in the 1950s do not tell the whole story of coffee planters' fortunes in that period. There were other additional factors which attenuated the effect the 'exchange confiscation' had on incomes they so vehemently denounced. Implicit subsidies granted to imports of industrial inputs for agriculture (such as fertilisers and farm machinery) in the form of preferential exchange rates were one of these. An assurance that the entire coffee crop would be bought alleviated the effect of shrinking demand and falling prices on producers' earnings.[90] And, as I will show in the next section, coffee planters were again able to adjust labour costs to price fluctuations in the 1950s. All these factors also account for the fact that coffee planters' average incomes in the decade between 1948 and 1958 exceeded the rise in income of all other agricultural producers by a wide margin.[91] This absence of a sufficiently rewarding alternative crop, in turn, contributed to the expansionist coffee cycle outlasting the coffee boom. As one observer noted, even in 1958–59 the 'farmers of São Paulo would have been up in arms, almost literally, at any proposal to reduce productive capacity by eradication'.[92] The authorities themselves recognised that successive exchange and price-support concessions to coffee planters only 'encouraged them to produce more coffee at a time when production was over-abundant'.[93] But they were unable to resist the political pressure exerted by the coffee sector for long so that it proved very difficult for them to avert the threat of overproduction.

The fact that coffee growers' incomes declined in the late 1950s is no proof either that they were defeated at last as a class. This decline

Table 3.2 Value of Brazilian coffee exports, purchasing power of the coffee sector and variations in dollar price and cost of living, São Paulo, 1953–61

Year	Average value of coffee bag (US$) Indices[a]	Coffee exports (million bags)	Value of coffee exports (US$) Indices[b]	Indices of returns from coffee (deflated Cr$)/cost of living index, São Paulo[a]	% variations in cost of living, São Paulo[a]
1953	100	15.6	100	100	16
1954	123	10.9	87	151	23
1955	87	13.7	77	1'?	17
1956	87	16.8	94	95	33
1957	83	14.3	77	92	14
1958	76	12.9	63	86	23
1959	60	17.7	71	59	43
1960	61	16.8	65	55	32
1961	60	17.0	65	54	43

Sources:

[a] W. Baer, *A Industrialização e o Desenvolvimento do Brasil* (Rio de Janeiro, 1975) p. 102, Table 5.9 for variations in purchasing power of São Paulo coffee sector, and p. 96, Table 5.8 for cost of living variations.

[b] J. W. Rowe, *The World's Coffee* (London, 1963) p. 30; I have calculated the indices of value of exports on the basis of nominal value in US$ given by Rowe.

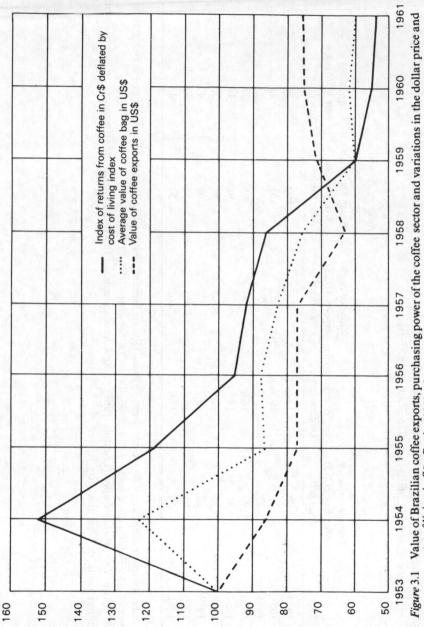

160

150

140

130

120

110

100

90

80

70

60

50

1953   1954   1955   1956   1957   1958   1959   1960   1961

——— Index of returns from coffee in Cr$ deflated by cost of living index
.... Average value of coffee bag in US$
- - - - Value of coffee exports in US$

Figure 3.1   Value of Brazilian coffee exports, purchasing power of the coffee sector and variations in the dollar price and cost of living in São Paulo, 1953–61

was not due to a greater transfer of resources to other economic interests but was the consequence of the deteriorating world market and of the domestic financial crisis, for which they themselves were partly to blame. The authorities had to maintain a difficult balance in their coffee policy, between two potentially conflicting goals: ensuring foreign exchange earnings without, however, jeopardising the country's competitiveness on the world market. Even if coffee policy was inspired primarily by the 'national' interest and implied the transfer of resources from coffee to industry, nonetheless, because of its central economic role, the coffee sector was not necessarily disadvantaged by this in either economic or political terms. As Maciel Filho had noted in 1952, 'the hegemony of [São Paulo] is determined by the number of *cruzeiros*... paid for coffee and for cotton'.[94]

The Limits of 'Technological Progress'

Until the early 1960s coffee defended themselves quite successfully against encroachments of other economic interests. Coffee growing, in the period, continued to be lucrative indeed. Those who have attributed the extinction of the *colonato* system and its substitution by casual wage labour to the adoption of more capital-intensive cultivation methods set the transition in this period.

Until the late 1940s an abundance of land and labour and the high cost of agricultural inputs usually stood in the way of mechanising Brazilian agriculture. In the 1950s government subsidies for farm machinery and fertilisers improved supply only gradually. Price guarantees and technical assistance by the government, as well as suitability for technical innovations, seem to have led to the partial mechanisation of some crops such as rice, wheat and sugar cane.[95] But coffee planters in São Paulo as well as in Paraná were, with rare exceptions, very reluctant to adopt new methods of cultivation until well into the 1960s. Only then, *after* the *colonato* had become extinct, did the introduction of technical innovations accelerate. In the 1950s there are several related reasons why coffee planters on the whole were uninterested in technological progress. Production is usually rationalised with the aim of maintaining or raising profit by improving productivity. One decisive factor influencing the decision to rationalise is the availability, discipline and cost of labour, another subsidiary one the cost of technical innovations. In the 1950s there was no shortage of labour and real wages of *colonos* declined. By comparison with the cost of labour agricultural inputs were expensive, a factor which gained weight toward the late 1950s as coffee prices declined.

Between 1952 and 1955, at the peak of the boom, rural wages considerably lagged behind the average rise in prices received by producers. Whereas real prices received by producers increased by 45 per cent between 1952 and 1954, to decline by almost 20 per cent the following year, over the same period real rural wages were slowly declining. Thereafter, up to 1961, real wages fell at a rate comparable to the decline in average real prices received by planters.[96] Accelerating inflation in the 1950s prevented the income from coffee being redistributed. There were several reasons why, despite rising inflation, planters were able to contain wage rises. For a start, landed interests had succeeded in vetoing protective legislation for rural workers, who were thereby excluded from the statutory minimum wage. Repeated readjustments of the minimum wage at the time, in fact, increased the gap between rural and urban wages and this certainly gave new impulse to rural exodus. Nonetheless, the decline in rural wages is an indication that, despite migration, there was no real labour shortage in São Paulo agriculture at the time.[97]

Diminishing labour costs obviated the need for labour-saving innovations. In effect, by 1958, coffee production in São Paulo was still heavily reliant on labour – as was shown, for instance, by the fact that on many estates the cost of one year's labour equalled or exceeded the average farm capital investment.[98] But innovations to improve the productivity of the land were also not adopted to any significant extent.

In the past, whenever coffee prices improved, the possibility of bringing new land under cultivation had been available and no effort was made to raise productivity through technical innovations, or to maintain or restore the fertility of the land. In the 1950s, the option of bringing virgin land under cultivation ceased to exist in São Paulo. Moreover, years of neglect of coffee trees had caused soil erosion and poor yields.[99]

In the early 1950s, some São Paulo coffee growers had attempted to draw their colleagues' attention to the urgency of renewing coffee production in São Paulo. Simultaneously, the São Paulo Secretary of

Agriculture in cooperation with the *Sociedade Rural Brasileira* initiated a Campaign for the Recovery of Coffee Agriculture.[100] But these efforts were for the most part overshadowed by the planters' primary concern with ensuring good prices for coffee through unflagging pressure on the authorities. More insistent and energetic calls for a 'coffee revolution' with the aid of more 'scientific' cultivation methods were heard in 1956, in response to growing foreign competition[101] but even then most coffee growers became somewhat more receptive only to the principle, but not the practice, of producing better-quality coffee from higher-yielding trees. For the most part, the 'planters who live on the asphalt' (*donos de fazenda vivendo no asfalto*), as a few of the more enterprising planters disparagingly called them, were uninterested. As one planter noted at the time, 'the rain and the hoe continue to be the two elements on which stingy planters rest their agriculture'.[102]

São Paulo's coffee yields had shown a tendency to decline since the war, while the area planted in coffee in the state expanded in the 1950s by contrast with other traditional coffee-producing states such as Minas Gerais, Rio de Janeiro and Espíritu Santo, where the trend after the war was to reduce the area and to increase coffee yields.[103]

The Agronomic Institute of Campinas had recently demonstrated that it was perfectly possible to obtain yields on old coffee land comparable to those achieved traditionally only on virgin soil. The so-called 'Campinas System' required the introduction of high-yielding coffee varieties, the regular use of chemical fertilisers, closer spacing of coffee trees, control of soil erosion through contour farming and partial mechanisation. Nevertheless, despite the campaign for coffee renewal, the demonstrations by the Agronomic Institute and the example of a few of the more enterprising planters, who adopted new cultivation methods on some old plantations in Valinhos, Campinas, Jaú, São Manoel and Itú, by 1958 little advance had been made in improving either the yields or the quality of coffee. That year only about 2 per cent of the tree population in the state were being cultivated in accordance with the new methods. Most of these trees were located in the old coffee region where soil erosion would not have paid to carry out new planting under the old extensive system.[104] Rather than adopt new cultivation methods, the majority of São Paulo planters responded to improved market conditions in the early 1950s by giving their existing trees better care, as

Table 3.3 Rural wages, average prices received by coffee growers and cost of living, São Paulo, 1948-61 (base 1952)

Year	Day-wage of resident worker[1]		Harvest rate (alqueire)[1]		Weeding task rate colono (1000 trees)[2]		Average price received by coffee growers[3]		Cost of living Index São Paulo[4]
	Index	Deflated	Index	Deflated	Index	Deflated	Index	Deflated	
1948	51	0.62	47	0.58	–	–	41	0.49	81
1949	59	0.71	65	0.78	–	–	54	0.49	83
1950	74	0.86	77	0.89	–	–	102	1.18	86
1951	87	0.97	91	1.02	–	–	96	1.07	89
1952	100	1.00	100	1.00	100	1.00	100	1.00	100
1953	107	0.92	104	0.89	116	1.00	124	1.06	116
1954	124	0.87	132	0.92	116	0.81	207	1.45	142
1955	152	0.91	106	0.63	166	1.00	200	1.20	166
1956	178	0.80	161	0.73	133	0.60	215	0.97	220
1957	205	0.82	186	0.74	–	–	222	0.88	250
1958	227	0.73	187	0.60	166[5]	0.54	162	0.52	307
1959	281	0.64	239	0.54	–	–	182	0.41	439
1960	367	0.63	332	0.57	–	–	244	0.42	579
1961	479	0.57	415	0.50	333[6]	0.40	336	0.40	827

Sources:

1. P. V. Sendin, 'Elaboração de um indice de salários rurais para o Estado de São Paulo, *Agricultura em São Paulo*, XIX, (II) (1972) p. 174, Table 3 and p. 176, Table 6.

2. Weeding task rates are given occasionally in the reports by regional inspectors of the São Paulo Secretary of Agriculture published regularly in *Agricultura em São Paulo* of the years 1951–6; no complete series is available, however.

3. São Paulo, Secretaria de Agricultura, Instituto de Econonia Agrícola, *Desenvolvimento da Agricultura Paulista* (São Paulo, 1972), p. 294.

4. W. Baer, *A Industrialização e o Desenvolvimento Econômico do Brasil* (Rio de Janeiro, 1975) p. 96, Table 5–8, the indices were calculated on the basis of yearly percentage increases in cost of living given by Baer.

5. O. J. Thomazini Ettori, 'Mão-de-obra na agricultura de São Paulo', *Agricultura em São Paulo*, VIII (12) (December 1961) p. 18.

6. *A Rural. Revista da Sociedade Rural Brasileira* (February 1961) p. 4; for the calculation of the indices of weeding task rates I have always taken the highest nominal wage given.

they had done on earlier occasions when prices rose. Trees were now weeded more regularly and more frequently and organic fertilisers were more widely used. But by 1958 regular use of fertilisers was still limited. Only 13 per cent of all coffee trees received chemical fertilisers, 29 per cent received manure, and over 50 per cent received no fertilisers at all and, moreover, the use of fertilisers on the whole was declining.[105] Though expanding coffee plantations in the state of Paraná constituted a threat to São Paulo's coffee production, the comparative advantages of Paraná's virgin territories were somewhat offset by uncertain climatic conditions and a poorer-quality coffee. It was mainly competition on the world market from African and Colombian milds which was responsible for Brazilian efforts to improve the quality of their coffee. Under the influence of government premiums to promote high-quality coffee, attempts were made to improve coffee selection. In Catanduva, for example, a group of coffee planters started a Movement for Homogenisation of Coffee by introducing a special coffee-selection procedure. A newly-founded plant hired young women to hand-select the coffee to achieve greater uniformity and to eliminate impurities,[106] an example followed somewhat later by the Alta Mogiana Regional Coffee Planters' Co-operative which introduced a similar selection process.[107]

In 1954, ECLA expressed serious doubts about coffee's future prospects and recommended controlling production through getting rid of marginal producers;[108] but until the early 1960s any proposal to uproot coffee trees fell on deaf ears. In 1958, the two FAO surveys confirmed that, far from improving, São Paulo coffee yields were likely to deteriorate further under prevailing cultivation methods.[109]

Even in the late 1950s, most coffee planters were still unwilling to get rid of ageing trees and to forgo their yields even if they were declining in order to renew coffee groves. The full restoration of coffee plantations meant temporarily foregoing production entirely. The introduction of new varieties, closer spacing and control of erosion through contour farming required the uprooting of existing trees.

In 1957 and 1958, 70 million trees were eradicated in São Paulo, but this was a very small fraction of the estimated 600 million sub-marginal trees in existence at the time. At that rate it would have taken 15 to 20 years to uproot all the trees with sub-marginal yields in 1958.[110]

More productive varieties were now available, such as *Mundo Novo* and *Caturra*. By 1958 an estimated two-thirds of new plantings were of the new varieties, but these new trees constituted a very small proportion of the tree population at the time. *Mundo Novo* accounted for 12.8 per cent of all existing trees and *Caturra* for only 1 per cent.[111] By contrast, better tree care and using fertilisers could be applied to existing trees, so did not require uprooting, to which planters were still adverse.

The way in which old trees were often replaced precluded the adoption of methods that would have raised the productivity of land and yields. Old trees were frequently replaced by interplanting new trees in the rows of established groves, by so-called *dobração* (doubling). Producers could thus harvest the old trees while waiting for the new ones to begin producing. But this practice prevented the introduction of contour farming and of closer spacing, perpetuating the old layout of the plantation. It was estimated that 3.6 per cent of the area put down to coffee in São Paulo in 1958 was interplanted with new trees, and that this practice had become very widespread over the previous few years.[112]

After 1957–8, instead of improving, coffee yields probably deteriorated further as, with falling prices, coffee planters again reverted to more widespread intercropping of foodstuffs with coffee to compensate *colonos* for their declining real wages.[113] A substantial increase in the cost of tractors and chemical fertilisers in 1958 surely further discouraged technical innovations.[114]

At least by the late 1950s 'technological progress' had advanced little on São Paulo coffee plantations, a situation that did not improve in the following years as market conditions became worse. Casualisation of labour was not therefore a consequence of technological progress.

Coffee Against Food Crops

In the late 1950s, more modern methods of cultivation were for the most part confined to the old coffee zone in the Northeast and central region of the state. Nonetheless, it is worth taking a closer look at these early technological experiments. They offer an insight into later developments that occurred in the 1970s, when the *colonato* system had already become extinct and was no longer an obstacle to mechanisation. At this point, technical innovations responded to new labour conflicts generated by the casualisation of labour, and served to consolidate it.

Where old coffee plantations were restored in the 1950s in accordance with new cultivation methods these were incompatible with the *colonato* system, though in ways different from those suggested by Graziano da Silva, for they undermined the traditional symbiosis between coffee and food crops.[115]

Planters who invested in restoring their declining coffee plantations, or who reverted to planting coffee on old coffee land, were neither romantics unwilling to accept the apparent end of the São Paulo coffee tradition or furious modernisers investing blindly in any innovation that happened to come their way. They were merely making new use of a valuable resource which they owned in a region climatically particular well suited for coffee. The recurrent frosts that had damaged plantations in the 1950s, especially in Paraná, had brought this point home. Physical and economic conditions were also favourable for other crops but, provided yields were good, the income that could be earned from coffee was still higher even by 1958 than that of any other major agricultural activity.[116] Land values were also rising steadily, and for coffee restoration to be profitable under this combination of circumstances, yields on reclaimed land had to be high. As I mentioned earlier, the 'Campinas System' was a combination of new high-yielding varieties with regular fertilising, erosion control and closer spacing of trees, which raised yields per tree and per area.

The new techniques affected seasonal labour demands, but this need not have made the *colonato* system obsolete. Coffee harvests had always been subject to fairly regular fluctuations in yields and labour requirements for coffee picking had, therefore, varied considerably. By comparison with the cultivation season, labour demand for the harvest could rise by anything between 15 and 70 per cent.[117] On occasions when there was a very large crop, *colono* family labour would be supplemented with casual wage labour. What was new about the 'Campinas System' was that it permanently increased the seasonal difference in labour needs. New varieties and regular use of fertilisers raised yields, and high-quality coffee had to be hand-picked.

The most common picking practices had been the so-called *derriça no chão* or *derriça no pano*, whereby the coffee berries fell either to the ground or onto a tarpaulin stretched out under the tree, and were separated from leaves and other impurities by winnowing. However, not all impurities could be eliminated in this way. Impurities and the unequal ripeness of the berries affected the quality of coffee. To obtain high-quality coffee, only ripe berries should be picked, by hand, going over the groves several times, which required more time.[118] More closely-spaced trees also required less weeding, though this saving was partly offset by the work involved in applying chemical fertilisers.[119] Greater seasonality of labour use, however, was not necessarily incompatible with the *colonato* system. Planters could have adapted hiring of *colono* families to cultivation rather than harvest needs, recruiting additional seasonal labour for coffee picking.

Crucial in making the *colonato* system obsolete was the effect new cultivation methods had on the former symbiosis between coffee and food crops. More closely-spaced trees and the tendency to plant new coffee trees among the rows of old groves made intercropping impossible. Moreover, intercropping became generally undesirable, anyway, in view of the aim to improve yields. Planters could grant their *colonos* a separate plot, *terra solteira* instead, as they had done before when coffee prices were good, but this became more difficult because of crop diversification in coffee plantations, especially when they were located near urban markets. Livestock and dairy farming followed by sugar cane, contributed increasingly to farm income.[120] In terms of land use, coffee and pastures were complementary, coffee occupying the higher ground less prone to frost and pastures being established in the low-lying areas where *colonos* formerly tended their plots. The introduction of such labour-intensive crops as sugar cane on coffee plantations also entailed competition for labour, especially during the harvest, and further intensified the seasonal peak in labour demand.[121]

Self-provisioning on separate plots was not only often infeasible but also undesirable because it meant that the *colono* family spent more time on the production of their subsistence than they would otherwise have done with intercropping. The *colonos* also objected to separate plots unless they received compensation for the extra labour time required. Short of resorting to other forms of labour contract, planters would instead directly provide their labourers with foodstuffs.[122] This, however, had two consequences, both of which undermined the rationale of the *colonato* system. For the coffee planter it meant that he could no longer appropriate the unpaid *colono's* labour expended on self-provisioning and the cost of the reproduction of labour rose accordingly. And for the *colonos* the handout of foodstuffs by the estate constituted an encroachment on their prerogatives. They lost the relative autonomy self-provisioning had given them, especially at a time when food prices were rising steadily. But if *colonos* no longer grew their own food, labour time was released which, together with an already reduced labour use during the cutivation season, further imbalanced the seasonal variations in labour demand.[123] Deprived of their self-provisioning rights, *colonos* sometimes abandoned the plantation to find work on other estates or, if they were lucky, in industry.[124]

In effect, on modernised and diversified coffee plantations, one solution was the so-called 'family task contract' (*empreitada familiar*), whereby labourers were hired in family units on a yearly basis to weed and harvest coffee and, instead of being allowed to grow food themselves, were given a certain amount of food in addition to a task- and piece-wage. On other estates the proportion of *colono* families in the labour force was reduced, and subsidiary crops were cultivated by wage labour paid by the day or the month (*diaristas* or *mensalistas*) hired on a daily or seasonal and yearly basis respectively. The FAO survey noted that in 1958 some coffee plantations had recently abandoned the traditional *colonato* system, replacing the *colonos* with day labourers, but that elsewhere coffee continued to be cultivated by *colonos* because of the advantages this system afforded coffee planters and labourers alike.[125] It is important to note, however, that in all the debates in the 1950s over ways and means of restoring coffee production, no-one ever suggested that the *colonato* system should be abandoned because it had become obsolete.[126] Moreover, by the late 1950s the proportion of coffee trees in São Paulo cultivated in accordance with the new land-intensive methods was extremely small. New cultivation methods in coffee can thus hardly have accounted for the end to the *colonato* system.

CLASS CONFLICT AND CHANGING PRODUCTIVE RELATIONS

In 1958, the population resident on São Paulo coffee plantations was constituted as in Table 3.4. As I will now show, two parallel developments in the early 1960s combined to bring about the disappearance of the typical *colono* family from coffee plantations and their replacement by wage labour instead. A substantial proportion of the *colono* and sharecropper families on coffee plantations fell victim to the massive coffee-eradication programmes which were enforced in

Table 3.4   Population on coffee plantations, São Paulo, 1958

Category	No.	%
Owner-operators with families	570 000	26.6
Colonos and sharecroppers with families	1 450 000	67.4
Other kinds of labour with families	130 000	6.0
Total	2 150 000	100.0

Source: 'A Industria do Café em São Paulo', *Agricultura em São Paulo*, VIII (3) (March 1961) p. 17. I have added together *colonas* and share-croppers.

the early 1960s. At the same time, the Rural Labour Statute was enacted in 1963, which defied agricultural employers' unlimited power to set conditions of work, which had permitted the high rate of surplus-labour appropriation due to which the *colonato* system excelled as a form of labour exploitation. By undermining control over labour the Statute challenged the *colonato* system itself.

Subsidised Coffee Eradication

Following the government's massive purchase of surpluses in 1957-8, for the first time the Brazilian Coffee Institute undertook to reduce (instead of only to limit) productive capacity. In 1959, the Coffee Institute proposed the so-called 'Three for One' plan, whereby for every three uprooted, one new tree would be planted.[127] This plan was a failure. Coffee planters felt that the negligible resources made available for uprooting bordered on an insult.[128] Instead, they continued to clamour for better prices and, more than ever, to complain about the government's coffee policy.[129] By 1960-1, however, Brazilian coffee stocks had reached the equivalent of more than two years' exports, and crops were still increasing. The 1961-2 coffee harvest was, with 35 million bags, the largest ever in the country's history and prices fell steadily.[130] In 1961, the government decided to act on two fronts: to stimulate coffee exports and to reduce coffee production. Export promotion alone was insufficient to absorb accumulating stocks, more so since an improvement in *cruzeiro* prices brought about by the exchange reform only served to stimulate production. In September 1961, President Goulart set up a *Grupo*

Executivo de Racionalização da Cafeicultura (GERCA, Executive Group for the Rationalisation of Coffee Growing), which was to help the Brazilian Coffee Institute formulate and implement an effective programme in the main producing states.[131]

The GERCA programme had three objectives: to eliminate low-yielding trees, to put the freed land to alternative use (particularly for food crops and industrial raw materials), and to modernise the remaining coffee plantations. This time the eradication programme was remarkably successful. Much of its success was due to the finanacial incentives offered to coffee planters, which were of two kinds: loans to finance most of the cost of uprooting trees (which were converted into grants once uprooting had been completed), and loans on favourable terms to diversify into other crops and to replant better coffee varieties.[132]

During the first phase of the programme, which went from 1962 to the end of 1963, the rate of uprooting in the country was over four times that of the second phase which lasted from January 1964 until June 1966. This difference reflected the erosion of government subsidies by inflation and the political changes that occurred in 1964, which involved a significant rise in the support price of coffee and allayed planters' worst fears about structural changes in agriculture.[133]

In the context of continuing over-supply, a third phase of the programme, with improved financial assistance and a stronger emphasis on diversification but with reduced price support, was initiated in August 1966. Coffee planters were now obliged to substitute specific crops for the uprooted trees if they wanted the benefit of a loan. This measure was designed to curtail a strong tendency to replace the coffee trees with pastures rather than food crops. Between August 1966 and April 1967, an additional 665 million trees were destroyed.

During the three phases of the eradication programme between 1962 and 1967, about one-third of all the coffee trees that had existed in the country in 1961–2 were uprooted. A further estimated 721 million trees were eradicated outside the GERCA programme over the same period.[134]

Coffee uprooting on such a massive scale was bound to affect employment in the coffee sector. In 1958, the FAO survey had already warned of the 'serious difficulties' that would arise from any coffee-policy that displaced the workforce from the plantations.[135] The survey did not spell out the nature of these difficulties but one

Table 3.5 Coffee tree eradication in Brazil and São Paulo, 1962–7

Period	Eradication	São Paulo	Brazil
		(million trees)	
June 1962 to July 1966	Total trees existing in 1961/62	1100	4300
	Percentage distribution	25.6	100.0
	Trees eradicated 1962/6	244	724
	Percentage eradicated	22.2	16.4
	Percentage distribution by state	33.7	100.0
August 1966 to May 1967	Total trees existing in July 1966	856	3576
	Trees eradicated	55	655
	Percentage eradicated	6.5	18.3
	Percentage distribution by state	8.4	100.0
Totals June 1962 to May 1967	Trees eradicated	299	1379
	Percentage distribution by state	21.7	100.0
	Outside GERCA programme	166	721
Total eradication GERCA + EX-GERCA		465	2100

Source: A. M. M. McFarquhar and G. B. Aneury Evans, *Employment Creation in Primary Production in Less Developed Countries*, Development Centre Studies, Employment Series 6, OECD (Paris, 1972) p. 75, Table III.15.

need only remember rising social tensions in the countryside at the time to understand their concern. In 1959, Carvalho Pinto, then Governor of the state of São Paulo, estimated that if two-thirds of all coffee trees were uprooted under the 'Three for One' programme, about 450 000 coffee workers would be made redundant.[136] Under the GERCA programme, São Paulo lost a total of 299 million trees between 1962 and 1967, apart from another 166 million that were uprooted independently. As a consequence, the number of coffee trees dropped by 42 per cent during this period.

Of all the trees uprooted under GERCA's auspices, the majority were disposed of during its initial phase between 1962 and 1963. Although no figures are available on the annual rate of voluntary eradication in São Paulo during this period, it is possible to estimate an annual average of 24 million trees on the basis of the total number of trees uprooted outside the GERCA programme. If such voluntary uprootings are added to those carried out under GERCA auspices, a total of 260 million trees (or 23 per cent) were uprooted between 1962 and 1963, before the 1963 Rural Labour Statute.

There are two ways of calculating the effect of coffee eradication on employment levels on São Paulo coffee plantations in 1962–3. The reduction of the tree population in the state by 23 per cent must have produced a corresponding rate of redundancy among coffee workers. If one takes as a basis a productive capacity of 2500 coffee trees/*colono*/year, one obtains a total number of workers made redundant of about 100 000 by the eradication of 260 million trees. Assuming, in addition, a dependency ratio of three, 400 000 persons living on coffee plantations would have been affected by uprooting. These 400 000 persons amount to 27 per cent of the total number of *colonos* and sharecroppers and their families resident on coffee plantations in São Paulo in 1958 – i.e., a percentage roughly comparable to the proportion of trees eradicated.

GERCA had foreseen that land freed from coffee should be planted in other crops, to increase the supply of food and raw materials for the domestic market and give employment to those made redundant by uprooting. But so long as alternative crops remained unspecified, this second goal was difficult to achieve, especially since coffee is particularly labour-intensive. As much as 27 per cent of the land cleared of coffee was given over to pastures, with 26 per cent to maize, 17 per cent to rice and the rest to other crops. Labour requirements for alternatives crops varied between 13 and 50 per cent of that for coffee.[137] Hence, widespread coffee eradication in São Paulo in the early 1960s substantially increased rural unemployment, giving a new impulse to the migration of rural labour into the towns.

The Politics of Accumulation

Roughly one-fourth of the labour force working on São Paulo coffee plantations in the early 1960s was made redundant by subsidised coffee eradication. The *colonato* as a system of labour exploitation, however, was made obsolete not by purely economic–technical developments but by processes that were essentially political in nature. The political power available to employers to set conditions for surplus labour appropriation plays a crucial role in shaping forms of labour exploitation. In the early 1960s, the whole structure of political domination in Brazilian agriculture came under attack, not only from those demanding effective land reform but also from those in favour of more moderate concessions. The effect such political events had in seemingly undermining landowners' traditional control over labour was decisive in inducing coffee growers to replace the *colonato* system by straight wage labour.[138] Although the Rural Labour Statute granting rights already enjoyed by industrial workers was merely a palliative to contain demands for more radical reforms, in the event these rights were conceived by landowners as an inadmissible threat to labour control. They reacted by adjusting the system of labour exploitation.

As I have shown, throughout the 1950s landed interests had effectively blocked any attempt in Congress to limit the landowners' uncontested domination in the rural areas. In the early 1960s however, growing pressure from outside Congress – coming not only from organised industrial labour which was shifting to the left, but also from organising rural workers who demanded far-reaching structural reforms in agriculture – transformed the political context in which the debate over the state of agriculture and the conditions of rural labourers developed thereafter.

In response to the political ferment surrounding the agrarian question Governor Carvalho Pinto succeeded in 1961 in having the São Paulo Legislature pass an Agrarian Revision Law designed to alleviate, through a land reform of sorts, the plight of rural workers and to improve the performance of agriculture. At the same time President Quadros, who had made structural reform a major campaign issue, created a Special Commission for Agrarian Reform composed of prominent national figures of diverse political persuasions, which was to continue the work begun by President Vargas' National Commission for Agricultural Policy in 1951.

Governor Carvalho Pinto's Law – which, carefully avoiding the ominous connotations of 'land reform', he referred to as a 'revision' –

imposed a tax on farms over 302.5 hectares which was graduated in accordance with farm land use. Subdivided public lands and unused private lands bought or expropriated by the state government, were to be made available to the landless who would pay for them over a ten-year period. Serious doubts were immediately raised, however, over whether the law would really solve the plight of rural workers and break up huge estates, rather than merely raise agricultural productivity.[139] Even so, landed interests were strongly opposed. It was rumoured, for example, that FARESP organised fund-raising among its members to finance a campaign against the project.[140] Deputy Leuzzi, the leader of the rural lobby in the Federal Chamber and a declared defender of São Paulo agriculture, accused unnamed industrial interests of wanting to benefit at the cost of agriculture and denounced the law as a 'trap for the workers and a serious threat for planters and the owners of the land which only serves to promote the struggle between the classes.' The way to go about protecting labourers, he now argued, was to grant them the benefits of labour laws, which he himself had so effectively opposed in Congress.[141]

Deputy Leuzzi's belated advocacy of protective legislation for rural workers as an acceptable compromise can be seen as a premonition of the fate of successive land reform bills submitted to Congress in the early 1960s. Confronted with the more serious threat of land reform, the representatives of landed interests in Congress, if not the landowners themselves, yielded to pressure to extend the labour laws to agriculture as the lesser evil in the end, although it curtailed freedom of contract.

The ill-judged and abrupt resignation of President Quadros in August 1961 and his succession by Vargas' protégé, João Goulart, after considerable resistance from sectors of the military and the dominant classes, increased the landowners' alarm. In Goulart's programme, land reform acquired special prominence which, in the context of growing rural mobilisation, now seemed for the first time to constitute a genuine threat.

By 1962, much of the radical debate over structural reforms had, in fact, shifted from the formal political arena to organising workers. Political mobilisation of various tendencies was advancing in the rural areas. The anxiety of the landed élite over to what extent President Goulart would be able and willing to incorporate these emerging rural masses into the political process without challenging their own hegemony, grew.

Rural Labour Mobilisation

Attention has largely focused on the growth of Peasant Leagues in the Northeast in the late 1950s, the region where poverty and disparities in land distribution were most extreme and where shifts in land use were threatening the limited security of tenure peasants had enjoyed.[142] Between 1945 and 1947, the Communist Party had organised Peasant Leagues round Recife until the Party was declared illegal and the Leagues banned.[143] A renewed attempt to set up Peasant Leagues was made in 1955, mainly among share-croppers and tenant farmers in the state of Pernambuco, under the guidance of the lawyer and state deputy, Francisco Julião. By 1960–1 these Leagues were radicalising and spread all over the state as well as in the south of the country. A regional and (somewhat later) a national organisation were set up, and, at the same time, links were established abroad, especially with Cuba whose recent revolutionary experience was viewed with sympathy by the leadership of the Peasant Leagues. Early in the 1960s, priests and Catholic activists began to organise leagues and rural unions of their own in an effort to counterbalance the growing influence of the Peasant Leagues, as well as the political work of the Communist Party, which after breaking with the Leagues in 1961 organised its own rural labour unions. After 1962, the Leagues, however, entered into decline, partly because of internal dissensions, partly due to the expansion of the Catholic and communist unions which absorbed former League members and partly because the Goulart government made gestures to promote rural unionisation from which the Leagues were excluded.[144]

The extraordinary organisational success and radicalism of these organisations, especially the Peasant Leagues, and the landed élite's violent reaction to their demands, has overshadowed rural mobili-sation elsewhere in the country, especially the southern central region (São Paulo, Paraná and Rio Grande do Sul). In this area, Church and communist sponsored rural unions were formed. The Catholic rural labour unions in São Paulo had their roots in a right-wing national movement of Workers' Circles in existence in Brazil since 1936, dedicated to counteracting communist influence in the labour movement.[145] In 1961, the São Paulo Federation of Workers Circles founded its first rural union in Presidente Prudente in the far west of the state. With the active co-operation of São Paulo's bishops, the organisation then founded a union in every diocese. These were incorporated into the São Paulo Federation of Rural Workers in late 1961. The choice of former Deputy José Rotta, who had been both President of the conservative Catholic organisation, the *Congregação Mariana* and an active member of the regional integralist (fascist) organisation as the Federation's President indicates these union's political orientation.[146] At the local level, some joint strikes seem to have been organised by Catholic and communist sponsored unions. Rotta, however, actively opposed the communists throughout the 1960s. In 1964, he welcomed the military coup as a 'victorious democratic revolution'.[147]

The Catholic-led Federation of Rural Workers were predictably moderate in their demands. They called for the statutory minimum wage for rural workers and agrarian reform based on land expropriation against 'just' compensation within the provisions of the 1946 Constitution, sharing the position of conservative opponents to land reform who well knew that, under such conditions, it was financially unviable.[148] By 1964, the Federation was said to control half of the approximate 200 rural labour unions in existence in the state of São Paulo.[149] In 1954, the Communist Party had sponsored the foundation of the Union of Peasants and Agricultural Workers of Brazil (ULTAB), with headquarters in São Paulo. With the rise of the Peasant Leagues and the church-sponsored unions, ULTAB intensified its organisational efforts in the countryside. The most powerful state federation within ULTAB was in São Paulo where it controlled the other half of the rural labour unions, together with the radical Catholic Agrarian Front, whose membership was, however, said to be considerably more numerous than that of the Catholic unions.[150] ULTAB supported the extension of protective legislation to rural workers and land reform by a constitutional amendment which would allow the government to pay for expropriated land in long-term bonds.

Another prominent rural labour organisation outside the Northeast was the Movement of Landless Agricultural Workers (MASTER), founded by Governor Brizola of Rio Grande do Sul to pre-empt the work of ULTAB and the Peasant Leagues in the state.[151] There are indications that the landless poor were also organising elsewhere in the country, under either Catholic or communist influence.[152]

The unionisation of rural labour had always met with implacable opposition from the landed élite, ranging from outright physical violence and coercion to obstructing Congress in any attempt to regulate and control rural unions. In 1954, for example, the Rural Confederation of Brazil had categorically opposed Labour Minister Goulart's plan to promote rural unions even though rural workers were, in theory, entitled by law to organise unions under Vargas' legislation of 1944. On this occasion, the Confederation, presided over by São Paulo Federal Deputy for the UDN Iris Meinberg, sent an irate memorandum to no less than the National Security Council in which it declared the 1944 rural union law void and rural unions consequently illegal, warning that such unions would only provoke agitation in the countryside.[153]

In the early 1960s, the Goulart government initiated a new campaign for rural unionisation in order to assert its control over the emerging rural labour movement as a new power base. In January 1963, Goulart had easily won the referendum reinstating the presidential system in the country and this gave him wider powers. By the middle of the year it was, however, clear that the President had definitely lost the support of the powerful landed interests and their representatives in Congress in the protracted land reform debate. In May that year, Goulart's contentious constitutional amendment was finally defeated. The critical issue around which increasing political polarisation was taking place, had all along been the notion of what constituted a land reform and how it should be carried out. The main difference between the 12 major land-reform bills and laws submitted to Congress in the 1960s was over the form of land expropriation. For a land reform to be at all effective in improving the lot of the rural poor, extensive expropriation and land distribution was required. The 1946 Constitution allowed land expropriation against 'previous and just compensation in cash' which meant that very large financial resources were needed for land distribution to have any effect at all. President Goulart had proposed a constitutional amendment instead that would permit the government to expropriate land against long-term bonds. Goulart had attempted to tone down his radical image and the main opposition parties (the PSD and the UDN) had in their rhetoric supported the need for structural reform. The President, however, failed in his conciliatory efforts. By mid-1963, he was being attacked both by the more radical wing within his own party (the PTB), as well as by the opposition which was becoming progressively more distrustful of his so-called 'responsible reforms'.[154]

By 1963, one of Goulart's foremost political aims was to win a new political base among rural workers. To achieve this it was necessary to counteract the influence of both the church and the communists in the countryside.[155] One way found was to incorporate the emerging rural unions into the state apparatus.

The successive bills submitted to the Federal Chamber of Deputies between 1954 and 1960 extending protective legislation to rural workers, while in part simply repeating existing but ineffective provisions, never contained any regulations of rural labour unions. Those that sprang up in the early 1960s operated outside any official framework. As rural unrest increased and the unions became better organised, the government as well as the landed interests became aware of the dangers of a genuinely independent rural labour movement. The landowners, however, clung tenaciously to their opposition to rural unionisation, whereas President Goulart recognised that this new constituency held real potential for his political survival.

The First National Congress of Agricultural Workers, organised by ULTAB with substantial backing from the Federal government took place in Belo Horizonte in November 1961. Representatives from the Peasant Leagues, from ULTAB and from MASTER, attended the Congress and President Goulart came in person. After serious political and ideological clashes between the more moderate ULTAB, which pursued a gradualist approach and defended reforming rent laws and extending protective legislation to rural workers, and the more radical demands of the Peasant Leagues, a call for radical land reform won the day.[156]

The Labour Ministry issued two decrees the following year, designed to regulate unionisation[157] and in order to regain the political initiative in the expanding rural labour movement, Minister Montoro in mid-1962 set in motion a government-sponsored Campaign for Mass Rural Unionisation. Labour Minister Pinheiro Neto the following year made explicit the political aims of this campaign, stating 'We hope through agrarian unions to find, finally, the instrument capable of lessening the growing social unrest that already has begun to make itself heard in the country districts'.[158] The various political tendencies within the rural labour movement, however, were not necessarily adverse to the Goulart government's endeavours to assert control over them.

The right-wing Catholic Federation under Rotta constantly sought government recognition for their unions and accused President Goulart of discriminatory practices. ULTAB seems to have benefited especially from the National Commission of Rural Unionisation (set up by the Labour Ministry in June 1963), with which it collaborated closely, obtaining official recognition of some of its unions.[159]

In mid-1963, latent antagonism between the different tendencies within the rural labour movement once more came to a head, this time over national representation. By July that year, five state Federations of rural workers had been granted government recognition, four of them conservative Catholic and one communist sponsored. In addition, ULTAB had eight Federations awaiting recognition. The four Catholic Federations had met in Recife in mid-year to set up a National Confederation of Rural Workers, but the ULTAB Federation questioned the legality of the meeting because they had not been invited in time to attend.[160] The government accepted this claim and the Labour Minister, together with the National Commission of Rural Unionisation, ULTAB, the PTB and others, called a new meeting for December that year at which ULTAB in alliance with the radical Catholic Popular Action and some Christian Democratic support, defeated the conservative Catholic tendency. Lindolfo Silva, the President of ULTAB, was elected first President of the newly-formed National Confederation of Rural Workers (CONTAG).[161]

Even before the second meeting, the Peasant Leagues appear to have been excluded from these initiatives to set up a national organisation of rural workers. As a result of the arrests of some of the original leaders of the Leagues the previous year, Julião had taken a personal stand against the presidential referendum.[162] This must have strained relations with the government.

In January 1964, CONTAG was officially recognised, thereby becoming firmly incorporated into the political structure of the Labour Ministry and thus under government control.[163]

A Rural Labour Statute had at last been passed the previous year. In addition to extending protective legislation to rural workers, it regulated rural labour unions along traditional corporatist lines.[164] President Goulart had succeeded with the unions, but as far as structural reforms in agriculture were concerned he had totally failed. Now he had little time left to derive political capital from the rural labour movement. After Congress defeated the constitutional amendment to facilitate land reform, in late 1963 SUPRA prepared a decree permitting land expropriations within 10 kilometres of certain development projects and alongside roads, railroads, dams

and irrigation projects. On 13 March 1964 President Goulart signed
the decree without even waiting for a constitutional amendment. But
time was up. Two weeks later the military deposed the President.

The Rural Labour Statute: A Challenge to Labour Control

It comes as no surprise that the landed interests should have been
irreconcilably opposed to land reform of the sort Goulart proposed.
However, they were also hostile to much more moderate reforms
such as protective legislation for rural workers which, through
institutionalising some of the rural workers' demands, would have
perhaps reduced political pressure for more radical reforms.

On 6 May 1960, on the opening day of the Chamber of Deputies'
sessions in the new capital of Brasilia, Deputy Ferrari presented yet
another bill extending protective legislation to rural workers. This
time he was more successful. Although the traditional representative
of landed interests in Congress (the PSD) was the majority party in
the Chamber, in July 1961 (a month before President Quadros's
unexpected resignation), the bill was approved by 204 votes in favour
and only 22 votes against.[165] After a number of amendments, the
Senate approved the bill on 14 September 1962, returning it to the
Chamber where it was finally passed in February 1963.

Rural workers had, in theory, been entitled to the statutory
minimum wage, paid annual vacations and notice prior to dismissal
ever since the Consolidation of Labour Laws was enacted in 1943,
but these rights had never been observed by landowners. The Rural
Labour Statute added some important new rights, granting rural
labourers job security and compensation for unjust dismissal for the
first time, which in 1954 not even President Vargas and his Labour
Minister (Goulart) had thought advisable to grant rural workers.[166]

Job security and severance pay had all along been singled out by
landed interests as the main cause for their opposition to protective
legislation for rural workers. Because it curtailed their freedom to
hire and fire, job security directly challenged rural employers'
control over labour. As one Deputy argued in April 1961:

> Job security transformed into law will generate distrust and
> threats, reactions of all sorts on the part of employers and well-
> conceived tricks by employees wanting to receive compensation
> for dismissal without just cause ... workers on large coffee plan-
> tations who are, by nature, already unstable and fascinated by the

adventure of nomadism, would feel even more strongly tempted by compensation always to search for new and distant places. I sincerely believe that job security would cause a series of misunderstandings in agriculture which would only add further to the large number of social misunderstandings that already exist, caused by the ambition of employers but many produced intentionally to disturb the existing order in preparation or construction of a new social and economic order. But the absence of job security should not exempt employers from payment of compensation to aid the employee.[167]

Even in the 1970s landowners still conceived of job security and severance pay as an affront to their authority and power:

> Compensation hangs like a veritable Damocles sword over the heads of landowners; it produces a sense of humiliation in employers who had to appear before a judge or a president of a rural labour union to talk as man to man to an employee who had only until recently been under his command.[168]

All the amendments that the Senate introduced to the Ferrari bill focused on labour control. The Ferrari bill had lacked any provision for rural unionisation, but the Senate proposed to place rural labour unions under government control along corporatist lines and, in addition, narrowed the scope of the law in a significant way. To avoid any misinterpretation, the Ferrari bill had named the categories of labour, including *colonos* and sharecroppers, that were to benefit from the law. In the final version of the Statute, however, the more generic notion of 'rural worker' replaced the earlier specification, giving way to protracted legal disputes about its applicability above all to sharecroppers, whose claims became doubtful.[169]

The Rural Labour Statute was a moderate concession to rural labourers made by a markedly conservative Congress in a context of political radicalisation in the countryside. Even as staunch a defender of the landed élite's political power in the early 1950s as São Paulo Deputy Iris Meinberg, the President of the Rural Confederation of Brazil, now advocated rural unionisation and the enactment of protective legislation for rural workers as a matter of political common sense:

> rural unionisation ... will direct... the legitimate demands of

rural workers ... at the same time serving to contain distortions in their behaviour motivated by social injustices and insufflated by professional agitators ... Rural unionisation, if adequately organised, will be in the countryside a powerful instrument for social peace in the same way as it is in the towns ... This is also true for the extension of the labour laws to agriculture, a measure which is not only legal because it is laid down in the Constitution but equally constitutes a moral imperative as a corrective of the undeniable iniquities of the present agrarian structure. We are no reactionaries ... We will not accept sterile class struggle in the rural areas. We are decided to prevent it by appealing to the indispensable transformations of the social and legal structure to be carried out in a climate of understanding inspired by the Christian wisdom of the people.[170]

Landowners, however, did not share the political pragmatism of their representatives in Congress.[171] Until then, they had had to contend only with the economic constraints of the government's coffee policy and the international market. Now they were confronted with a direct challenge of the very basis of their economic and political power, namely their unrestricted control over labour.

Coffee planters had warmly welcomed President Quadros' exchange reform of May 1961, and the well-financed coffee-eradication programme had met with approval.[172] The Rural Labour Statute, however, elicited all along protests from São Paulo landowners. Diverging from the political realism of the President of the Rural Confederation of Brazil, the state-affiliated FARESP and the independent *Sociedade Rural Brasileira* rejected the Statute. Landowners felt betrayed by their representatives in the Federal Chamber, whose sense of urgency in approving the bill had prevented them from having any influence in drawing up the Statute.[173] FARESP argued that the law smothered free enterprise, surprisingly, however, *not* that of landlords but above all that of peasants – since genuine workers were in the minority in agriculture anyway – who would be prevented from fulfilling their irresistible desire to work on their own account as tenants or sharecroppers. 'In our system', so FARESP argued, 'to strangle free enterprise constitutes a crime against democracy!'. The SRB shared FARESP's misgivings and used the opportunity to extract new advantages from the government by pleading that 'in order to be able to comply with the law, landowners must obtain greater government support, price support, the permission to export, etc.'.[174]

The explicit inclusion of *colonos* and sharecroppers under the provisions of the Statute challenged the form taken by surplus labour appropriation under these labour systems in several ways. The provisions regarding job security and severance pay applied directly to *colonos* and sharecroppers who were on annual contracts. Job security implied that if a planter wanted to get rid of a *colono* or sharecropper, he could do this only by paying compensation. In addition, while the Statute permitted discounts for rent and meals as well as for foodstuffs provided by the employer from the statutory minimum wage, food crops grown by the working family itself could not be deducted.[175] Since coffee planters were far from abandoning the *colonato* system or sharecropping, these provisions were felt to be a threat to prevailing patterns of exploitation. The more ambiguous wording of the Statute as it was finally enacted, extending its benefits generically to 'rural workers', did not exclude the *colonos*, however, from the effects of the law.

Struggle on Two Fronts: Against Labour and the State

The enactment of the Rural Labour Statute in 1963 coincided with renewed protests by coffee planters over government coffee policy.[176]

At the beginning of the year, members of the SRB had condemned the 'political leaders of leftist subverted mentality' for wanting to wipe out coffee production. Coffee planters were now subjected not only to one but to two confiscations, namely the contribution quota and the artifically-low coffee exchange rate. With the help from official coffee policy, 'Brazilian coffee producers were now being defeated by African pygmies'.[177]

The coffee planters' restiveness over 'exchange confiscation' (reintroduced through multiple exchange rates) was increased by the uncertainty surrounding the government's formulation of crop regulations and marketing arrangements for the year 1963–4. The Brazilian Coffee Institute's administrative board had approved a coffee plan for that year that acknowledged the demands for better prices. Early in June 1963, however, conflicting rumours suggested that the President might refuse to approve the proposed prices. In mid-June, an announcement came that President Goulart had, in effect, vetoed all provisions in the coffee programme designed to improve the producers' returns from coffee.[178]

In the following two weeks coffee planters in Paraná and São Paulo succeeded – with the full support of local commerce, banks as well as county administrations – virtually to paralyse commercial activities in the major coffee regions of the two states for several days. The confrontation over coffee policy served other sectors as well to manifest their own hostility to the Goulart government. A committee of representatives of the coffee sector went to Brasilia to negotiate the revision of coffee policy with the President, backed by the growing protest movement.[179]

At the end of June an agreement was eventually reached that satisfied most, if not all, the coffee planters' demands.[180] In September of the same year, the coffee sector was even more satisfied when, after yet another severe frost and drought in Paraná, the government raised domestic prices by 25 per cent, granted crop finances of up to 70 per cent and promised to get rid of the contribution quota for the following year.[181] As exports expanded in response to growing foreign demand and international prices improved sharply, coffee planters, especially in São Paulo, had no further grounds to complain.

It has been argued that the coffee sector supported the ousting of President Goulart by the military in 1964 basically because it was dissatisfied with official coffee policy.[182] I want to argue, instead, that coffee planters and exporters were indeed sympathetic to the military coup, but for other than immediate economic reasons. Months before the coup, coffee planters had achieved a substantial victory in their confrontation with President Goulart over coffee policy. The impending land reform and the enactment of protective legislation for rural labour, however, aroused their intense hostility against the Goulart government.

Landowners regarded the Rural Labour Statute as a genuine threat to their traditional privileges although it failed to mitigate labour disputes precisely because they refused to comply with it. Thus in October 1963, the largest ever rural strike occurred among sugar-cane workers in Pernambuco over non-compliance with the Statute, which affected about 200 000 labourers and heightened landowners' fear that 'insubordination ... [was] destroying the labour hierarchy'.[183]

São Paulo's landowners were also organising by 1963 to confront the clamour for land reform, 'a manouver that aimed at implanting communism in the country',[184] and as strikes were becoming more frequent in that state as well. In May 1963, for example, a total of 12 strikes are said to have occurred on São Paulo sugar plantations.[185] And one long strike had taken place at the large sugar mill, Nova América, in Assis the previous year. It had began as a protest over non-fulfilment of the collective agreement for sugar mill workers. When the mill owners promised to observe the agreement, the strike was called off only to be resumed a month later, this time including plantation workers and receiving support from unions in the nearby town of Assis. The workers now demanded a wage rise and the elimination of discounts for rent and, in addition, protested over police violence, declaring their solidarity with strikers at another sugar mill. The mill owner reacted by mobilising support from local politicians, denounced the strike as illegal and as a communist plot and had the plantation and the mill surrounded by police to prevent strikers re-entering. Finally, he evicted all workers from their houses, thereafter hiring only casual wage labourers who lived away from the mill, a form of reprisal for challenges over non-compliance of legal provisions, that was becoming a common practice among landlords in the early 1960s.[186]

Coffee planters, on their part, were well aware that unemployment produced by large-scale coffee eradication created fertile ground for rural unrest. In February 1963, the SRB appealed to the state governor, Adhemar de Barros, for help in view of the 'agitation which has now become manifest on numerous estates in the different regions of the state provoked tendentiously among workers...'. The landowners asked the Governor 'to stop the disorder brought to this state and to prevent the actions of those extremist revolutionary elements who are at their head. The perturbations arising now on the plantations will certainly induce landowners to abandon their activities which are so fundamental for the equilibrium of the economy'.[187]

In this climate of deepening social and political antagonism in the countryside, coffee planters threw their support behind the military coup, only to be sadly disappointed thereafter. Landowners felt blighted in their hopes as much by the military government's coffee policy as by its approach to the agrarian question. Their major political grievance was not, however, the largely innocuous Land Statute passed by President Castelo Branco shortly after the coup, but the Rural Labour Statute which successive military governments did not revoke.[188] The military government intervened or dissolved the rural labour unions and rural leaders were driven underground or went into exile, making it more difficult for workers to claim their rights. Nonetheless, the Statute was maintained, and even though rural employers could now evade protective legislation with impunity, it became the source of constant labour disputes.

In mid-1965 a serious disagreement over coffee policy also developed between the government and the Brazilian Coffee Institute. The latter put forward proposals to improve the *cruzeiro* price so as to stimulate exports, but the government overrode these on the grounds that this would only stimulate inflation. Instead, the contribution quota was maintained, marketing conditions for coffee deteriorating again after an improvement in the minimum price had been granted the previous year.[189] Subsidies for coffee eradication were, however, raised.

In mid-1966, amid loud protests from the Brazilian Coffee Institute, the government maintained the minimum coffee price for the new season at the previous year's level which, in real terms, represented a 40 per cent decline. Despite pressures from the coffee lobby, the government seized the opportunity of a small crop to reduce their level of support. As one foreign observer noted cynically: 'Here again is one of the advantages of non-democratic government in a country like Brazil'.[190]

In 1967, the Delfim Netto era began, a period of mixed blessings for coffee planters. Delfim Netto was one of the country's leading experts on the economics of coffee. He had been very critical of coffee valorisation and blamed price support for the decline in the Brazilian market share. As new Finance Minister he took it upon himself to implement his own recommendations. During the following six years, Delfim Netto's main goal was to increase Brazilian coffee production and to recover the country's share in the world market. One of his first actions consisted of reforming the structure of the Brazilian Coffee Institute. The Administrative Board representing coffee interests was deprived of its powers which were transferred to the Board of Directors, to the Ministry of Industry and Trade and to the National Monetary Council headed by the Finance Minister himself.

Coffee planters experienced the Delfim Netto era as one of unprecedented centralisation of coffee policy making from which they were now virtually excluded. This allowed the military government, especially in the second half of the 1960s, to impose some very unpopular measures indeed. By the early 1970s, however, the aggressive export drive pursued by the Finance Minister, coupled with two severe frosts, also bore fruit for the coffee planters. Prices rose especially after 1972 and the government gave substantial financial incentives for coffee renewal.[191] Landowners' insistent demands for at least a revision of the Rural Labour Statute to the effect of abolishing job security, however, went unheeded.

Throughout the 1960s and 1970s, landowners, prominent among them São Paulo coffee planters, had demanded a revision of the Rural Labour Statute. One of their main demands was that the *Fundo de Garantia por Tempo de Serviço* (FGTS, a Provident Fund) be extended to rural workers. Industrial workers had been deprived of their job security in late 1966 when the FGTS was introduced, by which employers' contractual responsibility to their workers were substantially reduced.[192] This fund facilitated the hiring and firing of workers in creating a more flexible labour supply. Landowners argued that this alone would 'eliminate the fear landowners had of having to pay large compensations to their permanent labourers'. Only by introducing the FGTS could the expulsions of rural workers from estates cease. The military did not respond to these appeals.[193]

In 1975, a proposal to replace job security in agriculture by the FGTS reached the Chamber of Deputies, but without success. At this point CONTAG, under the more progressive leadership of José Francisco da Silva, vigorously opposed any such change. The FGTS would only heighten workers' job insecurity and augment the mass of casual workers.[194]

The End of the *Colonato* System

The Rural Labour Statue was not revised to any significant extent, but landowners could evade the law, and they did. Nonetheless, although political repression made it more difficult for rural workers to press for compliance with the Statute, they could not be deprived of their awareness of their new rights. Labour disputes increased.[195] By the 1970s landlords were forced to admit that they had, after all, lost some of their power over labour. As one São Paulo landowner complained:

I feel that the labour laws are badly interpreted by some leaders because when those laws did not exist there was more respect on the plantation. The planter gave orders and they were obeyed.

After those laws [the workers] would go to court over anything. In the old times it was very unlikely that the worker could create problems with his boss until the law [was introduced]. If there was a problem it was solved on the spot, without those intermediaries, those lawyers.[196]

The Rural Labour Statute, however, contained a valuable loophole that allowed landowners to reassert their control to a degree. As one Federal Deputy had predicted with remarkable foresight as far back as 1956 a Statute:

would produce discord among people in the countryside, between labourers and employers without doing the former any good ... the employers' natural vengeance would be to fire rural labourers en masse. The trap of the law consists in the article that allows employers to choose the task system in order to escape the contractual obligations established by the law.[197]

The Statute had suffered innumerable modifications before it was finally enacted in 1963, but landowners had succeeded in preserving this possibility. Casual labourers – i.e., workers hired on a temporary basis and/or for specific jobs, the so-called *avulsos, volantes* or *provisórios* (spare, itinerant or provisional workers) – were not entitled to any of the benefits laid down by the Statute save the minimum wage.[198] In 1973, the Rural Labour Statue was substituted by Law 5889 of June that year. Instead of getting rid of some of the Statute's noted deficiencies with regard to the legal status of casual wage labourers, the new law merely excluded this growing category of labour even more effectively from protective legislation. The beneficiaries of the new law, which neither took away nor added any significant rights, were now defined as 'rural employees', as opposed to the earlier 'rural workers'. 'Rural employees' were labourers who worked directly for a rural employer on a non-casual basis (*não eventuais*). Casual workers comprising the so-called pseudo-tenants and task-workers, by contrast, were at most entitled to the minimum wage, holiday pay and overtime. In January 1974, Law 6019 defined casual or temporary work as that which did not exceed 90 days. If, however, a labourer worked for a rural employer indirectly (i.e., was hired by an intermediary to work on the former's estate) he or she was not entitled to any of the benefits of the new law.[199] By a new turn of the legal screw, the growing contingent of casual rural workers which had been generated by the 1963 Rural Labour Statute was at last legalised.

The political mobilisation of the rural masses had not effectively challenged the private ownership of land, but the Rural Labour Statute did, however, at least contain a redefinition of the obligations incumbent on landed property. Landowners, unable to have the Statute revoked or changed, had in the 1960s instead opted to transform their form of labour exploitation to reassert their property rights. If the law covered permanent workers but left casual labourers unprotected, the way found to evade the law was to hire the latter in the former's place. Whether in reprisal for having been taken to court by their workers, or in order to avoid future labour disputes, landowners in the 1960s started to dismiss the permanent labourers they could dispense with, hiring casual workers instead. Some opted for new uses of their land such as cattle raising or highly-mechanised temporary crops which demanded little labour.[200]

The extent to which landowners were able to dispense with permanent labour depended on the labour process and labour needs characteristic of the crop they produced. In 1970, São Paulo coffee plantations, which still absorbed the largest proportion of the agricultural labour force in the state (31 per cent) relative to the other main crops, had the smallest percentage of casual labour in their total labour force.

São Paulo landowners had been especially emphatic in pointing out how inadequately the Rural Labour Statute dealt with *colonos* and sharecroppers. And this was for a reason. Between 1958 and 1970, the structure of the labour force engaged in coffee cultivation changed radically. The *colonato* system disappeared and the proportion of sharecroppers shrank dramatically, whereas that of wage labour rose from 6 per cent (including families) to 37 per cent (excluding families).[201] The absolute number of owner-operators with their families growing coffee declined by two-thirds in this period, but their proportion in the labour force engaged in coffee cultivation more than doubled.

Independent of the effects of legal provisions on job security, around a quarter of the many *colonos* and sharecroppers had been made redundant by coffee eradication by the 1960s (sharecroppers being probably affected more by eradication than *colonos* because the former tended to be hired especially for low-yielding coffee estates). Those workers who continued working in coffee were to a

Table 3.6 Agricultural labour force by category for selected crops, São Paulo, 1970

Crop	Total	Owner-operators with paid family members		Permanent wage workers		Temporary wage workers		Sharecroppers and similar	
	no.	no.	(%)	no.	(%)	no.	(%)	no.	(%)
Coffee	310 518	169 600	54.6	85 784	27.6	29 384	9.4	25 750	8.2
Oranges	35 596	17 438	48.9	10 877	30.5	5 703	16.0	1 589	4.0
Cotton	151 801	104 644	68.9	14 554	9.5	21 308	14.0	11 295	7.4
Rice	70 412	54 686	77.6	5 853	8.3	5 950	8.4	3 923	5.5
Sugar cane	89 966	23 381	25.9	39 077	43.4	25 118	27.9	2 390	2.6
Beans	16 988	14 881	87.5	616	3.6	1 026	6.0	465	2.7
Maize	188 314	145 325	77.1	17 758	9.4	16 977	9.0	8 254	4.3

Source: Brazil, Ministério do Trabalho, Secretaria de Emprego e Salário, Governo do Estado de São Paulo, Secretaria de Economía e Planejamento, 'O trabalho volante na agricultura paulista' (1977) I, p. 94 (mimeo).

Table 3.7   Labour force on coffee plantations by category,
São Paulo, 1958 and 1970

Category	1958		1970	
	no.	*(%)*	*no.*	*(%)*
Owner-operators with families	570 000	26.6	169 600	54.6
Colonos and sharecroppers with families	1 450 000	67.4	25 750	8.2
Other workers with families	130 000	6.0	–	–
Wage workers (resident and non-resident)	–	–	115 168	37.0
Total	2 150 000		310 518	

Sources: 'A indústria do café em São Paulo, *Agricultura em São Paulo*, VIII (3) (March 1961) p. 17 for the size and composition of the population residing and working on coffee plantations in 1958; Ministerio do Trabalho, Secretaria de Emprego e Salário, 'O trabalho volante na agricultura paulista', p. 94.

large extent transformed into permanent wage labourers paid by the month and to a lesser degree into casual wage workers. The pattern of labour demand on coffee plantations had not changed substantially because new cultivation methods had been adopted only on a very limited scale.

The Rural Labour Statute constrained coffee planters' use of labour under the *colonato* system in a special way. Job security and severance pay affected coffee planters especially, because the *colonato* and sharecropping were annual systems. Contractual conditions, i.e. the task-rate for coffee cultivation or the share in production, were renegotiated yearly, ideally in accordance with market conditions and price levels. Job security made re-negotiation of the terms of the contract more difficult. Another contentious issue was the extent to which food grown by the workers themselves could be discounted from the statutory minimum wage. And yet another area of uncertainty was whether family members of the *colono* were to be considered as employees in their own right, with all the attendant benefits this entailed.[202] By substituting *colonos* by permanent *wage* labourers, the latter two problems could be overcome without jeopardising labour supply. Under this new arrangement, the head of the family is hired on an individual basis as a permanent wage worker and has an entitlement to all the rights, at least if he is registered, which even in the 1970s was not necessarily always the case. This permanent labourer lives together with his family on the estate, but the rest of the family are not protected by the labour laws. Family members continue to work in agriculture but they are typically hired on a temporary basis for special tasks, often paid a piece-rate. Hence, the families of permanent workers became a kind of resident pool of casual labour, which reduces the need to hire such labour from outside the estate. Moreover, they tend to be lower paid than workers brought in by a contractor from neighbouring towns. Often these family members are not allowed to work outside the estate.

Permanent resident workers were also no longer allowed self-provisioning beyond a small kitchen garden. Initially, after the enactment of the Statute, planters had used general intimidation or the prohibition of self-provisioning to persuade *colonos* to abandon the estate of their own accord to avoid having to pay compensation, and had replaced them with permanent and/or casual wage workers. But self-provisioning became generally undesirable because the foodstuffs grown by the workers could not be discounted from the minimum wage.

The Rural Labour Statute and subsequent legislation made two of the sources of the efficiency of the *colonato* as a system of labour exploitation, namely the labour of women and children and the work that went into self-provisioning, not only visible but also accountable. If the surplus labour extracted from women and children in coffee production and in self-provisioning had to be paid for on an individual basis because family members could no longer be subsumed under a family contract and self-provisioning could not be discounted from the statutory minimum wage, then the *colonato* system had lost its meaning. Significantly, when in the early 1970s coffee planting was resumed as prices improved and better financial incentives were made available by the government for coffee renewal and plant care, São Paulo growers demanded, unsuccessfully, that a 'family contract' be reintroduced, which might permit rural employers to use all family members – meaning, of course, without having to pay separate individual wages for them.[203] Also in the 1970s, planters proceeded to mechanise cultivation on a larger scale in order to diminish their dependence on labour and the endless disputes this involved. More permanent workers were dismissed and the use of casual labour increased. At this point, coffee became at last a monoculture in the true sense, namely a cash crop for export cultivated by gangs of casual workers incompatible with food crops.[204]

As Delfim Netto had already written in 1962:

We have accumulated a sum of technical know-how that goes from selection of high-yielding and more resistant varieties to cultivation and fertilising techniques which make it possible to increase yields of our coffee at least threefold within a relatively short time. Efforts in this sense make it possible today to conceive of a highly-mechanised coffee production where labour needs arise only during the harvest.[205]

But landowners had to pay a price for this change. So long as harvests are unmechanised, planters remain heavily dependent on casual labour, even if only on a seasonal basis. Complaints by São Paulo landowners about the unreliability of casual labour, of the poor quality of their work and the general disorganisation of the rural labour market became common in the 1970s. By evading the Statute they had hoped to re-establish labour discipline. The unforeseen consequence was further loss of control. If employers shirked their legal responsibilities, then labourers felt neither economic nor moral compulsions to work well. As one landowner summed up their new problems in 1977:

He (the *bóia-fria*, i.e. casual labourer) is a person without responsibility; he feels no motivation to make a reputation as a worker ... This is the worst aspect, I think in the long run of the existence of the *bóia-fria: the creation of a citizen who knows no responsibility to anyone or anything.*[206]

Technical innovations, then, rather than having been the driving force that transformed productive relations in São Paulo coffee cultivation, were coffee growers' response to changing social relations of production brought about by labourers' challenges to traditional forms of domination. These in turn produced new conflicts and contradictions.

4 New Forms of Labour Exploitation and New Conflicts

'The disadvantage of the poor is always to work.' Da Yandira, casual worker in São Paulo (1973)

An understanding of the conditions that led coffee growers to replace the well-tested *colonato* system with resident and casual wage labour required two levels of analysis. The coffee growers' economic success was shown to depend as much on their ability to enforce low labour costs as on the influence they were able to exert over official coffee policy. Labour costs and coffee policy were conditioned by the coffee growers' power to defend their interests against encroachments on profits by both labour and the state. But to the coffee growers' dismay, the military coup of 1964, which they themselves had helped to instigate, was followed by a decline rather than a reassertion of the coffee sector's political power, although in compensation plans for a genuine land reform were warded off.

Rising political agitation in the countryside, coupled with the Goulart government's endeavours to co-opt the restless rural labourers, led to the enactment of protective legislation for rural workers which, contrary to the landed interests' hopes, the military government proved unwilling to withdraw. But the landlords were nonetheless able to regain some of the ground they seemed to have lost, albeit at the cost of jeopardising labour discipline, by creating a new type of worker, namely the *volante* or casual wage labourer.

Not all casual wage labourers working on São Paulo coffee plantations by the 1970s were direct victims of the landlords' refusal to comply with new contractual obligations – some had been evicted from plantations because coffee had been uprooted, others had abandoned them in search of better wages and working conditions elsewhere. Many of the workers who continued working in agriculture were unable, however, to find a permanent job on an estate because of the protective labour laws. The military government made little attempt to enforce the law, but the very possibility of

being taken to court by labourers demanding their rights was perceived by landlords as a constant threat. The hiring of casual wage
labour through labour contractors was the way found to overcome
this threat. Under the new system of hiring, the workers lacked any
demonstrable contractual link with the estate.

Little attention has been paid until now to the crucial role played
by the labour contractor in the new productive relations, to the way in
which the labour process has been reorganised and to the new
problems that have arisen over labour discipline and quality of
work. These are, however, central to an understanding of landowners'
motives for adopting casual wage labour as well as of the new contradictions that have emerged with it.[1]

THE LABOUR CONTRACTOR: AN INSTRUMENT OF CAPITAL

The 'law about people no longer living on the estates' was how Da
Alzira, a casual worker on a large coffee plantation in São Paulo in
1973, aptly referred to the Rural Labour Statute, thereby underlining
the feelings of many casual workers about what protective legislation
really meant for them. Worker interpretations of the events leading
up to their departure from the estates are a combination of memory
and myth informed by a sense that their destinies have been
governed by forces which, though clearly identifiable, have nonetheless
escaped their control. On the whole they thought that the enactment
of the labour laws induced the coffee planters to get rid of their
colonos. Significantly, only in the late 1970s did some ex-*colonos* or
sharecroppers (and especially some labour contractors) begin to
regard the progressive mechanisation of coffee weeding as a potential threat to their work opportunities.

The first step many coffee planters are said to have taken was
to forbid self-provisioning. As one of the older workers,
Sr Sebastião, explained:

> Before it was better; in those days I had enough to eat; my capital
> [*cabedal, sic*] were the animals I raised and there was more than
> enough; thus I did not have to buy anything... Nowadays it is
> much worse. If you analyse the situation well, with the wages we
> earn..., what ruined those estates were those laws the govern-
> ment passed. I think it was still Getúlio, those laws demanding

that time worked be indemnified, that vacations be paid. In order not to pay, the landlord began to dismiss the workers. In those days the estates were full of people, now they work with people from outside . . . First of all they began to take away the food plots; people then thought that without them they could not manage. With the laws they [the landlords] had to pay compensation for dismissal; therefore they began to do this [forbid food crops]. The people had no strength to react; it is the landlord who is in command. The people thought they could not manage and left of their own accord. The strength of the household is this – maize, rice, beans, fat – now nobody has anything.

With the introduction of the 'wage' (*o salario*, meaning the statutory minimum wage), the *colonos* were no longer allowed to grow food crops. It is generally believed that when President Vargas decreed the 'wage' and enacted the 'rights' (*os direitos*, as the labour laws are known generically), landlords 'became afraid to hire workers' and closed the gates of their estates. For many of the workers the critical issue was, however, job security. As one worker put it, this was the 'law protecting against expulsion'. The timing of protective legislation is often unclear, but the connection between the enactment of protective legislation and their displacement from the estates is indelibly imprinted on the workers' collective memory.[2] Most workers attribute the 'rights' to Vargas even though many of them knew that, while Vargas proposed extending labour laws to rural workers (his intentions were widely known and debated amongst them at the time), the Rural Labour Statute was only enacted nine years after his death:

> It is said that he, Getúlio, left the laws signed and afterwards they were forced to print them. There was already then at the end of Getúlio's government much talk that there had to be a wage for rural workers, but on the estates it was said that the wage would not come; but then, when Getúlio died, the wage appeared. It was said that the wage would not come, that there was no governor capable of such a thing. Afterwards it was said that what had been signed had to be fulfilled, but things did not improve. Shortly after price controls ended.

Vargas 'knew how to please the rich but also helped the poor'. This was how Georgina, a single mother of five, aptly characterised his ill-fated populist politics. Had he lived, the landlords would not, it is believed, be enjoying the government's protection as they now do simply to evade the laws. As it is, with the passing of protective legislation, the landlords simultaneously deprived the workers of their former right to a food plot and then, through dismissals from the estates, they denied them also the benefits of the new rights. Consequently, the alternative left for those unable to find employment outside of agriculture, was to work as *gente de caminhão de turma*, 'people who travel on gang trucks', who are like *viralatas*, like stray dogs, working one day here and one day there, and lacking any 'rights'.

With the casual wage labourer also came the labour contractor who now hires labour for the estates and mediates relations between landlords and labourers. The *turmeiro*, as he is generally known in the area of research,[3] must not, however, be confused with the *empreitero* who traditionally supplied extra labour to São Paulo estates for special non-recurrent tasks. The *empreitero* typically hired young single men who, because they lacked family attachments, were unable to find employment as *colonos*, or resident wage workers. These gangs of single men, mainly of temporary migrants from other states, were usually taken to the estates by the contractor for a week during which they lived in quarters specially prepared for them.[4] Nowadays, by contrast, most workers, married men, women and even children, who cannot find employment in town, must work as casual wage labourers in gangs recruited by contractors.

One main function of the modern contractor is to help landlords evade their legal obligations towards their workers, imposed by the labour laws. One contractor in the region of Cravinhos put this well:

> When the wage came, that was the end of the worker as *colono* ... when the wage came people realised that they had nothing, that they had at times worked for 30 years on an estate and had nothing, they hadn't earned Sundays, holidays, the annual bonus. Hence they wanted to leave the estates because they had nothing. A war began between *colonos* and landlords. The *colonos* caught the landlords unaware and took them to the courts and the landlords had to pay everything.[5]

By law permanent workers must be registered, i.e. possess a *carteira professional* (employment book) signed by the employer and which states the date at which he/she began working on the estate and the wage received. This serves as legal proof of an existing contractual relationship which the worker can use to claim his/her rights before a court of law. Even in the case of resident workers, landlords will often go out of their way to avoid signing the employment book. Hiring casual wage labour through a contractor is, however, a safer and more effective way of evading contractual obligations. Casual labourers are entitled to the minimum wage but lack all other rights and, above all, can be dismissed without any onus on the employer for they, it is claimed, have no employer. The contractors recruit them, transport them to the estates, often allocate and supervise the work and they hand out the wages. Since the contractor neither owns the estate where they work, nor assumes any legal responsibilities himself for the workers – he merely hires for a third party – the contractual position of casual workers is, at best, ambiguous. As one woman worker who was unregistered, although she and her gang had worked on the same estate for years, explained, 'the *patrão* [landlord] has nothing to do with the gang. The contractor does not own an estate, a property. We have two employers and none registers us'.

In the mid-1970s, there were about 15 contractors supplying labour to estates surrounding Jaguariuna, a town of approximately 10 000 inhabitants near the city of Campinas. Workers living in Jaguariuna provided labour for the whole range of crops grown in the area which included sugar cane, cotton, coffee, citrus fruit and some maize as well as cattle raising.[6] Significantly, all the contractors who had worked, or were still working, in the town had begun their careers at or after the turn of the 1960s. Initially there had been only one contractor who began by supplying labour to a newly-opened horse-breeding estate at the beginning of the 1960s. He was successful and well regarded. After a number of years, he sold his truck and bought a taxi in the town, a job that produced far fewer headaches.

All contractors who succeeded in the business possessed some capital when they began labour contracting which enabled them to buy their own trucks and to pay wages if and when payment by an estate was delayed. Either their families had been small-farm owners or cattle dealers or they themselves had been estate administrators who had made money by not entirely legitimate means. Two brothers who now work as contractors, for example, not only swindled the estate out of quite a substantial sum of money, but also, on their dismissal, took their employers to court and obtained healthy compensation on top. It is generally recognised that a simple *colono* could never become a labour contractor. Two contractors had gone bankrupt for lack of starting capital to buy a truck, having had to rent one. The owners of a truck, however, more than succeeded in staying in business. Many have either renovated and extended their houses or moved into newer ones. Some have even bought a car. Only one contractor, the one working with the gang I studied, seemed to have started with literally nothing although he possessed other valuable assets which distinguished him from the ordinary workers. He was literate and was also a harsh, shrewd and self-assured man. Of all the contractors, he seemed to have had the best technical knowledge of agriculture. His family were sharecroppers though his brother had been somewhat better off. He himself had worked for some time in the municipal administration of the town as a clerk, but disliked the dependence this implied. He started out with a rented truck but soon was able to buy one.

Indeed, more is required to recruit labour and be hired by an estate than the initial capital. The contractor must gain the confidence of workers as well as of landowners or their administrators and for this he needs to be experienced in agricultural work. The respect a contractor enjoys among his workers depends to an important extent on his ability to organise work and impose labour discipline. On the quality of work he is able to deliver depend also his chances of finding work for the gang on an estate where work conditions and wages are good.

Exempting landowners from any legal obligations *vis-à-vis* their workers, however, is not the modern contractor's only function. Generally, besides hiring and transporting the workers to the estate, he also supervises their work. Under the *colonato* system work intensity and labour discipline were largely enforced by the workers themselves due to the incentive wage. Now the quality and pace of work (save for piece-work during the harvest) is set by the contractor in his role as overseer. But though his functions are fundamental to surplus appropriation by the estate, the contractor is not an employee but an independent entrepreneur. His commitment to the landlord and the labourers is determined by his own business interests, which coincide with those of neither; his position requires of him the impossible, namely to satisfy the conflicting expectations of both. The contractor's ability to make money depends on the labour he is able to extract from the gang through efficient allocation and supervision of work, for only in this way is he able to find employment for his gang. But he must also comply with the workers' own expectations regarding levels of effort and pay and these do not coincide with the landlords' demands. As an intermediary, the contractor is well placed to perceive this. As one contractor aptly put it, 'the worker wants money and the landlord wants work [but] for the landlord however much you work it is not enough and for the worker however much he earns it is never good enough'. Consequently, his position is wrought with tension: 'our work is of much envy: there is a lot of envy here', as one *turmeiro* complained.[7]

The power with which their independent mediating role endowed contractors and the danger this entailed for landowners' control over labour supply became overt at times when labour was scarce. Thus, by 1973, a relative labour shortage, especially in the industrialised centre south of the country, produced by the economic boom of the late 1960s, had for the first time pushed rural daily wages in São Paulo above the statutory minimum level. Labour scarcity became particularly acute at harvest time. Contractors were able to drive up wages by playing off one estate against the other. As a consequence, during the cotton harvest of 1974, for example, the picking piece-rate in the area more than doubled that of the previous year. Landowners were well aware that while labour contractors played a valuable role, they also posed a potential threat which needed to be contained.

The following year landlords in the neighbouring town of Mogi Mirim, bordering an area where expanding sugar plantations were absorbing increasing numbers of workers, made the first attempt to set up what was euphemistically called a 'labour cooperative'.[8] This idea had been launched in 1972 at a Congress called by the Federation of Agriculture of the State of São Paulo[9] and in 1977 the São Paulo Labour Department started a pilot project creating labour cooperatives in 12 towns in the interior of the state.[10]

The stated aim of the scheme was to organise the labour market in order to overcome the problems caused by the alleged 'inconstancy' of the workers and the contractors' command over the uncertain supply of labour during seasonal shortages. Supply of labour was to be adapted to peak demand during the agricultural year. During the slack periods, in areas of monoculture, excess labour was to be employed in subsidiary jobs, as artisans and gardeners in the parks of the towns in which the workers lived. Workers' incomes were to be raised by eliminating the labour contractor, who was presented as the culprit for their miserable wages, and family earnings were to be improved by offering complementary jobs to women and children, such as laundry work at the cooperatives for women, and packing and selecting of produce for children. The cooperatives were also to provide transport to the place of work. In reality, these so-called cooperatives were no more than government sponsored labour-leasing agencies, whose main purpose it was to regulate labour supply in accordance with rural employers' needs. The cooperatives exempted landowners once again from any contractual links. Some of the benefits of protective legislation, such as an annual bonus and holiday pay, in proportion to the time worked, were to be included in the wages which were negotiated between the employer and the cooperative. But obviously no provision was made for job security or compensation for dismissal. In a way, the scheme transformed the workers into their own employers placing them in the extraordinary situation of aiding landowners to evade contractual obligations towards them.[11] It would provide employers with a flexible labour force without the inconvenience and cost of coping with uncertain supply.

Nonetheless, the scheme did not prosper, apparently also for lack of funds. The casual labourers who formed the membership could hardly be expected to assume the running costs of their cooperative. If, on the other hand, the share of their wages withheld by the con-tractors was used to finance them, then it was unlikely that a reorganisation of hiring along these lines would improve their wages. That the workers' own interests were hardly the issue is also revealed by the fact that at no time was any attempt ever made by the authorities to use the existing rural labour unions for this purpose.[12] The autonomy of these unions, limited as it was, would have defeated the purpose of the scheme, namely to reassert control over labour. It is worth noting in this respect that rural unions in São Paulo were again becoming more active in the mid-1970s. Some 60 of them negotiated the first collective wage agreement in 1976, albeit under close government control.[13]

Landowners themselves had already devised other ways of dealing with excessive labour mobility that would ensure labour supply and quality without challenging the legal exclusion of the workers.

Contractors in the area of Jaguariuna operated under a variety of arrangements with regard to forms of payment and continuity of work. Large estates, in particular those growing more than one crop (for instance, coffee, maize used for fodder and cattle; or, as in another instance, citrus fruit, cotton and cattle) tended to work with what were called *turmas firmes*, i.e. permanent gangs whose members were casual labourers only in a legal sense. The core of the gang I studied had been working on the same estate for years. Until 1973, the administration had taken the precaution of having the workers sign a three-monthly contract which they had to hand in when a new one was issued, but the 1973 law made even this unnecessary.

For estates of a certain size, a permanent gang had obvious advantages. Workers were familiar with the jobs that had to be done. The contractor would select the best workers he could find to guarantee his own job and, appreciating the opportunity for work all year round in an area of seasonal fluctuations, the workers would apply themselves assiduously to their tasks. Four contractors in the area operated arrangements of this kind. Others, though also working all year round, nonetheless shifted from one estate to the other every few weeks and a few contractors, the so-called *turmeiros de verão*, only worked during the harvest season.

Regional differences in cropping patterns, once casual wage labour spread, came to influence the duration for which workers were hired by contractors. In regions of policulture, such as Jaguariuna, where seasonal fluctuations in labour demand were comparatively smaller than in monocultural regions, permanent gangs were more common and workers were typically hired by the week. In monocultural regions, however, such as the areas where sugar-cane predominated and seasonal labour needs vary greatly, contractors haggle amongst themselves for workers at true auctions every morning during the harvest, whereas during the dead season the workers are often out of work, unless they find employment in town.

The productivity of the sugar mills depends on adequate labour supply for cane cutting more than other crops. Cane supply must be carefully adjusted to mill demand to avoid either idle capacity or a decline in sucrose content due to delayed milling. Consequently, sugar mills have found other ways of ensuring sufficient labour. In an attempt to settle workers in their neighbourhood, some of the large mills in São Paulo, for example the Usina Nova América and the Usina Santa Lina in the Assis area, built genuine company towns. The houses were sold in instalments to workers who, in exchange, entered into tacit agreements to work for the mills when required. Simultaneously, in the mid-1970s, to improve their performance, mills were considering re-settling workers on the estate. At peak times, some of the mills would also keep back part of the workers' pay until the end of the season to prevent them from abandoning work before the harvest ended.

In the Jaguariuna region only the harvesting of coffee and cotton was paid for by production. All other tasks were paid for on a time basis, either *por dia contado* (per day) or *com domingos e feriados* (including Sundays and holidays). Under the latter arrangement, however, only those labourers who did not miss a day during the week were entitled to the Sunday pay. The risk of losing not only the day's wage but also the Sunday pay acted as a disincentive to absenteeism.

In the late 1970s, a new form of hiring spread in Jaguariuna. This entailed hiring workers on a casual basis but transporting them in a truck belonging to the estate and driven by an estate employee. This represented yet another attempt to bypass independent contractors at a time when the supply of labour in the region was being squeezed by competition from a growing number of small industries such as a ceramics factory, a hammock factory and a chicken freezing plant.

Although contractors were supposed to conceal the landlord's legal responsibilities to the workers, they themselves resorted to the courts if an opportunity arose to turn the labour laws to their own advantage. In Jaguariuna, some had claimed compensation for being dismissed from an estate before becoming contractors and two others went to court in the late 1970s, and not primarily on behalf of their workers, when they and their gangs were dismissed. At the same time, however, contractors used diverse means, from blacklisting and insults to outright intimidation, to discourage workers from going to court over rights in case their own deceptions came to light.

The contractors' reputation among workers depends on securing the best possible wage arrangement. Also, their profit often depends directly on the number of workers they hire. Contractors were paid under two different systems. Either the estate paid the transport costs in addition to a daily rate for supervising the work. In this case the contractor was not entitled to withhold any of the workers' pay. Or the estate paid either the transport costs or the overseer's daily rate, which the contractor supplemented by deducting his commission from the workers' daily wages. The same system operated for piecework during harvests. It was, however, generally believed that all contractors not only withheld a commission but more than their due. Allowing the contractors to pay the workers enabled them also to swindle the estates. Several cases of contractors were known who charged estates for non-existent workers and then split the difference with administrators. For obvious reasons it is difficult to know the contractors' exact income, but some of those operating in Jaguariuna were declaredly earning around five times a worker's wage.

The contractors knew no loyalties save to themselves. Highly individualistic and enterprising individuals, they manipulated the language of both classes, of landlords and of labourers, to suit their own interests. If, through the landlords' refusal to raise wages, they ran the risk of losing workers to other contractors, they would accuse the landlords of exploiting the workers; but when the workers failed to meet the contractor's expectations they, in turn, would be denounced for their ignorance and laziness. The contractors are ambiguously situated between landlords and labourers, but they are also divided amongst themselves. Competition over labour and jobs is intense, the goal being always to secure the best workers and the best estates. Contractors who had managed to obtain a relatively permanent job for themselves on an estate went out of their way to prevent others from taking their place by spreading rumours about the poor quality of another's gang. Only if a contractor succeeded in controlling a local labour market did he cease having to face competition from others. There was a large labour contractor who dominated the market in a nearby town and who used to hire extra transport, drivers and overseers for the gangs he could not supervise himself, but none of the contractors in Jaguariuna, however, had the financial power to attain a monopoly.

THE 'PEOPLE OF THE GANG TRUCKS'

The option of using casual wage labour had given contractors enough power to constitute a threat to the landlords' own control. The new labour system failed also in two other respects. Firstly, the hiring of labour through contractors did not conceal the landlords' contractual obligations in the eyes of the workers; and secondly, the movement of workers from the estates to the towns and their subsequent transformation into casual wage labourers undermined labour discipline and quality of work.[14]

The casual workers were not easily convinced of their lack of 'rights'. When they were being paid the statutory minimum wage in

São Paulo in the 1970s, their main grievance concerned the non-payment of their annual bonus and of compensation on dismissal. The general feeling among casual labourers was that they 'knew their rights but it is no good because they won't pay'. Disputes over 'time worked' and compensation were constant and much discussed among workers. Employers and contractors lived in permanent fear of being taken to court by workers claiming their rights. The principal concern of employers themselves was to prevent workers from accumulating 'time worked', which might have entitled them to compensation. The contractor, for example, took the special precaution of never dismissing workers overtly. Instead, if he wanted to get rid of a labourer, he would intimidate him or her until he or she left of his or her own accord thus foregoing any rights.

This tension over the 'rights' between workers, contractor and landlord is also apparent from the way in which the workers define themselves. The labour contractors most consistently conceived of themselves and of their gangs as *volantes*, i.e. 'workers without a patrão [boss]' and therefore, also without any 'rights'. The workers, by contrast, in defining their occupational status, would refer to themselves collectively as the 'people of the gang trucks' (*gente de caminhão de turma*) or individually as day labourers (*camaradas*) or agricultural labourers (*lavradores* or *trabalhadores rurais*). The majority of workers rejected the term *volante*, either because of its association with the lowly social position of temporary workers in former times or because of the absence of rights the word is nowadays associated with. The ambiguity surrounding the legal position of casual labourers, particularly when they work in a permanent gang, was aptly expressed by Da Maria who defined a *volante* in the following terms:

> wherever he can manage he will go, wherever he can earn more, there he will go. He will work *por dia* [time-work] when he can find it, he will do piece-work; it's not a bad thing. People who work with a gang truck work on the contractor's behalf; if the worker gets hurt the contractor is responsible. Now, a *volante*, if he gets hurt, nobody is responsible; there are a few *volantes* here [in the town] but most people work on gang trucks; they are employees of the contractor. Those who are *volantes* have no contractor.

Da Amelia, in turn, underlined the pejorative connotation of *volante*:

To be a *volante* is dreary. The *volante* is a person who stops nowhere, who goes from one place to the other, who does not want to work. We go on the truck but we are permanent workers even though we are not registered. To be called a *volante* is almost like being called an errant. We who work on the land are agricultural workers, we have a profession.

But above all, both those who regarded themselves as *volantes* and those who refused to be included in that category were agreed on one crucial point, the *volantes'* absolute lack of any 'rights', said to result from the 'inconstancy' of their work.[15] Whereas landlords and contractors alike use the term precisely to underline their workers' lack of rights, the labourers themselves are less easily persuaded of this: 'they say [that we are *volantes*] to stress that we have no rights at all. On the *fazenda* Jatobá they told me that I was a *volante*, that I had no 'right', only to the work, but I did have 'rights'. I went to Mogi [the court in Mogi Mirim] and we won the case'.

The three other popular labels applied to casual workers (*bóias-frias*, i.e. cold meals, *pau-de-arara*, or *birolos*) add insult to injury. Each harp upon one of the visible signs of their condition as casual workers – the quality of their food, their mode of transport and their clothes – all of which are sources of acute self-consciousness and shame. The women prepare the midday meal in the early hours of the morning before going to work, but by the time the workers eat their food, sitting on the ground in the fields covered with dust from the rich red soil, it is cold. The trucks – and, by extension, the workers themselves – are often called *pau-de-arara*, a term that arose during the mass migration from the Northeast to the Centre-south of the country, because workers travelled perched on narrow benches at the backs of the trucks like parrots on a rod in a cage. For some this designation has an even harsher connotation which expresses their disaffection with special force. When the trucks appeared, some workers ironically referred to them as *pau-de-arara* also because they brought to mind a punishment meted out to thieves in jail. As they steadied themselves on the back of the truck, the workers would hold onto the roof looking not unlike thieves when being punished by the police who string them up by their hands and knees bent across a stick. Finally, the workers' characteristic dress, earth-stained trousers and shirts for men and skirts over their trousers for women and large straw hats over scarves hiding a good part of their faces and necks to protect them from the sun, serve as reminders of the traditional rustic clothes made of a rough fabric called *birola*, which the rural population wore in the old days. All these terms are accurate descriptions of their situation, but because they are seen as symbols of their subordinate class position, the workers are intensely resentful if others use them. They themselves may joke about their misery (like one girl who sarcastically insisted that she was proud of being a *bóia-fria*, but that next time anybody called her that she would call them a *bóia-quente* (hot meal). But when coming from social superiors these designations are felt to express contempt.

It is difficult for workers to prove their rights because not only those who do decide to launch a legal complaint but also those willing to act as witnesses in court, are blacklisted. Sr Luiz, the contractor of the permanent gang I studied, argued time and again:

> The labour laws exist but only for those who are registered; it is better to come to an agreement ... to tell the administrator that one had been working on the estate for some time and ask that they pay something; he [the administrator] will then talk to the landlord and the latter will surely give something. To meddle with the courts only creates trouble. Afterwards everybody knows that he launched a complaint and he gets a bad name.[16]

Yet all this cajoling by contractors is necessary precisely because, particularly in permanent gangs, the workers refuse to accept that they lack rights. Many workers may be discouraged from suing an employer because this can ruin their chances of finding work elsewhere, because they can hardly afford the expenses and loss of earnings repeated visits to the courts entail, and because they are sceptical about winning a court action anyway. But there are always some workers, generally men rather than women, who do take legal action against the landlord. Some of the male workers I knew had in the past gone to court mostly over unpaid compensation, vacations and bonus, one of them three times. Three of the women who had at some time worked in the gang had also taken legal action when they were dismissed from another gang after a few months of work and had received compensation for the time they claimed they had worked.

The most spectacular case – and one that was widely discussed among workers in the region – was that of four permanent resident labourers who had worked for over 20 years on an estate owned by

President Kubitschek's ex-Finance Minister, Sebastião Pais de Almeida. In the mid-1960s, the estate had already dismissed about 30 families, but those remaining had been promised registration. After years of waiting, the workers themselves demanded their registration and they too were dismissed. They took the landowner to court and, in the first instance, won their case. The landlord then appealed against the sentence and the case went to arbitration in São Paulo. While awaiting the outcome, two of the workers joined the gang. Cases like this not of casual but of permanent workers being dismissed solely to prevent them from accumulating *tempo de serviço* (time worked), were not infrequent, and only served to heighten the casual workers' general awareness of the landlord's responsibility for their own lack of rights.[17]

The mediation of social relations of production by the labour contractor also has failed to conceal from the workers that it is above all the landlord who appropriates their surplus labour. Casual workers may often be ambivalent when it comes to defining who is their *patrão*. This does not, however, mean that they are abdicating their rights. Workers are unanimous in their belief that contractors have become rich at their expense, but nonetheless feel that it should be the landlord, and not the contractor, who ought to register them.

Although the workers and the labour justice tend to hold landlords responsible when legal action is taken by workers, contractors are nonetheless never quite at ease.[18] Landlords try to shift responsibility to labour contractors when they are sued. While it is the contractors' recognised function to conceal the landlords' responsibility, paradoxically it is in their own interest to leave no doubt about who the *patrão* is, namely the landlord, when a labour dispute flares up. In one instance, a contractor, together with his gang, went so far as to threaten to sue the employer for compensation if they were dismissed from the estate. In insisting on the landlords' ultimate responsibility, the contractors set casual labourers even more firmly against them. In the end, the workers see the contractor as just another landlord's agent. As Da Ditinha lucidly described the new authority structure:

> Dona Amelia [another worker] told me the other day that we who work on the land have to maintain four families: we have to produce some profit for the *patrão* [the landlord], some for the

administrator and some for the overseer. And what is left for us? Little is left for us. And this is true! I started thinking about what she had told me and it is true. If you stop to think, the *patrão*, the administrator, the overseer, they only look on. As the *turmeiro* [contractor] said, his job is only with the eyes. The administrator gives orders to him and he gives orders to us.

The *colonos'* transformation into casual labourers hired through a contractor has transformed the authority structure introducing yet another person who lives at their expense. It has made it more difficult for the workers to claim their 'rights'. Those who continue to work in agriculture have little choice but to work as 'people of the gang trucks' for 'what do the poor have in life? Only their labour power'. Nonetheless, the contractor has failed to conceal the true source of their exploitation from them.

WORKERS' RESISTANCE TO LABOUR DISCIPLINE

The truism that 'the disadvantage of the poor is always to work' does not, however, mean that those who must work for their livelihoods must work well. The landlords' persistent refusal to comply with the laws endowed the 'rights' with a disruptive potential which jeopardised labour discipline and the quality of work and which, in the role as overseers, the contractors were never quite able to overcome. The quality of the labour force is as important to capital as is the abundant supply of cheap labour.

Analyses of labour disputes often tend to focus on organised collective action to the detriment of the more subtle acts of individual resistance at work.[19] For a number of reasons, which I will discuss later, spectacular forms of collective action by workers, such as strikes, were rare. This, however, does not mean that the workers offered no resistance to exploitation at work. Quite apart from the issue of 'rights', wage levels and labour discipline were constant sources of conflict. Landlords may have succeeded in shedding most of their legal responsibilities towards their workers, but they failed to create a docile and committed labour force. By increasing job insecurity and making them entirely dependent on a daily wage the transformation of *colonos* and sharecroppers into casual labourers has undermined their identification with their work thereby eroding their work standards. Workers may be committed to seeking work but they are no longer committed to working well.

Under the *colonato* system, the pace and quality of work were ensured by the incentive wage. Then, the main area of dispute was over the reward for work or the share in production. But once an agreement had been reached between landlord and workers, the organisation and standard of work were largely enforced by the workers themselves, for their earnings depended, in part, on the effort they made. As Da Alzira recalled: 'Work was done with greater care because it was on our own account. If one did something wrong, if one did a plantation badly, the damage was our own. Now people have all become disorganised, there are some in the gang who do their job well, others do it badly'. Labour rotation and the disappearance of the wage-incentive characteristic of the *colonato* system, together with the loss of self-provisioning rights, have combined to erode workers' identification with their jobs. As Sr Dito thought, 'if you work in a gang you can't love your work'.

Because the new work relations do not in themselves contain an incentive to work well, work standards must be enforced by an outsider (usually the contractor) and are, therefore, potentially always open to dispute. In effect, the contractor's role as overseer in charge of labour discipline is as full of contradictions as is his function of concealing workers' 'rights'. Landlords are never satisfied with the work produced and workers are never content with the size of their pay packets. While this may also have been true in the old days, once contractual conditions for the year were agreed, the *colonos* would (save when they went on strike over harvest piece-rates) get on with their work. Embodying the contradictions between landlord and labourer, the contractor can never reconcile their opposed interests because to do so would jeopardise his own job.

The workers were unanimous in thinking that the work they did was for the landowner and not for the contractor who merely hired them on behalf of the estate. Hence, the most bitter recriminations were reserved for landlords, not contractors, and work relations were rife with conflict and incessant demands over wages, which were always considered too low.

The relative shortage of labour in São Paulo agriculture in the mid-1970s did provide workers with some leverage to resist what they regarded as unwarranted demands at work. Their challenge of labour discipline usually took the form of individual rather than organised collective action. Moreover, the political obstacles to collective action may even have made individual resistance to labour discipline all the more frequent at the time.

Attitudes to and behaviour at work are not determined solely by market forces. The proverbial 'worker' is never entirely free of social ties, nor is he always a man. He or she is not only a party to productive relations, which always entail some measure of coercion, but is also part of a wider network of social relationships which affect his or her commitment to and behaviour at work in different ways. Social values regarding gender roles and a work ethic existing independently of immediate economic constraints, modify significantly the effects of market forces on standards of work.

The particular labour gang I came to know most closely was unusual in some respects. First, by contrast with the average labour market participation rate for women in the region at the time (25 per cent) in the gang 80 per cent were women. The labour contractor was unusually exacting and harsh to the workers. Also, as a permanent gang, a significant number of its members had worked on the estate for years and they were paid by the day, including holidays and Sundays. The labourers may well have regarded their greater job security as an advantage over the more typical temporary gangs, but they also felt more keenly their lack of 'rights'.

The gang worked on an estate of approximately 1300 hectares of rich, red soil located near the town of Campinas. Roughly one-third was planted with 250 000 coffee trees, another third was in pastures for raising cattle and breeding race horses and some maize for forage and, occasionally, some dry-land rice, to sell to resident workers whose numbers diminished visibly in the second half of the 1970s, was also grown. The owner of the estate, Adhemar de Almeida Prado, died in 1976 without an heir, upon which the workers remarked on the irony of having so much land and no heir. He had belonged to one of the old distinguished planter families of São Paulo, was President of the São Paulo Jockey Club and also a banker. He had purchased the estate in 1959 when its former owner apparently went bankrupt. At that time coffee had been the main, crop and it was cultivated by *colonos* who then lived in three different *colonias*. Shortly after buying the property, some of the old coffee was uprooted and replaced by new trees, in accordance with modern, more land-intensive methods of cultivation.

Table 4.1 Temporary wage labour in agriculture, by age and sex, São Paulo, 1975 and 1980

	1975				1980			
	Under 15 years	(%)	Over 15 years	Total	Under 15 years	(%)	Over 15 years	Total
State of São Paulo								
Men	12 583		174 766	187 349	15 754		146 166	161 920
Women	5 797		32 901	38 698	7 037		52 250	59 287
Total	18 380		207 667	226 047	22 791		198 416	221 207
% of Women	31.5		15.8	20.6	30.8		26.3	26.8
Campinas Region								
Men	315		13 616	13 931	–		–	–
Women	407		4 429	4 836	–		–	–
Total	722		18 045	18 767	–		–	–
% of Women	56.3		24.5	25.7	–		–	–

Sources: For 1975 figures computed by the Instituto de Economia Agrícola of São Paulo from the periodical samplings done by the Instituto in the months of January, March, June and November of labour demand, wages, crops, etc. on selected estates. These figures refer to November 1975. I am indebted to José Graziano da Silva for these data. For 1980 Brazil, IBGE, *Censo Demográfico*, 1980, Mão-de-obra (São Paulo) published in *Senhor*, 167 (30 May 1984).

In keeping with the region as a whole, by the 1970s production on the estate had been diversified by combining cattle raising with the cultivation of coffee. Coffee was now tended predominantly by casual wage labour brought in from outside, as well as by the wives and children of some of the remaining resident wage workers. In the 1960s Almeida Prado had donated part of the land to the state of São Paulo for a university campus and later, when the land had been valued, some tracts surrounding the new university were sold off as part of a high-class residential neighbourhood. Almeida Prado also set up a construction firm which undertook the layout of the residential area and the building of its drains, streets and some of the residences that sprang up in the 1970s. At the same time the estate also went into floriculture, presumably to take advantage of growing demand for ornamental plants from the housing estate. Despite diversification, coffee continued to be the main crop besides cattle and race horses.

There is a beautiful old mansion on the estate, 'a very old house, from the time of the slaves; it was the slaves who built it . . . only the roof had been renovated' and, as one worker remarked, 'for two people who use it, 54 rooms!' The mansion is surrounded by a luxurious park, next to which there is an airstrip for small aircraft which was occasionally used when the owner came from São Paulo on his weekly visits to check on the running of the estate. During the late 1960s, the plantation earned a certain local notoriety when first the King of Norway and later Queen Elizabeth of England paid brief visits to inspect the horses.

The estate was run by a resident administrator under whom were three overseers in charge of the stables, the plantations and the gardens respectively. Two of the *colonias* still remained, though some of the houses were being pulled down, ironically with the help of the gang. Semi-skilled workers such as tractor drivers, minor overseers and personnel in charge of the stables lived in the remaining houses, but the bulk of the field hands were brought in from outside by one and, at times, two labour contractors.

The main work of the gang consisted of weeding and harvesting coffee. But during the off season or when other jobs needed doing, they also undertook a variety of other tasks on the estate such as pruning old coffee trees, planting new trees, spreading fertiliser, draining low-lying areas for pasture planting, weeding pastures, sowing, weeding and harvesting rice, harvesting maize for forage, or cleaning out the stables. On occasion, a group of women were sent to the housing estate to work on road construction and on the digging of ditches for drains as well. Some of the tasks were particularly onerous, either because they entailed working knee-deep in water or because they demanded particular strength. Others, such as cleaning bricks from demolished houses or ripping up a badly-laid road, were regarded as downright useless.

The wages paid to this gang roughly corresponded to average levels for the state as a whole, though at times they were slightly higher than those paid to most of the gangs operating out of Jaguariuna. The workers appreciated the advantages of working in a permanent gang and of being paid for the whole week. Despite an improvement in real wages in the 1970s the workers still complained constantly about their prevailing conditions of life and work.

WORKING WOMEN

Gangs that work permanently on one estate or that are composed predominantly of women are unusual but not exceptional in the region. I have already indicated the advantages for large estates of hiring a permanent gang. Four of the gangs in Jaguariuna, all of which were relatively permanent, were made up mainly of women. The contractors were quite explicit about some of the reasons why they preferred to work with women, others can be inferred. Although they rarely admitted this openly, some contractors felt entitled to withhold a larger commission from women's paychecks. One contractor alleged that men would resent being paid the same wages as women. More generally, however, contractors regarded women as more docile and better workers than men. The contractor of the gang in question, who incidentally did pay equal wages, repeatedly made this point: 'A woman subjects herself more to the job. Women work more because they have a sense of self-respect, a sense of shame. Men do not have this; they say, if the contractor calls me to order I will do the same to him; they [the women] have no voice to talk back'.[20] As the women themselves recognised, 'men don't have the patience women have'. Men are also quicker than women to leave a gang on the slightest pretext. There were always some gangs the

RUA BARÃO DE OLIVEIRA CASTRO 17,
APTO 402
RIO DE JANEIRO, RJ 22460
(011)-(55)-(21)-294-0243

ELIZABETH ANNE KUZNESOF

DEPT. OF HISTORY
UNIVERSITY OF KANSAS
LAWRENCE, KANSAS 66045

U.F.F. NITERÓI
INSTITUTO DE CIENCIAS HUMANAS

workers regarded as better than others, either because of the form of remuneration, the work intensity, the type of jobs, the distance to work or the degree of job security. The main reasons behind workers changing gangs consisted of excessive demands being made by the contractor, being called to order for slow or poor work, and wage differences. Women were not insensitive to these but they ideally preferred to stay in the same gang as long as wage differences were slight because they were reluctant to go to work among people they did not know. Men, by contrast, were permanently on the lookout for jobs that offered the benefits of protective legislation and for better pay.

But there were limits to the women's forbearance as well. Late in 1973 wages paid to this gang began lagging behind those of other gangs. Under the pretext that the statutory minimum wage would only be readjusted the following May, the estate refused to raise wages, thereby turning against the workers what had been their instrument of struggle when rural wages were lower than the official minimum. The gang grew restless and eventually 14 of the women left to work elsewhere. This was doubly upsetting for the contractor. In failing to persuade the estate of the need to raise wages, he had lost some of his good workers.

Control over the supply and reliability of labour is fundamental to the efficient organisation of work. A contractor's power and prestige was partly reflected in the extent to which he himself could control hiring as opposed to having to depend on the worker's initiative. In this gang, hiring was surrounded by a genuine ritual exalting the contractor's authority. He would never seek out workers in their homes, as many contractors did, but expected them to come to him for work. The most he would do – and that reluctantly – was to send a message through another worker to offer a place in the gang. The workers understood the difference between asking for work or being asked to work in the gang and, obviously, preferred the latter. The extent to which contractor and labourers were able to maintain their stance depended on the situation in the labour market. To prevent any unforeseen departure, the contractor also controlled the workers' movements. If a worker intended to leave the gang he or she was expected to give due notice. Since workers provided their own hoes (all other implements belonged to the estate), one way in which the contractor could check on their intentions was to see if they took their hoes away in the afternoon, for usually these were left on the estate. A distinction was made between legitimate and illegitimate reasons for abandoning the gang which affected the worker's chances of coming back later. Differences in wages, which did not entirely depend on the contractor, were regarded as justified grounds for going somewhere else, whereas complaints about the nature of the tasks were not, for such complaints could damage the reputation of the contractor in the region.

The greater docility of women was not only reflected in their greater stability in a gang, but also in work standards. Men often disliked working among women because it was thought that women tended to work harder and with greater perseverance than men. The women themselves stressed that they were *teimosas* (stubborn, persistent) whereas men now lacked *coragem* (courage) to work. Though they recognised that they, as women, often worked harder than the men, it never occurred to them to demand a higher wage than that paid to the men. Instead, they welcomed the fact that the estate seemed to acknowledge their greater efforts by paying them the same as men.

Women tended to work harder than men when they were paid the same day wage. In addition, cotton and coffee picking, which was formerly done by the whole family and which is paid by result, is now generally carried out by women and children alone. Payment by result entails hardly any rest. Men often reject work paid by result on the grounds that, because of their proverbial nimble fingers, women are better at it. Although women are well aware that piece-work is more demanding, they are nonetheless more willing to take it upon themselves than men.[21] Finally, women are less likely to take legal action against their employers.

But despite the acknowledged advantage of employing women owing to their greater efficiency, they are a minority in the agricultural labour force of the state. In São Paulo agriculture women were hired partly to fill jobs abandoned by men who moved into more attractive jobs. This contrasts, for example, with the practice of the labour-intensive multinational assembly plants which are being transferred to third-world countries of seeking precisely cheap, docile *female* labour for unskilled jobs but rejecting men although they are available.[22]

In São Paulo, occupational opportunities for men were better than for women. Women who 'need' to earn a wage could work either as maids, where the hours are long and the wages no better than for agricultural workers, or, in the case of young girls, they could seek work in local small industry where the wages are somewhat better, where they are sheltered from the sun and rain, but where they are also unlikely to enjoy social benefits.[23] Men, by contrast, could work in the building sector where work is equally insecure but where they can earn considerably more than in agriculture, or they could find jobs in industry which usually does legally register adult men.

Market forces – that is, the nature of labour demand – may partly account for regional variations in participation rates by gender but they do not serve as an explanation for the behaviour of the supply side. In the case of São Paulo agriculture, regional differences in the participation rate of women have to do with the fewer occupational opportunities available to them outside agriculture. When men become scarce, the demand for women and children may grow. But market forces alone do not explain women's labour market commitment nor their characteristic behaviour in the work situation, i.e. that women exhibit a tendency towards higher standards of work than men which in turn is related to women's specific attitude toward working for a wage. As I will argue, both are rooted in their social definition as women.

The exclusive use of women for such tasks as coffee and cotton picking on a piece-rate basis is attributed to their special aptitude for these. However, these jobs have only recently been typified as feminine. Moreover, the variety of agricultural tasks carried out throughout the agricultural cycle by gangs in the region were in no way related to their gender composition. The women in this particular gang did all the jobs they were ordered to do, with the possible exception of lifting heavy weights. As Da Antonia explained,

> now women do anything; before they didn't, now they do because they have to work in a gang. If they order us to do it, we have to do the job [for] ... if we say that we won't they won't give us work ... Those who work for a day-wage have to do what they are told. If we are sent to quarry stones, to dig a ditch, we go.

Paradoxically, women's greater diligence at work goes together with a lower labour-market commitment relative to men. If market forces alone were to account for attitudes regarding and behaviour at work, women's lower commitment to seek paid work would have the opposite effect, namely of raising women's wages and/or lowering standards of work, for there would be fewer women available on the labour market and hence their bargaining power would be greater.

The reasons for women's lower labour-market commitment as well as for their higher work standards must be sought in the cultural values defining gender roles. These women have worked all their lives not only at home but also in the fields under the direction of a typically male family head. As *colonos*, however, women were generally excluded from doing wage work directly for the estate, which men often did. That women now also work for a wage has neither changed the domestic division of labour nor has it altered the definition of woman's paid work as subsidiary to that of men, who continue to be regarded as the family providers: 'The one who has to maintain the family is the husband, the wife works to help the husband'. Thus men work for wages because they are men, women only when their help is needed. Nowadays this need often arises for there never seems to be enough money to meet the family's needs which, moreover, have changed with the move to the towns:

[Women] need to work, it is impossible [not to] because we have to pay a rent. In those days when I lived with my parents [on the estate] it was better ... everybody grew crops. Before they [the crops] were ours, there was [an] abundance, we raised animals, now we buy everything. In those days the estates were full of people, now they are empty. Everybody went to town to pay rent. They only hire people in an emergency.

Men's commitment to seek work is socially constructed as an inherent part of their maleness. They will endeavour to find secure employment which will entitle them to social benefits and, ideally, will enable them to provide for their families. By contrast, women regard working for a wage as an obligation imposed by circumstances. Though often needing to work for a wage to make ends meet, they felt uneasy about having to do so. Some women had grown accustomed to working outside the home and welcomed the opportunity to escape from the repetitiveness of domestic chores which, moreover, are unpaid. To work in the company of other women was more fun than being at home, not least because domesticity in town meant increasing social isolation. But at the same time, they profoundly resented the double burden. As they saw it, 'God made the world in six days and Sunday for rest, but we work Saturdays, Sundays and all we earn we eat'.

For these women a typical working day starts between three and four in the morning. If they also work, the men and children get up at about five. Most of the time before leaving for work is taken up with cooking the family's midday meal and with tidying up the home. If there is no gas cooker this means that a fire has to be lit, often in the yard in the dark. Breakfast is eaten, if at all, standing up and then, around six o'clock, all the working members of the family leave. Those who work in a gang go to a stop where the contractor picks them up in his truck. Work starts at seven and goes on until five with a one-hour lunch break and a half-hour coffee break somewhat later. If they are doing piece-work they hardly stop to eat. Around six, they are back home. After changing their clothes, the men either sit down to watch television or go to the bar. The women prepare the evening meal, go down to the river to fetch water, do some urgent washing, feed the family, clear up and, when they can manage, drop into bed. On Saturdays, work goes on until one o'clock. The afternoon is used to clean the house and do the washing. On Sundays women can get up a bit later and they may even be able to take a nap in the afternoon. A few of the women even did washing on the side as an additional source of income.

The women resent their husbands no longer seeming to be able to provide for them so that they have to work for a wage as well. As they say, 'it is a good thing to find a man who doesn't allow us to work, but if we work it is no good having a husband'. They equally resent having to do what used to be considered men's work such as digging ditches:

we have already dug so many ditches, there aren't any more men in the world. I think there are more women now in the world. The men there are take up other jobs, they don't go after weeding any more, they seek better jobs where they earn more and don't have to make such an effort. For women, there is only the possibility to work as a maid and they earn the same as in the fields.

When a group of women was finishing up a ditch some men had left half done, one of them suggested bluntly: 'one ought to cut off his thing, his penis and give it to the dog to eat; cut it off totally, the balls, all of it to give it to the dog to eat; [they] have no courage!' Considering the conditions under which the women work and the meagre wage they earn, it is not surprising that if they had the choice, many of the married women would cease to work for a wage and stay at home. This is a decision many of their husands would endorse because of the negative reflection having a wife who has to go out to work has on their own ability to provide for the family. The men do not, by contrast, have this option. Their socially-defined role as bread-winners prevents them from staying at home. Women, however, even when they stay at home, are never idle for they have all the domestic chores to do.

The difference in commitment to the labour market between women and men has a number of consequences for women's behaviour at work. As long as they have a husband who works 'women [who] earn little ... are content. Not men, they look out. Men want to earn more, but then they have to because they are heads of households. They have to provide for everything, that is why they hope to earn more'. Since the worst jobs are typically paid the least and because women feel less compulsion to maximise their earnings than men, they end up doing the worst jobs. Lower pay for women is then justified by defining the jobs they do as feminine. Women are socially destined to be above all wives and mothers who depend on their husbands for their livelihood. For this reason, except when they are the sole supporters of a family, women tend to be less motivated to seek paid work. And the image of women as dependent on and being provided for by a man also serves to legitimise the lower wages they earn.

Women's lesser commitment to the labour market may explain why they are more easily satisfied with what they earn but it does not provide an immediately obvious reason for why, once women work for a wage, they exhibit higher standards of work than men. I have argued elsewhere that women's subordinate position in so-called productive labour is only one of the consequences of the role ascribed to women and the social meaning attributed to it, in the re-production of social inequality in a hierarchical society.[24] As I will show in Chapter 6, the transformation of these men and women into casual wage labourers eroded the authority structure in the family but this did not enhance women's autonomy nor has it altered gender roles in any substantial way. Rather, wage work means just one more burden for these women. Their subordinate position within the home and in society at large is extended to the work situation in an objective as well as subjective sense.

Georgina, the single parent of five children from five different men, exemplified the special problems women's subordination entailed for those who support a family alone. It was also she who denounced her specific oppression as a woman most explicitly:

It is said that women will have to work building roads now, with those machines; that the time will come when men will not be needed any more. But now, earning less than the men a woman is a slave of the men, but that little by little it will change. In the end we will be independent of the men. We will not need the men to provide for us. Then the women will earn the same as men and it will be better. Then we will not suffer as we do now, as I, who have to go to the fields, look after the children. Earning like the men it is easier. There on the estate we do the same as men, slowly, but we do.

Be it clear that I do not attribute the women's specific behaviour in the work place simply to some sort of generic submissiveness and resignation characteristic of women in an unequal society. Such an interpretation would be doubly misleading. It would not only underestimate the enormous pressure placed on these women as women *and* as members of a class. It would also conceal the women's subtle but persistent forms of resistance against the demands made on them at work. To assert themselves, these women have to overcome not only one but several related forms of domination, namely at home, at work and in society at large. Being denied a voice of their own within and outside the home, it is very hard for these women to make themselves heard at work. Objective oppression is reinforced by subjective self-image. The social definition of women's paid work as subsidiary only increases their difficulties in asserting themselves. Not any allegedly greater skill for jobs which require speed and endurance nor any inherent deference to men account for their higher standards of work, but their subordinate position in the family which is actively endorsed by their men, and which places them at a disadvantage with regard to men at work as well.

To sum up, these women need to go out to work because their husbands' wages are often insufficient to provide for the family's needs.[25] While for cultural reasons women are less committed to seek paid work, once they do work for a wage, they tend to work harder than their male counterparts. With their greater tolerance for labour discipline comes higher productivity and more careful work. Because they are less bent on maximising their earnings, women are less likely to change gangs, which is a special advantage in the case of permanent gangs. On the other hand, their lesser work commitment makes them more flexible as workers and therefore easier to dismiss, especially since they are less likely than men to take legal action. This, coupled with the employers' image of women as ideally confined to the home, may explain finally why women are preferred for permanent gangs but also why they exhibit a lower participation rate in the labour force than men.[26]

WOMEN AS WORKERS

Nonetheless, these women do not accept passively all the demands made on them at work. Women workers share with their male counterparts a basic disagreement over the levels of effort imposed by the estate. Therefore, irrespective of whether a gang is composed of women or of men it cannot do without an overseer, usually the contractor, to enforce labour discipline.

Distinct differences could be detected in the standard of work among the women themselves, not only because some were more skilled than others but also because some were more willing than others to work well. In effect, the contractor needed to be constantly on guard to prevent slowing down and negligence. Occasionally, he would have to go to town and leave the gang on its own. Some of the older women assured me that they continued working as before irrespective of whether or not he was there, but he nonetheless took the precaution of leaving without being seen just in case they might use the opportunity to have a rest.

The contractor usually spent a good part of each day walking through the groves checking on how work was progressing. When the women heard him approaching, they would warn each other and work especially hard, above all avoiding being caught standing around. When the contractor is absent though, they clearly feel easier about stopping for a while.

Contractors were well aware that levels of effort depended on their own ability to impose discipline. It was precisely because, even among the women, levels of effort were always open to dispute that standards of work depended on the contractor's skill in enforcing labour discipline. When a gang works poorly, be it composed of women or men, the overseer is usually blamed for failing to fulfil his function properly. What distinguishes women from men at work, however, is their different responsiveness to the contractor's demands, although there are distinct limits to what even the women workers are prepared to take. For example, when the estate administration attempted to control individual daily ouput, not only did the contractor resent this implied criticism of his own efficiency, but when he tried to get his gang to speed up work, the women refused to comply. They did not believe him when he tried to frighten them by telling them that the administration was writing down the names of anyone seen stopping work:

> Nobody is [made] of iron, nobody can resist working all day without stopping. We work a little, stretch our bodies a bit and bend them again. He says this to frighten us so that we will work without interruption.

When wages in the gang lagged behind those of other gangs, the women's discontent rose visibly. As Da Cida, indisputably the hardest worker amongst them, declared, 'nobody is obliged to get up early in the morning to work for free for the *patrão*'. Wage differences between gangs could sometimes induce the women to change their jobs and some of them did indeed leave, but those who stayed worked clearly with less enthusiasm:

> He [the contractor] does not make any effort to obtain better wages for us, hence we will work but not yield. When they pay well we work cheerfully. The days are gone when we worked cheaply because everything has gone up.

Work standards set by the contractor/overseer are not only open to challenge but are constantly renegotiated in a sort of wrangle between the women and himself.

Much has been written on the existence among workers of a kind of work ethic, a subjective notion of what level of effort is appropriate for a given wage.[27] A work norm existed among these women workers but not in relation to wages in any absolute sense. Instead, and depending on the bargaining power of both parties, the standard of 'reasonable effort' was renegotiated all the time. Any concrete normative standard was always the outcome of the interaction between divergences in work performance among the workers themselves and the contractors' ability to manipulate and exploit these differences to raise output. Rather than with ethics, this process has to do with relative power and politics.

The workers agreed that when they work for a time wage, they should do so accordingly, *de acordo, conforme*, i.e. at a slower pace than when paid by results. Working badly is thought of as 'robbing the *patrão*' and is reprehensible. They should not, as they say, 'swallow the landowner's day (*chupar o dia do patrão*). Thos who are aware of their 'duty' (*obrigação*) will allegedly work irrespective of whether or not the overseer is there. To work excessively hard, however, is 'to work beyond one's nature', which is criticised. Those thought to exceed the standards of 'reasonable effort' are disdainfully referred to as the 'landlord's arse lickers' (*puxa-saco do patrão*). Even the contractor is open to such criticism if he imposes too fast a pace or fails adequately to defend the workers' interests.

These notions of what constitutes an appropriate work effort are also informed by the principle that equal pay requires equal work. Since all members of the gang earn the same wage, they should by rights also work the same amount, though this is clearly not the case. Those who are thought to work too slowly neither escape censure, for they are believed to take it easy at their fellow workers' expense. This egalitarian norm does not, however, specify a concrete general pace or standard of work.

The workers were well aware that the notion of 'equal pay for equal work' did not apply to the division of labour in society at large. After all, the wealthier people are, the less they have to work. The 'rich', including the landlord, do not work at all precisely because they are rich and even the contractor, who only looks on, earns more than they do. Workers often questioned the justice of a wage differential operating between skilled and unskilled occupations: 'The job of a doctor is work, he operates but it is lighter than our own work. Our work is killing... but his is as well'.[28] was how Da Antonia, not without a dose of humour, vented her sense of injustice over inequalities in effort and wealth.

However, the notion of 'equal pay for equal work' with its egalitarian implications within the gang, aided, above all, the contractor, in exploiting the differences in performance among the women themselves, in setting a standard of appropriate effort and in enforcing faster work.[29]

In discussing why she disliked lagging behind the other workers, Da Cida's argument was as follows: 'What do I come to the fields for? Don't you think that those who pay do so for us to work? I want to earn [my living by] working, sweating. I don't want to earn the money for free'. This notion of duty is not, however, shared by all the women. If left to their own devices, some get on with their work whereas others slow down. Nonetheless, Da Cida also felt she constantly had to justify working harder than anyone else to conceal her eagerness to please the contractor which elicited critical remarks from her fellow workers.[30]

Differences in work performace, a source of friction among the women themselves, arose from both the contractor's preferential treatment of those who worked well and the different strategies adopted by the women themselves with regard to labour discipline. The contractor made every effort to hold onto good workers, not only because, as individual workers, they contributed towards improving his reputation *vis-à-vis* the estate administration, but also because their presence in the gang raised the general standard of work. Although he would have liked to, he could not reward hard work with better pay. So, instead, he offered special favours to good workers, such as buying them a new hoe or offering work to their children at the adult wage. As a result, not only did the workers stay on but also, in order not to be indebted for such favours and hence constrained in their freedom of movement, they would work even harder to make up for their children's slower pace.

Faster workers often explained their greater dedication to work by arguing that they disliked working slowly because it made them languid (*preguiça*) and even more tired than when they worked at full pitch. Others, however, resented the faster workers because it forced them to work harder themselves:

On this estate the gang works in the rain, it works a lot ... because they pay an equal wage, so they exert themselves more. The men ... say that they do not like to work among the women [for] women exert themselves too much, they kill themselves for others. Does the *patrão* feel sorry for us? I work at my own speed. When [we] used to work for ourselves [as *colonos*] I worked so much, now I don't keep up with the others, I work according to my own nature ... Da Amelia, Da Antonia in the old days worked much more. I felt ashamed. He [the contractor] would shout ... Those who make so much effort, push for the side of the *patrão* (*puxa para a lado do patrão*). In the afternoon they are exhausted, not me. They say that working slowly produces langour (*preguiça*). I couldn't care less. They always pay the same, there has been no shortage of work. In the old days, yes, because the estates were full of people, but now there is no lack of work. You can go elsewhere if you don't like this one, you can, we're not registered.[31]

The contractor usually tried to ensure the standard and quality of work by shouting quite viciously at those who were behind which was a source of anger mixed with shame for the women. Or he attempted to cajole poor workers into leaving the gang. With equal pay workers tended to level standards of effort and without the overseer's control, the levelling tended to be downwards. To ensure his position in the market, the contractor must seek to enforce a standard of work that is satisfactory to the estate. He achieves this by establishing proper labour discipline, but also by turning the workers' own egalitarian ethos against them. The result is a level of effort lying somewhere below the best workers, but clearly disadvantageous to the slower ones among them.

Divergent attitudes to and behaviour at work do not arise, however, from any fundamental differences in consciousness among the women. All the women were aware of their exploitation by the landlord and they shared a basic sense of common identity and solidarity. Nonetheless, some were more assertive about it than others. The tacit rule is that nobody should stand out although in practice there are exceptions. One woman felt very resentful precisely because someone rightly pointed out that she was stronger than anyone else:

The wage is one and the same. I don't mind working digging the ditch but why do they say that one is stronger than another. The wage is one. I don't like them saying this. This is ugly even for myself, it is ugly, it makes me feel ashamed when people say that I am more than the others. It is true, but there is no need to say so.[32]

Confronted with the combined power of the landlord and the contractor, the women could react in different ways. Some were critical of the injustice and disloyalty of those who worked very hard, others were more pragmatic in their response. Da Tereza, for example, complained that fast workers 'harm the poor weak ones who suffer ... Everyone exerts herself for him [the contractor] so that he won't be able to say that they are earning their money at the *patrão's* expense ... He says that badly-earned money is badly-spent money, that money must be earned with sufficient work ... The profit of the *patrão* is for the gang to work a lot'. Da Cida, however, thought that one should make the best of a bad situation. After all, 'we have to lick the arse of the rich, we have nothing. It is ugly to be scolded, he says that one is a tramp [but] he has nothing to say about me'.

Workers' solidarity is permanently eroded by their own sense of powerlessness and the contractor's endeavours to pitch them against each other to further his own ends. Under these circumstances, some women opt for individual promotion by complying with labour dis-cipline, although censure from fellow workers sets limits to this strategy. Or they resist individually despite the contractor's control because the obstacles to collective organisation and action, which I will discuss below, are immense. Nonetheless, not even those women, most eager to comply with the contractor's demands, accept any imposition he makes.[33]

Labour discipline depends on more than merely the efficiency with which the overseer is able to supervise the execution of work. Because resistance is always latent, the labour process must be organised in such a way that it becomes difficult for workers to slow down or waste time. But even with his considerable technical knowledge and experience of agricultural work so vital for the tight organisation of the labour process, the contractor was still unable to prevent workers from using every opportunity to take a rest and pursuing their own interests rather than those of the estate. A few examples will suffice.

With consummate irony one of the women made a point of only pulling out the mature and of concealing the young weeds 'in order not to finish the race because otherwise we'll be out of work. One must kill the father and leave the offspring. The adult one you weed, the little one you cover up'.

Stopping work because of rain and the setting of the piece-rate for the coffee harvest were particularly contentious issues. It was never quite clear how hard it had to rain before work could legitimately cease. Different contractors dealt with the issue in different ways. One gang did not work when it rained but did not get paid; another was paid only for the hours it worked on rainy days. The gang I studied was paid for the whole week, so although the workers were eager to stop at the slightest hint of rain, the contractor insisted that they carry on until it literally poured. Hence, rainy days were restive days among the workers and the pace of work declined.

With the exception of the coffee harvest, work was usually paid on a time basis. Piece-work, while speeding up the pace had the dis-advantage of endangering the quality of work. At the onset of the harvest, the estate would have the gang work for a week or so on a time basis to assess yields and would then set the piece-rate accordingly. Some workers disliked piece-work because they had to work harder to maintain their previous wage, whereas others preferred it because when the crop was good it enabled them to increase their earnings despite having to work at double the speed: 'Working for a piece-rate one earns considerably more but in the end the result is the same or even less and you work and work and don't even have the time to eat and when piece-work is over there may be no work'. But all the workers united in their resolve to work as slowly as possible while piece-rates were being set.[34]

During the harvest, paid by result, three tasks in particular were sources of constant friction between workers and contractor. Disagreements could easily arise over the picking and leaving of coffee on the trees. From the piece-workers' point of view, it is time consuming to pick trees clean and quicker and more profitable to move on before all the coffee has been picked. But, apart from wasting valuable coffee, leaving berries on the trees encourages a wood-boring disease and this too can undermine the estate's profits. Secondly, workers may mistreat the trees in their eagerness to keep up production. After picking the berries that can be easily reached by ladder, the workers often beat the branches with a stick so that the remaining berries fall to the ground. It is in the landowner's interests that the sticks are used lightly, whereas to keep up their speed, the workers tended to beat the trees rather too hard. And finally, the contractor had to ensure that the coffee was properly winnowed and that no impurities were left in the sacks. But winnowing is tiring and time consuming and if impurities like stones and earth are left in the sacks they increase the weight, although they also adversely affect the quality of the coffee. Close control by the contractor was therefore necessary to uphold an acceptable standard of winnowing, but the workers would, while taking care to pick up every berry that had fallen on the ground, carelessly include impurities. After 1977, in effect, a time wage was introduced during the harvest in an attempt to ensure greater care. Now, instead of throwing all the berries together on a tarpaulin stretched out under the tree, the ripe ones are picked by hand to improve the quality of the coffee. Although it was generally understood that work paid on a time basis could be taken at a more leisurely pace, on this occasion the workers complained that their 'miserable *patrão*' not only denied them piece-work when the crop was good because he feared they'd earn too much, but that he set such high standards that some of them had had to work during their mealtimes, an imposition they felt was unwarranted in this case.[35]

It was also becoming more frequent, as bargaining power increased, for workers simply to walk out on the job before the end of the day if they regarded the work and/or the wages as unsatisfactory. But generally, only young men took this form of action which others saw as evidence of the young's lack of courage to work. The women were usually far too constrained by sexual norms to follow suit.

CONCLUSION

The option for casual wage labour and the landlords' dependence on the labour contractor, while exempting them from legal contractual obligations, brought new problems of labour control for which there are no easy solutions. Disputes over workers' 'rights' and labour discipline became the order of the day. The workers had lost their former identification with their work. The landlords' refusal to grant them any of the 'rights', coupled with a relative labour shortage at the time, produced a perceptible decline in the quality of work. But these circumstances did not erase gender-determined differences in work attitudes and standards of women's work remained higher than men's. Nonetheless, women did not comply with all demands at work.

Extra-economic factors account for women's characteristic behaviour and for that of employers toward them. The women workers' identity is a function of their domestic *and* their class position. For cultural reasons these women are more efficient workers than men because their submissiveness makes them more responsive to labour discipline. This does not mean, however, that as workers they are unaware of their double exploitation at home and at work. As members of the exploited class, they share a working class consciousness which challenges prevailing power relations and which informs their multiple forms of resistance to work discipline. But in contrast with men, whose class consciousness may vary in clarity, the women workers' consciousness is inherently contradictory.

Class antagonism is certainly not lost in these women workers. More difficult to establish is the frontier between resistance and submissiveness. For historical reasons, these women share with their men a special sense of powerlessness to which is added, however, a feeling of vulnerability especially in the extra-domestic domain which is specific to them. These women have to struggle against two forms of exploitation and two forms of domination so that the pressures to comply are all the greater in their case. Nonetheless, they resist for, as one woman stated: 'The days of the slaves working all day are long gone'.

It was essentially in response to increasingly hostile labour relations and decreasing standards of work that certain aspects of coffee cultivation were becoming mechanised in the second half of the 1970s. One labour contactor, for example, had given up his job because, as he explained, 'it is impossible to work with these people anymore, they are very proud'. The labour contractors had failed on two fronts. They had failed to conceal the landlords' legal responsibilities and they had failed to impose a rate of surplus labour appropriation comparable to that of the former *colonos*. These casual workers had indeed become 'citizens who know no responsibility to anyone or anything'.

Class consciousness has often been inferred from the nature of workers' politics. In the early 1960s, the state played an active role in Brazil, first in channelling political mobilisation by rural workers and later in repressing it. Political repression did not, however, suppress the antagonism between labourers and landlords and by the 1970s workers' hostility towards employers was unmistakable. Confrontations between workers and landlords mostly took the form of individual or unorganised collective resistance to work. Despite profound discontent, organised collective action was very rare. While class consciousness is a necessary condition for collective action by workers, common identity and purpose do not invariably entail collective action because such action also depends on how the workers *perceive* their power to overcome oppression. In other words, forms of struggle are shaped not only by changes in the structural position of workers within productive relations, but also by their perception of the relations of power that prevail. It is necessary, therefore, to examine how the workers themselves experienced the transformations that occurred in their conditions of life and work and the way in which the new patterns of domination find expression in their class language.

5   Memory and Myth in the Making of Workers' Identity

'Landowners (*solemn*)
– The order is to expel those who mistreat the innocent trees!

Colono men (*melancholic and tame*)
– Rascals those who abused of the innocent fruit, retaining them in the insatiable storehouses, burning them in the clandestine fires of dawn!

Landowners (*harsh*)
– Foolish are those who talk without knowing the supreme laws of History!

Colono women (*irritably, several voices at the same time*)
– History! The ignorance of the humbled, the smartness of the scholar!'

   Mario de Andrade, *Café* – Concepção Melodramática (em tres atos) (São Paulo, 1933, 1939, 1942) in M. de Andrade, *Poesías Completas* (São Paulo, 1966) p. 348

The new form of labour exploitation was then not simply the result of the coffee growers' uncontested pursuit of profit under changing technical conditions. The workers' reactions were crucial in shaping the new productive relationships. But if the workers did play an active role, one should enquire also into how they experienced this process themselves. The issue is not only to document the workers' presence in history but to capture their own images of their past which forms part of this history.

Oral history has limited utility as a source of 'hard facts' on the undocumented history of dominated and excluded social groups, but it may advance our understanding of their experiences in other ways. Images of a 'fact' formed by thought are an integral part of the 'fact' itself. The present conditions the memory of the past in the same way as memories of the past condition present perceptions and

159

actions. The omissions as well as the emphases in accounts of the past not only highlight those events and experiences that are of relevance in a social group's class-specific view of its history but also offer insights into the sociopolitical reasons for this specific memory. Lastly, accounts of the past contribute also to an understanding of present perceptions and actions, and thus suggest future possibilities.

When I began research among this labour gang, my intention was to study the workers' present conditions of life and work and, by collecting life histories, to reconstruct the causes of their transformation into casual wage labourers. Early on I was made forcefully aware of the class-specific nature of their history. A national election was set for November 1974. This seemed a good opportunity to discuss politics with them. To my surprise, the workers appeared totally oblivious of the 1964 military coup which had abolished democratic liberties, produced widespread repression and instituted an artificial two-party system. When asked if they remembered the 'revolution' (a term which unequivocally and painfully evokes the 1964 military coup for other sectors of Brazilian society), the older workers invariably described the revolution of 1932 between the Mineiros and Paulistas when an uprising by São Paulo liberals against the first Vargas government was defeated after an armed conflict which partly took place in the region where they had lived. One woman even recalled a yet earlier event, the passing of the Prestes Column in 1924 (*sic*). She was a child at the time and lived with her family near Amparo on an estate:

A man passed by, of average height and long hair. Our house was at a distance from the road. The man said that something strange, a plane would pass above the trees hunting down the horses and the people. When the plane arrived everybody was frightened, came out to see. Nobody saw where this man came from nor where he went. He arrived and asked my mother whether she didn't have a sip of coffee and a piece of bread. He said that we shouldn't be frightened, that the worst came behind, a great war with much spilling of blood. Nobody had seen this man, had seen him pass by. What he said all came true, the war came. The landlords were against Getúlio, above all those of São Paulo.

The end of slavery in 1888, however, marks the first milestone in the workers' historical memory. Though they were no longer slaves, the labourers identified with their slave ancestors, if not on account of their ethnic origin. The gang contained workers of all extractions, Portuguese, Italian, Spanish, African, and several mixtures. It was their class situation which led these workers to compare themselves with the slaves and identify with their plight. Slavery, in fact, marked 'the beginning of the suffering of the poor.' Hence, 'we are slaves, only that they no longer beat us. First they used to beat us, for the rest it is all the same'. Patterns of domination have changed but domination itself persists and the world is still divided into 'we, the poor' (*nos, os pobres*) and 'they, the rich' (*eles, os ricos*), an opposition based, as before, on prevailing property relations.[1]

CLASS OPPRESSION OR GOD'S DESIGN

At first, some workers attributed the existence of rich and poor to God's design. As Da Cida put it, 'I think that God made them [rich and poor]; there are rich and poor'. This seemingly fatalistic interpretation of social inequality and domination as God-given soon turned out to be a combination of the workers' individual sense of powerlessness and their initial distrust toward someone who so visibly did not belong to 'us, the poor'. As I got to know the workers better, this attribution of their poverty to destiny gave way to an interpretation that unequivocally and insistently blamed the landowners' power and monopoly over land for their own expropriation and consequent obligation to work for them. Da Maria explained this in the following terms:

This business of rich and poor began a long time ago when the land was not sold. The *ladinos* [the shrewd ones] fenced in the land and the others were left with their mouths open and worked for the others. In those days the most cunning appropriated everything. The others were fools. Now this is no longer possible; when you are poor it is difficult to become rich. Working one does not become rich.

Having been deprived of the land, the poor have nothing but their labour power to sell for their livelihoods. 'They [the rich] don't work, they are not used to it. That is why they need the poor. The poor don't have the land, they need the rich'. Another two women concluded that only when one dies, can one hope for one's own piece of land and even that has now shrunk from seven to five feet. 'One works and works and does not even have the money for the coffin when one dies'. It is not the work in the fields as such which accounts for their poverty, but the circumstances under which they have to work. The main cause of their poverty is that, being deprived of land, they are forced to work for others, in their case the landlords who 'pay the least to those who work most' and who, therefore, do not themselves have to work.

The class language of these workers reveals bitter antagonisms, apparently rooted in the consequences their expropriation has for their ability to reproduce themselves as workers rather than in their structural position as landless labourers in the sphere of productive relations. But this appearance is misleading. The wider social order which is composed of rich and poor alike is seen to have arisen as a result of the rich having the power to appropriate all the land. As a class in opposition to the landlords, these workers regard themselves as *trabalhadores* or *lavradores*, i.e. rural labourers who are distinct, for instance, from *operários,* industrial workers, who do enjoy social benefits but who, like themselves, belong among the poor. A few even spoke of themselves as *nossa classe*, as *classes baixas* (our class, the lower classes).

The society is split into those who work and those who don't need to work because they reap the profit from those who do. In other words, 'the rich live with the profit from the poor, there have to be rich and poor ... The landlord does not work because he owns the estate, he has the power not to work'. As Da Maria explained, without the poor:

agriculture, crops, I think they would not exist, because you see, someone who is rich, not even if he knew how to, not even jokingly, would take a hoe to work. But you see that the bread of everyday comes from the dust of the earth, doesn't it? It comes from the hands of the poor ... Thus, the rich wants money and we, the poor, want food. Now, if everybody was rich nobody would want to work ... Those who are rich, even those who are somewhat better off, don't want to have anything to do with work, they will prefer to pay somebody else, the poor, to making an effort themselves, because they think that working is a sacrifice. Now, people like us who are poor, who need to work, we face it. We have already been born for this struggle.

Above all else, being poor for these workers means being expropriated and hence forced to work for those who own the land. What distinguishes the poor from the rich is not their respective standards of living as a consequence of their unequal access to the means of production, but the monopoly of the rich over the land. Those who are somewhat better off, like a labour contractor who would own a house and a truck, are regarded as belonging to neither the rich nor the poor. Contractors, like shopkeepers, are 'middling people', *remediados*, who, although not owning land because they own property, none the less do not work. The workers recognise that there are those who are even poorer than they themselves. All the poor need to work, but those who are unable or unwilling to work, are consequently, poorer still. Despite these internal gradiations, however, the all-encompassing opposition is that between rich and poor, those who don't work and those who do.

Knowing that they as workers were the only genuine producers was a source of neither pride nor self-esteem. As Da Cida remarked bitterly, 'I would like that the poor came to an end so that only the rich were left and they had to work as well. The rich live at our expense and on top they trample on us.' Hoeing is considered 'the most worthless job, the worst job [being] the one in the fields'. The workers' alienation is reflected in all spheres of their lives. Because their work lacks value, all the attributes of their being rural workers are sources of intense shame. The food they eat is the 'food of the poor' (*comida de pobre*) and disdained by the rich; their houses, the 'houses of the poor' (*casas de pobre*), are worthy only of sneers from the better off. As one girl joked, 'it is no good to be rich, you would have thieves. We have nothing to fear. In the houses of the poor a thief only gets a fright.' The devaluation of their labour fills the workers with shame because it is an indication of their powerlessness *vis-à-vis* the rich, who not only live at their expense but who also treat them with contempt. 'We are ashamed because we are poor. Those *que pode* [who have the wherewithal, the power], what should they be ashamed of?' Landlords have not only used their power to appropriate land, but have also used it ever since to defend their privileges.

The workers regard education as an indubitable asset. Parents attempt to send their children to school because, potentially, education improves their occupational opportunities out of agriculture and reduces their general sense of social exclusion. But more often than not, schooling is cut short because the children have to go out to work at an early age. Hence, education for their children is a desirable, though usually unattainable, goal. But they don't see it as the reason for the landlords' control over the land or as a sufficient requisite in overcoming their own poverty.

Experience has shown them that, given prevailing power relations, as a rule 'the rich are born rich [and] those who are poor die poor as well'. Or, as Da Cida put it, for the poor to become rich is as likely to happen as for her son to become a woman.

The landlords' wealth is obviously not always newly acquired. The inheritance laws have played their part in perpetuating the power of the rich. As Sr Dito saw it, 'the rich rose through profit but also to a certain extent thanks to their parents. Without your parents you do not get rich nowadays . . . now, the wealth of the father came from his own father and his robbery'.

Though the workers account for their class position in explicitly secular terms, there are nonetheless frequent allusions to God's will, destiny and a pervasive sense of powerlessness which would seem to suggest they locate the roots of their oppression in another world. Alongside the secular class language there is, in effect a religious language which, however, rather than contradicting secular explanations of exploitation serves to account for those aspects of their condition for which the rational secular theory provides no answers.[2]

I will discuss the workers' religious belief system only in so far as it pertains to the workers' class consciousness and politics. The Catholic church and its agents were regarded as allies of the rich. The workers were profoundly anti-clerical and yet, with the exception of a few Pentecostal converts, they defined themselves as Catholics. Their attitude towards religious rituals was, to say the least, ambiguous. Most of them rarely went to mass, but all of them had their children baptised and most were married in church. These rituals were as much social as religious, for the workers felt that had they disregarded them, their spiritual well being would not have been jeopardised in any way. Hardly any of the parents had their children take Holy Communion. Their anti-clericalism was accompanied by a highly externalised form of popular piety and devotion, with most of the workers going fairly regularly on pilgrimages to the shrine of Nossa Senhora Aparecida, the country's patron saint, and to the shrines of other saints, in search of help and protection.

The local priest had few friends among the workers and was much criticised for trying to use his position to get rich, for keeping his charity work to a minimum by charging for his services whenever he could, and for looking down on the poor. Da Tereza disliked him because 'in the church he knows us and outside he does not even greet us. When a rich [man] comes along he gives him a great embrace. Everybody is equal. Because we are poor, he does not need to trample on us.' Many shared this sentiment and felt that a priest was, after all, a man like any other and there was no inherent reason why he should be revered. It was a standard joke that during confession priests would generally keep young girls for hours while hardly listening to the older women. In Jaguariuna, rumour had it that the priest would use the courses held for young couples about to be married (which had recently been introduced) as an opportunity for making indecent overtures to the young men!

This widespread anti-clericalism did not, however, preclude a form of religiosity which offered religious explanations for events that apparently had no immediate cause in this world and which allowed the workers to appeal to God through the mediation of the saints for help in specific areas. While the workers attributed the social order – i.e., the existence of the poor who have to work for the rich – to the power of the rich, the very existence of humanity and the world itself was due to God's design, 'without God nobody would live in this world'. The existence of God is explained in equally pragmatic terms: 'If there were no God, we would not know why we are here'. God and God's will are adduced when there are no obvious worldy explanations for events and for phenomena that occur by chance rather than by any rational design.

The workers do not see their domination and exploitation as a class as God's design. Such chance events as why they as individuals were born poor are, however, attributed to God's will: 'God wanted *me* to be less than you'. Events without any obvious secular explanation are seen as part of a person's destiny; and God is the only designer of destinies: 'God thought that we [the family] could not be rich, only poor. This is our destiny. If you are born in this way you will die in this way'.

Because their labour power is the only resource they possess, good health is vitally important to the workers who rely on it to work and to earn their livelihoods. As they say, 'health is the wealth of the poor'. There is some evidence that general health standards may have fallen when the workers were displaced to the towns. It is no mystery to them that those who work most eat worst and that hard work and poor food are weakening and generally detrimental to their health. As casual rural labourers they were not entitled to the benefits of the national health-insurance system. Therefore, they either had to resort to the local doctor who was expensive, to the chemist, or be treated as *indigentes* (the indigent) in the *Santa Casa* of Campinas. The workers feared the *Santa Casa*, which served as the local teaching hospital, because they thought that if a patient died there the body would not be returned to the relatives. Whereas the workers condemned their socio-economic conditions for undermining their strength, and blamed the rich for having to work for a meagre wage, they failed to see how this could account for one worker falling ill when the others stayed well. Good health was definitely seen as evidence of God's grace: 'Without God we wouldn't be alive. God gives us strength to work so that we are able to earn', for 'God gives us health to be able to work'.

Since God is seen not only to provide good health but also to cure illness, the workers will resort to supernatural agents to obtain a cure. The regular pilgrimages to the shrines of saints or of the virgin are often for recreation but mainly to appeal for protection and help when someone in the family falls ill. They may resort to the local pharmacist or doctor for specialised medical help, but often they appeal to the supernatural for additional protection, for life, good health and death all depend ultimately on God 'who knows our destiny . . . We do not know it. We are here because of God's will. He allows us to stay while he wants.'

A number of religious and magical strategies are available for dealing with problems ascribed to the will of God. As nominal rather than practising Catholics the workers conceived of neither the priest nor the Church as efficient agencies for obtaining help or even, since 'the priest does not save anyone', salvation. Instead they appeal directly to the saints, who are regarded as the proper intermediaries with God. The usual way of appealing to God for help is to make a 'promise' to a saint. The person who is affected by an illness, or a relative, promises to perform a ritual act, usually entailing a visit to the saint's shrine with a photograph, candle, or piece of cloth belonging to the person in question, if a cure is forthcoming.

As I mentioned earlier, a few of the workers had converted to Pentecostalism which, besides demanding strict observance of a set of moral rules regarding drink, sexual conduct and dancing, did offer direct access to God. But above all, Pentecostalism teaches passivity and acceptance of the sufferings of this world as a path to salvation, which held some appeal only for a few of the workers. Da Antonia, for instance, had recently renounced her Pentecostalism on the grounds that she had felt too insulted by a quarrel with another woman to turn the other cheek. Although this sect is thought of as less contemptuous of the poor than the Catholic church, many of the workers objected to the sense of moral superiority often displayed by its followers. Apart from some of the labour contractors, none of the workers resorted to any of the Afro-Brazilian cults of which Umbanda was the most popular. In fact, they saw these cults as evil and were particularly afraid of Umbanda and Macumba. There are other magical agents, however, which are frequently used and which are compatible with popular Catholicism. These include *curadores[as]* and *bençedeiras[os]*, who are people endowed with special healing powers. And finally, the occasional so-called missionary priests who set up their own services during which they allegedly perform miracle cures, are yet another presence of the supernatural. But, as distinct from the saints, these missionary priests and the healers enjoy only the qualified confidence of the workers, who are quick to suspect them of lining their own pockets at their expense.

Misfortunes such as a fire or the break-up of a marriage are sometimes attributed to an ill-disposed neighbour having resorted to black magic. The appropriate avenue of redress is then through the *curadora*. One way in which the workers distinguish between good and bad magic is on the basis of whether or not the mediating agent charges for his or her services.

A clear distinction is drawn between problems that can generally be solved by their own initiative and those outside their control which require help from the saints or from a magical agent. Da Ditinha appealed to a saint for a television set and for her daughter's success in an examination. In this fortunate case, she won the television in a lottery and the daughter passed her examination, but to have asked God for a wage raise would have been totally inappropriate: 'I do not appeal to the Saints in regard to the wage. This depends on them, the landlords. Other things I ask of God, of God himself. The saints are like us, God makes miracles. We have to demand everything we want of the landlord. The saints, if they want to do a miracle, they must seek the order from God'.

Since their common exploitation is neither God-given nor a matter of fate, any improvement in, or transformation of, their condition as a class can only be achieved in this world. The possibility of another world in which sins are punished and good deeds rewarded, of heaven and hell, is very doubtful because of lack of any evidence: 'They say that those who die and are good go to heaven, that those who are bad do not go, but I don't know this. I have not yet died and those who die do not return to tell us.'

The women tended to be more inclined than the men to believe in some sort of other world where one can find salvation and sinners are punished for their wrongs. But even they were unwilling to describe what it might be like, on the grounds that they had never been there. Significantly, it seemed to be precisely those women who were the most self-effacing in their family relationships and the most compliant at work, who were also the most likely to hold a strong belief in God and in their salvation in another world. The less power they had in this world, the more they pinned their hopes on the next. Da Ditinha thought women were more religious than men 'because women suffer more . . . Men don't care, they only think about their work, to have fun. Not all of them, there are also men who are religious'. But even women who seemed to have given up all hope of improving their lot in this world could conceive of drastic secular solutions to their oppression. One woman, who had been betrayed for years by a husband who was giving some of his earnings to his lover, was close to despair: 'I like to work only early in the morning but with God's help it'll go . . . I think that everything comes from God, otherwise life doesn't progress'. When asked why some got on better than others, she felt that 'it is surely because He thinks that one has already deserved it. I think that I haven't deserved it yet. Everything has its day, its hour: my hour has not yet arrived. Either I will improve or I will die to rest. If God does not bring an improvement, then He will take me from this world to rest'. Access to heaven depended, she thought, not on regularly attending mass where people only looked down on you because of your clothes, but on following the 'rules', for religion could be practiced very well at home. Nevertheless, despite her sense of resignation, she had on one occasion beaten up her husband's lover and on another flew into a rage: 'the poor could all die when they are born so that the rich have to suffer as well. Who would grow the crops for the rich to buy?'

The more assertive women were much more sceptical about the afterlife. Although the workers all acknowledged that there were conflicting views about the existence and nature of another world and attitudes were not always clear-cut, most of the women as well as the men, while sharing a deep belief in God, thought that life's rewards and punishments were confined to this world. As Sr Dito, with a firm sense of realism and some irony, asserted:[11]

I don't believe that people go to heaven . . . Where does a person go who dies? He returns to the soil. They say that those who deserve it go to heaven and those who do not deserve it go to hell. I'll tell you, there is no other hell than that of the worker who lives here on earth. Greater suffering than that of the people of the fields who go from here to there, is none . . . If there was a hell who should go there? The rich, of course. The poor deserve the heaven, the rich ought to go to hell because it doesn't matter how good they are, they always take advantage of the poor no matter the miracles they make.

Thus, rather than a path to salvation, death is often conceived of as the moment when a person finally comes to rest: 'for those who die it is not a bad thing, for those who are left behind it is worse . . . Our hope is the cemetery itself'. Or, as Da Maria explained at greater length:

Those who are in command are the *tubarões* [sharks]. The *tubarões* are the rich, the politicians, the government party . . . The poor are always defeated. They are like slippers [*pe de chinelo*], you put them on when you want and throw them off when you like. The poor only straighten themselves out when they die, then they do not eat, they do not think . . . Heaven and Hell? I believe the hell is where we find ourselves here, it is our life now because people think and try to improve but it never turns out right; because if there was a hell we would already be in it; heaven is when we die. When we die we do not eat, we do not struggle, we do not think . . . Who can tell? Those who go do not tell. When one dies one is put into the hole . . . the soil benefits, one becomes like manure.

Those who have failed to keep a 'promise' to a saint or who have shown disrespect for their parents do not, however, find rest when they die, or at least not until someone else fulfills the promise on their behalf, or the injured parents grant forgiveness. Until then, they will appear to the living as lost souls, *almas perdidas*, restless and unable to find peace.

Death has a political meaning as well, for it is the great equaliser which knows no difference between rich and poor. As Da Amelia exclaimed on hearing the news of the landlord's death, 'Good God, he was so rich, and I thought that the rich do not die'. The inevitability and unpredictability not only of death but of ill-health serve to assert the common humanity of all people irrespective of worldly power. As one man noted:

> One should show deference and have a good time. We all die, don't we? And when you fall ill, you can be whatever you want, you are worth nothing... Everybody is equal, we are all brothers, everybody dies, stinks the same. One should think about working, drinking and eating.

It is because everyone shares a common human condition that the workers so often use animal metaphors to denounce their oppression by the rich: it is unacceptable to treat the poor as if they were 'dogs', 'animals', or 'beasts' because they are human as well.

The rich may try to pretend that social inequality is of the nature of things, that wealth is the sign of special inherent abilities which the rich have and which the poor lack. But the poor know better. One landlord tried to persuade me of the inevitability and immutability of social inequality with a proverb the workers never used, i.e. 'God made five fingers and none of them the same. There must be a difference!' Da Antonia, however, expressed the feelings of most of the workers by urging that the 'rich and poor should all be equal. Each one should have something to live on, not be so poor. Each one should have a piece of land, a little house to live in'.

Because people are by nature equal, it is thus possible to conceive of change and improvement in this world. Workers may become impatient with the saints or even with God when their appeals seem to be to no avail: 'God is not right, there should be some distribution. I did not want to leave school, I said that God was not just. There should be some distribution.' It is also this egalitarian element in Catholicism which, while more often than not suppressed by the official church, has made the Basic Christian Communities organised by the progressive clergy in Brazil in recent years so successful among the poor. Although the workers in Jaguariuna had not come into contact with this movement, I suspect that it would be well received because of the explicit aim of such communities to provide an organisation for collective action to overcome social injustice.[3]

Finally, religion also provides moral values which are reinforced by the notion of sin. Some of these values encourage deference and an acceptance of one's condition, others condemn behaviour that is opposed to community cohesion, while others still may put in question the very source of the oppression of the poor by the rich. To kill is regarded as a mortal sin, although it may be justified in self-defence. For a few, a husband or wife's infidelity is a sin, mainly because it could deprive children of their food. But everyone agreed that stealing, speaking ill of someone without reason and envy were sins. While these may have been conceived of as universal values, in practice they were only applied by the workers to denounce insolidary behaviour amongst themselves. It was obvious to everyone that the contractors' comfort and the landlord's wealth had been acquired by robbery, but this did not make them sinners who would be punished, for to profit at the expense of the poor and to appropriate the labour of others was only an expression of their power in this world.

In conclusion religious language, rather than expressing class conflict in religious terms, serves these workers to account for individual contingencies. Only God knows why one particular person happens to be born rich and another poor. Religious language instead of constituting a class language in itself, thus complements the workers' secular language of class. The placement of a particular individual within the relations of exploitation is, like individual misfortune, attributed to God's design, but the workers' oppression as a class is unequivocally seen as of the making of the rich.

FROM THE AGE OF PLENTY TO A TIME OF MONEY: THE DOMINANCE OF THE MARKET

The clarity with which the workers described the roots of their oppression varied from worker to worker. Few could match the acuteness of perception of Sr Dito, a 50-year-old man, who told me that:

> What gives the landlord his profit is labour. Not the land. Without labour it does not give anything. That's logical. It is the profit of capital. But if you do not apply labour it does not give anything. You have to be a fool not to perceive that. If you leave the capital in a corner you should see what comes of it. If you do not weed the land, you should see what happens, nothing! To me all that is produced is produced by the labourers. The landowners think that we are all suckers.

All would have agreed with him. Sr Dito, like most of his fellow workers, men and women alike, is illiterate and has never belonged to any organised political movement. Some of the workers remembered the *colono* strikes in the old days but had had no part in the union-isation of rural workers in the São Paulo area, which had preceded the military coup of 1964. Information among them about the mobilisation of rural workers in the Northeast, the Peasant Leagues and the rural unions, as about the campaign for mass unionisation in the early 1960s, was either exceedingly vague or non-existent. Neither were they aware of the Cuban revolution or knew anything, for instance, about Allende's recent death. Their perception of exploitation rested largely on their own life and work experiences.

Basically, the workers derived information from two sources, their fellow workers, which occasionally included the labour contractor though he did not elicit much confidence, and television, which to an extent had come to replace the radio. None of the workers read newspapers. Television was used mainly for watching endless soap operas (*tele-novelas*) which undoubtedly served to familiarise the workers with other, often highly extravagant, life styles,[4] but they paid little attention to news bulletins. Apart from the language in which news items were presented being quite impenetrable to the workers, the issues that were discussed were of little relevance to them or to their lives. This is hardly surprising for, until the late 1970's, television was systematically censored and all programmes that were in any way critical of the military government and/or could be thought to incite popular unrest were banned.[5] The government was only too well aware of the dangers of arousing popular interest through showing such programmes to the workers. Even election broadcasts were only given limited coverage and were of little interest to them unless the cost of living or wage policies were discussed. They were profoundly distrustful of outsiders. For the most part, they only really listened to and trusted their fellow workers and would frequently preface their remarks with words like 'the gang said' or 'the women said', as if in some way this substan-tiated what they had to say. For example, whenever someone denounced the landlord for profiting at their expenses, none of the other workers ever disagreed. On being told by a fellow worker of how a whole hierarchy of beneficiaries lived from their labour and of how much they received in contrast to their own miserable wages, Da Ditinha did not hesitate to agree:

I started thinking about what she had told me and it is true. If you stop to think, the landlord (*patrão*), the administrator, the overseer, they only look on. As the contractor said, his job is with the eyes. The administrator gives orders to him and he gives orders to us.[6]

The workers' consciousness as a class and a common identity have been formed by shared experiences of work as *colonos* or sharecroppers on the coffee estates, reinforced by their collective and compulsory transformation into casual wage labourers. Indeed their class consciousness and politics are informed not only by the workers' common perception of their current oppression as casual labourers, or even by the power and coercion in the hands of present-day land-lords, but also by the way they recall the sociopolitical processes leading up to it. The distant past of slavery has now only symbolic meaning in the workers' collective memory; the crucial turning point is the abolition of the *colonato* system when they were forced to leave the estates for the outskirts of the small towns in the interior of the state of São Paulo.

The gradual improvement of real wages which the workers experienced during the 1970s at first sight might seem to contradict their acute sense of exploitation and their profound discontent at their new conditions of life and work. By moving to the towns, the workers also, however, lost a number of other benefits in kind, such as housing and self-provisioning, which they had received over and above their money wage when they were living on the estates.

It is notoriously difficult to calculate the value of self-provisioning, for not only must the foodstuffs produced be taken into account but also the labour that went into it. Moreover, the statutory minimum wage, which became effective in agriculture in 1963, was implemented only in the early 1970s. In 1963, the rural daily wage amounted to only 58 per cent of the legal minimum wage.[7] During the second half of the sixties, this gap gradually closed. For the first two years after the enactment of the Rural Labour Statute rural daily wages in São Paulo rose proportionately more than the official readjustment in the legal minimum wage. Therefore, the wage freeze imposed by the military government after 1964 by readjusting the minimum wage below the annual increase in the cost of living affected rural workers in São Paulo less than industrial labour. By the end of the decade the gap between the rural daily wage and the mimimum wage had narrowed to about 20 per cent.[8] During the same period, however, with the exception of 1965-7, the prices received by coffee growers rose proportionately more than the rural daily wage. In 1964-5 coffee prices paid to growers rose by 149 per cent, while the nominal rural daily wage increased by only a little over 100 per cent. After 1967 and until 1970, rural daily wages again lagged behind the prices rises received by the coffee growers.

In the early 1970s rapid economic growth produced a genuine, if modest, improvement in rural workers' real incomes. By 1973, the relative labour shortage created by the economic boom for the first time pushed rural daily wages in São Paulo above the legal minimum wage and prices for export crops were rising. By 1973, also for the first time in the country's history, however, Brazil had to import black beans, one of the basic staples in the popular diet. By 1975 the cost of living was again rising at an annual rate of 40 per cent, reaching almost 80 per cent by 1979. Nonetheless, the real rural daily wage continued to rise slowly until 1979, even though in most years less than coffee prices, which more than doubled when the coffee regions were hit by the exceptionally severe frost in 1975-6. At the end of the decade, the onset of the recession produced by the debt crisis, however, once more began to erode the rural workers' income.

As far as real wages are concerned, the 1970s may be regarded then as a genuine improvement over the 1960s. But the real wage index does not capture the full meaning for the workers of their displacement from the estates.

As significant as the strictly economic changes in determining how the workers experienced their transformation into casual wage labourers was how the social and political implications of their departure from the estates affected their control over conditions of life and work and how they interpreted the political process underlying this change.

The workers' historical memory is divided into two radically distinct periods: the old days, the 'time of plenty' (*tempo de fartura*) when they lived on the coffee plantations and the present, the 'time of money' (*tempo de dinheiro*). The comparative advantages of each period are, however, far from clear cut: before, food was plentiful but there was no money; now there is money but it has no worth: 'What is the good of a wage rise if food has already gone up twice?' When they lived on the coffee plantations as *colonos* or sharecroppers, money wages were low. At that time 'work was very cheap', but they

Table 5.1 Prices received by farmers, by coffee growers, day-wages of casual labour and statutory minimum wage and cost of living, São Paulo, 1960–71 (base 1960 = 100)

Year	Prices received by Farmers[1]		Prices received by Coffee growers[2]		Day-wages of casual labour[3]		Statutory minimum wage[4]		Cost of living index
	Index	Change (%)	Index	Change (%)	Index	Change (%)	Index	Change (%)	
1960	100		100		100		100		100
1961	141	41	137	37	155	55	139	39	137
1962	235	66	238	73	230	48	139	0	210
1963	404	71	482	102	361	56	222	59	364
1964	813	101	1204	149	740	104	444	50	683
1965	1058	30	1158	–3	1406	90	699	57	1104
1966	1496	43	1158	0	1882	33	889	27	1623
1967	1716	14	1567	35	2307	22	1112	25	2106
1968	2103	22	2386	52	3363	45	1366	22	2604
1969	2868	36	3600	50	3700	10	1652	20	3215
1970	3491	21	6076	68	5010	35	1980	19	3826
1971	4419	26	5208	–14	6428	28	2383	20	4212

Sources:
1. P. V. Sendin, 'Elaboração de um índice de salários rurais para o Estado de São Paulo', Table 2, p. 171.
2. R. Araújo Dias, 'Problemas Atuais da Economia Cafeeira', Agricultura em São Paulo, XIV, (1/2) (1969) Table 5, p. 45; the series given by Araújo Dias ends in 1968; the 1969 and 1971 indices were calculated using average domestic prices for processed coffee paid in Paraná, São Paulo and Minas Gerais per bag of 60 kg; they may not be strictly comparable with Araújo Dias's price series who does not indicate which prices he used; Anuário Estadístico do Café, Coordenadoria de Estudos da Economia Cafeeira, 11 Brazil, (Rio de Janeiro, December 1977) p. 374.
3. P. V. Sendin, 'Elaboração de um índice de salários rurais', Table 6, p. 176.
4. Conjuntura Económica (November 1983) 37, (11), Table 9, p. 40; refers to São Paulo.
5. Conjuntura Económica (February 1971) 25, (2), p. 195; the index for 1971 refers to January of that year, constituting probably an underestimate of the annual average.

176

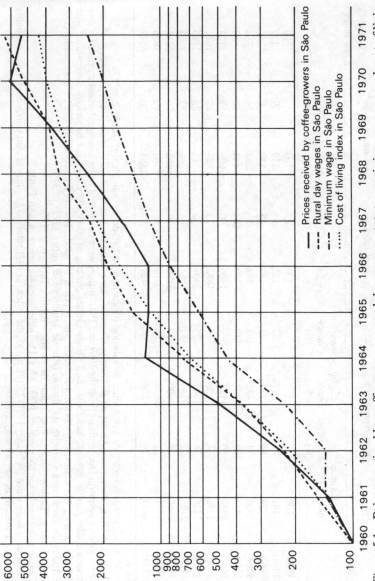

Figure 5.1 Prices received by coffee growers, rural day-wages, statutory minimum wage and cost of living index, São Paulo, 1960–71

needed little money because they grew their own food. Self-provisioning, though a source of surplus labour appropriation, had sheltered the workers from the food market. Despite rural wages reaching those of unskilled industrial workers in the 1970s, many workers still felt that this did not fully compensate for what they had lost by leaving the estates. They had had to work from morning till night to feed themselves and earn their wage, but as Da Alzira complained:

> I believe that at the time of Getúlio [Vargas] we lived better. Before there was no money but it was a time of plenty . . . Now we have nothing left . . . We had chicken, pig. Now there is always money but one does not find anything to buy. In one way things have become worse, but in another they have improved. At that time you would not see the face of money. Now, when Saturday arrives you have money although I don't know why things become more expensive all the time.

Workers in the sugar-cane area of Pernambuco, in contrast to those of São Paulo, recall their period of living and working on the sugar plantations as one of captivity as opposed to the freedom they now enjoy as casual workers (*clandestinos*) living in town. The Rural Labour Statute had similar effects in other parts of the country, but how particular workers perceived what effects leaving the estates had on their lives varies in accordance with the conditions under which they worked as resident labourers before. Viewing their expulsion from the plantations as a move towards greater freedom relates to the heavy restrictions they experienced as *moradores* (residents). They were permanently at the landlord's beck and call, especially since, rather than stipulating what tasks had to be performed in an annual contract, these would be set on a piece-work basis as and when they occurred. As *clandestinos* they may lack any 'rights' but they are at least free to work when and for whom they please. *Moradores* had the right to self-provisioning, but even this had been constantly threatened by the encroachments of sugar cane. The workers in the sugar-cane districts of Pernambuco therefore conceive of the contrasting experiences of 'captivity' and 'freedom' in terms of the amount of control they are able to exercise over their labour power. In São Paulo, instead, leaving the estates and the loss of self-provisioning is seen primarily in terms of loss of control over food supply due to the resulting food dependence on the market.[9]

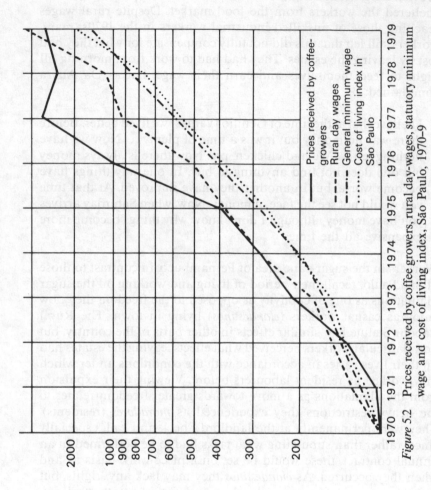

Legend:
- Prices received by coffee-growers
- Rural day wages
- General minimum wage
- Cost of living index in São Paulo

Figure 5.2 Prices received by coffee growers, rural day-wages, statutory minimum wage and cost of living index, São Paulo, 1970–9

Table 5.2 Prices received by coffee growers, day-wages of casual labour, statutory minimum wage and cost of living, São Paulo, 1970–9 (base 1970 = 100)

Year	Prices received by coffee growers[1]		Day-wages of casual labour[2]		Statutory minimum wage[3]		Cost of living index[4]
	Index	Change (%)	Index	Change (%)	Index	Change (%)	
1970	100		100		100		100
1971	105	5	128	28	120	20	118
1972	135	28	–	–	143	19	136
1973	219	62	181	41	166	16	155
1974	289	31	290	60	201	21	207
1975	402	39	399	37	285	41	271
1976	1050	161	508	27	410	43	393
1977	1842	75	907	78	588	43	563
1978	1613	−12	1088	19	834	41	781
1979	1783	10	2177	100	1203	44	1374

Sources:
1. *Conjuntura Económica* (May 1979) 33, (5) p. 170.
2. For 1970 and 1971 P. V. Sendin, 'Elaboração de um índice de salários rurais', Table 6, p. 176; wages for 1973 to 1979 are those paid by the coffee estate studied.
3. *Conjuntura Económica* (November 1983) 37 (11) Table 9, p. 40; refers to São Paulo; the indices were obtained by dividing monthly minimum wage by 30.
4. The cost of living indices were calculated on the basis of the rate of inflation in consumer prices given by W. Baer *The Brazilian Economy, Growth and Development*, 2nd edn (New York, 1983) p. 118.

But the workers' relative standard of living cannot be assessed only by measuring the purchasing power of their incomes as regards basic foodstuffs, for this would conceal how their move to the towns has also changed their *needs*.

Estimates show that the lowest income group, to which these rural workers belong, spend no less than 50 per cent of their income on food. Despite the increase in real wages in the 1970s, the workers showed growing concern over rising food prices and deteriorating nutritional standards. Being able to remember a time when food was plentiful and provisions assured undoubtedly heightened their anxiety over food supplies caused by rising inflation. The recurrent

Table 5.3   Rural day-wages (deflated by cost of living index), São Paulo, 1970–9

Year	Day-wages of casual labour (Cr$)	Day-wages of resident labour (Cr$)	Minimum day-wage (Cr$)
1970	2.33	2.24	2.95
1971	2.45	2.36	2.95
1972	2.71	2.57	2.97
1973	3.28	3.11	2.65
1974	3.75	3.40	2.55
1975	3.61	3.34	2.77
1976	3.74	3.01	2.95
1977	4.11	–	3.01
1978	3.56	–	3.09
1979	4.75	–	3.87

Sources: J. Graziano da Silva and J. Garcia Gasques, 'Diagnóstico inicial do volante em São Paulo', Departamento de Economía Rural, UNESP, Botucatú (São Paulo, 1982) p. 95 for day-wages of casual and resident labour for the period 1970 to 1976; day-wages of casual labour for 1977 to 1979 are those paid the gang studied deflated by the cost of living index for São Paulo; minimum day-wages were calculated by dividing monthly minimum wages by 30 and deflating the result by the cost of living index for São Paulo.

shortages of black beans in the mid-1970s deepened their nostalgia for a time when they themselves largely controlled the supply of food. Equally important to how these workers perceived their loss of self-provisioning rights were their feelings about status and their resentment over the unequal distribution of food between those who do and those who don't work. When commenting on an extended and much-publicised strike by university teachers in late 1979, one of the women's main objections was that those who worked most had to eat the worst food:

> The government could open its hands for the poor and not for those professors there. They have their lives under control, it is not so much sacrifice. They only sit, theirs isn't hard work. They can manage well eating once a day. Now, in the fields you need to eat three times a day. We have no land to grow food and we earn this miserable wage. The poor die of hunger.

Table 5.4 Purchasing power of day-wages measured in basic foodstuffs, Campinas, 1973–9 (kg/day-wage)

Foodstuffs	November						
	1973	1974	1975	1976	1977	1978	1979
Rice	4.16	5.55	4.62	6.04	9.38	5.81	6.66
Beans	2.50	4.44	4.81	2.61	4.12	4.25	5.92
Oil	2.32	2.59	2.99	3.64	3.70	3.15	4.28
Macaroni	4.54	4.65	5.65	6.40	8.40	6.97	8.88
Coffee	1.21	1.57	1.25	0.70	1.02	0.92	0.99

Source: Day-wages and food prices are those received and paid by a sample of the workers belonging to the gang I studied. In November 1973, for example, a day-wage would buy 4.16 kg of rice *or* 2.50 kg of beans.

Her conclusion about the poor having to starve was a rhetorical point which became a reality only in the 1980s when galloping inflation and the recession made living conditions very much worse. In the 1970s, though, São Paulo's rural workers were the least poor of the poor. Even in agriculture there was no shortage of work in the state, and the regional minimum wage paid in São Paulo was the highest in the country. But the nutritional value of the workers' diet seems to have deteriorated none the less. Food, rather than work, loomed as the most constant and pressing concern.

When they lived and worked on the plantations their main staples were rice, black beans and maize. Pork and chicken provided meat and fat and sometimes they even had a goat. Their main beverage was coffee. A traditional maize dish called *polenta* has now disappeared from their diet on the grounds that it takes too long to prepare. Macaroni and bread are used as substitutes, especially for beans and/or rice when their prices rose. Ideally, the workers should have chicken or beef, at least on Sundays, but following a sharp rise in the price of beef, meat too has all but disappeared from their meals.

Now, the basic diet consists of rice and beans accompanied by a few vegetables, such as cabbage or onions, to give the meal some flavour and only very rarely any meat. The diet lacks animal proteins which are substituted by plant proteins, mainly black beans. The workers feel particularly resentful, however, about the unequal distribution of food: 'The rich do not work because they have what they need to live on and they have the poor to work for them ... The rich don't work because they already have [enough] to eat and the poor work and only have this little to eat'. The irony of an export agriculture unable to feed its own workers properly was not lost on them. As they would say, 'a crop like coffee that needs so much work is only for drinking. It goes abroad. Coffee produces so much profit for the boss', but then 'the poor are like circus animals. Don't the artists live at the expense of the animals? Well, we are like animals, we have to earn a little and a lot for them'.

The workers not only resent the quality of their food and its unequal distribution, but also the circumstances under which they now have to eat it. In the old days on the estates, the women would bring a hot meal to the fields. Now, by the time they eat, the food they have brought along is cold. The food should be warm and tasty and, above all, it should provide the energy they need to work. The poor need to work in order to live and to be able to work they must be healthy and strong and for this they need to have proper food: 'What allows us to live is our health; being healthy one is willing to work, to eat'. But not all food provides enough strength to wield a hoe all day. There are two kinds of food: *comida* (food) i.e. the main staples, and *mistura* (mixture), supplements that are added for taste. None the less, this classification has been distorted by the market as well; workers find that meat, the source of strength *par excellence*, is now a supplement:

> It is necessary to eat food, otherwise one does not resist. With bread one does not resist, bread has no weight ... Macaroni does not sustain one, neither *polenta*. It makes people weak. Rice and beans and *virado* [beans with ground maize] is strong; rice alone has no strength. Rice without beans is like macaroni. Meat is better than eggs; eggs are no good either.

In the 1970s, in response to the sharp rise in meat prices, there was a substantial expansion in cattle raising and the gang worked for months draining the lowlands of the estate for pasture planting, but they were well aware that the meat their labour produced would not be for them. As Da Antonia joked, 'in addition to being *bóias-frias* [cold meals] we will become rabbits ... Soon we will begin eating salad [made] of grass'.

Not only do the workers have to eat nutritious food in order to work properly, but different jobs require different degrees of effort and hence different amounts of food. Consequently, when they don't work they feel hunger less, but when they are hungry they cannot work: 'The poor, when they don't work [on Sundays] they never get hungry, but when they work, meal time never seems to arrive'. But obviously this connection between one's ability to work and the food one eats does not apply to the rich. They do not do manual work and nonetheless eat well: meat every day, warm and varied food and they can even afford the throw food away. *Comida de pobre*, the food of the poor, consists of rice and beans every day, eaten cold in the fields. Those who do not work are strong and the workers are weak, as Da Rosa, a woman of about fifty complained: 'My nerves have been weak for some time. I get this trembling when I am in the fields; but then we sleep little, work a lot and eat poor food. Working with the hoe all day, we must feel weak'. But it is not only the rich who prosper at their expense. The contractor also lives off their labour and, hence, he can, as it were, afford to live close to the butcher's whereas they have to travel very much further for their meat. The final irony came when the price of coffee went up so much that the coffee workers could no longer afford it and had to drink mate tea instead. They drink such beverages with a lot of sugar, a cheap source of calories.

The numerous social pressures of town life have also created new needs and status requirements which make extra demands on their limited means. When they lived on the estates the workers' housing was provided by the landlord, but in town most of them have to pay rent. When they first arrived in town some of the workers were able to buy plots and build houses of sorts with the compensation they had received on their dismissal from the estates. The money rarely amounted to what they were entitled to by law, but most did not even receive this. The added burden of the rent was felt especially by the women in that it often meant that they had to go out to work for a wage. Job insecurity increased their anxiety over having to pay a regular rent. Those who owned a house were at least protected from eviction in the case of unemployment.[10]

Life in town has recently provided the workers with some comforts they did not enjoy when they lived on the estates. At the beginning there had been neither electricity nor running water. Electricity was eventually installed upon an organised request by the workers themselves. Running water arrived somewhat later in the neighbourhood following an electoral campaign when local politicians tried to capture the workers' votes by improving basic services. Initially, only a few families had wells in their backyards. Some allowed their neighbours to draw water but this was a source of friction and most women did their washing in the nearby river. Electricity and water have to be paid and there is always the danger of services being cut off if bills are not settled on time. As yet there is no sewerage and the streets are unpaved, becoming almost intransitable when it rains. Not all families have running water. Despite having to pay for the services, the women regard them as a great improvement because they alleviate their domestic chores and leave more time for other tasks. With electric lights they can now do their mending at night.

Traditionally food was cooked on wood-fired, brick-built stoves which were situated in a corner of the house or in the backyard. But because firewood is now scarce and must also be bought, gas cookers now gradually replace these stoves. The purchase of a gas cooker and of bottled gas entailed substantial expense, but it has facilitated cooking the meal before leaving for work in the mornings, especially on rainy days. Electric lights, running water, household appliances such as the gas cooker, and the rent are added expenses which being part of urban life cannot be avoided even if this means going without sufficient food.

The workers' changing consumption patterns have, however, gradually come to include also durable consumer goods such as television sets and even fridges, which appears to contradict the workers' ostensible difficulties in providing themselves with adequate food. Da Maria compared the quality of life in town and on the estates in the following terms:

Many say that it was better before, many say that it is better now. I think that it is better now. Before, when you were ill it was home remedies. We had no means, it was very far away, if you cut your foot, it would swell . . . There was no pharmacy, nothing. Not now. They suffered a lot but we no longer suffer as much. It was always the same thing. You married without a trousseau, made the bed on the floor, stuck four poles in the ground, placed some sticks across and covered them with bamboo and over them went a mattress of straw and you slept. I knew this . . . shoes only for going out. I remember until today my mother's white wedding shoes . . . there was abundance for those who had plenty but not for all ... We bought clothes in a shop once a year, everything we bought yearly ... My brother says that by contrast with the old days we who are poor are rich. We have enough to eat, we don't go barefoot. It's true we have to work [but] domestic work is easier now. Then if you needed rice, coffee, you had to husk it, water was far away.

This woman's optimistic assessment, however, was not shared by all. Although everyone experienced the new social pressures of the consumer society in similar ways, by no means all were capable of adequately satisfying their new needs.

In the old days, the workers had few belongings: some pots and pans, working implements, blankets and a few clothes. Owning little also allowed for greater mobility. They could move from one estate to another in search of better working conditions with greater ease. But, above all, having few possessions and simple clothes did not reflect on their social standing in the way it now does. 'There was no luxury as there is now. Nobody minded [*reparava*] the others' appearance'. In the old days, they hardly ever wore shoes, now 'you are already born with shoes on your feet'. When they lived on the estates, visits to the nearby towns tended to be limited to the occasions when annual purchases were made. For the rest, social relations were confined to their fellow workers whose living and working conditions were no different from their own. Contact with the planter was usually distant and sporadic. Moreover, he belonged to the 'others', the rich, and his life style did not challenge their own self-regard. The workers' move to the towns changed all that. Town life not only introduced them to new consumer goods but also brought them into close contact with other social groups, a permanent reminder of their own inferiority precisely because the superior status of even the slightly better off is reflected in their access to these goods. In the urban context, the quality of the workers' homes, their clothes and their food, have acquired symbolic meanings which contribute towards undermining their own self-respect.

The 'demonstration effect of the consumption patterns of the rich' does not account by itself for the emergence of new 'wants' among low-income groups,[11] for poverty not only creates material hardship but also produces a sense of indignity among the poor. Frequent encounters with the better-off who look on the poor with contempt has given the workers a sense of shame over the visible signs of their subordination, the poor quality of their clothes, the precariousness of their homes, the inadequacy of their food. Their inability to shed the symbols of that condition enhances their sense of inadequacy and powerlessness at being workers of the fields 'who do the dirtiest job but also earn the least'.

Conspicuous consumption is not a privilege of the rich. But while for the rich it entails a choice, for these workers the option between eating adequately or suffering the disdain of the well off is hardly a genuine choice. Pressure to improve at least their appearances is felt especially keenly among the young. Many of the young girls working in the gang would wrap up their hands with pieces of cloth to prevent calluses and to protect them from the sun. In this way, their hands would not give them away as agricultural workers in town. As one girl explained, they wanted to appear to be more than they were (*aparecer mais*) so that the young men in town would not regard them with disdain. As one of the men remarked in describing their lot, 'the disease of the poor are calluses and colds. The poor work with the hoe so that the colds will run away, the rich hide'. The girls were also ashamed of carrying their hoes home from work. Not only their work clothes but their clothes in general were a source of embarrassment and some of the older women were even reluctant to go shopping in town because they thought people would sneer at their looks. I was told of one gang that worked for a large cooperative farm of Dutch settlers in which the labourers dressed up for work because there were these other people around. Some even refused to visit their better-off relatives because they felt humiliated by not knowing how to eat properly with a knife and fork.

Although as *colonos* and sharecroppers they had had to live and work under harsh conditions, most of the workers felt that then at least they had had more control over their lives. Now, in addition to having to work so hard for so little pay, they are also permanently reminded that they have no social worth. But ultimately, this sense of inadequacy derives above all from the powerlessness their condition as rural workers is seen to convey and the social contempt with which such weakness is rewarded. The better-off are referred to as those *que pode, que tem poder* which means they can both 'afford something' and that they 'have power'. By conflating the two ideas, possessions become simultaneously the consequence and the manifestation of power. Those who own property or possessions do so because they have the power to afford them. The poor not only have nothing because they lack power, but having nothing also underlines their powerlessness. Or, in the words of Da Cida, 'we are nothing because we have nothing, only our children, my crowd of children'. In the old days what one was seemed to depend, at least to an extent, on the effort one made at work. Now, one's social worth appears to depend entirely on what one has. In town people 'mind' (*repara*) about one's clothes, one's home, 'they say that our home is shabby (*mal arrumada*), that we are badly dressed, they say, look at those old shoes but they don't realise that our circumstances don't allow us to dress any better'.

Constant exposure to the contempt of the better-off has had a divisive effect among the workers themselves. Durable consumer goods were bought in response to the subtle social pressures of town life, but not all the workers were equally well placed to satisfy these new needs. Families who owned their houses and who had several of their members earning a wage were able to acquire some of these goods and, consequently, assessed their new circumstances most favourably compared with the lowest-income families who felt so much more nostalgia for the 'abundance' of the past. Without the introduction of hire purchase, however, none of these families would have been able to buy durable consumer goods such as television sets, furniture, clothes and fridges. Even food is generally bought on credit by the week or the month, although this raises the price. Clothes and domestic appliances are always bought on hire purchase.

Most of the older women hardly ever bought any clothes for themselves and merely wore what others who had 'more power' had given them, thereby sacrificing their desires to the family's well-being. Men occasionally bought trousers and shirts but it was above all the young who needed to be well dressed. Everyone required at least two sets of clothes for work in case one got wet and, since winter temperatures could drop to freezing point at night, they also needed some warm clothes. The houses were generally very draughty since the roofs were covered only with tiles and the windows had shutters but no glass. Often, there were not enough blankets to go around, but even so, they also needed a set of clothes for when they went out. Married women rarely did go out because they had little time and no appropriate clothes, but men regularly went to the bar and the youngsters went out with their friends. Moreover, girls could no longer marry without a trousseau and young men were expected to provide at least bedroom furniture and kitchen appliances. In the old days, no wedding presents were given but marriages were celebrated with large feasts. Now, only the witnesses and the family participate in the wedding meal and the relatives and friends bring presents to the reception afterwards and are served cold drinks and a few snacks. The wedding dress is usually hired. The quality and quantity of food and drink offered at a wedding reception has become a delicate issue for while unable to offer much, serving too little is a poor reflection on the social standing of the family and elicits disapproving comments in the neighbourhood.

The craving for social recognition was even more pronounced in the purchase of household appliances. Families with children old enough to contribute to the family income were first to buy a television set, generally at the children's request. At first neighbours would come and watch but not for long, for they soon felt that the owners of the set were beginning to resent their presence and to look down on them. If they could possibly afford to, they would eventually buy a set themselves. An even more obvious example of social pressure inducing consumption is the decision to buy a fridge, usually justified by the need to keep meat even though *per capita* consumption was going down. Thus, one woman ironically suggested to another who was considering buying a fridge 'you can cool your legs a bit'. Most people, however, thought they needed many other things before a fridge: 'A fridge? Nonsense! We hardly have anything to keep cool. This is only for those *que pode, que tem poder* [who have the power to afford it]. We need blankets for the beds, the cold is coming now'.

The case of Da Alzira, who lived in a rented house and who had recently had to give up a plot of land for which she had begun to pay, provides a good example of how changed social relations have imposed new needs. This woman was timid rather than socially ambitious and the house in which she lived with her husband who drank, a teenage son and two daughters was too small even for the little furniture they possessed. She eventually decided to buy a fridge because one of her daughters wanted cold lemonade and she herself was reluctant to continue asking her neighbour for ice on the grounds that 'some will give gladly but others won't'. She finally made up her mind when she paid the last instalment for a television set bought earlier to keep her daughters at home in the evenings, enticed into the purchase by a sales woman who had offered it to her without a down payment.[12]

But there are financial limits to such spending. By 1979, when inflation was becoming a serious threat, even women who had been among the first to acquire fridges admitted the essentially symbolic nature of such an acquisition:

> Have you seen the price of meat? This is the first thing that dis-
> appears from the map. Our wage is not sufficient to buy meat. We
> don't starve but we buy that little food with the wage but *mistura*
> we cannot afford. For the last three months we haven't bought any
> meat ... The fridge, even before, we didn't make much use of it
> and now we can't.

Some of these socially-induced purchases were made at the expense of better food. It could well happen, as a widow, Da Antonia, pointed out, that if you pay your debts on Saturday, 'on Monday you have to play the guitar without strings', i.e. work without proper food. Debts incurred under hire purchase arrangements imposed special constraints on their tight budgets. Most of the families nearly always had some outstanding instalments and, seduced by the apparent facilities offerred by hire purchase, some certainly overreached themselves at times. 'Poor people are shit; if you don't spend money you have nothing and if you do you have debts'.

In a society in which social power rests on property and is expressed through possessions, the struggle for material possessions is a struggle for social meanings and social recognition. In the urban setting, self-respect and social acceptability no longer seemed to be earned by working hard but primarily by owning possessions. Hence, workers were impelled by a new compulsion to consume which only served to increase their dependence on the market rather than alleviating their feelings of inadequacy. Low wages have therefore caused an under-consumption of food rather than of consumer goods and, in comparison with the 'abundance' of the past, a consequent decline in nutritional standards. Life in town did offer some comforts to everyone and families with favourable dependency ratios were able to acquire some of the consumer goods, but for most the new conditions of life only served to emphasise their position as a subject class.[13]

As I indicated above working conditions also changed. Despite relatively full employment in the 1970s, the most obvious result of leaving the estates was the loss of job security throughout the year that this entailed. Less obvious, though equally important, was the effect that the casualisation of labour had on work performance and on the length of the working day. While as *colonos* or sharecroppers they had worked from sunrise to sunset, they now work the statutory forty-seven hours a week with a further two or three hours everyday for travel to and from work, for which they are not paid. As *colonos* or sharecroppers they worked long and arduous hours, but because they themselves set the pace they enjoyed a sense of freedom they now miss. As Sr Nicanor thought:

> Entertainment, before on the estates there was more. There were dances every Saturday, but it has all come to an end. The people have come to an end, agriculture, the crops, the people ... people were free then, they had more time. There wasn't this business of the wage [the minimum wage] and there were *dias de Santo* [religious holidays]. Now there are no religious holidays .... [We were] free because people grew their provisions, had their animals. If you missed two days it did not matter. If one morning it rained and you lay in your bed your crops grew all the same ... With *colonos* and sharecroppers it was all the same, they all worked for results, that is they worked hard. They forced themselves to work hard to do their job, but work was not on account of the landlord. It was on their own account.

And they generally preferred this to straight wage labour because it was 'of their own accord' and 'the harder you worked the more you had at the end of the year'.

Workers' perceptions of work in the past in comparison with the present are, however, mediated by their ability, both then and now, to make ends meet. In much the same way as access to consumer goods nowadays depends on a family's capacity to work, so too were the *colonos* or sharecroppers of those days to a large extent dependent for their success on the size and composition of their families. Because half of what they produced went to the landlord, sharecroppers with small families were particularly conscious of the price they paid for their relative freedom, for the lower a family's capacity to work, the smaller was its return. Small *colono* families were often similarly hard pressed to tend both the coffee and their food crops to grow enough to eat. They are likely to recall the hard work of the old days and the exploitation of self-provisioning with particular scorn: 'When the time to grow food came we worked overtime [*sobre tempo*], that is on our own account and earned nothing, as *colonos*'. Because landlords preferred *colonos* with large families, however, small families were rare, but those that did exist had a hard time.

By contrast, although family size and composition continue to affect family income, it is more difficult now to raise a large family in town and small families are no longer handicapped in the same way they were previously because, so long as work is readily available, each worker earns a separate wage. And they can now work at a more leisurely pace and still rely on a secure income. As Da Florencia told me:

We were *colonos* and tended 6000 coffee trees, the two of us alone [they had no children] and grew food. We harvested two to three carts of maize, beans. We harvested little, and no rice; the soil was poor. When we finished our task in coffee, my husband would also work for a day-wage for the estate. I wouldn't. When it was finished I would stay at home. We ourselves tended the food crops, both of us together. The contract was for the year. Good God, how we worked! Early at five in the morning we were in the field. The neighbours did not help. We had a pig, chickens. I think it is better now. We earn more, are paid already on Saturday. Before it was much worse. Now it is better to live. Between the two of us we can eat. We don't eat well but we can eat. Food was better then, now it is weaker. Now, as to life, to clothes, the house, we hardly had anything at all. Now there is more comfort. You cannot buy many good clothes now either but is is easier. In those days there was no hire purchase and you made a greater effort. Now, you work for the day, you work more slowly. Only when you work by results you work more. Then, if we wanted to leave the estate we even had to pay a fine [i.e., before the end of the contract]. Not now. If you leave he has to pay on top. In those days we worked and earned very little and did not receive any money, only those slips, 'orders' to buy; you did not see the money; when you shopped you gave it to the merchant. Not now. When Saturday comes you receive money. As *colonos* there was an overseer who would walk the fields but not all day, only once or twice a day. Who distributed the work was the family head. There was more entertainment. We went out more. There were dances, prayers, feasts, anyone on the estate would hold dances, prayers. Here in town there aren't any more dances, life is too difficult. Then you had no expenses, you would prepare something to drink, coffee with something at night, all what people had. Now you have to pay for everything. In those times you ate and drank and paid nothing'.

Colonos and sharecroppers regarded the use of a plot of land for growing their own food as a right though they recognised it as a source of surplus labour appropriation . Only those who experienced real difficulties in growing enough food failed to conceive of their present dependence on the market as a new form of constraint. Inversely, only those who own their houses or who, through the favourable composition of their families, were able to acquire certain consumer goods, regard their present situation as in any sense an improvement.

Only because landlords are, however, unwilling to hire workers under the conditions that prevailed in the past and because today's casual labourers are paid the lowest wages being, moreover, treated with such contempt, do they regard working in a factory as a desirable alternative for it may allow them to shed some of the hardships and indignities associated with working in the fields. When these workers left the estates, some of their relatives had managed to move to the city of São Paulo where they found work in industry and are thought to be better off. But as the economic boom was coming to and end, migration to São Paulo no longer was a viable alternative. Instead, the children of these workers were leaving agriculture for new factories which were moving into Jaguariuna in search of cheap labour. A few of the young men managed to get jobs as drivers, but most of them, including the girls, became unskilled workers. Wages were distinctly better than in agriculture, partly because they did an inordinate amount of overtime.

The main aspiration of most of the men was to hold down a secure job, though ideally many would have also liked access to a plot of land for their own use. The women were more interested in owning or renovating their houses and in working fewer hours. Parents' aspirations both for themselves and for their children reflected as much a desire for security as for social mobility. For the parents, however, there was little hope of improving their lives.

It is hardly surprising that at a time of economic growth the lowest income groups should also have experienced improved job opportunites. The workers became firmly incorporated into consumer society but their relative position did not change. Between 1970 and 1980, the *per capita* GDP in Brazil (measured in 1981 US dollars) rose from $1386 to $2477, yet during the same period the percentage share in total income of the lowest 50 per cent of the population declined from 15.62 to 14.56.[14]

Living and working conditions have changed in many and sometimes immeasurable ways. Some of the workers moved to town in search of better wages, others were forced off the estates by coffee eradication, others still were dismissed by landlords eager to evade protective legislation, but none became casual rural labourers by choice. Nor is the need to work for landlords who refuse them their 'rights' and pay such a miserable wage a matter of fate. They clearly identify the political events that forced them to work as casual labourers and which are to be blamed for this.

THE VARGAS MYTH: GOVERNMENT VERSUS STATE IN CLASS POLITICS

Through a fusion of reality and myth, the workers had come to view their departure from the estates as inextricably linked to the Vargas government. Vargas's suicide in 1954 is thought to have ended the brief interval in history which was not adverse to them as a class. Although the 1963 labour laws were enacted in response to growing political agitation in the countryside over land reform these workers did not conceive of the 'rights' as a gain that they themselves had won. Vargas introduced workers' 'rights' because he was sensitive to their needs, yet they remembered him not only for the 'rights' but for the scope of his political vision and for their own sense of defeat and loss when he died:

> Getúlio was good to the poor. There they killed him. At that time there were no vagrants on the roads. All the poor were singing. He left those laws, that the poor were no dogs, that the workers could not be dismissed, that they [landlords] had to pay compensation . . . They killed him because they were furious.

Had Vargas lived, the workers felt sure they would not be oppressed by the landlords as they are now. Da Maria, who was so militant that the labour contractors were afraid of her, thought that 'in the old days we had no rights at all. If you were not permanent they would dismiss you. You didn't even have the right to a coffin. That is why I say, in one respect it is better now. First the people had no rights, now they do'. The workers believe that it was when the Vargas government 'established the rights' and compelled the landowners to pay minimum wages that food crops were abolished and the workers were expelled from the estates.

Vargas's death is seen as the dastardly deed of the *tubarões* (sharks, the rich) whose interests he was threatening: 'When someone wants to do some good for the poor, there come the rich and kill him . . . like Getúlio, he was very much in favour of the poor and they killed him'.[15] Never in their experience were landlords benevolent. A few landlords in the old days did sometimes grant favours, in the case of an illness, for example, or to some of the more hard-working *colono* families to try and discourage them from leaving the estate at the end of the agricultural year. But any help always had to be paid back in the end. Social relations between the landlord and the workers were distant most of the time. They often employed bodyguards (*capangas*) to protect themselves from possible transgressions by the workers. Now, because of the mediating role of the labour contractor, the landlords have become even more remote. The right to a plot of land may have to some extent legitimated landed property in the past, but when landlords withdrew this right and, in addition, refused to honour their new obligations, this heightened the workers' sense of being exploited and called into question more forcefully the landlords' exclusive claim to the land. Landlords are now regarded with even greater scorn, as witnessed from the following conversation between Da Antonia and Da Carmen:

> *Da Antonia*: 'If I were President . . . I would make all the poor rich and would put all the rich to work, all with the hoe'. *Da Carmen*: 'They wouldn't resist for a week . . . can you imagine, to put one of those *tubarões* [sharks] there in the ditch to work. One should tie them all up like pigs and throw them in the river. Then the poor would be rich; with the money we give the rich the poor could eat'. *Da Antonia*: 'You already want to kill!' *Da Carmen*: 'But they kill the poor all their lives, it is all for that'.

The workers realise that it is unrealistic to pin their hopes on a government or President. Vargas's death is there to prove that Presidents who are well intentioned towards the poor have little chance of implementing their plans. As Da Antonia thought:

> The government does not do anything right, the government does not know anything; it should control prices and set wages and

stop talking. If I were President I would control prices and raise wages very high. You poor would live well. As it is the poor only go to the fields to work.

But Da Carmen remained unconvinced: 'I would not vote for Antonia. Once she has got rich she'll forget us'.

In contrast to the powerful memory of Vargas's death, the military coup of 1964 which deposed the Goulart government, the heir to Vargas's populism, went by largely unnoticed by these workers. The only perceptible effect was to reinforce their general lack of interest in governments and Presidents which dates from Vargas's death. When Vargas was in power 'the people shouted and he listened. Look now, the people shout, the price of meat, and the government does not listen'. Since Vargas died and more so after 1964, the government has ceased to listen and the people have lost their voice. The Vargas myth has left a deep imprint on workers' political identities, not only because his particular brand of populism and dramatic suicide captivated the imagination of the poor. The strong nationalist element in Vargas's rhetoric, for example, found no resonance whatsoever among these workers, but they continue to demand price controls which played an important part in his economic policy. The workers' collective memory thus retains only some elements of Vargas's policy, relevant to them as a class. What really gives the Vargas myth its enduring force is the indifference with which all subsequent governments have regarded the conditions of rural workers. João Goulart and Janio Quadros did gain some credit for trying to implement a land reform, but their efforts were curtailed by the *tubarões* and by their own shortcomings: 'He [Quadros] wanted to act too fast. He should have gone more slowly . . . that is why they cancelled his mandate'. But both these politicians are of minor significance in comparison with the powerful figure of Vargas who stands out not only as the only man in the history of the agricultural working class ever to have listened to their grievances and died for their cause, but also because no other government has ever listened to them since.

The Northeast state of Pernambuco is the only region of the country in which Vargas's memory has been partly eclipsed. This is because as state governor of Pernambuco, Miguel Arraes played an active role in defending the interests of rural workers in the years leading up to the military coup. Pernambuco then became the only state in which the Rural Labour Statute was upheld, at least for the first months. The sugar workers of Pernambuco thenceforth came to associate their 'rights' with the name of Miguel Arraes. This reinforces my point that Vargas's populism and image persists among workers of other regions precisely because no other political figures have emerged whom they perceive as identifying with the interests of the working class. Moreover, because Vargas died, the workers were never given the opportunity to recognise the limitations of his conciliatory politics.[16]

Vargas' death underlined the historical exclusion of the poor from the political process, an exclusion that still prevailed in the 1970s. The Vargas myth perpetuated the workers' sense of defeat and consequent scepticism towards any subsequent governments, or even the state as such.

Rural workers were never treated as full citizens; until the early 1980s illiterate people were denied the right to vote. Literacy can mean many things depending on the political context, but in Brazil the exclusion of illiterates served to reinforce the silence of the powerless. In the early 1960s, for instance, the local dominant class saw the literacy campaign which was undertaken mainly in Pernambuco as a threat to their control by large numbers of new voters. Until the 1980s, ironically, while voting was compulsory, the illiterate were obliged to abstain.[17] Some of the workers in the gang were registered voters but their very notion of a citizen (*cidadão*) as a well-heeled town dweller underlines the traditional exclusion of rural workers from political power in Brazil.

In the build up to the national legislative election of November 1974, the workers' sense of exclusion was manifest in their lack of interest in the electoral process and the absence of information about the nature of the election and the offices at stake. They felt that if elections could affect their lives in any way, then local elections deserved their attention for only at the local level could they realistically expect to exert any influence to obtain improvements for themselves. By contrast, they regarded national elections as totally futile:

> It is more interesting to register [as a voter] for the election of the Mayor. For that of Deputy it is of little interest for the people who work in the fields. The only one who can give us any help is the Mayor. He is the one who can give the labourer a hand.

This highly instrumental attitude towards voting and elections could vindicate those who traditionally opposed enfranchising illiterate sectors of the population on the grounds that their ignorance made them easy prey to political manipulation and hence would entail the corruption of representative democracy. But since these workers have in any case been excluded from the political system and since, with the possible exception of Vargas, those in power have never represented their interests, they were not convinced that theirs was a genuinely representative political system in the first place. For this reason, they see no point in voting.

In the old days on the estates, workers who had the vote probably voted, through a mixture of fear and calculation, for the candidate the landlord supported, and this certainly would not have made them any less sceptical about the usefulness of electoral politics. Nowadays, nobody controls their votes. They just vote, if at all, for the candidate who offers them the most. Even the decision to register as a voter is not a purely political act, for a voter's card is needed by anyone wanting to apply for a job in industry.[18] Because the electoral process lacked legitimacy as far as their interests as rural workers were concerned, the vote had no political worth and was traded for immediate advantage irrespective of the candidate's ideology and politics. Thus, Da Rosa, for instance, who had once canvassed for a candidate in a municipal election without being rewarded for her services as promised, emphatically maintained that next time she would insist on payment in advance and, moreover, would canvass for whoever paid the most. In national elections no such control can be exercised over rewards, and hence it is useless to vote.

The 1974 national election took place in a climate of mounting popular discont with the military government. In all the major cities of the country, the official opposition party (the MDB) won a series of impressive victories, which came to be known as the 'vote of distrust' of the military regime.[19] The workers in the gang, however, remained unremittingly indifferent to the election. Some attributed this to their own ignorance about the purpose of the election, but many were excluded anyway on the grounds of illiteracy. They were all nonetheless convinced that even if they did vote it would make no difference whatsoever to their lives:

> I don't quite understand this business. Sometimes I ask at home... For the poor it is no good to have anybody up there. To put the others in a good place so that we should work. I don't know but if I could vote I wouldn't. They couldn't care less. They

say, look after yourselves. If I could I would not vote for anybody. See, you make an effort and once he has become mayor, the poor should look after themselves. It is like marriage. You are courted by a young man and he says this and that. Then you get married and he doesn't do anything of what he promised. He says, look after yourself. With the government it is the same. They promise and promise, and afterwards they don't do anything.

Although the woman quoted above was unacquainted with the technicalities of a national election, she clearly understood that for rural workers elections merely perpetuated their own exclusion. Their indifference arose from the conviction that a national election would make little difference to them as workers which, in turn, discouraged them from becoming better informed. One of the women explicitly questioned the grounds of denying the vote to illiterates: 'We do not know how to read. There are many who say that those who do not know how to read are illiterates, that they know nothing, but when I don't understand I ask'.

Although some of the workers, especially the women, withheld their vote alleging ignorance, they all agreed that in the form and context in which it was held, the election was of little use to them:

The people here did not go so much for the person but for the party. I think it makes no difference. Even if you change the one who does the flogging, the whip will always remain the same. Something might change for those who win. For us labourers everything will remain the same.

Underlying whatever reason the workers gave for failing to be aroused by the national election, usually their self-professed ignorance or absence of franchise, is the conviction about the worthlessness of their vote. Municipal elections, however, did interest the women at least as much as the men, for the issues at stake were of direct concern to them, as the special beneficiaries of any improvements in urban services. By contrast, at the national level, the women are far more likely to hide behind their ignorance and reliance on their husbands' knowledge. A very sceptical view of politics is common to both men and women, but the sexual division of labour does reinforce the role of women as bystanders. Demands made to the federal government are usually concerned with wage and price levels and hence more relevant to the men, who are expected to engage in wage employment and to provide for their families.

The workers could hardly ever remember what parties the various candidates had represented in previous elections, and most did not even know to what party Vargas had belonged. Those who did know the names of the two parties created by the military government in the 1960s – the government party, the National Reform Alliance (*Aliança Renovadora Nacional*) (ARENA) and the official opposition, the Brazilian Democratic Movement (*Movimiento Democrático Brasiliero*) (MDB) – identified *neither* of them with the concerns of the poor. ARENA was almost unanimously regarded as the party of the government and/or of the rich. The MDB was not associated with the government but neither did it represent the poor, even if it did sometimes pretend to speak on their behalf:

> This is all nonsense. They are all arselickers to the boss. ARENA is the boss's arselicker. It is said that ARENA belongs to the landowners. Those who are in front, the MDB . . . how do they call them? They say it belongs to the poor but I do not believe it at all.

The occasional support which some of them rather reluctantly gave to the official opposition did not dispel their more general misgivings about elections as such.[20]

The workers' highly sceptical attitude towards elections ultimately controlled by a government hostile to their class interests, at first sight seemed inconsistent with the way in which these same workers were forever placing their hopes in this same government.[21] When it came to formulating their demands, time and again the workers would appeal to the government for help:

> Brazil is large. It is like God. It is difficult for God to look after the whole world. One is happy, another one isn't happy. With us it is different. We don't have to look after anybody, only take care of our work. The government can do a lot of things but it can't deal with all the people. The government passes a law, the landowners make another one. In order to deal with the landowners the

government has to kill a good number of them. It is the fault of the landlords, of many of them, not of all of them. The landowners and the shopkeepers do what they want. It is no good the government controlling prices in order to help the poor. It does not get anywhere with the shopkeepers. The government doesn't get anywhere with these people.

Here, the government is conceived of as standing above the interests of landlords and shopkeepers. The workers appeal to a potentially well-intentioned but constrained government. Not only price controls and wage rises are demanded of such a government, but also action to discipline landlords and to force them to grow food crops, to abandon cattle raising and to implement the labour laws.

But there are clear limits as to what can realistically be demanded of such a government. For explicit political reasons, land reform involving the redistribution of land is rarely envisaged as a possibility and even more rarely demanded. A few of the workers believed that Janio Quadros and João Goulart had been deposed by the landowners because they threatened to carry out just such a land reform, but even those with no memory of Goulart's ill-fated programme regarded the possibility of land redistribution as highly unlikely.[22] On one occasion, one of the women complained that employers were only able to squeeze them as they did because the poor had nowhere else to go, whereupon another woman came up with the solution: 'it needs a land reform. Then even the priests have to work'. When I asked her what a land reform was, she explained that 'it is a landlord who has a large estate and distributes one *alqueire* [24 200 m^2] to each worker to cultivate'. She went on to explain how 'here the soil is good, you could grow beans, maize. You would need two *alqueires* to live. Two people could cultivate two *alqueires* very well. It depends on the soil. It would be enough to live, and a good little house, running water'. Upon which another woman exclaimed 'O God, when will this happen!' The first speaker then ended the conversation categorically with: 'It does not happen because the landlords don't like it ... and there are landlords who don't even have children and mistreat the others'.

The workers consider it equally unrealistic to ask for a return to the *colonato* or sharecropping systems for although they themselves would like to have the access to the land, they are convinced that landlords wouldn't hire labour on that basis. And, to live on an estate under present conditions (i.e. without usufruct rights, with lower wages than those paid to casual workers and, in addition, having to pay rent) is clearly out of the question. Moreover, unregistered resident workers without 'rights' are liable to be victims of chicanery and given the worst jobs. If indeed they were to acquire a plot of land at this stage, it may be too expensive to cultivate for the soil has become depleted and fertilizers are expensive. Under such circumstances, it may be just as well to work for a wage in a gang, but the wages would need to be raised.

Behind the apparent contradiction between the workers' sceptical view of the government and their hope that it might respond to their appeals for help lies the memory of the Vargas government and its promise of at least temporary solutions. There is no ambivalence towards the present government. Because the Vargas government appeared to lack any specific class base with Vargas' conciliatory populism seemingly raising him above the interests of the classes, the Vargas myth has given rise to the notion of an ideal state. It thus becomes possible to conceive of the state as ideally representing the interests of neither the rich nor the poor, but only favouring one or another class under particular concrete circumstances, as witnessed in remarks like, 'that government protects the rich a great deal'. Moreover, the considerable political autonomy of local overlords in rural areas in earlier times and the tendency for landlords in the region to vote for the opposition in protest against the government's 1974 agricultural policy, give further credence to this distant and basically neutral view of the state. If landlords are autonomous from the government, then it is reasonable to assume that the state stands above the dominant class, i.e. the 'rich' as a whole, and if the state also stands above the 'poor' then it must, so the logic goes, stand above all classes. This notion of an ideal state existing over and above its partisan practices is what makes it possible for workers, despite their scepticism, to appeal to the government for help. Nonetheless, the workers showed no sign of losing their firm hold on reality. With inflation devaluing their wages daily and landlords refusing them their rights, they must surely question why their demands were never met. The workers resolved this contradiction by drawing a distinction between concrete governments and an ideal state. They were sceptical of elections because they associated them with Vargas's death and because ever since his suicide no real governments have ever regarded their interests in an unequivocally favourable way. For structural as much as for contextual reasons, real governments only very exceptionally listen to the poor. The class position which governments assume in practice and the class background of politicians, invariably deprive the poor of any chances of making themselves heard.

The *tubarões (sharks) and the graúdos* ('big shots' specifically landowners, merchants and industrialists) are thought of as constantly watching over the government to ensure that their own interests are safeguarded or, what in the workers' view amounts to the same thing, that the workers are kept in their place. Populism has shown that the President could become the *pai dos pobres* (father of the poor, as Vargas was called), but its defeat also proved that the rich will use the government to promote their own interests whenever they can. The populist alliance and its successive defeats has reinforced the workers' conception of the government as simultaneously standing above and promoting class interests:

> Like the Federal government, when one General leaves another comes in. It is all the same family. There is nothing to be done. Here in Brazil there is no way of doing anything because of those *tubarões*. If one comes along who wants to change things, the *tubarões* don't let him. The government is on their side. The government goes for money; there is nothing that can be done.

The rich gain their control over the state through the positions of power they secure for themselves. Because the rich are powerful, the government is bound to be on their side and from this vantage point there is no room for hope. Because the government represents the interests of those who have power, appeals to it for help are bound to fail. 'It is the rich who are the most powerful' because 'of the money. Money gives power. With money you can buy everything, even death'.

The workers failed to distinguish between politicians and the rich which only adds to their sense of political exclusion and belief that since politicians are not workers themselves, they have no reason to defend the workers' interests. Here Vargas and, to a lesser extent, Janio and Jango were seen as the exceptions who, because they were either killed or deposed for their defence of the poor, only go to prove the rule. They were never quite clear why, as non-workers, these politicians espoused their cause, but their defeat seemed to obviate this question. Under normal circumstances, once elected, politicians are only out to fill their own bellies (*encher a barriga*):

For them the election is a great thing. For us it is no good. I only sign the ballot not to leave it empty. At the time of the election they are all friends, they do everything for us. They do not disdain the poor. But afterwards they do not care any more, poor us. For the poor the right thing to do is not to vote for anybody. To vote for you who are rich ... afterwards the poor are like beggars in the street. When they [politicians] pass close by they say 'what a disgrace is that'. There are few who are not presumptious.

As a logical consequence of perceiving the sociopolitical reality in class terms – society is made up of 'we, who work' and 'they, who don't work and profit from those who do' – the workers can only conceive of a reformist solution if there is something like the notion of an ideal state which stands above class interests.

The experiences of each new generation of workers are, to an extent, specific to them. In this light it might be useful to look at how the political opportunities which opened up in Brazil almost simultaneously with the recession in the late 1970s and early 1980s, might have influenced the political perceptions of the new generation of casual workers. The emergence of a political alternative that defends workers' interests could have any one of two contradictory effects. It could either overshadow the Vargas myth by giving the workers real hope of a government that is responsive to their needs. But unless the growing discontent generated by the recession is contained through a policy of genuine redistribution, it could also lead to even greater political disaffection, but this time without the Vargas myth to attenuate class antagonisms.

National politics played a crucial role in shaping these workers' class identities. Their formal or informal political exclusion has served to create a sense of utter scepticism towards politicians and the government, which may ultimately constitute a threat to those in power themselves.

CLASS CONSCIOUSNESS WITHOUT POLITICS

Despite the workers' acute class consciousness there was little evidence of concerted class action precisely because of the way in which landlords were seen to use their power to defend their class privileges. This does not mean that in their attempts to improve their conditions the workers never considered strategies beyond appeals to an unresponsive government. In addition to the individual forms of resistance to exploitation at the work place and to occasional collective attempts to restrict output (as in the setting of piece-rates), the notion of organised joint action to obtain certain improvements was not alien to them. But exactly what collective political solutions were envisaged depended directly on how they assessed their chances of success.

The word 'revolution' was known, but it did not imply a radical alteration of the *status quo*. Informed by childhood memories of the 1932 revolt in São Paulo against Vargas's taking of power, for them it essentially meant armed conflict, the purposes of which they ignored and which merely filled them with fear. One worker did conceive of a 'general strike', although he was very doubtful about its feasibility:

The poor in order to have strength needed to have courage for unity. The poor have no unity. If they all united they would overthrow the rich. Here ... there are more poor than rich. If you organise a meeting (*reunião*), a strike, you could finish with it all. Then all the rich would have to be beaten, all of them would have to be beaten (*apanhar, entrar no cacetete*). Those six policemen there would not react. How can they react if there are five policemen and 100 poor. They can kill one of them, but not all. You take the scythe, invade ... but there is no unity. One must strike, one must fight [reinforcements from elsewhere?] but that is why it must be general. The unity of all those of the estates would be necessary to do this. In the whole of Brazil there are more poor than rich. Of every three there are two who are poor ... You would have to go against the rich [not the middling people, the *remediados*], the capitalists [*sic*], the landowners, the shopkeepers who are all thieves. Industrialists are capitalists. Our punishment is that President there, that Governor. The landowners are also our punishment. But the government, none of them punishes those there. At one time who put those Presidents there were the big shots themselves. Now it is the army. Now there are no more elections.

Although the strategy was clear, this worker saw no chance of a general strike succeeding. For a start, rural workers were in a minority and many of them were women and children who were unlikely to strike.[23] Moreover, the working class was divided, for people like stonemasons could hardly be expected to participate in a strike for land. And, last but not least, the government had the support of the army.[24] This sense of powerlessness had on another occasion accounted for the same worker's reluctance to tell his fellow workers how he had managed to win a court case against his employer, for he was afraid that they might tell on him.[25]

None of the other workers I knew conceived of joint action in such radical terms. Most of them, especially the women, were generally even reluctant to demand a wage rise for fear of jeopardising their jobs. Some of the workers had distant recollections of *colono* strikes, although they thought that there had been none in the region since the 1930s. But even those who had never participated in or even heard of earlier strikes, were quick to capture the idea, though convinced that strike action was not possible now. Nonetheless, I was told of two instances in the mid-1970s in which women who had previously worked in the gang had participated in collective movements. In the first case, the estate in question had wanted the gang to work on Holy Friday. They refused and, headed by one of the women, threatened to go on strike unless they were given the day off with full pay, and the estate eventually agreed to their demand. In the other instance, the woman who spoke for the gang demanding a wage rise, was fired in reprisal and nothing further came of it.

The workers see class solidarity as fundamental in overcoming their powerlessness and in effecting change, but with the same intensity with which they emphasise the need for unity, they also regret its absence. These workers had never been unionised. The rural unions that sprang up in the early 1960s had been either co-opted or destroyed by the military government. In mid-1975, a rural labour union office was, however opened (with government approval) in Mogi Mirim to which Jaguariuna belongs. It was headed by a labour lawyer who had been put in charge of the main union office of nearby Araras in 1967 by the military government when the union was reopened in response to growing unrest among sugar workers. But the Jaguariuna workers showed little enthusiasm for this union. Unions were typically conceived of as agencies for dental and medical assistance, rather than for the defence of class interests.

The workers thought they lacked unity because they did not have the strength for joint action. As one worker explained:

Unity? There is none because they are fools, they are afraid that the landlord will fire them, that they will not find any other job, that they will not find a house in town . . . Therefore, the thing is to keep quiet and look like fools . . . Here, if all united if all together went to the landlord and asked for the wage to be raised, he might agree, but if only one goes he would fire him . . . Don't you see there in town, in the factories, they strike and solve everything, but all of them together. But on the estates there is no way (there is no unity) because in the factory the work must be done. Now, on the estates the job can be left for another day. With the hoe, weeding, our work has no value because of this.

One of the women felt that although she would have no part in organising a strike, she would join in if one began. Although the men were equally reluctant as the women to become involved in collective action, they were usually better informed as to what strikes entailed. To a certain extent the women depended on their husbands for their political information, but the husbands encouraged such dependence for they could not possibly countenance independent political action by their wives. The worker's assertion that 'a woman is the most timorous (*amedrontado*) animal to strike . . . She has no idea of striking, has no experience . . . women all the things they do, they carry out in contact with the husband' reflected wishful thinking on his part as much as women's subordination by men.

What deterred the workers from taking joint action was the risk of becoming known as trouble makers and hence losing their jobs. It was futile to demand better wages because 'they wouldn't pay more. They would prefer to stop work if the poor won't work for that wage. They would plant pasture and put cattle . . . The poor don't strike because they have no strength'. The powerlessness of the poor is the consequence of the power of the rich. Few dared to stick their necks out to demand improvements having nothing to fall back on if reprisals were taken against them, rather than because of a lack of solidarity *per se*:

> The rich, if they wanted . . . could kill all the poor . . . To organise a strike, it could be done but the lower classes have no unity and then it's no good. You get a bad name so that you wouldn't find a job to work.

As yet another worker asserted, 'the poor do not want to strike, not because they are afraid, but because they are afraid of hunger', for the estate could easily hire another gang.

It could be argued that in a situation of relatively full employment there was no reason to fear dismissal and being left without a job. For a day-labourer who earns strictly by the day, to lose even one day's work is, however, a threat. During the *colonato* period, bargaining power was greater because the contract was annual. Most strikes occurred at the onset of the harvest when labour needs were greatest and when coffee growers would have run into serious difficulties finding replacements. As casual labourers working on a daily basis, it is often preferable to pursue an individual strategy, either working as little as possible without being fired or working hard to take advantage of the small favours the contractor offers to good workers. Obviously, such individual strategies militate against unity. As the workers themselves put it, now it is 'each one for himself and God for all'. But ultimately it is the power of the landlords, not an absence of class consciousness, of an awareness of their common exploitation, that informs the workers' sense of impotence and jeopardises the unity that joint action demands. This mood of fear is powerfully reflected in a grim tale Da Ditinha related to me:

> We are afraid that a stronger power may come and take us and beat us. There was a time, when my parents were still alive, when people said that. They told me that there was a time when the little children were dying of hunger, that it was a hard time, there was nothing to eat. Thus they got together and went to the government. Government and President is the same thing, isn't it? They went to ask for a little help. The President said 'go up there onto the hill and wait'. They went and waited. The little children were happy. But then my parents told me he sent a bomb and finished it all. That was the only thing he could give them.

And then she asked 'do you think this is a joke or is it true?'

6 The Exploitation of Family Morality

'Coffee growing demands not the contribution of casual labour but, indeed, that of 'well constituted' families, of at least three hoes.' *Boletím do Departamento do Trabalho Agrícola*, XI (72) (São Paulo, 1932) p.11

'The selection of rural workers and of helpers is the task of the administration. A well-colonised plantation, with well-constituted families, strong people, well disposed to work, who know the job, will do well . . . The worker must have his family with him on the plantation. The single worker is restless, a nomad, he does not put down roots, he has no incentive. Rural life more than life in town imposes organisation in families.' *RSRB* (October 1938) p.27

By contrast with the *colonato* system, when labour was hired and worked in family units, today's casual wage workers sell their labour on an individual basis. Nonetheless, these men and women continue to reproduce themselves as workers within families. Their attitudes to work continue to be mediated by their socially defined and contrasting family responsibilities. Until now I have focused attention on the labourers' experiences at work and on their class politics. However, changing productive relations have also challenged family morality and gender relationships. The workers' class consciousness was seen to have been informed by their perceptions of the political process that made them into casual labourers. Similarly, because the workers' social identities are shaped also by gender relations, when changing productive relations challenged these, their gender consciousness created new contradicitons between women and men within the family.

The efficiency of the *colonato* system rested to an important extent on the exploitation of the family as a work unit. Now, by contrast, each worker sells his or her labour power individually for a wage. Nonetheless, because wages are very low, the need to pool efforts within the family persists. Clashes between traditional family norms and new economic conditions place strains on the family which undermine its cohesion. The *colonato* system drew on and reinforced a family organisation in which cooperation was self-understood, whereas the present system of casual wage labour rests on a family organisation in which not labour but income is pooled. Individual wage labour has failed to convert men, and to an even lesser extent women, into formally free agents on the labour market released from all family commitments. Nonetheless, individual wage labour has strained the traditional authority structure and cooperative spirit of the family because, although all able-bodied members were forced into individual wage work, the need to share earnings persisted and gender roles have not been redefined.

It is generally recognised that neither the nuclear family nor gender hierarchy were created by the industrial revolution or by capitalism for the sake of capital accumulation. But one relevant question remains. What is it in the advance of capitalism that, although challenging gender roles and changing family forms, nonetheless makes for the extraordinary resilience of the family and gender hierarchy? How do we explain the paradoxical coexistence in class society of an ethos of individualism, self-reliance and personal achievement along with the persistent mediation of the individual's place in society by family ties and origin? As Barrett and McIntosh have argued, there has been an 'underemphasis on the extent of the cultural hegemony of familial ideology . . . "the family" . . . is not only an economic unit, nor merely a kinship structure; it is an ideological configuration with resonance far beyond these narrow definitions'.[1] We need to look more closely at these ideological configurations.

There are at least two sides to the question of the persistence of the working-class family – namely, bourgeois class interests, both economic and ideological, in maintaining the nuclear family, and, equally significant, the forces and motives that account for the working-class adherence to it. In the past decade, extensive research into the evolution of the working class family and gender hierarchy in capitalist society has pointed to the contribution made to the cheap reproduction of labour power by the domestication of women and by the family.[2] Still, this research has shown little awareness of the strains capitalist development has generated within the working-class family. A more recent exchange over the political meaning of the working-class family's persistence under capitalism, in particular for the condition of women, has made explicit the contradiction embodied in an institution which is the source of women's subordination and yet, at the same time, is able to offer support and solidarity to family members in the face of economic hardship.[3] This new perspective challenges the idea that the family is a collectivity of reciprocal interests, a pooling of efforts for the benefit of all members,[4] and suggest the need to examine the effect that economic change has upon power relations *within* the household, to trace historical linkages between economic processes and the family structure.

Research on the subordination of women during the expansion of capitalism in Latin America has raised doubts about the extent to which female wage labour gives women greater autonomy.[5] It is uncertain whether capitalist development, understood as the generalisation of the cash nexus, will undermine traditional links of personal dependence and subordination based on gender. But which are the connections between women's subordination, the family and forms of labour exploitation? In this chapter I will examine the contradictory effects the transition from family to individual wage labour had for the household structure, gender hierarchy, the sexual division of labour and the position of women. I will argue that socioeconomic change does not occur in an ideological vacuum but that family morality and gender hierarchy play a part in economic change because they give meaning to the new conditions for those concerned. The effect of capitalist expansion on the position of women cannot be properly understood if we only measure the access women gain to former male privileges such as paid work. Subordination is a social and political relationship which is historically determined by the circumstances of men in relation to women in society. Hence, it is essential to investigate changing conditions for both women *and* men and to see how these affect their mutual relationships.

THE CAPITALIST EXPLOITATION OF THE FAMILY

The introduction of free labour into São Paulo agriculture in the mid-nineteenth century is exceptional in that, from the very beginning, it rested on the coffee growers' preference for hiring labour in family units. Even under slavery, by contrast with other enterprises run with slave labour where the proportion of women was insignificant, on coffee plantations women and children from the age of five helped bring in the harvest.[6] When coffee growers first formulated a system under which free labour was to be hired, they drew on this earlier experience. They adopted the sharecropping system not only because they expected the incentive wage to ensure discipline and harder work from labour, but also because the family constituted a labour reserve which could be bought well below the market rate. As I have indicated above, coffee growers usually explained their preference for family labour by arguing that immigrants accompanied by their families were less prone to abandon the estate. Yet this is, at most, a partial truth. It conceals the ideological notion of the family as a corporate unit which the coffee growers themselves shared. To the coffee growers it was inconceivable that a person could abandon his family. In addition, this notion of the family offered the planters substantial material benefits. It provided them with a cheap and readily available labour reserve. Revealingly, coffee growers did at times prohibit immigrants and their families from working outside the estate.[7]

An ideology of family solidarity and cooperation enabled the coffee growers to exploit the whole immigrant family to the full. As one observer lucidly commented in 1877:

> The colonisation that has really been useful for us has been that of Germans and Portuguese. The German *colono* is always hardworking and honest and when he has a large family he offers an incalculable advantage. The head of the family endeavours to demonstrate in practice the English proverb that 'time is money', and together with his family they make time their property in such a way that even when they are working in the coffee grove for the planter, they make use of the weeds that grow there to feed their pigs and chickens, and when they return home the children begin to work. All of them go to school and when they rest they remove the maize kernels from the cob, build fences, cultivate the food plot, raise chickens and pigs and calves which are the source of their subsistence. The wife and daughters prepare the famous maize bread, which is the basis of their food.[8]

This ideology of family solidarity was shared by the immigrants as well. The workers resented, for example, the clause establishing solidary responsibility for the debt, not only because this aggravated their difficulty of redeeming their debt, but also because families were often forced by their communities of origin to take in strangers in order to rid them of a financial burden, 'people with whom they had nothing to do', as the workers objected.[9]

Like the initial sharecropping contract, the labour-leasing system that was tried out in the 1860s to overcome problems of labour productivity and discipline and the *colonato* system that eventually replaced it, both presupposed the hiring of labour in family units. The coffee planters' preference for family labour, moreover, reinforced a family organisation among the workers in which the household head supplied, mobilised and coordinated the family labour force and which implied a particular sexual division of labour and reproductive behaviour.

Contracts based on the nuclear family as a separate residential unit specified the economic functions of the household, namely joint labour in coffee cultivation and the growing of food strictly necessary for family consumption.

It is difficult to assess the quality of intra-household relationships retrospectively, but it is, however, possible to gain some insights into family morality as implied and enhanced by the family-labour contract.

The *colonato* as a wage-incentive system put a premium on work commitment by, and cooperation among, family members and reinforced their interdependence. It strengthened the commonality of interests of the household but it also underlined an authority structure and sexual division of labour that gave the husband/father preeminence over all other members. The allocation of family labour was decided by the husband/father, as household head, and followed a division of labour by sex and age.

The contract was always signed by the head of the family, who also received the family earnings. From an early age, children of both sexes were expected to contribute their share in looking after small animals and in helping with the harvest. The wife was primarily responsible for the domestic chores and for cultivating the food plot, aided by the adult men when they had time left over from their main task of tending the coffee trees, which required several weedings. Although each case varied according to the size and composition of the family, men, women and children worked together during the harvest and women were usually assigned half the number of coffee trees allocated to the men.

The husband/father's pre-eminence and authority over the family members arose partly from his relative autonomy in organising and coordinating the family's labour. In terms of work or the allocation of earnings nothing seems to point to husbands/fathers deriving material benefits from the control they exercised over family labour and income besides the gratification and responsibilities entailed in the authority itelf. No information is available on the distribution of income and resources within the household or on decision making beyond the organisation of work. The income the family received was based on the work of the family as a whole and did not, therefore, distinguish between the contributions of the different members. Although sometimes food surpluses were sold and men would do odd jobs for the estate for a daily wage, there is no indication that these additional earnings were attributed individually.

At the level of meaning, however, an important dimension of the exercise of authority is made explicit. Tasks done predominantly by men and tasks done by women were conceptualised in significantly different ways. Weeding coffee and cultivating crops were regarded as *serviço da gente*, i.e. 'our own job' as opposed to work done for a daily wage directly for the estate. Consistent with this classification, the coffee harvest paid at a piece-rate was also considered as 'our own job', even though the product was for the landlord.

Within the category of 'our own job', a further distinction between coffee weeding and food growing reflects an authority structure underlying the familial division of labour. The husband/father allocated jobs to the members of his family. Work intensity depended, in principle, on each family member's responsiveness to the wage incentive. Coffee weeding was, therefore, regarded as *trabalhar por conta* 'working of ones own accord', for 'one stopped when one wanted'; there were no set times and nobody set the pace of work. The weeding was done primarily by men. Hence, men enjoyed the relative autonomy that payment by results allowed. The workers were aware that they had to work very hard for this autonomy, but they nonetheless welcomed the opportunity to increase their incomes. By contrast, food growing, which was done predominantly by women, was seen as *trabalhar para a gente, plantar para a gente*', working or growing food for ourselves', i.e. for the family as a whole. Although the women also 'worked of their own accord', it was not the absence of supervision, but rather that the whole family would benefit from their work which was seen as its distinctive trait. Men's and women's work were not conceptualised as simple opposites within one single frame of reference, one autonomous, the other subordinate. Instead, in the case of men their control over their work was conceptually emphasised although the product belonged to the estate and they also worked for the family whereas in that of the women it was the beneficiaries, namely the family, who were stressed.

The food plot given to workers under combined cash-crop and self-provisioning systems has often been regarded as a form of payment in kind.[10] This obscures, however, the labour invested in self-provisioning which not only reduces money wages because the workers feed themselves, but also constitutes a source of surplus labour appropriation, especially of the women. By conceptualising self-provisioning as 'work for ourselves' the labourers themselves seemed to share in this mystification, although some of the women were aware that they earned nothing for the labour they invested in growing food.

The husband/father's control over the allocation of family labour may not have had any apparent material payoffs, but the different conceptions of men's and women's work reveal a particular authority structure embedded in the ethos of family cooperation. As I will show later, this endorsement of the husband/father's authority by the *colonato* system, however, also made the transition to casual wage labour particularly painful for the men.

The preference of coffee growers for a system of family labour impinged on the workers' family structure in yet another way. Coffee growers not only preferred families to single workers, but also favoured large families. The greater the proportion of workers to consumers in a family the greater its productive capacity. Because coffee cultivation was paid at a fixed task rate per thousand coffee trees under the *colonato* system, the workers' family income depended not only on the number of trees tended by the family but also on the task-rate set by the landlord. Coffee growers based the rate on a family containing at least three adult workers. As one experienced planter rejoiced in 1877:

These families are truly patriarchal both because of their size and their morality, solidarity and love of work . . . The families from the Tyrol are still the most advantageous ones for the landlord because of their size. This advantage is considerable: the greater the number of workers, beyond accelerating emancipation of the *colono* [from the debt] which is an edifying example, it offers the landlord a better guarantee because the collective responsibility of all warrants the whole payment of the debt even if some family members are forgetful of their obligations.[11]

The coffee growers' interest in the size and composition of immigrant families influenced demographic behaviour by placing a premium on fertility and this, in turn, affected the sexual division of labour. Although having a large number of children might have placed a considerable burden on the mother and father initially, it did mean that after the first few years the family's productive capacity increased each year. By contrast, a family with only a few children was disadvantaged throughout its life cycle.[12] A mother with a large number of children would be fully occupied with child rearing for a considerable part of her life and would have little time left for extra-domestic activities. But fully to appreciate the lives of these women with long child-bearing careers, one must also take into account how society regarded their specific responsibilities, for the burden and dependence of prolonged child bearing could be eased to an extent if they were accorded due social recognition. Under the *colonato* system, the work that went into housekeeping and child rearing was, in fact, acknowledged as essential and valued accordingly. As a French observer noted in 1879:

> The conclusion to be drawn is that . . . the larger a family the greater is the help it can offer its head to redeem himself of the initial debt . . . The helping hands of his children constitute a natural aid, the more precious the more numerous they are, and the woman, while she minds her own business, is also productive in the home, without her presence being indispensable in the fields, something that will become necessary if the family is composed of only a few members.[13]

As I mentioned earlier, the advantages of large families also had consequences for the class structure in general. Only families with a high productive capacity could hope to redeem their debts. In this way the *colonato* system contributed towards differentiation among immigrant families.[14]

The *colonato* as a system of family labour also had direct political consequences, for it influenced the organisation of the large *colono* strikes that took place in the early part of this century:

> [the labourers] did not adopt the system of head or leaders because this would have meant reducing to misery and persecution some of the most valuable members of this union. They acted in groups of four or five families in accordance with the friendship within these groups, having not one leader for this group but rather one family in charge of transmitting the thoughts of the secret collective leadership which was the one that solved all the problems.[15]

As the division of labour increased on the estates, so the coffee growers selected labour more consciously, offering different contractual arrangements in accordance with whether the worker had a family and its size.[16] As I noted earlier, gangs of men hired for one-off jobs were called *turmas de solteiros*, 'gangs of bachelors'.[17] The constitution of a family affected the employability of its members. *Camaradas* were less secure in their jobs than *colono* families[18] and this must have made marriage all the more attractive as well. But the labour system already influenced marriage in another way. The choice of a marriage partner was reduced by the family's initial indebtedness and the landlord's attempts to recoup his investment. The parents, particularly the father, intervened in choosing a partner for their children and then, on their marriage, the young couple would leave the family to set up a separate hosuehold. To protect their investment, landlords would prohibit marriages with young men from other estates unless the bridegroom's employer was willing to pay off the bride's debt.[19]

Subsidised immigration continued until 1927, when coffee growers gradually also started hiring national labour, first on a temporary basis for specific jobs but eventually also as *colonos*. As the family labour system was extended to include national labourers, landlords were delighted to discover that the *caboclos* (as the native rural population is known) not only were not as idle, immoral and undisciplined as they were assumed to be but adhered to the Christian family ideal as well:

> I still have to say what I have heard about the morality of the national labourer. It is good, very good. Well-constituted families,

mutual respect among the spouses, deference on the part of the children toward their parents... Isn't it remarkable that in the wild *sertões* [backwaters] and distant lands, where civilisation only rarely arrives, an institution such as monogamous marriage should have been preserved... Isn't it extraordinary that an institution which is justly renowned as the flower of Christian civilisation should have persisted in the nature of such a race despite the wilderness of the environment in which they live?[20]

Under the *colonato* system, as under the sharecropping contract that preceded it, the extra-familial economic structure ensured a corporate labour organisation within the family reinforced by a family morality that encouraged cooperation among family members as well as endorsing the husband/father's authority within it. The quality of intra-familial relations is, however, unknown. The transformation of the *colonos* into casual wage labourers hired on a temporary and individual basis was to pose a threat to this family morality and its authority structure. The present labour system does not enforce a particular family organisation but, nevertheless, assumes the pooling of resources within the family by paying an individual wage well below the cost of reproduction of its members as individuals. This new household is composed of labourers working for an individual wage. The onus of keeping the family together to permit the pooling of resources then falls entirely on the family members themselves and, when under certain circumstances this becomes too great, the family disintegrates. Moreover, individual wage work has deprived husband/fathers of some of the main attributes that legitimated their authority within the family, thus further straining the traditional family organisation.

FROM FAMILY TO INDIVIDUAL WAGE LABOUR

Not only men, but women and children from the age of about 12 became casual wage labourers working in gangs. Contributions from all the able-bodied members of the family are needed to make ends meet. As Da. Maria explained:

We have to work. [The husband's wage] is not enough because we have to pay rent... Before when we lived with our parents [on the estate] it was better . . . everybody planted food. Before there was an abundance, we raised small animals. Now we have to buy everything. In my youth the plantations were full of people, now they are empty.

Migration to the towns and incorporation into the money economy altered not only material conditions but the quality of social relations as well. In retrospect, many of the workers feel that the *colonato* system enhanced solidarity within the household but also among neighbours.

Kin and friendship ties which provided important links in the workers' move to the towns and in their search for work, were often strained by the unfamiliar conditions of town life. Da Alzira, an older women, regretted that:

Before it wasn't the same . . . it was everybody together . . . the families all together, not like now, one here and the other there. For me it was better before; everybody was united, neighbours combined well, they lived all together, prepared bread together, combined well. Now it is difficult to find anybody to do anything together. There is mistrust. First there was trust. One day you gave flour, eggs to me, the other day you had confidence in me and I would give to you. Now, nobody does anything together anymore. Now, I don't know why this is so, first we combined, now nobody combines anymore.

Periods of change in which there is little noticeable improvement are known to often evoke 'golden age' images of the past. While offering some insights into past experiences, such views are just as likely to be expressions of dissatisfaction with the present as they are fond memories of the past. Life on the estates was far from idyllic. The whole family worked from dawn to dusk and although relationships between households may have been more intense, they were not necessarily harmonious. It is difficult to reconstruct the frequency and depth of social conflict between families in the past, especially since there was so much overlap on the estates between neighbourhood and work relationships. But symbolic language even today still attributes certain illnesses and misfortunes to the envy of neighbours. The incentive wage system, for example, was hardly conducive to inter-family solidarity. Especially during the harvest, competition could become intense. Families who finished their quota of coffee picking could earn extra money helping the ones who were lagging behind. The slower ones bitterly resented this because it meant they were deprived of part of the income from the grove they had tended all year. On the other hand, there were many ways in which families cooperated and strike action, as I showed above, occurred. Households exchanged days of work and sometimes joined forces to help a family over a particular job organising a *mutirão*, with no reward other than to partake of a collective meal. Now, by contrast, it is, as the workers say, *cada qual para si e Deus para tudos*, 'each one for himself and God for everybody'.

Just as shared experiences did not entirely preclude social conflict in the past so, despite widespread nostalgia for the harmony of the past, mutual help and a common identity are not absent from the present. But the new poverty of the towns has affected relationships among workers and between neighbours in specific ways. The need to keep up 'appearances' puts new demands on scarce resources and this makes it more difficult to offer help. Hence, to avoid the embarrassment of having to face those to whom one has denied help and the frictions that may ensue, neighbours will tend to keep as much as possible to themselves.

The workers now live in dwellings ranging from bare and squalid huts to very modest houses at most, which have sprung up in irregular clusters along the trail of the rural workers' displacement to the towns. In Jaguariuna there are three such neighbourhoods in which rural workers are housed, two on the edge of the town and the third separated from it by a main road that leads inland from the city of Campinas. It is in this latter neighbourhood that most of the workers I came to know lived. The social composition of the neighbourhood is relatively homogeneous; the best off being the four bar owners, followed by the stonemasons and those who own their own homes and the local industry's unskilled workers. The majority of the residents, however, are casual rural labourers. There are no shops in the area so food and consumer goods have to be bought in town, which is about half an hour away on foot. Although migration from the countryside did, to some extent, scatter the rural population, a number of the families living in the neighbourhood have known each other for many years. Some of the families are related and a certain amount of intermarriage has created new kinship ties. Despite fewer feasts and religious festivals and less entertainment in general, public occasions such as weddings, wakes, prayer sessions which a family might organise to celebrate a particular saint's day and pilgrimages, all provide opportunities for getting together. Neighbours might even organise to demand better urban facilities from which they could all benefit, as they had done a few years earlier when three workers succeeded in mobilising the whole neighbourhood to obtain electric light.[21]

Conceptually, neighbours are those who live close by. Friends, on the other hand, are those with whom one has grown up and who enjoy special privileges in one's home. They do not need to ask permission to come in and may make use of whatever one has. Colleagues are those with whom one has developed a long-standing friendship at work and who enjoy one's trust but who must, however, ask before coming into one's home. There are certain basic obligations one has toward them all irrespective of any return. Neighbours must and do help in the case of an emergency such as a sudden illness and must offer their respects when someone dies. This is one of the reasons why it is regarded as important to have neighbours. And, being a natural resource, water must be shared. But changed material conditions have contributed to the workers' sense of isolation by restricting mutual help in other respects. Food has now become too scarce to share generously and it is no longer possible, nor can workers afford, to offer work days to someone else without pay. Neighbours may still cooperate in the building of a well, for instance, which would serve them both; and help which does not involve expense, such as giving a neighbour leftovers to feed a pig, is offered without expecting anything in return.

Nonetheless, strong feelings of reciprocity which had informed social relations among equals in the past and which demanded that unless favours could be returned in kind, they shouldn't be asked, has also become a source of conflict. As Sr Dito asserted:

In the old days there was that unity. Nowadays, there is no unity. Nowadays it is everyone for himself. In the old days when you asked for anything, there was the *mutirão* [joint work]. Nowadays people do not want to have anything to do with that. Nowadays people only want to get on as they can. It is no longer as it was. People help, in case of an emergency; when a neighbour dies, you rush to ask whether they need anything, but otherwise there is no way. In the old days one helped each other in everything, it was one for the other. Nowadays, it is each one for himself.

Favours or help must be recognised, i.e. acknowledged and reciprocated. Indebtedness, which is seen as either meanness or incapacity and inferiority, is feared because it may mean being denied future help. Obviously, reciprocity operates differently with social superiors. In this case, while favours still produce a sense of obligation, retribution can always be relegated to God. When a social superior offers help one is unlikely to be able to repay, the appropriate way of thanking him or her is to say *Deus lhe pague*, 'may God pay you', which is regarded as much stronger than the simple, but significant, *obrigado*, obliged.

The new material constraints on mutual help cause conflict also because they threaten the workers' already fragile self-respect. The more worried they are about their social image, the more self-conscious and defensive they tend to become. For example, they will take offence for the slightest reason, such as having the help they have offered not duly recognised or even being denied a greeting when they meet someone they know. Paradoxically, as Da Maria pointed out, now that one depends more than ever on the other's help, it has become almost impossible to obtain assistance:

> One needs the other. You must take care what you say. I don't quarrel with anybody. She [a neighbour who was too easily offended] does not know how to make up to the people, she does not know how to please others, she says what she thinks she has to say ... In the old days everybody worked in the fields, the estates were full of people, nobody needed anyone, only in case of death. You did not depend on others, you had everything, a place to wash the clothes, rice. Not now, you need the others. That is why a person cannot be harsh.

To be unwilling or unable to oblige when asked a favour immediately creates ill-feeling on both sides. The person refusing the favour is made to appear stingy and proud; and the one to whom the favour is refused feels resentful and somewhat ashamed. To keep to themselves and to refrain from asking for help thus becomes the safest strategy for preserving their self-respect. Da Cida, for instance, insisted that she did not quarrel with her neighbours because:

> I hardly see them, I do not ask for anything; they may refuse to do it. If they don't do it you must keep quiet but this is disagreeable. You must be quiet because they are not obliged to do you a favour. Good neighbours don't quarrel, they don't get easily upset.

Disagreements do, however, occur when favours are not fully appreciated or if an offer of help is suddenly withdrawn,[22] in which case the rules of reciprocity operate in reverse and then, to preserve one's self-esteem, one must give as good as they get. As Da Maria put it: 'The better a person wants to be to me, the better I want to be. The worse a person wants to be to me, the worse I want to be'. Disrespectful behaviour is penalised by retaliating in kind and by exposing the culprit to public censure. Public opinion, through gossip, is the final arbiter of social conduct. Infractions of social norms, in fact, only cause offence and are the source of censure when by becoming public they acquire social significance. Because self-respect rests so importantly on the social recognition others grant, any act of disrespect needs to be publicly known to become an offence. This is why, despite their sense of social isolation, the workers have an intense fear of being talked about; slander is frowned upon only if it is undeserved. Generosity earns social recognition and, ideally, the rules of reciprocity which inform social interaction underpin a sense of equality. But, intensified by the social compulsion to keep up appearances, material hardship militates against reciprocity and hence also against equality as a basis for solidarity. The result is a permanent tension between solidarity as an ideal and the reality in which a worker's self-respect is constantly endangered by the absence of reciprocity.

Most of the workers look upon their neighbourhood with a mixture of disgust and shame, not only because it lacks many features of a proper town but also, and especially, because it is seen as a place of perpetual quarrels and fights. Pent-up frustrations, combined with high levels of aggression and low tolerance make physical outbursts virtually inevitable.[23]

Faced with such a harsh and tense social environment, one might reasonably expect family and relatives to provide the last, but essential, bastion of support and solidarity. But, on the contrary, the circumstances brought about by the transition to wage labour have also placed severe strains on intra-familial relationships. The quality of family relations is now further than ever from the ideal of family and kin solidarity. As Sr Dito recalled:

The husbands felt bad when the women had to go out to work with the trucks. When these gangs began, people changed. It is not the world that changed, it is the people who changed. Even the mode of living of the people changed. Before there was no jealousy, everybody was united, the neighbours. The coffee groves had numbers and each family had its own. Everybody was united. There was competition among them . . . When weeding started all the families started work at the same time, everybody in their grove. The family had only the name of the family head, there was only one head, only the head of the household. The gang trucks brought many novelties. They brought separation between husband and wife, quarrels between husband and wife. They brought lack of respect, the wife lost her fear of the husband and the husband became distrustful. When I join a gang there may be 20 to 30 women. There is always a woman who will say, 'your husband likes that woman there'. Women have a weak brain.

The family and household continue to be coterminous, those not belonging to it being regarded as 'people from outside' as opposed to 'somebody of the house'. Family/household members continue to be expected to pool their incomes: 'the family are those who help us to work, whose wages belong to us'. Households are predominantly two-generational, containing either both parents or a mother with their unmarried children. Children are expected to remain in their parents' home until they marry and to contribute all their earnings to the family income. On marriage they will set up a household of their own. It is rare to encounter dependent grandparents in a household. Married adults try to live on their own for as long as they are able to earn a living, which is often until they die. They regard going to live with their children as a distinctly unattractive prospect. If this becomes necessary, however, it is the sons rather than the daughters who are responsible for the care of their ageing parents. Daughters are supposed to look after their husbands and husbands are generally unwilling to take in their parents-in-law. Consanguines are socially differentiated from affines, the former belonging to one, the latter to the 'others'.

The boundaries of specific kin obligations outside the nuclear family are difficult to define. A certain amount of visiting takes place between relatives, usually between consanguines, unless a couple visits a relative of either of them. Relatives, usually even as far removed as second cousins, are expected to help in cases of need and if, for whatever reason, their assistance is not forthcoming this is deeply resented. Such expectations and obligations to help extend also to 'ritual kin' who are acquired through baptism or marriage. Although people certainly don't always abide by this rule, ideally, ritual kin were in the past and continue to be chosen from among relatives or acquaintances of the same class.

But geographical mobility makes contacts between close kin more difficult. In general, workers are able to maintain regular contact only with relatives who live close by. Travel is time consuming and expensive and children are frequently unable to visit their parents for years on end. Moreover, since the older generation of workers is usually illiterate, contact through letters is also impossible. An equally important obstacle to contacts between kin is social differentiation. Although better-off relatives could be of help in principle, they are instead often regarded with a combination of unease and shame, precisely because they are better off. Da Amelia, who was the only member of her family who still worked in agriculture complained that:

> They [her brothers who live and work in town] don't pay any attention to me and I don't run after them. Since my father died [18 years ago] I haven't seen any of them. They are better off than I, they own cars. I don't care if they don't come ... My daughter is a *grã-fina* [fine lady]. Her husband works in a bank. They have a car. They don't come to visit; her husband doesn't allow her to come.

Social advancement tends to put a strain on parental bonds, especially in the case of married daughters. Because, as men, sons possess social status of their own which they can share with others; they are more likely than daughters to maintain family ties and might even help their siblings to advance. Women, by contrast, can derive status only from their husbands and therefore have none to bestow on anyone else.

Because sons are expected to care for their aged parents if needs be, some parents give this as a reason for preferring them to daughters who, in addition, are thought to be more difficult to raise as respectable women. This does not, however, mean that parents' relationships with their sons are more intimate than with their daughters, provided they have remained at the same social level. As a matter of fact, practical assistance tends to flow more frequently from mothers to married daughters rather than to sons. In the specifically feminine sphere of child-bearing, a mother will assist her own daughter when she gives birth but not her daughter-in-law, unless the latter lacks female consanguines living close by. But such assistance rarely extends to child-minding if the daughter goes out to work, for the mother will often have to work for a wage as well.

The nuclear family/household constitutes a distinct social unit within which, ideally, effort and earnings are pooled. Even if married children continue living with their parents for a time, or if old parents find refuge with married children, each nuclear unit would normally operate its own economy in which food is purchased, cooked and eaten separately. If, for some reason this is not the case, conflicts (generally over allocation of resources) can easily arise. An important symbol of a family unit is the stove and if more than one family unit is living under one roof, each will endeavour to have its own stove.

Married children bridge the gap between the co-resident nuclear family and relatives living outside the household. Though in a different way, adopted children also blur the boundaries between family and household. Unlike married children who are genealogically close but residentially set apart, adopted children are more distant genealogically, but nonetheless form part of the household. Although families are getting smaller, it is still fairly common for a couple to raise someone else's child or children along with their own; these are usually the children of a female relative who has died. The moral obligation to look after such children does, however, also carry certain material implications. Adopted children are expected to repay the investment made in their upbringing as soon as they are able to contribute to the family income. But the right acquired by the household through caring for the child does not necessarily go uncontested. A surviving parent may well reappear when the child has reached working age and, on the basis of his or her parenthood, claim it back to put to work for him or herself. In one such case a foster mother went so far as to go to court and was told by the judge that he would calculate the cost of the labour she had invested in raising the child for the biological parent to reimburse. The parent was in no psition to pay and so the child remained with her. One way of preventing parents reclaiming their children is through legal adoption, *com papel passado* (to hand over the document, a procedure said to *cortar o sangue*, cut the blood), but parents are not keen on this. Because there is often no clear fit, in cases of married and adopted children, between genealogical kinship ties and material obligations and rights grounded in the household, their presence in the household is a potential source of conflict.

The workers' new socioeconomic conditions have left the nuclear family/household intact as the typical ideal unit of social reproduction. In practice, however, the individuation of work and the loss by the household of one of its main former functions (namely, joint work) have affected family organisation in several important ways. Unlike the *colonato* system where labour arrangements militated against individual family members pursuing individual strategies, individual wage work by all able-bodied members now militates against corporate goals. Before, women and children may not necessarily have always endorsed and accepted the authority of the household head, but now, however, in traditional cultural terms, there is little left to legitimate the husband/father's authority within the family, especially since wage work by the wife and children also further challenges his authority. Coupled with the continuing need for the household to pool its resources, the resentment this creates in men has opened new areas of conflict within the family, which can only partly be overcome by the personal disposition of its members. Before, the family was kept together as a corporate unit by extra-familial constraints; now individual projects constantly conflict with the economic imperative to co-operate.

Even in the 'prosperous' 1970s, the wages men earned as casual labourers were generally insufficient to provide for their families. Because the women's wage was often lower still, they were even more dependent on the family. Earning a daily wage the equivalent at most of 3 kg of rice and 1 kg of beans, the individual worker could barely provide for the social subsistence (which includes housing and clothes, etc. apart from food) for one or two dependents and herself. The mutual dependence of family members thus persists but the individuation of labour, on the other hand, fosters personal aspirations, threatens the traditional authority structure and often frustrates a consensus of needs. As Sr José, an older worker of Italian origin, recalled:

> As *colonos* the family worked all together. Women and men did all the same work. Where one went all the family went. The head, the father, contracted with the estate. The head received the money. It was he who arranged everything... The harvest was done by everybody together. It wasn't like at present that only women harvest the coffee... the number of coffee trees contracted depended on the size of the family and these had to be tended all year round... the family worked together, not like now in the gang. The gang scatters everybody now. One goes in one direction,

the other in the other. We [the men] also worked for a day-wage ... women would go to weed rice, beans on the family plot. The landlord did not want to hire women for the day in order to protect the family plot. Only the men would go and work for the estate directly; and it wasn't like now either, everybody earning the same. The weaker [families] earned less, that was already set down in the contract book ... At that time things were bad because there was no money. You worked and worked and had nothing. The family was more united everywhere because at that time it was not like now, women commanding in the home. At that time it was the family head who was in command. What he said was done ... Also there was no fighting because there was little money, we bought few things.

Now contractors hire family members on an individual basis. Husbands/fathers may attempt to influence their wives and children's work options and arrange jobs for them but, in practice, women make decisions for themselves as well as for the young children who usually begin work alongside their mothers, from whom they learn how to do the job. Ideally, earnings are pooled and administered by the husband/father in his role as head of the family, but sons, in particular, are often reluctant to hand over their entire wage, preferring to pay room and board alone and keep the remainder for themselves. Wives and daughters do, however, give all their wages over to the family but, as one of the women pointed out, family finances are not necessarily administered by the husband: 'It is the family head who should control the money. In many places the head of the household is the man, in many it is the woman. If the husband is irresponsible, spends all the money on silly things, the woman has to take control'. One of the attributes of the family head is to control the family's income. If the woman assumes control over earnings, she also becomes the family head.

As provider, the husband is expected to pay the running costs of the household, the *despesas* – i.e., food, rent, water and light bills. The wife's and children's wages should, in principle, be reserved for occasional special expenses, such as clothes, a piece of furniture, doctor's bills, and so on. In addition, husband and sons are entitled to spending money for cigarettes and drinks and girls should receive some money to accumulate a trousseau. The only one not entitled to spend anything on herself is the wife/mother who sacrifices her entire income for the well-being of her family. Moreover, women are always afraid that their husbands might spend more than their legitimate share on excessive drinking or other women, thereby jeopardising the rest of the family's survival: 'robbing the innocent children of their food', as it is put. It is for these reasons that women sometimes take over the administration of the family finances.

Wives and daughters also must go out to work for a wage. But that they no longer work under the direct surveillance of their husbands/ fathers undermines the latters' authority and provides new grounds for marital conflict. Women are thought to have lost respect for their husbands and the gangs, with their dubious morality, are regarded as inappropriate places for respectable women to work. Labour contractors have a reputation, which is not entirely unfounded, for taking advantage of their position to seduce women workers. In the gang I studied, one young girl who was the contractor's lover eventually became pregnant, lost the child and left.[24] Her fellow workers generally thought that she was treated with special favour by the contractor, but whereas neither the men nor the women would have wanted such a situation for their own daughters, they nonetheless did not ostracise the girl for it. Later the contractor was said to have had an affair with a married woman.

Estates would sometimes dismiss whole gangs because of the effect the advances some contractors made to the women had on labour discipline. A belief that women without the protection and control of their men succumb easily to the advances of other men, fuelled the husbands' fears, based upon traditional sexual values and on the difficulties they now feel they have in enforcing them. Ideally, married women should stay at home and only men are free to go wherever they like, but many women now have to go out to work. Traditional moral norms gave men exclusive rights to and control over their wives' labour and sexuality. Needless to say, there was never a perfect fit between the 'ideal' morality and the practice. Landlords and administrators were a constant menace to the *colono* women and cases of pregnant daughters having to get married were not unknown. But a wife's fidelity was assured, not least because she never escaped her husband's vigilant eye. Under the *colonato* system, the women's labour was as important to their husbands as their procreative capacity. Now, although a woman's sexual services are, of course, desired by her husband and although men want to have a few children to prove they are men, as important to men is the access they gain through marriage to a woman's domestic and extra-domestic labour.[25] Some of the women noted cynically that men no longer marry women for their beauty but to have them working for them. After all, a man can obtain a woman's labour without pay only if she is his wife (either legal or consensual) or his daughter. This cynicism surely also expresses a deep sense of emotional deprivation coupled with a lack of communication between spouses, often intensified by the new strains in conjugal relations which are especially painful against the background of the love and affection which often informed the union early on. From the point of view of the men, a wife's infidelity is not simply an attack on the husband's pride; it also threatens to deprive him of her labour, for if she has another man she is bound to leave home, or at least so they think.

A husband's jealousy is one of the main causes of fights among spouses, and often leads to physical violence of which the women are the victims. One hears constant complaints about the neighbourhood being no place to raise respectable daughters and about how morals are not what they used to be. Time and again stories are told of women who have run away with other men. But men's fears that their wives might go off with another man, or that unmarried daughters might bring the family into disrepute and land it with an additional mouth to feed seem to be less founded than women's fears that their husbands might forsake their family responsibilities. The incidence of alcoholism among men is high, desertion by men is not infrequent and men do have women 'on the side'.

There were cases of young girls going off the rails, who had, as they put it, 'lost' themselves. A few became single mothers and although this certainly tainted their reputations, once back on the straight and narrow they usually managed to find husbands. It is not unusual for a girl to elope with a young man when there are conflicts with the parents, usually because they demand too much work of her or because they keep postponing the wedding so as not to lose their daughter's services. Usually they marry soon after. Parents will initially make a show of hurt pride, but they are usually soon reconciled, since couples who elope do at least save them the expense of a regular wedding. Men who have extra-marital affairs do so mostly with women whose relationships with their husbands are problematic, or who, through being separated or widowed are no longer under a man's control. They well know that otherwise they have the retaliation of a husband to fear. I know of only one instance of a married woman who lived with her husband running away with another man. Men fear their wives infidelity because it challenges the authority they have over them. Apart from the emotional pain and physical violence this may entail, women also fear their husbands' alcoholism and infidelity because it diverts the family income. No woman would involve herself with another man unless she derived some material advantage from it. As the lover of one of the women workers' husbands rather candidly put it, 'I am not such a fool as to offer my backside for free'.

THE CULTURAL CONTEXT OF ECONOMIC CHANGE

There is no immediate reason why economic hardship in itself should generate conflict rather than reinforce solidarity within the family/household. Kin relationships and the authority structure within the family are, however, invested with cultural meanings. How people experience socioeconomic change is informed not only by material facts but also by their previous socioeconomic circumstances and by the ideological and cultural values attached to them. With regard to family morality, the economic individuation of household members has been mediated by a gender ideology that defined the relationship between women and men in a characteristic way. The transition to individual wage labour has challenged these cultural norms in various ways. The former *colonos* have experienced changing productive relations not as autonomous individuals but as social actors enmeshed in social relationships endowed with specific reciprocal obligations and rights. Therefore, economic change has had consequences at three different, though related, levels of meaning. At the first, most objective, level, women's and men's respective conditions of work have changed. At the second, social level, new relations of production have altered relationships between men and women. Since gender is a social relationship, if the circumstances of the partners in the relationship change, then the relationship itself will also be modified. At a third but no less important level, the specific meaning of change for those concerned depends also on previous cultural norms of conduct and the expectations that are informed by them. This cultural dimension shaped responses to change in a very material way.

Men and women have been affected by their transformation into casual wage labourers in fundamentally different ways. For a number of reasons men have felt the additional pressures of their new conditions of life and work more intensely than women. Some of these reasons are connected with the greater uncertainty of work, some with the difficulty of fulfilling their role as providers, but most with a growing sense of loss of authority and control. First and foremost, men have lost the relative antonomy they possessed to allocate family labour and organise work. In the process, men have also often lost the right to control the family income. This perceived loss of culturally significant elements of men's social identity as husbands and fathers has undermined their authority within the family which, in turn, has intensified their sense of insecurity and lack of self-respect, making the men all the more distrustful of their wives and children. Job insecurity and low wages make it objectively more difficult for men to fulfil their role as breadwinners for the family. In the old days, although women contributed substantially to family subsistence, the husband nonetheless remained the uncontested household head. Now, not only do the women have to go out to work, but the men's position of authority has been challenged as well. Hence the danger of being left by their wives seems all the more real.

The transition to wage labour has affected women differently. For a start, they had no authority to lose. Instead, their incorporation into wage work has meant an increase in their responsibilities in comparison with the men. The domestic sexual division of labour remains unchanged so that work for a wage is added to the domestic chores. Moreover, once the women work for a wage, they exert themselves more. But women's paid work continues to be considered as subsidiary to that of their husbands. Hence, because men are more strongly committed to working for a wage, they are also more directly affected by the conditions of the labour market than women. For a woman it is far less of a tragedy to be out of work than it is for a man.

For those women who do not go out to work, either because they cannot leave their small children alone, or because their husbands earn enough to keep them at home, the division of labour by sex has been intensified. These women have been effectively domesticated. For those women who work for a wage, however, tasks have been redefined by gender and a new general division of labour between the sexes has emerged, with women doing what are regarded as the worst jobs.

In terms of workload, women who work for a wage are now worse off relative to men than they were under the *colonato* system. Formerly, the whole family worked from dawn to dusk. Now, the women work from dawn to dusk and the men work the statutory work day for which they are paid. Nonetheless, from a purely subjective viewpoint, their transformation into casual wage labourers seems to have been much more painful and distressing for the men because of the loss of self-respect that it entailed. Whereas wage labour has increased the women's burden relative to men, it has not affected their sense of self as women (i.e., as wives and mothers) in any significant way. On the contrary, precisely because their social identity has remained intact, they must now bear the double burden.

The wives feel resentful and have new misgivings towards their men, essentially for failing to fulfil their traditional responsibilities as husbands. As Da Maria complained, 'it is a good thing to find a man who does not allow one to work, but working it is no use to have a husband'. The ideal husband is a man who works, does not drink and is respectful to his wife. Nowadays, however, such men are thought to be few and far between. The women recognise that the life of a married woman is very hard, yet all the girls nonetheless want to get married, to 'give it a try'. They marry often out of love but they also hope for the comfort he will provide and that, clearly, is in short supply. They want a provider to take care of them and, for this reason, they actively support the family form that is at the root of their subordination. But they often soon discover that their husband cannot, or will not, provide for them. Because the family ethic that designates the role of breadwinner to the husband/father and exempts him from the domestic chores is so deeply ingrained in the society,[26] when the husband fails to provide adequately for the family's needs forcing the woman to go out to work for a wage in addition to her domestic responsibilities, she naturally feels resentful. The women blame the landlords for their miserable condition as casual wage labourers, but they also see their own need to work in a gang as a failure of their husbands. Women *do not* object to domestic work *per se*, but to their burden being so much greater than the men's.[27] When men marry they expect the woman to take care of the home and this is what they get. If she is also a wage earner they get an additional bonus. Women marry to be provided for, but they often don't even get this and consequently have to work for a wage too. Men lament the authority they have lost, women the added burden they have gained.

If they could, many women would stay at home, but domestic work is unpaid and, in addition, staying at home in town often means confinement to the house. Domestic work is neither invisible nor regarded as inferior by these workers, but with their incorporation into wage work, domestic labour has lost value in a relative sense. During the *colonato* period, a woman's work at home (and, when feasible, in the fields) was considered the proper and adequate contribution by women to the family economy. Now they have to work more than men to satisfy family needs, and it is in this sense that domestic work has been devalorised. Paradoxically, while 'the woman is always useful in the fields and at home [and] always works more', she is no longer valued in the way she was before. So long as wages are as low as they are and domestic work is unshared, their incorporation into wage labour offers women no more personal autonomy than they had before and they are acutely aware of being worse off than men.[28] Nonetheless, the women seem to bear their double burden with greater ease than the men their loss of authority within the family and of control over their lives.

Generalised wage work has affected family size but has not put motherhood, women's basic defining attribute, into question. Expectations as to number of children have dropped because even though children of working age can contribute to family earnings, small children can no longer be taken to the fields and stop their mothers from working themselves. Ideally, one should have two or three children, but no more: 'The thing is to close the factory gate, close it and lose the key'. Coitus interruptus is probably the most frequently used method of contraception: 'you have to shoot and miss' as one woman described it graphically. Some women, particularly the younger ones, take the pill or use the IUD provided by an international population control agency. Although most women are aware of the various contraceptive methods, their knowledge is at best confused because accurate information and regular free gynaecological service are unavailable. An abortion does not seem to elicit any moral qualms but again the conditions under which it is often carried out and the expense it involves make it rare. One woman commented jokingly that when the contractor had taken the young girl who was his lover to a nearby town allegedly to *tirar um quisto* (to remove a cyst) it was, in fact to *tirar um Cristo* (to remove a Christ, i.e. to have an abortion).

Though smaller families are now preferred, both men and women are still highly committed to having children. If they are unable to have a child of their own, they will consider adoption. One woman who had adopted a boy expressed the sense of loss and inadequacy felt by women who cannot have children as '*bananeira que não da cacho merece ser cortada*' (a banana plant that does not give bananas should be cut down). Motherhood constitutes a woman's essential attribute. A man ceases to be a man in a social sense if he does not work, unless there is no work and even then he feels the impact on his sense of self. A woman ceases to be a woman if she is barren. Women's transformation into wage labourers has not undermined their procreative role. Their burden has often increased but their sense of self is unimpaired.

Da Cida remarked of her husband, who had been unable to work for some time, that 'he was not meant to be a man. A man should not like to stay at home. Women must like to stay at home. I don't like it ... God made a mistake'. The husband was himself very uncomfortable at not being able to work, not only because the family had to make do without his wage but also because he felt it degrading to have to stay at home: 'If I was a woman nobody would find it wrong that I stay at home. Being a man I think myself that people are beginning to say, "won't he ever get well?"'.

The greater versatility of women, while involving hardship, provides them with special resources with which to confront life. As the women themselves often assert, they have more 'courage' than the men. But their greater resilience has drawbacks as well, for it means that they tend to put up with what is expected of them. Women are believed to suffer more, but having more patience, they tend to bear their lot.

The men often cope with their demoralisation by turning to alcohol. This the women find particularly painful. Deserting their families is yet another way in which the men try to deal with economic hardship and a sense of having lost control.[29] About one-third of the women I knew were living without a man in the household. Some were widows but others had been deserted by their husbands who had either gone to live with another woman or whose whereabouts were unknown. Among those husbands who did live with their wives, some drank or were unfit to work. A few of the women who had been deserted by their worthless husbands welcomed the change, for they felt it was 'better [to be] alone than in bad company'. Others may have considered leaving a husband who was no good and who also beat them but, as one woman explained, 'women who have a weak head will leave. I am calm, I stay. It is painful to leave, [but] to stay is difficult as well'. In one sense it is more difficult for the men to live on their own because they are incapable of cooking and washing for themselves and so they will always attempt to attach themselves to a woman. For women with small children it is almost impossible to make ends meet on their own, but there are also ideological reasons why they are less likely to leave the home. Men literally have to 'earn' their rightful place in the home, whereas it is the women's 'natural' place. Men might abandon the home when they feel they have failed. For women, abandoning the family *constitutes* the failure itself. If a woman leaves her husband she will be blamed as much by her fellow women as by the men:

> A woman who leaves her husband, people always say that she is bad, irrespective of whether she had reason to, people say that she is bad. That is why you have to think before leaving. But at times you do wish to leave, one gets fed up. Many women who leave, like my sister, left because they had a reason. She starved, had no clothes to wear, and people said that it was she who was wrong.

Women are also constrained from leaving home by the special bond which is thought to exist between mothers and their children. It is, therefore, very difficult for a woman to leave her children behind. As Sr Dito asserted:

> It is worse when a mother leaves or dies. It is much worse. A woman when she leaves the home, the children feel it more deeply. A mother may reprimand children more but the children are more loving with their mother than with their father. When the father leaves the house trembles, when the mother goes away the house crumbles. Mother you have only one, the father nobody knows who he is. You see, when a woman is left alone and has small children, if she finds a man, marries, the children will soon call him father. Now, if a man sets up with another woman, it is difficult for the children to call her mother. They will say, you are not our mother, you are our step-mother. The man carries the name. Now, the things have changed, women receive their money, the children as well.

In contrast to the man's central role in supporting his family, fathers are assigned a marginal role in relation to their children. Because parenthood is conceptualised in such biological terms and because of the ideological emphasis on the biological difference between women and men with regard to childbearing underlying the special 'nature' of motherhood, fatherhood depends importantly on co-residence and on the fulfilment of the man's role as provider. Both are potentially fragile bases for fatherhood.

The maternal and paternal bond are conceived of as differing in quality and in intensity. Children owe respect to both parents, they are expected to obey and not talk back. But expectations regarding conduct towards one's mother are more exacting: 'They must respect their father and even more their mother because the mother suffers more. Also, the mother feels greater love for her children. A mother will go without food in order to give something to eat to her children'. Because the wife/mother is conceived of as the natural centre and binding force in the family, a husband/father's desertion may increase economic difficulties but does not threaten the persistence of the household as such. When a mother/wife leaves, however, the father will either attempt to find a substitute wife or disperse the children among relatives.

It is difficult for women with children and without a husband to reconcile domestic duties with the need to earn an income, but they do their utmost to succeed. Da Zahira, a widow of about 35 with four of her six children still alive and living with her, one of them working like herself, commented with disapproval that 'on the truck a man said that if he were in my position he would have abandoned the children. Love does it all. What do you think of that, when the father dies to go off? Not me, I show them a happy face'.

Men are seen as the 'natural' providers of the family's needs, women as endowed by 'nature' with special skills to care for and raise the children. Women's special skills are not necessarily incompatible with wage work outside the home. Men, however, depend on women for all domestic services. As one woman put it, they think it is shameful to help at home although they eat the same as women, which is why, men will always try to have a woman at their disposal: 'a man does nothing. He has to pay for it. If he has a lot of money he has a maid'. Women, however, are often very dubious about allowing a new man into the house. He may be no better than the first and, in addition, if there are daughters in the household, he may take advantage of them. These women who take over as the genuine heads of their households may, in the end, hold more autonomy than anyone else, but under the circumstances they pay so heavily in material and emotional terms that it is hardly a choice.

The individuation of labour has challenged traditional gender roles and the authority structure of the family without freeing either men or women from the constraints imposed by the family. Despite the economic redefinition of the family members' roles in more individual terms, they must stick together and pool their resources if they are to make ends meet. As before, married women are motivated not by personal aspirations but by family needs to seek wage work outside the home. The married men's greater individuation as expressed in their control over the family budget, when they exercise it, and in their generally greater freedom of movement is also more apparent than real.[30] This apparent freedom conceals the constraints imposed on men by the ideology of the male breadwinner. Casual wage labourers are probably the 'formally free' labourers *par excellence*, totally deprived as they are of any 'rights'. But precisely because they are the most 'unprotected' of all workers, they also reveal most clearly the sharp contradiction between the individuation of labour through the advance of capitalism and the ideological construction of men as family providers and women as wives and mothers. The women do not necessarily benefit from their husbands' loss of authority by acquiring more autonomy themselves, because the ideology of the male breadwinner is constantly reasserted by society at large and the men are not prepared to abdicate the power that it bestows on them.[31] In the case of these rural workers, new economic circustances have not produced a redefinition of gender roles. Instead, one is impressed by the strength and good humour of the women which contrasts with the sense of defeat exhibited by many of the men. Women resent the double burden they must carry, blaming both the landlords for not giving them subsistence plots and their husbands for not providing adequately for them. Husbands blame the adverse economic cirumstances on the power of the landlords but often vent their frustrations on their wives and children. One outlet for men's pent-up anger at their powerlessness is domestic violence, though it is difficult to know to what extent conjugal conflict ending in physical violence also occurred in the past. As one woman complained:

There are people who really hit. He [the husband] when his foot got bad, the beatings he gave me and the children got bread only on Sundays. In the fields I ate only rice and beans. There were many people who felt sorry for me and would give me bread ... this village is a place of much confusion. I hit her [the husband's lover] because she made me starve. Just think of it, to work the whole week and have to starve on Sundays ... Now the situation is much worse; now they [the men] are all scoundrels. When we lived on the estate some men were like that, by far not all of them.

Obviously not all men are scoundrels but many are eventually unable to resist mounting pressures and will beat their wives and children. When the men feel their inadequacy most keenly they may attempt to reassert their authority through use of physical violence.[32] Women are surely not exempt from the urge to hit back but they usually have less strength. There are circumstances which are generally believed to justify a beating, as when a child is disobedient, a girl goes around with too many men, or a wife is suspected of having another man. But women get the worst of both worlds: a husband is as likely to beat up his wife when he fears her recriminations for his infidelity as when he suspects her of being unfaithful to him.[33] Women fear drunkenness not only because it eats up family income but also because it often precipitates physical violence.

Children, especially sons, will usually come to the aid of their mothers in a fight. In one instance, a father shot his own son for trying to prevent him from returning to the bar where he had already got drunk (most men have small firearms or knives at home). In another case, a son stabbed his drunken father who was trying to beat his mother. Another woman with a number of small children attempted suicide when she could no longer bear her husband's assaults.

These are extreme cases. They are only the most dramatic manifestations of the extraordinary strains produced within the family by a socioeconomic system which endorses a family structure and ideology that subordinates women to the power of men but, at the same time, undermines this family by depriving husbands of the material conditions to properly comply with their assigned role as family providers. These strains are particularly acutely felt by these men because they are experienced against a background in which their family authority was hardly ever contested, at least by extra-familial economic forces.

THE FAMILY: SUPPORT, CONFLICT AND SUBORDINATION

The transition from the *colonato* system to casual wage labour was not a passage from an idyllic life of plenty, of personal gratification and social harmony to one of misery, demoralisation and violence. Such a picture would be inaccurate. The *colonato* was a labour system based on extreme exploitation of family labour. As a family labour system, it reinforced a particular family form with its own set of social relations and moral values. The *colonos* were aware of their exploitation and resisted it when they could. At present, individual wage work has partly undermined this corporate family organisation but, because of very low wages, cooperation between family members is as vital as ever. New productive relations have, at the same time, strained intra-familial relationships as labourers have become individual wage earners and men, in particular, have been deprived of some of their prerogatives. The earlier experience of the *colonato* in which family cooperation was actively enhanced only serves to underline the present disunity.[34]

Historical changes in levels of interpersonal violence have sometimes been taken as indicators of the progressive or regressive nature of historical change.[35] In this particular instance, however, the transition to individual wage labour was not one from less to more interpersonal violence, but rather a transformation in the kinds of violence. Under the *colonato* system women were firmly subordinated to men's authority and probably rarely challenged it. Relations among *colono* families were both solidary and competitive and individuals would easily get into fights, usually over affronts to them or their families. For the most part, the landlord administered a form of rough justice and generally only used the police to defend his own interests. A loss of self-respect, particularly acute among the men because of their loss of control, has deepened the men's anger and now also affects their relations with their wives who seem to be challenging their authority as well. These new strains within the family and between neighbours also contribute to the workers' general lack of unity.

The introduction of the *colonato* system and the transition to casual wage labour on the São Paulo coffee plantations and its effect on the workers' family structure is one example of how economic processes can be influenced by ideological and cultural forces. In this case, coffee growers organised production around a specific model of the family, and in so doing created material constraints which served to reinforce this family form as a set of moral values and social relationships. The workers' reaction to economic change was, in turn, mediated by their belonging to this kind of family and the social roles within it assigned to them. The contradictions that mark this process are the compounded result of economic pressures as they are experienced in the light of social values and expectations.

Wage labour has affected women and men in different ways because the transformation in productive relations was mediated by former cultural values regarding gender roles and the sexual division of labour that resulted from them. Women also perceive the causes for their present situation differently from men. While sharing the men's general interpretation of their common exploitation, they blame their husbands for the heavier burden they must now bear and are also keenly aware of being more exploited than the men. By demanding of their husbands that they fulfil their traditional role of providers, these women, however, are endorsing the very institutions which are at the root of their exploitation and subordination as women – i.e.,marriage and family with a gender hierarchy and sexual division of labour within it.

This endorsement could be taken as a sign of their basic conservatism and the acceptance of dominant family values by the working class. This set of values – the aspiration to marry whatever the consequences, for women to stay at home, for men to provide for their families, for girls to be respectable – coexist, however, with a considerable tolerance towards those who fall short of these ideals. Those who infringe moral norms, particularly regarding sexual behaviour, may be regarded as *semvergonha* (shameless) but so long as they do not constitute a threat to one's own or one's family's livelihood and status, they are looked upon with leniency. Once she had left the gang, the contractor's lover had an affair with her aunt's husband and after having his child went to live with him. Her aunt was understandably deeply affected by all this, but the women in the gang and in the neighbourhood did not ostracise her. Of the young woman who had five children by five different men (none of whom supported her) and who now lived in poverty with her aged parents, it was merely thought that she was silly to get herself into such difficulties.

Beyond the purely ideological constraints, material pressures also reinforce the nuclear family as the appropriate form of social re-production. In a society in which all aspects of life are structured around the nuclear family, even if it harbours considerable conflicts of interest and hardship for the women, alternative forms of living are difficult to envisage and even more difficult to put into practice. Moreover, the complex articulation of the family with the socioeconomic order is much more obscure than class antagonisms, exploitation and power relations that sustain it in societies such as Brazil where social inequality is so overt. Finally, one should also not underestimate the extent to which emotional ties and dependences among family members hide the underlying exploitation, which cannot prevent but may aggravate personal conflict and suffering. There are a significant number of women heads of household, many with no desire to acquire a new husband. Even so, these female-headed households are usually not by choice, for everybody is aware how very difficult it is, at least materially, to get along without a male provider in the family. Both women and men are caught in an institution strained by deep conflicts and contradictions but, so long as their general exploitation continues, they are unable to extricate themselves from it. The result is extreme exploitation of the women and further demoralisation of the men.

As I indicated above, capital organises its strategies of accumulation on the basis of existing social institutions, such as the nuclear household, which can serve its interests. At the same time, through extreme exploitation, it may also undermine them. In this particular case (which is not so different from the experience of the working class in the early decades of the English industrial revolution and from times of crisis of capitalism), the spread of casual wage labour in agriculture has not only uprooted and demoralised the workers, but has had a negative effect on the productivity of labour as well. But then, capital sometimes fails to foresee the contradictory effects the pursuit of profit may have.

Postscript: The Limits of Exploitation

This book tells an open-ended story. The conflicting interests of landlords and labourers could never entirely be reconciled. The 1970s saw a significant shift in agricultural production from coffee to other cash crops such as sugar-cane, soya beans and oranges which during the peak of the harvest season now absorb almost half of São Paulo's seasonal agricultural labour force.

Brazilian agricultural policy in the 1970s pursued three goals – namely, increased production of sugar cane as a substitute source of fuel to ease the balance of payments disequilibrium, of soya beans and oranges for export and of food crops, which, however, proved to be irreconcilable. Favourable market conditions for some export crops and the Proálcool programme introduced in 1975 for the production of ethanol as a fuel for cars, buses and trucks coupled with preferential access by large agricultural producers to government subsidies for technical innovations in cultivation disadvantaged food crops grown mainly by small and medium farmers. As a consequence, the segmentation of agriculture into an export and fuel-producing sector and one growing food crops for domestic consumption deepened. Land became more concentrated, the cultivation of export crops and sugar cane became more mechanised and energy intensive, some food crops stagnated and others even declined and the seasonality of labour use intensified as conditions of work and pay of casual labourers deteriorated by the end of the 1970s.[1]

One result of these trends was a food problem. As Homem de Melo showed, by the late 1970s, domestic supply of basic staples as measured in calories and proteins available per inhabitant per day, either stagnated as in the case of maize, or declined most notably in that of beans and manioc.[2] The agricultural exports drive and the energy import substitution programme may have contributed to improving Brazil's trade balance, but insufficient domestic food production stimulated inflation, which, by 1983, had reached over 200 per cent.

The Proálcool programme transformed the state of São Paulo into the country's main ethanol producer, providing 61 per cent of national output. And in São Paulo, the Riberão Preto region, formerly prominent for the quality and quantity of coffee it produced, has now become the most important ethanol producer of the country. Bordering on its huge sugar cane plantations is an extensive orange growing area which together have concentrated almost 150 000 casual rural labourers in the small towns scattered throughout the region.

In 1984, as I was finishing this book, a succession of much publicised strikes of casual rural labourers occurred in the sugar cane and orange growing region of the state which shook landowners and government officials alike. It is appropriate, in ending this book, to take a look at these strikes. They highlight the deepening contradictions in Brazil's agricultural development. The living and working conditions of these labourers are little different from those of the coffee workers I have described, although a politically relevant feature of sugar cane and orange workers in São Paulo is their extraordinary regional concentration.

In the 1970s, real wages in São Paulo agriculture had improved somewhat. By the turn of the decade, they began to decline and living standards deteriorated. A nutritional study carried out in 1979 among a sample of casual rural labourers in the Riberão Preto area revealed serious deficiencies. Only 17.5 per cent of the men had a daily calory intake of 3000 Kcal and only 36 per cent of the women achieved 2200 Kcal, respectively regarded as adequate for these workers. The remaining men and women showed nutritional standards that were below 80 per cent of the calory intake they required.[3]

Cane-cutting, paid by production, is one of the most arduous tasks in agriculture. It demands strength and endurance. Mill-owners were aware that deficient nutritional standards affected productivity of labour. Instead of improving wages, however, some sugar-mills introduced food schemes to overcome low productivity. In late 1982 the São Paulo sugar-mill Santa Adelaide began providing its workforce with a 'warm and balanced meal' against a small payment. As it was found shortly after, the labourer's income had also risen, as it was pointed out, 'because they were now able to exert themselves more'. And, by providing the workers with a warm meal, the mill saved women workers the extra hour they had previously wasted on preparing the meal which they could now use to work longer in the fields! The experiment was hailed as a model for other sugar mills to follow for it had succeeded in breaking the 'vicious circle of inadequate food producing poor physical conditions which entailed poor wages leading to inadequate food'.[4] But this is obviously a matter of perspective. The income of workers, even if they are paid by production, depends essentially on wage rates and these, in turn, are determined by the bargaining power they have to extract better wages from landlords.

As the harvest season began in mid-May of 1984, the 10 000 sugar-cane cutters of Guariba, a small town of 25 000 inhabitants located in the heart of sugar-cane country, went on strike. At the same time, 12 000 orange pickers in the neighbouring town of Bebedouro also went on strike in demand of better wage rates. Both strike movements began in the towns in which the workers lived rather than at the place of work and were accompanied by extensive rioting and violent clashes with the police that attracted national attention.

The sugar-cane workers' discontent exploded when the new cane-cutting system that had been introduced the previous year and which reduced a cutter's daily output without a corresponding increase in the piece-rate, was maintained for that year's harvest.[5] As the Guariba cane cutters, among whom were many women and children, went on strike, rioting triggered off by a substantial increase in water rates, broke out in the town. The dispute, in fact, involved the whole town. While pickets on the outskirts of the town were intercepting the gang trucks as they arrived to take the workers to the fields, a growing crowd in the town centre proceeded to set alight and demolish the water company's two buildings, along with a truck and a van that belonged to it. When the military police arrived and opened fire into the crowd, killing one bystander and wounding another fourteen workers, the riot reached its peak. The crowd now marched on the nearby supermarket looting and destroying it. For the rest of the day, the atmosphere in the town remained tense although there was no further destruction. But in the evening some workers set fire to a sugar-cane field as a warning to mill-owners if they did not meet the labourers' claims.[6]

As an expression of workers' grievances in the absence of genuinely representative political organisations through which to channel demands, riots are not a novelty in Brazil. The Guariba workers attacked the three culprits responsible for their deteriorating living standards, the water company which had raised rates, the mill-owners who had cut their wages and the supermarket where food prices were going up by the day.

Indications are that the strike and riot began as a spontaneous protest movement. Some observers suggested the presence of outsiders but the local rural labour union leader admitted his own lack of contact and influence among the casual rural labourers. This absence of leadership among the workers was in fact seen with considerable concern by some. It made the protest movement all the more difficult to contain. Union leaders, labour lawyers and politicians made their appearance only the following day at a rally called to consolidate and extend the strike movement and to define the workers' demands. At the rally threats were heard that all 100 000 sugar-cane workers in the Riberão Preto region would be called out in support of the strike. At the same time a list of demands was drawn up including the return to the previous cane-cutting system, the provision of receipts for cane cut to allow workers to control their earnings, a rise in the piece-rate, payment of overtime for travel to and from work, paid sick leave and the provision by the mills of work tools such as machetes, files, gloves and work clothes which the workers had hitherto had had to buy themselves.

As a first concession, mill-owners agreed the same day to return to the five-row system. The next day, as the tension and small confrontations continued in Guariba, mill-owners were ready to sit down around the negotiating table with workers' representatives and eventually accepted most of the labourers' claims. Three days after they had gone on strike, the Guariba labourers returned to work having won the strike.

The agreement on wages and work conditions negotiated with mill-owners was in principle applicable to sugar-cane workers in the whole state. For the most part, however, mill-owners elsewhere could be persuaded to raise wage rates and improve working conditions only when and where workers threatened to follow the Guariba workers' example or actually went on strike. The following weeks saw a number of strikes not only of sugar-cane workers but also of labourers on coffee plantations in different areas of the state. A number of these strikes were accompanied by riots and the destruction of a market and gang trucks. In all cases landowners were forced to make concessions.

The orange pickers of Bebedouro's strike was also successful initially. Orange growers agreed to raise picking rates, but it turned out that a substantial proportion of the raise was discounted for payment only at the end of the season as a means to ensure labour supply. Discontent spread again among workers. Mill-owners in the area of Guariba and Barretos similarly adopted reprisals against the workers. Instead of paying them on a weekly basis, as before, by July payments were made monthly which created new difficulties for the labourers.

By August it was clear that, as a prolonged drought was increasing unemployment among rural labourers, the Guariba and Bebedouro agreements were not generally observed. Renewed rumours spread of strikes and mill-owners got together in anticipation of new labour disputes, hoping to confront them in a more organised fashion. Simultaneously, there was talk of further mechanisation of the sugar-cane harvest.[7] As regards the workers, if inflation continues to erode rural wages and rural unemployment rises agricultural labourers may become either more defeatist or more desperate. If their livelihood is further threatened new outbreaks of rioting and violence may occur which pose more severe problems even than unorganised strikes. Under such conditions rural employers may at last be persuaded, with some pressure from the state, that adequate wage agreements must be negotiated to restore labour discipline and productivity, and rural unionisation may be promoted to channel workers' discontent. The events of 1984 are only one expression of the contradictions created by an agrarian structure which deprives its own workers of their livelihood. As long as these conditions prevail, more or less latent conflict will persist in São Paulo agriculture.

Notes and References

Preface

1. M. Palacios, *Coffee in Colombia, 1850–1970: An economic, social and political history* (Cambridge University Press, 1980); L. W. Bergad, *Coffee and the Growth of Agrarian Capitalism in Nineteenth Century Puerto Rico* (Princeton University Press, 1983); W. Roseberry, *Coffee and Capitalism in the Venezuelan Andes* (University of Texas Press, 1983); C. LeGrand, *Frontier Expansion and Peasant Protest in Colombia; 1830–1936* (University of New Mexico Press, 1986).
2. G. M. Sider, *Culture and Class in Anthropology and History, A Newfoundland Illustration* (Cambridge University Press, 1986).

1 The Introduction of Free Labour in São Paulo Coffee Plantations

1. An earlier version of this chapter written in collaboration with M. M. Hall has been published under the same title in *The Journal of Peasant Studies*, special issue 'Sharecropping and Sharecroppers' edited by T. J. Byres, 10,(2/3) (January/April 1983).
2. 'Bericht des schweiz. Generalkonsuls in Rio de Janeiro an den schweiz. Bundersrath über die Auswanderung nach Brasilien', *Schweizerisches Bundesblatt*, X. Jahrgang II, 34, 24 July 1858, pp. 183–8, quoting the speeches of an immigration agent named Mota on behalf of emigration to Brazil.
3. E. Viotti da Costa, 'Colônias de parceria na lavoura de café: primeiras experiências', in her *Da Monarquia à República: momentos decisivos* (São Paulo, 1977); W. Dean, *Rio Claro: a Brazilian Plantation System, 1820–1920* (Stanford, 1976); J. S. Witter, 'Um estabelecimento agrícola no estado de São Paulo nos meados do século XIX'. *Revista de História*, 98 (1974); S. Buarque de Holanda, preface and notes to T. Davatz, *Memórias de um colono no Brasil* (São Paulo, 1941).
4. Vergueiro had begun to replace sugar cane with coffee in 1828, but activities were limited by the small number of slaves he owned. In 1840, he made a first attempt to reorganise the plantation, introducing 80 Portuguese families to replace his slaves. This experiment failed because of the political upheavals of 1842. Not discouraged, however, by 1847 he had founded an immigration company, *Vergueiro e Companhia*, and with the aid of a three-year loan from the provincial government, hired a group of 64 German families, J. S. Witter, 'Um estabelecimento agrícola'; W. Dean, *Rio Claro*, p. 88.
5. J. Vergueiro, *Memorial acerca da colonização e cultivo de café* (Campinas, 1874) p. 4. S. G. Kerst, *Über brasilianische Zustände der Gegenwart, mit Bezug auf die deutsche Auswanderung nach Brasilien und das System der brasilianischen Pflanzer, den Mangel an afrikanischen Sklaven durch deutsche Proletarier zu ersetzen* (Berlin, 1853).

6. J. P. Carvalho de Moraes, *Relatorio apresentatado ao Ministério da Agricultura* ... (Rio de Janeiro, 1870) p. 5. In view of the glowing terms in which São Paulo agriculture was presented to the immigrants, they presumably preferred the contract offering them a 50 per cent share in the net profit to one paying them a fixed piece-rate per unit of coffee produced.

7. Le Comte Auguste von der Straten-Ponthoz, *Le budget du Brésil* (Paris, 1854) pp. 102–04. A similar contract was signed between Senator F. A. de Souza Queiroz and a group of immigrants in 1852. Interest on outstanding debt was charged only after four years, the contract was for five years, and the planter agreed to let out land to the labourers on one of his plantations once the contract had been completed. E. Viotti da Costa, 'Colônias de parceria', pp. 175–77. The number of coffee trees assigned to each immigrant family depended on the number, sex and age of its members. J. P. Carvalho de Moraes, *Relatório apresentado*, p. 7.

8. A significant number of immigrants were said to have managed to pay off their debts within the first years and move on to establish themselves on their own. J. P. Carvalho de Moraes, *Relatório apresentado*, p.7; *Allgemeine Auswanderungs-Zeitung*, 39, Rudolstadt (25 September 1857); J. J. von Tschudi, *Viagem às provincias do Rio de Janeiro e São Paulo* (São Paulo, 1953) pp. 135, 149. The President of the province, Saraiva, reported in 1855 that of the initial 900 immigrants that had settled on Vergueiro's property in 1847, by 1855 about 670 remained. The rest had either fulfilled their contracts or indemnified the planter for the costs incurred on their behalf. By 1867, however, an emissary of the Prussian government, H. Haupt, noted that only under very favourable circumstances – such as fertile plots, a large family, the absence of diseases – could an immigrant family succeed in repaying its debt within a reasonable time. H. Haupt, in Sociedade Internacional de Imigração, *Relatório,* I (1867) p. 39.

9. J. J. von Tschudi, *Viagem às provincia*, pp. 135, 166.

10. J. J. von Tschudi, *Viagem às provincias*, p. 135; J. P. Carvalho de Moraes, *Relatório apresentado*, pp. 55–56.

11. J. P. Carvalho de Moraes, *Relatório apresentado*, p.5; it was argued that this would allow labourers to tend a larger number of coffee trees (p. 59).

12. 'Relação das colonias existentes na provincia de São Paulo no ano de 1855', an anonymous manuscript dated 8 March 1856, in the archive of the Instituto Histórico e Geográfico Brasileiro, Rio de Janeiro, lata 71/7. There were 117 731 slaves in the province in 1854. How many were engaged in coffee cultivation is not easy to say, but they surely constituted a majority. J. F. Camargo, *Crescimento da população no estado de São Paulo e seus aspectos economicos* (São Paulo, 1952) II, p. 12.

13. J. P. Carvalho de Moraes, *Relatório apresentado*, p. 10.

14. E. Viotti da Costa, 'Politica de terras no Brasil e nos Estados Unidos', in *Da Monarquia à República*. Liberals opposed to the landowning interests rejected it, arguing instead for the donation of land to

immigrants as an incentive to attract foreign settlers to civilise the country. Cf. J. de Souza Martins, *A imigração e a crise do Brasil agrário* (São Paulo, 1973) pp. 51–4; W. Dean, 'Latifundia and Land Policy in Nineteenth-Century Brazil', *Hispanic American Historical Review*, LI (4) (1971).

15. Those who were attached to the plantations were a relatively unimportant group of *agregados*, a kind of retainer allowed the use of marginal estate land in return for occasional labour and other services. M. S. de Carvalho Franco, *Homens livres na ordem escravocrata* (São Paulo, 1969). Cf. P Eisenberg, 'O homen esquecido: o trabalhador livre nacional no século XIX. Sugestões para uma pesquisa', *Anais do Museu Paulista*, XXVIII (1977–78).

16. J. J. von Tschudi, *Viagem às provincias*, p. 136. Tschudi was an envoy of the Swiss Federation, sent to Brazil in 1860 to inspect the conditions of Swiss sharecroppers. He was himself a landowner in his native country and reported sympathetically that the planters were well satisfied with the modification of the contract since these offered them a solid guarantee for the capital invested.

17. *Allgemeine Auswanderungs-Zeitung*, 43, Rudolstadt, (23 October 1857) pp. 188–9. The Swiss Consul-General David was exceptional in his sympathetic attitude towards the immigrants. One of his predecessors was Charles Perret-Gentil, who was an immigration agent as well as Senator Vergueiro's brother-in-law and business partner. Perret-Gentil's immediate predecessor had been dismissed after having misappropriated the funds of the Schweizer Hilfsverein in Rio de Janeiro. R. A. Natsch, *Die Haltung eidgenössischer und kantonaler Behörden in der Auswanderungsfrage, 1803–1874* (Zurich, 1966) pp. 171–2.

18. T. Davatz, *Memórias*, contains a detailed account of the events. See also the collection of documents reproducing reports by several observers in *Schweizerisches Bundesblatt*, X. Jahrgang II, 34 (24 July 1858) and XII. Jahrgang III, 61 (28 November 1860). The immigrants' discontent was aggravated by the fact that for a significant number their local governments had advanced transport costs free of interest and commission, for which they were being charged by Vergueiro.

19. T. Davatz, *Memórias*, pp.105–6.

20. *Deutsche Auswanderer-Zeitung*, Bremen, 83 (22 October 1857), quoting a report of the Brazilian Imperial Colonisation Agency on the Ibicaba revolt. J. J. von Tschudi, 'Bericht des schweiz. ausserordentlichen Gesandten in Brasilien, Herrn v. Tschudi, an den Bundesrath über die dortigen Verhältnisse der Kolonisten, vom 5. Oktober 1860', *Schweizerisches Bundesblatt*, XX. Jahrgang III, 61 (28 November 1860). Tschudi pointed out that part of the blame for the difficulties belonged to the immigration agents who had not selected the labourers properly and had recruited many disabled people simply to earn the commission. But he particularly blamed the immigrants themselves, who did not show the necessary interest in their work. Tschudi had omitted these aspects in his report to the Imperial government, 'in order to emphasise those points which arise from the

conditions in Brazil', *Schweizerisches Bundesblatt*, XII. Jahrgang III, 61 (28 November 1860) p. 269. T. Davatz, *Memórias*, p. 100; M. J. Valdetaro, 'Colônias de S. Paulo', in Brazil, *Relatório de Repartição Geral das Terras Públicas apresentado em 31 de março de 1858* (Rio de Janeiro, 1858) p. 91.

21. *Allgemeine Auswanderungs-Zeitung*, 43, Rudolstadt (23 October 1857) p. 189.

22. The theme is prominent, for example, in the works by J.S. Witter and S. Buarque de Holanda, as well as in W. Dean's *Rio Claro*.

23. R. A. Natsch, *Die Haltung eidgenössischer und kantonaler Behörden*, makes this point quite clear.

24. A. Marshall, *Principles of Economics* (London, various editions).

25. S. N. S. Cheung, *The Theory of Share Tenancy* (Chicago, 1969).

26. T. Holloway, 'The coffee *colono* of São Paulo, Brazil: migration and mobility, 1880–1930', in K. Duncan and I. Rutledge (eds), *Land and Labour in Latin America* (Cambridge, 1977). It is unlikely that São Paulo planters did not know average coffee yields. They had the Paraíba Valley experience to go by. In any case, no entrepreneur can exactly predict future markets and prices.

27. J. D. Reid, Jr, 'Sharecropping and Agricultural Uncertainty', *Economic Development and Cultural Change*, 24, 1979; J. D. Reid, Jr, 'Sharecropping as an Understandable Market Response: the Post-Bellum South', *Journal of Economic History*, 33 (1973) which contains a number of sharecropping contracts similar to those used in São Paulo. See also *The Journal of Peasant Studies*, special issue 'Sharecropping and Sharecroppers'.

28. J. Martinez-Alier, 'Peasants and Labourers in Southern Spain, Cuba, and Highland Peru'. *The Journal of Peasant Studies*, 1 (2) (1974).

29. As José Vergueiro, p. 5 pointed out in 1874: 'I understand colonisation can only progress if carried out in families. One estimates that each family is composed of an average of five members'.

30. J. P. Carvalho de Moraes, *Relatório apresentado*, Appendix 5, p. 2.

31. A. Ramos, *O café no Brazil e no estrangeiro* (Rio de Janeiro, 1923), p. 104, 358.

32. The clause contained in the early contracts that half of any food crop surplus belonged to the planter, which was intended to discourage labourers from growing food in excess of their basic needs and in detriment to work in coffee cultivation, was soon abandoned as ineffective. J. P. Carvalho de Moraes, *Relatório apresentado*, p. 57.

33. C. Heusser, *Die Schweizer auf den Kolonien in St. Paulo in Brasilien* (Zürich, 1857) pp. 28–9. Among others, Kerst, *Über brasilianische Zustände*, p.70, considered the planters' selling of the crop a grave disadvantage. The 'exhorbitant deductions' made by the planters, convinced him that the 'labourers would be better off it they received their share *in natura* and sold it themselves, instead of having the planter... as their intermediary... Of course, it could then occur that the labourers compete with the planter'. Cf. also E. Viotti da Costa, 'Colonias de parceria', p. 174. W. Dean, *Rio Claro*, pp. 105–7, maintains that an average family could repay its debt within five years or less,

and in addition accumulate some savings. Other authors have estimated that it took an average of nine years. According to Dean an average family of five members would tend about 3000 trees, yet most accounts indicate that this is an overestimate.

34. J. J. von Tschudi, *Viagem às provincias*, pp. 164–5, reports another work stoppage on the plantation Boa Vista in Amparo in 1858. The labourers were harvesting green berries along with the ripe ones to speed up the work. Reprimanded by the planter, who threatened pay deductions, they stopped the harvest. Another case is that of Portuguese immigrants on a plantation in the area of Rio Claro, reported in S. Machado Nunes, 'Colônias na provincia de S. Paulo', in Brazil, Ministério do império, *Relatório... 1860*, p. 15. M. J. Valdetaro, 'Colônias de S. Paulo', p. 94, reports that on the plantations Bery and Cavatinga most Swiss and German labourers were lazy and careless in the fulfilment of their duties, to the point of abandoning work entirely. Cf. H. Haupt, *Relatório*, I, p. 39: 'The labourer in sharecropping ("*obreiro colono por parceria*") will moreover be a very bad worker, because he necessarily loses the love of work which gives him no result, nor independence. In this case, he will seek to avoid his duties and deceive the planter. Soon a feeling of enmity will grow up between them, and in many cases deplorable scenes will result'.

35. S. Machado Nunes, 'Colonias no provincia', pp. 2–3. Cf. also J. P. Carvalho de Moraes, *Relatoria apresentado*, p.86. J. J. von Tschudi, *Viagem às provincias*, p. 183, n.69, reported that on the plantation São Lourenço some families tended no more than 500 to 700 coffee trees. When asked why, they replied that they were overburdened by their debts and thus not interested in cultivating coffee. Their food plots produced sufficient for them to live on.

36. M. J. Valdetaro, 'Colônias de S. Paulo', p. 91.

37. M. J. Valdetaro, 'Colônias de S. Paulo'; J. J. von Tschudi, *Schweizerisches Bundesblatt*, XII. Jahrgang III, 61 (28 November 1860).

38. Data on the number of coffee trees tended by immigrants either on an individual or family basis, are scarce. According to Carvalho de Moraes, *Relatório apresentado*, pp. 70–1 it was initially expected that a labourer could tend up to 3000 coffee trees in the case of mature groves between five and 12 years of age, provided he weeded them four to five times a year and had no other duties. In this case, additional labour for the harvest would be required. If the labourer, however, simultaneously grew food crops, he could not tend more than 1000 trees, while women took on between 500 and 600 trees of five to 12 years of age, since 'in general labourers do not pay their debts with anything else but their income from coffee and for this reason they will try to tend as small a number of trees as they possibly can, in order to have more time for their own crops and to benefit from other activities. This is one of the reasons why in this province the work of a free labourer is considered less efficient than that of a slave' (p. 86). Cf. also E. Viotti da Costa, 'Colônias de parceria', pp. 173–4, and J. J. von Tschudi, *Viagem às provincias*, pp. 46–50, 183. J. P. Carvalho de Moraes, *Relatório apresentado*, 'Mapa de São Jeronimo', published data on a

plantation run under the sharecropping system which lists all the families that settled on the estate between 1852 and 1869, giving their size, composition (number of workers and consumers), income in that period, and date of arrival and departure. Of the total 141 families, 40 per cent had paid their debts and made a profit by 1869, 4 per cent had merely repaid their debts, and 56 per cent continued indebted. On the basis of these data it is possible to calculate, if not the number of trees tended per labourer, at least the labourers' earnings per month for those families who had repaid their debts. The amount of outstanding debt is not given for those who continued indebted at the time. We can also calculate the consumer/worker ratio in order to determine the comparative productive capacity of the families. Since the greater the number of labourers in a family in proportion to the consumers, the greater would be its productive capacity, this should be reflected in the monthly earnings of its workers, provided that they worked at full capacity:

Monthly earnings per worker from coffee cultivation by consumer–worker ratio of the family: plantation São Jerónimo, 1852–1869

C/W ratio	1.0–1.4	1.5–1.9	2.0 and over
Mil. reis	6508	7714	8111
No. of families	25	20	16

(I have excluded three families from the total of 64 with favourable results; one was a widow who married another immigrant and joined her accounts to his; the other two were single individuals.) The earnings given refer to income from coffee cultivation, with which debts were paid. Harvests varied from year to year, but it may be assumed that over the years earnings roughly expressed the number of trees tended. As the table indicates, productive capacity of the families is inversely related to the number of trees tended by each of its workers as expressed in monthly earnings, a further indication that immigrants did not respond to the economic incentives of the sharecropping contract.

39. *Allgemeine Auswanderungs-Zeitung*, 40, Rudolstad (2 October 1857).
40. J. P. Carvalho de Moraes, *Relatório apresentado*, p. 21.
41. J. P. Carvalho de Moraes, *Relatório apresentado*, p. 21. If we define debt peonage in its strict sense as being the intentional burdening of labourers with a debt to tie them to a property, this does not apply to the case of São Paulo. Cf. W. Dean, *Rio Claro*, pp. 97–8, and E. Viotti da Costa, 'Colónias de parceria', p. 169. The aim planters pursued in charging immigrants with their transport costs and food advances was to recover their initial investment. Stability of labour on the plantation was a welcome by-product. Significantly, an 1852 contract stated both length of contract *and* amount of debt, E. Viotti da Costa, 'Colónias de parceria', p. 177. It was also not infrequent that immigrants moved from one plantation to another, taking their debt with them.

C. Heusser, *Die Schweizer auf den Kolonien*, p. 1. The Vergueiro contract included a clause allowing for transfer of immigrants. Planters, it is true, were accused at times of treating immigrants like white slaves, H. Haupt, *Relatório*, I, p.40. However, Tschudi was probably correct when he noted: 'I have not observed such a tendency on any of the plantations I visited; all planters declared that their greatest interest was in seeing their labourers free of debt' – surely not least because this would have meant that labourers worked in coffee cultivation. *Viagem às provincias*, p. 186.

42. J. J. von Tschudi, *Viagem às provincias*, p. 143.
43. J. P. Carvalho de Moraes, *Relatório apresentado*, pp. 19–20.
44. J. P. Carvalho de Moraes, *Relatório apresentado*, pp.18–20.
45. J. P. Carvalho de Moraes, *Relatório apresentado*, p. 12 and Appendix 2 for an 1868 labour-leasing contract; cf. M. J. Valdetaro, 'Colônias de S. Paulo, and S. Machado Nunes,'Colônias na provincia', for descriptions of contract changes.
46. P. Denis, *Brazil* (London, 1911) pp. 216–17
47. J. P. Carvalho de Moraes, *Relatório apresentado*, pp. 20–1
48. Ord. Libro 4°. Titl. 45, of the *Ordenações e Leis do Império de Portugal*, various editions.
49. Lei de loção de serviços of 11 October 1837, in *Coleção de Leis do Império do Brasil*, VIII (1837).
50. S. Machado, Nunes, 'Colônias no provincia', p. 10, reports the case of one German and two Swiss labourers of the Laranjal plantation in the area of Campinas, arrested in São Paulo and condemned under the 1837 law to pay double their debt for having refused to fulfil their sharecropping contracts. He notes, however, that in another case a similar sentence was overruled with the argument that the 1837 law did not apply to sharecropping. He concluded that 'if immigration according to the sharecropping system is to increase in São Paulo . . . it will be indispensable to pass special legislation regulating the sharecropping contract and furnishing an easy means to resolve quickly the conflicts between labourers and planters', 'Colônias na provincio' p. 20. Cf. J. J. von Tschudi, *Schweizerisches Bundesblatt*, XII. Jahrgang III, 61 (20 November 1860)p. 260, for another case. Tschudi was highly critical of the practice of applying the 1837 law to share-cropping contracts, suggesting that this opinion was shared by a number of São Paulo jurists. J. J. von Tschudi, 'Denkschrift an Seine Exzellenz den Senator João Vieira Cansansão de Sinimbu, Minister der Auswärtigen Angelegenheiten', *Schweizerisches Bundesblatt*, XII. Jahrgang III, 61 (20 November 1860) p.197. Finally, the police chief, Tavares Bastos, who was ordered to investigate the events on the Ibicaba plantation in 1857, suggested that the 1837 law be adapted to the sharecropping contract, 'Relatório de Tavares Bastos sobre colonização em S. Paulo', in T. Davatz, *Memórias*, pp. 231–40.
51. As José Vergueiro, *Memorial acerca*, p. 5, noted 'However, this same contract, as positive as it is, does not satisfy the *colono*, who detests being subjected to it; and since he does his daily job under constraint, he tries exclusively to make use of the plot of land [which he

is assigned] because he has no hope of owning it someday'. Tschudi suggested a further reason for the immigrants' unresponsiveness to the new contract. With rising coffee prices in 1860, it was in the planters' interest to pay a piecerate rather than share of growing net revenue. For the labourers it was the reverse; at a time of rising prices, labourers would have benefited more from a sharecropping than from a piecerate contract. J. J. von Tschudi, *Viagem às provincias*, p. 157. It must be kept in mind that the piecerate was established annually, while the share was defined by contract, which usually remained in force until the debt had been repaid.

52. J. J. von Tschudi, *Viagem às provincias*, pp. 176, 183. Both long-term productivity and life of coffee trees depend on the number and quality of the weedings. At the time, the average number of weedings was five to six a year, including *coroação* before the harvest and *esparramação do cisco* after it. Although contracts by the 1860s usually stipulated its number, weedings could still be done with greater or lesser care. If weeds were removed by only lightly hoeing the ground, the soil would harden and become impermeable to the rain, besides not allowing adequate ventilation. São Paulo, Secretaria da Agricultura, *Inquérito agrícola sobre o estado da lavoura cafeeira no estado de S. Paulo* (São Paulo, 1904) pp. 56–7.

53. For the debate on immigration systems, between Jaquim Bonifácio do Amaral and José Vergueiro, see *Gazeta de Campinas* between January and July 1870. Vergueiro was totally disillusioned with privately-sponsored immigration. In addition to the Ibicaba revolt, in the 1860s the Swiss Federation had sued Vergueiro and Co. for the restitution of passage money advanced by the cantons to the immigrants and eventually the company declared bankruptcy. R. A. Natsch, *Die Haltung eidgenössischer und Kantonaler Behörden*, pp. 207–8. In the early 1870s, the Angélica plantation, also belonging to Vergueiro, was sold off to creditors, the London and Brazilian Bank. The English managers are alleged to have been 'drunken incompetents' who brutalised the labourers and led the estate once again into bankruptcy. It is reported that in 1876, Angélica's administrator was murdered by some labourers. G. B. Marchesini, *Il Brasile e le sue colonie agricole* (Rome, 1877). Joaquim Bonifácio do Amaral, in contrast, travelled to Europe in 1870 to recruit labour personally. He complained, however, of the scant support he had received from other planters in this undertaking. *Gazeta de Campinas*, 24 July 1870. Cf. also J. B. do Amaral, 'Introdução do trabalho livre'.

54. P. de Turenne, 'L' immigration et la colonisation au Brésil', *Revue Britannique* (February 1879) p. 453. J. B. do Amaral, 'Introdução do trabalho livre'.

55. A. Lalière, *Le café dans l'Etat de Saint Paul, Brésil* (Paris, 1909) Appendix.

56. The law included the important proviso that until children became 21 years old they could be used by their mother's owner. Though technically free, the *ingenuo's* condition was in practice that of a slave. The Rio Branco law would have little practical significance until 1892, when the first of those born under it would become 21.

57. The most thorough study is in R. W. Slenes, The Demography and Economics of Brazilian Slavery: 1850–1888', Ph.D. dissertation (Stanford University, 1975) pp. 120–78.

58. Since the mule teams which the railroads replaced had sometimes required as much as 20 per cent of the plantation labour force to operate, the number of slaves made available for field work was quite significant. E. Viotti da Costa, *Da senzala á colonia* (São Paulo, 1966) pp. 154–77.

59. Planters were no longer 'stubbornly sticking to tradition and routine' as they had previously done, but were now employing various foreign and domestic machines to replace 'their scarce and expensive labour'. São Paulo, *Relatório apresentado . . . pelo presidente da provincia . . . 5 de fevereiro de 1871*, p. 42 Cf. A. de Queiroz Teles, 'La culture du caféier à São Paulo, Bresil', *L'Economiste Francais*, VI, 49 (7 December 1878) pp. 718–20 for a description of the production process at the time.

60. J. Vergueiro, *Memorial acerca*, p.22.

61. *Informações sobre o estado da lavoura* (Rio de Janeiro, 1874) p. 149; the Dutch traveller Van Delden Laerne commented in 1885 that during the preceding ten years the planters had been able to increase significantly the productivity of their slaves who were now 'better treated, better fed and cared for', but who 'must work harder'. C. Van Delden Laerne, *Brazil and Java: Report on Coffee Culture* (London 1885) p. 91.

62. In 1870 Carvalho de Moraes had suggested as an afterthought that the Imperial Government at least 'grant the planters who introduce free labour a subsidy of 30 $000 to 40 $000 for each child under the age of 14 years who comes in the company of his parents', *Relatório apresentado*, p. 103.

63. O Lavrador, *Gazeta de Campinas*, 20 February 1870.

64. Congresso Agrícola, *Coleção de documentos* (Rio Janeiro, 1878) pp. 47–8. On the Congress, see P. L. Eisenberg, 'A mentalidade dos fazendeiros no Congreso Agricola de 1878', in J. R. Amaral Lapa (ed.), *Modos de produção e realidade brasileira* (Petrópolis, 1980).

65. J. Vergueiro, *Memorial acerca*, pp. 7–8; M. Hall, 'The Origins of Mass Immigration in Brazil, 1871–1914, Ph.D. Dissertation (Columbia University, 1969) pp. 38ff. has a detailed discussion of the politics of the *Sociedade Central de Imigração*. Influential coffee planters allied with the Prado family founded their own association in 1886, the *Sociedade Promotora de Imigração* to organise subsidised immigration of labour directly for the coffee plantations.

66. Martinho Prado opposed settlements for 'the establishment of "nucleos" is going to interfere with satisfying the need for workers on the plantations', M. Hall, 'The Origins', p. 101. His brother, Antonio Prado, shared Martinho's aversion: 'Experience has demonstrated, at least in the province of São Paulo, that the establishment of immigrants on the plantations is the best system (by contrast with the colonisation by means of nuclei of smallholders) because, after three or four years, the family established in this way, if it is abstemious, serious and hard working, will have been able to accumulate sufficient money to purchase land on which their labour will be all the

more fruitful as they will be acclimatised.' Antonio Prado, letter published in the *Correio Paulistano*, 20 August 1889, quoted by B. Sallum Jr. *Capitalismo e cafeicultura, Oeste-Paulista: 1888–1930* (São Paulo, 1982) p. 108. As one observer noted in 1892, 'The large landowner has never seen with good eyes the distribution of small plots of land to the immigrants', A. L. Rozwadowski, 'São Paulo', in *Emigrazione e colonie; raccolta di rapporti dei rr. agenti diplomatici e consolari* (Rome, 1893) p. 161. W. Dean, *Rio Claro*, pp.185–6 suggests that government colonisation schemes were often used to bail out bankrupt planters.

67. Decreto no. 2827, 15 March 1879, in *Coleção de Leis do Império do Brasil* (1879).

68. The strike broke out on 9 June. The *Tribuna Liberal* of 11 and 13 September 1878 carried detailed reports by the Police Chief sent to investigate the events, as well as information from a special investigating commission.

69. They drew up a list of nine demands: that the planter fulfil his promise to provide new houses within six months; that foodstuffs be charged at current prices; that they receive the total amount of flour from the maize ground at the planter's mill; that they not be forced to abandon their food plots for new uncultivated land; that they be paid for the replanting of trees; that medical expenses be shared by the planter; that tarpaulins for the harvest be provided free of charge; and that a school teacher be provided free. *Tribuna Liberal*, 11 September 1878.

70. J. B. do Amaral, 'Introdução do trabalho livre'; *Tribuna Liberal*, 11 and 13 September 1878. The previous year a group of German labourers which Amaral had recruited in the neighbouring province of Santa Catarina had gone on strike and some of the leaders had been sentenced to jail.

71. J. B. do Amaral, 'Introdução do trabalho livre', pp. 284, 252.

72. C. F. Van Delden Laerne, *Brazil and Java* pp. 213, 217. The question is also discussed extensively in *Congresso Agrícola*.

73. Brazil, *Anais da Câmara* V (1884) pp. 541–3. In 1884, his brother, Martinho Prado, defending a bill introduced in the São Paulo assembly to subsidise the entire costs of the passage of immigrants, stated clearly the purpose of such a measure: (1) to replace the slaves with free labourers and prepare for immediate emancipation; (2) to allow immigrants to arrive free of debt; (3) to permit planters to employ free labour without having to advance money. São Paulo, *Anais da Assembléia* (1884) pp. 34, 224.

74. *Anais da Câmara* V (1884) p. 540.

75. *Anais da Câmara* IV (1888) p. 323.

76. *Anais do Senado* (1887) annex to III, p. 6; another source estimated that between 1882 and 1888 a total of 103 571 immigrants had entered the province through official channels. F. P. Lázaro Gonçalves, *Relatório apresentado à Associação Promotora de Imigração em Minas*, (Juiz de Fora 1888) p.

77. C. F. Van Delden Laerne, *Brazil and Java*, p. 354.

78. A. Castro, *7 ensaios sobre a economia brasileira*, (Rio de Janeiro, 1971) II, p. 78.
79. Decreto 213 (22 December 1890) in *Decretos do Governo Provisório*.
80. Decreto Federal 1162 (12 December 1890) 'Dos crimes contra a liberdade do trabalho, in *Decretos do Governo Provisório*.
81. F. Mosconi, 'Le classi sociali nel Brasile e le loro funzioni', *La Riforma Sociale*, VII (1897); F. Dafert, 'A falta de trabalhadores agrícolas em São Paulo', in Instituto Agronómico, *Relatório*, (1892) p. 206; F. P. Lázaro Gonçalves, *Relatório apresentado*, pp. 10–11, noted that freedmen demanded high salaries and were widely considered insubordinate and unreliable; L. Couty, *Etude de biologie industrielle sur le café* (Rio de Janeiro, 1883) pp. 120–8.
82. M. Hall, 'The Origins', pp. 144–7.
83. The theme is a common one, for example, among the planters in the *Inquérito Agrícola*.
84. J. P. Carvalho de Moraes, *Relatório apresentado*, p. 100, notes that a number of prominent planters introduced immigrant labour in the 1860s. Pp. 77–86 describe the different types of contract used on the plantations run with free labour in 1869. The separate payment of cultivation and harvest might have been introduced initially to counter the labourers' complaints about low profit from young groves when tended under the sharecropping arrangement. J. B. do Amaral, Visconde de Indaiatuba, 'Introdução do trabalho livre em Campinas'.
85. P. Denis, *Brazil*, p. 202.
86. Labourers were often more interested in the clauses in their contracts relating to food crops than in those determining wages. P. Denis, *Brazil*, pp. 202–3.
87. E. Bonardelli, *Lo stato di S. Paulo del Brasile e l'emigrazione italiana* (Turin, 1916) pp. 71 ff.
88. G. Maistrello, 'Fazendas de café – costumes', (São Paulo), in A. Ramos, *O café no Brasil*, p. 564.
89. J. B. do Amaral, 'Introdução do trabalho livre', p. 244 F. P. Lázaro Gonçalves, *Relatório apresentado*, p. 28; G. Maistrello, 'Fazendas de café-costumes', p. 559. Planters regarded labourers contracted in family units as cheaper. He also noted in 1922 that the 'tending of the coffee groves is preferably done by families of *colonos* with annual contracts, but unfortunately they are not always sufficient and almost all the planters must resort to extra personnel. Needless to say, employing such labourers [*camaradas*] in weeding or harvesting increases quite noticeably the costs of the fazenda', (p. 562). Planters usually employed single men as *avulsos* – labourers recruited exclusively for the harvest or special tasks such as pruning – or as *camaradas* for coffee processing and transporting. They were paid on a monthly wage basis, as young families generally were. Large families were hired as *colonos*. Carvalho de Moraes, *Relatório apresentado*, p. 66; *Bollettino Ufficiale della Camera Italiana di Comercio ed Arti* (BUCICA) (February 1903) p. 73; D. Jaguaribe Filho, *Algumas palavres*, pp. 19, 32.

P. Denis, *Brazil*, pp. 216, 318–23, noted that Italian immigrants were not only more hardworking but also made their women work. They were expected to make all able family members work, while Brazilians were usually employed as single wage labourers.

90. G. Maistrello, 'Fazendas de café-costumes', pp. 558–9, calculated in 1922 the incomes of three immigrant families with different consumer/worker ratios, and showed that at the prevailing wage levels a family with only one worker could not make ends meet. At the end of the year, the large family would have cleared Rs. 1:130 $000, the family with two workers Rs. 620 $000, and the small family would lose Rs. 140 $000.

Family size	No. of workers	c/w ratio	Trees per family	Annual weeding	Harvest earnings	Extra work	Annual expenses
				Rs.	Rs.	Rs.	Rs.
10	6	1.66	16 000	2:400$000	480$000	600$000	2:350$000
5	2	2.5	7000	1:050$000	240$000	460$000	1:130$000
4	1	4.0	3000	450$000	70$000	120$000	780$000

With weeding wages calculated on the basis of large families, those with a small number of workers, even exerting themselves proportionately more, would do comparatively worse. Earnings from extras refer to day wages received for odd jobs not stipulated in the contract.

91. F. P. Lázaro Gonçalves, *Relatório apresentado*, pp. 20, 28. For a typical *colonato* contract, see the *Bolletino Ufficiale della Camera Italiana di Commercio ed Arti* (BUCICA), São Paulo, II, (4) (February 1903).

92. L. Couty, *Etude de biologie*, pp. 166–7, comments on the planters' aversion to producing maize, rice, beans, and to raising animals in a country importing a large part of its foodstuffs from abroad. Cf. BUCICA, XV (July 1917) p. 10.

93. São Paulo, *Relatório apresentado . . . pelo Presidente da provincia . . . 17 de janeiro 1887*, pp. 120–2.

94. A. de Zettiry, 'I coloni italiani dello stato di S. Paulo', *La Rassegna Nazionale*, LXX (1893) p. 78; A. L. Rozwadowski, 'San Paolo', in *Emigrazione e colonie: raccolta di repporti dei rr. agenti diplomatici e consolari* (Rome, 1893) p. 177; *Emigrazione agricola al Brasile. Relazione della Commissione Italiana 1912* (Bologna, 1913) p. 232

95. P. Denis, *Brazil*, p. 205; A. Ramos, *O café no Brasil*, p. 209.

96. P. Denis, *Brazil*, p. 205. Strikes usually occurred at the onset of the harvest, since a delay at that point would immediately affect the quality of the coffee.

97. E. Viotti da Costa, 'Colónias de parceria', pp. 171–2. In *Da senzala á colonia*, Viotti argued somewhat differently, attributing the failure of sharecropping to the high cost of production of coffee on account of its very labour-intensive nature, low level of mechanisation, and low coffee prices, with consequent small profit margins, which discouraged both employers and labourers. W. Dean, in *Rio Claro*, while

initially agreeing that the sharecropping system was in fact more profitable than slave labour, attributes its failure to the fact that after the first years free labourers could be kept working only by the use of coercion or by offering them more favourable contract conditions. He suggests that the former would have required backing by the government which was unavailable, the latter the planters themselves were unwilling to grant, ideologically incapable as they were of dealing with a genuine proletariat on a purely contractual basis.

98. M. J. Valdetaro, 'Colónias de Paulo', p. 93, quoting a planter whose labourers worked little and badly.

99. The *colonato* itself has received considerable attention recently. Interpretations that differ substantially from my own (and from one another) are: V. Caldeira Brant, 'Do *colono* ao bóia fria: transformações na agricultura e constituição do mercado de trabalho na Alta Sorocabana de Assis', *Estudos CEBRAP*, 19 (1977); J. de Souza Martins, *O cativeiro da terra* (São Paulo, 1979); C. R. Spindel, *Homens e máquinas na transição de uma economia cafeeira* (Rio de Janeiro, 1980); T. H. Holloway, *Immigrants on the Land: Coffee and Society in São Paulo, 1886–1934* (Chapel Hill, 1980); B. Sallum Jr, *Capitalismo e Cafeicultura, Os**este-Paulista: 1888–1930* (São Paulo, 1982); C. Vangelista, *Le Braccia per la Fazenda, Immigranti e caipira' nella formazione del mercato del lavoro paulista (1850–1930)* (Milan, 1982).

100. Two of the most influential statements of the respective positions are A. Passos Guimaraes, *Quatro séculos de latifúndio* (São Paulo, 1964), and Caio Prado Jr, *A revolução brasileira* (São Paulo, 1966).

101. The most vehement recent claim that the *colonato* was pre-capitalist is J. Gorender, 'Genese e desenvolvimento do capitalismo no campo brasileiro', in E. de Morais Filho *et al.*, *Trabalhadores, sindicatos e politica* (São Paulo, 1980). It would be difficult to deny that under the *colonato* free workers were obliged to sell their labour power in the market.

102. Francisco de Oliveira, 'Economia brasileira: crítica à razão dualista', *Estudos CEBRAP*, 2 (1972).

103. S. Silva, 'Agricultura e capitalismo no Brasil', *Contexto*, 1 (1976) p. 31.

2 The Symbiosis of Coffee and Food Crops

1. W. Cano, *Raízes da concentração industrial em São Paulo* (São Paulo, 1977) p. 41; São Paulo coffee production rose from 2.9 million bags in 1890 to 10.2 million in 1901 to 15.4 million in 1907.

2. C. C. Fraga, 'Resenha Histórica do Café no Brasil', *Agricultura em São Paulo*, (hereafter *ASP*) X, (1), (January 1963); R. Araujo Dias, 'Problemas atuais da economia cafeeira', *ASP*, XVI (1/2) (1969) pp. 35–7. Until the 1950s coffee earned an average 50 per cent of Brazil's foreign exchange, with peaks, as in 1924 at 74 per cent.

3. J. de Souza Martins, *O Cativeiro da Terra* (São Paulo, 1979) and more recently, A. M. da Silva da Silva, 'Família e Trabalho na Cafeicultura', *Cadernos de Pesquisa*, 37 (São Paulo, 1981) attribute the *colonato* system to the absence of a labour market, the abundance of land and the

shortage of capital on the part of the planters. But this system consolidated precisely when a labour market had been constituted. Moreover, they disregard labour conflict as a primary factor. B. Sallum Jr. *Capitalismo e Cafeicultura, Oeste Paulista; 1888–1930* (São Paulo, 1982) interprets this combined cash-crop and self-provisioning system as a way of reducing the reproduction costs of labour; he does not, however, consider the important incentive element and the role played by the family.

4. K. Kaerger, *Brasilianische Wirtschaftsbilder, Erlebnisse und Forschungen* (Berlin 1892) p. 335. Dafert, another German, who was Director of the Agronomic Institute of São Paulo, wholeheartedly shared this view. F. W. Dafert, *Ueber die gegenwaertige Lage des Kaffeebaus in Brasilien* (Amsterdam, 1898); L. Couty, *Etude de biologie*, noted similarly that 'many planters affirm that colonisation under present conditions [the *colonato*] is the most secure and least expensive labour system, the most secure because it determines production costs in proportion to production and the least expensive because the labourers on a plantation cost less per month than Chinese or any other kind of wage labour, providing in addition a variety of products' (pp. 166–7).

5. In the early 1890s falling exchange rates had kept prices in domestic currency high. By 1896, even the price in milreis declined sharply. M. Hall, 'The Origins', p. 153. The world stocks in July of every year had increased from an average of slightly over 5 million bags between 1895–1900 to more than 11 million after 1902 as compared with an annual world demand of 14 million bags by the end of the century. A. Delfim Netto, 'Foundations for the Analysis of Brazilian Coffee Problems', in C. M. Pelaez (ed.), *Essays on Coffee and Economic Development.* (Instituto Brasileiro do Café, Rio de Janeiro, 1973) pp. 65–6.

6. A. de E. Taunay, *Pequena História do Café no Brazil* (Departamento Nacional do Café, Rio de Janeiro, 1945) pp. 295–312, for the debates and proposals made at the time to stem the price slump.

7. Quoted by A. Delfim Netto, 'Foundations' p. 66.

8. W. Cano, *Raízes da concentração*, pp. 70–4; coffee was marketed through *comissários* (brokers) who sold coffee either directly to the exporters or passed it on to *ensacadores* (packing houses), against a commission. *Ensacadores* mixed different kinds of coffee to obtain the various blends which were then re-packaged and sold to the exporters. These medium grades could be sold at much cheaper prices than the mild (*fino*) coffees. Unscrupulous merchants sometimes passed off medium grades as mild coffee making large profits in the process. Until the First World War the broker's function was not restricted to mediating between the coffee producer and the merchant. He also financed coffee planters to a large extent and even the formation of new plantations. Many of the brokers were severely affected by the price slump and the deflationary policy adopted at the turn of the century. The *comissário* lost importance with the expansion of banking and government intervention in the market. Early in the century only the *corretores* and exporters remained. In the late

nineteenth century the *comissário* houses were exclusively Brazilian owned, but all exporters with the exception of two (Holworth & Ellis and J. F. Lacerda Franco, which was associated with the *comissário* house belonging to Vergueiro & Co.) operating out of the port of Santos were foreign. When in 1906 the first coffee-support programme was adopted by the state government a large number of new export houses appeared associated with the *comissários* and national exporters began to outnumber foreign dealers. Betralda Lopes, 'Comércio de Café, Através do Porto de Santos (1870–1974)', in E. Carone (org.), *O Café*, Anais do II Congresso de Historia de São Paulo (São Paulo, 1975) pp. 75–64.

9. A. Castro, *7 ensaios sobre a economia brasileira*, II, p. 61.
10. Until abolition new land was cleared and new coffee planted mostly by slaves or free *empreiteros*; thereafter immigrant labourers were used who usually became *colonos* later. On new plantations, the virgin soil yielded much more abundant food crops. J. P. Carvalho de Moraes, pp. 68–9; P. Denis, *Brazil*, p. 213; A. Ramos, *O café no Brasil, Relatório' Apresentado*, pp. 210–12; G. Maistrello, 'Fazendas de café-costumes, pp. 556–7, 572–3; São Paulo, Secretaria da Agricultura, *Inquérito Agricola* p. 43; J. Brandão Sobrinho, *Apreciação da situação agricola, zocotécnica, industrial e commercial em Riberão Preto* (São Paulo, 1903).
11. P. Denis, *Brazil*, pp. 206–7, who probably coined the term 'nomadism', reports that some 40 to 60 per cent of the labourers left their plantation each year. Even on one well-run estate, between 1895 and 1930, half the *colonos* stayed for less than 4.5 years. M. S. Beozzo Bassanezi, 'Fazenda Santa Gertrudis: uma abordagem quantitativa das relações de trabalho em uma propiedade rural paulista', doctoral dissertation, Faculdade de Filosofia, Ciencias e Letras de Rio Claro (1973) p. 153. W. G. McCreary and J. L. Bynum, *The Coffee Industry in Brazil*, US Dept of Commerce, Bureau of Foreign and Domestic Commerce, Trade Promotion Series 92 (Washington, 1930), p. 24 estimated that *colonos* with intercropping entitlements were paid approximately 25 per cent less for tending the coffee trees than those who were denied this possibility.
12. W. Cano, *Raízes da concentração*, p. 41, table 2.
13. A. Delfim Netto, 'Foundations, p. 66; C. C. Fraga, 'Resenha Histórica'.
14. A. Ramos in *O Estado de São Paulo* (28 May 1902) argued that planting continued.
15. A. de E. Taunay, *Pequena História*, p. 297; Prado attributed the difficulties coffee planters experienced during the first coffee crisis to excessively high interest rates (12 per cent) and high labour costs, advocating increased immigration. The *União dos Lavradores* (Association of Agriculturalists) in 1903 also opposed the law prohibiting new planting, at least until other estates agreed to ban planting. J. Love, *São Paulo in the Brazilian Federation 1889–1937* (Stanford University Press, 1980) p. 223.

16. F. Ferreira Ramos, *O Café, Contribuição para o Estudo da Crise* (São Paulo, 1902); this is a collection of articles published in the *Correio Paulistano* in 1901 and 1902. Francisco Ferreira Ramos was the brother of Augusto Ramos, the author of the classical study of coffee in Brazil and abroad.

17. For critical analyses of government intervention programmes in the coffee market see A. Delfim Netto, 'Foundations', C. M. Peláez, 'An economic analysis of the Brazilian Coffee Support Programme: theory, policy and measurement', in C. M. Peláez (ed.) *Essays on Coffee*; C. C. Fraga, 'Resenha Histórica'; C. Furtado, *The Economic Growth in Brazil* (University of California Press, 1963); W. Cano, *Raízes da concentração*, pp. 42–7.

18. M. Palacios, *Coffee in Columbia*.

19. C. C. Fraga, *Resenha Histórica*'; W. Cano, *Raízes da concentração*, pp. 41–4.

20. P. Denis, *Brazil*, p. 199.

21. C. F. de Lacerda, *Estudo da Meiação, Parceria, etc. e das suas Vantagens* (São Paulo, 1905) pp. 25–6; P. Denis, *Brazil*, p. 200.

22. J. P. Carvalho de Moraes, *Relatório apresentado*, p. 66; BUCICA (February 1903) p. 73.

23. M. S. Beozzo Bassanezi, 'Fazenda Santa Gertrudis'; W. Dean, *Rio Claro*, p. 170. These craftsmen were overseers, carpenters, stonemasons, pruners, operators of the coffee-processing machinery, ploughmen, etc. See also *Boletim do Departamento Estadual do Trabalho*, I (1 and 2) (1911–12) for a description of categories of labour.

24. P. Denis, *Brazil*, p. 216. As A. Ramos noted in *O café no Brasil*, 'The second disadvantage [of mechanical weeding] is of an economic order and is caused by the imbalance between the number of labourers needed for tending the coffee trees and those required for the harvest. This latter demand is much higher. In other words, in the interval between the harvests there is an excess of not a few workers of those used during the harvest and unless the estate has available supplementary jobs to occupy these, it will be unavoidable either to dismiss them with the risk of being short of labour during the following harvest, or to keep them paying them just the same. In this second case, having considerable time left over, the workers who do the weeding are not interested in the *carpideira* and disdain it' (p. 104).

25. M. Hall, 'The Origins', and M. Hall, 'Emigrazione italiana a San Paolo tra 1880 e 1920', *Quaderni Storico*, 25 (1974) for a more detailed account. These observers – mostly diplomatic personnel – were not opposed to emigration nor were they particularly hostile to São Paulo or Brazil but they considered the living and working conditions on the plantations unbearable, significantly worse than in other countries of large-scale Italian settlement. Perhaps the most famous report and which helped provoke the 1902 Italian ban on subsidised emigration to São Paulo, is A. Rossi, 'Condizioni dei coloni italiani nello stato di San Paolo', *Bollettino dell'Emigrazione*, 7 (1902).

26. S. Coletti, 'Lo stato di S.Paolo e l'emigrazione italiana', in Ministero degli Affari Esteri, *Emigrazione e colonie: raccolta di rapporti dei rr.*

agenti diplomatici e consolari (Rome 1908) vol. III, p. 375. Coletti argued that it was not the fall in prices but the acquisition of plantations at fabulous prices and the formation of new ones on credit at high interest rates which led planters into financial difficulties. See W. Dean, *Rio Claro* for a plantation which weathered the crisis well.

27. F. Mosconi, 'Le classe sociali nel Brasile e le loro funzioni', *La Riforma Sociali*, VII (1897); F. Dafert, 'A falta de trabalhadores agrícolas em São Paulo', in Instituto Agronómico, *Relatório* (1892) p.206; F. P. Lázaro Gonçalves, *Relatório apresentado*, pp. 10–11, on the problems of freedmen; L. Couty, *Etude de Biologie*, pp. 120–8; Congresso Agrícola 1878, p. 47. C. Vangelista, *Le Braccia per la Fazenda*, studies the movement of rural wages in relation to immigration into São Paulo. She argues that because wages did not always respond to labour supply it is unwarranted to speak of a free labour market in São Paulo agriculture in the early decades of the century. She sees this imperfect labour market as segmented into a sector of immigrant labour and another one of national workers. However, she neither explains this nor does she analyse the way in which the *colonato* system permitted the adjustment of money wages to coffee prices.

28. W. Dean, *Rio Claro*, pp. 181–4 suggests that the murder of Diogo Salles, the then President's brother, at the hands of the son of an Italian *colono* and the spectacular trial that followed contributed to the ban by Italy.

29. The letter by an Italian immigrant from the Veneto working on the estate Angelica in 1889 is probably exemplary in the way it reflects the profound disillusionment that followed the high hopes he had set in Brazil as a country of abundance and high earnings. 'Der Traum der weissen Sklaven-Brief eines italienischen Emigranten aus Brasilien', published with a commentary by Friederike Hausmann in *Freibeuter*, 30 (January 1987) pp. 101–10. It is taken from a collection of such letters published by E. Franzina, *Merica! Merica! Emigrazione e colonizzazione nelle lettere dei contadini veneti in America Latina 1876–1902* (Milan, 1979). Until the turn of the century Italian immigrants came predominantly from northern and central Italy and were of rural origin. E. Sori, *L'Emigrazione italiana dall'unitá alla seconda guerra mondiale* (Bologna, 1979)
T. Skidmore, *Black over White, Race and Nationality in Brazilian Thought* (Oxford 1974) p.136, suggests that Brazil was less successful than, for example, Argentina, in promoting its image abroad in the 1890s to attract immigrants.

30. By 1935 only a relatively small number of the 150 000 Japanese immigrants were working on coffee plantations. The largest group of Japanese were market gardeners for the city of São Paulo although most seem to have started out as wage earners. A smaller group grew coffee. maize, cotton and tea in the interior of the state while a last group had established themselves on a large settlement founded in 1912 on the coastal plain of Santos near Registro under a contract of the São Paulo government with a financial group in Japan. F. Maurette, *Some Social Aspects of Present and Future Economic*

Development in Brazil, ILO, Studies and Reports, Series B. 25 (Geneva 1937) pp. 93–4.

31. P. Denis, *Brazil*, p. 214. The average annual rate of immigration into São Paulo in the first decade of the century was somewhat under half that of the years preceding the war. W. Cano, *Raizes da concentração*, p. 308, Table 71.

32. T. W. Merrick and D. H. Graham, *Population and Economic Development in Brazil, 1800 to the Present* (Baltimore, 1979) p. 96. By comparison with Argentina and the United States, the return flow from Brazil was much less (21 per cent as compared with 33 per cent and 40 per cent respectively).

33. Quoted by P. Denis, *Brazil*, p. 226 from the Secretary of Agriculture's report for 1901 and 1904 respectively.

34. P. Denis, *Brazil*, pp. 227 and 231 for the colonies created by 1908 and the negative attitude of settlers toward plantation work. W. Dean, *Rio Claro*, p. 186 notes that in the county of Rio Claro which had more sponsored colonies than any other at the time, there were a total of 12 such settlements with some 1 800 families living on them at the turn of the century.

35. W. Cano, *Raízes da concentração*, p. 61; in 1905 the tariff was introduced on foodstuffs which raised prices but also stimulated production so that by the First World War Brazil was self-sufficient in maize, rice and beans. P. Denis, *Brazil*, pp. 202–3 and S. Coletti, 'Lo stato di S. Paolo e l'emigrazione', p. 41 note the value *colonos* attached to intercropping of foodstuffs.

In the above-mentioned letter ('Der Traum der weissen Sklaven') by an Italian immigrant on the estate Angelica which denounces the hardships he has encountered, little money, unbearable heat and a ceaseless struggle against the weeds which threaten to overtake all useful crops and which requires ceaseless hoeing, there is also a description of the foodstuffs he planted: maize, black beans, potatoes, tobacco, pumpkins, water and sweet mellons in the coffee rows and rice on a separate plot.

36. São Paulo, Secretaria da Agricultura, *Inquérito Agrícola*, pp. 29, 71; C. F. de Lacerda, *Estudo da Meiação*, p. 25 noted that 'at present the planter keeps the labour strictly necessary in order not to have his plantation deteriorate; and if, by chance, he needs an extra job to be done he will be forced to resort to wage labour.

37. A. Ramos, *O café no Brasil*, p. 106; A. Delfim Netto 'Foundations', pp. 65 and 126, notes the virtues of the *colonato* in allowing planters to reduce nominal wages.

38. The origin of these national small holders is yet unclear. A. A. Kageyama *et al.*, *Diferenciación campesina y cambio tecnológico: el caso de los productores de frijol en São Paulo*, I, p. 2. *L'Emigrazione Italiana dal 1910 al 1923*, pp. 294–5, note that during the war there were still very few smallholders of immigrant origin.

39. A. A. Kageyama *et al.*, *As Transformações na Estrutura Agrária Paulista, 1818–1976*, Unicamp, IFCH (Campinas, 1981) pp. 33–4.

40. A. A. Kageyama *et al.*, *As Transformações*, pp. 31–6 insist that the process began in the first decade of this century comparing the land-tenure structure of 1904–5 with that of 1939–40.
41. M. Hall. 'The Origins', pp.144–7 for a careful analysis of the evolution of wages at the time. Improving exchange rates at the turn of the century created a peculiar set of circumstances. It reduced planters' earnings from coffee in domestic currency. For the workers, the gold value of wages improved while the nominal value probably declined along with deteriorating working conditions. For a calculation of *colono* incomes on one estate between 1885 and 1911 see W. Dean, *Rio Claro*, p. 175 and P. Denis, *Brazil*, pp. 211–212 for the effect of rising exchange rates on wages. F. W. Dafert, *Ueber die gegenwaertige Lage*, p. 50 notes the financial burden planters brought on themselves by excessive borrowing when credit was abundant in the early 1890s and the advantage of paying labour in paper currency when the exchange rate was low.
42. C. F. de Lacerda, *Estudo da Meiação*, p. 7.
43. C. F. de Lacerda, *Estudo da Meiação*, p. 14; as he noted, 'sharecropping [was] a sure means to rid ourselves of the deficits and to guarantee a profit over expenses, whatever the price paid for coffee'. However, 'the idea of sharecropping, even if well received was considered impracticable by many planters. There was no lack of questions and objections regarding the ways and means required to reach a general agreement not only on the share but also on the work of processing and transport'.
    J. Brandão Sobrinho, *Apreciação da situação*, tried to demonstrate by means of complex cost-benefit calculations (which, however, rested on the false assumption of high product prices and low wages) that sharecropping was much more advantageous *for both planters and labourers*. For similar calculations see also 'L'Agricultura nello Stato di S. Paulo', *BUCICA*, II (5) (March 1903) pp. 94–101.
44. C. F. de Lacerda, *Estudo da Meiação*, p. 15.
45. C. F. de Lacerda, *A crise de lavoura. Estudo das causas da crise do café e dos meios de combatela* (São Paulo, 1903) pp. 4–5.
46. C. F. Lacerda, *Estudo da Meiação*, p. 13. Lacerda did suggest, in his essay *A crise de lavoura*, p. 8 that 'in order to valorise coffee it would be sufficient that Brazil refrained from harvesting one coffee crop; then we would have our fortune made. But the state and the railways ... would not be able to live, which is the reason why they demand such sacrifice of us.'
47. M. Piza, 'O trabalho na lavoura do café (1929) conference presented to the SRB that year, pp. 5–6.
48. See W. Dean, *Rio Claro*, pp. 179–83 for the nature of the conflicts between planters and labourers in the area of Rio Claro; for a more extensive analysis of forms of violence, conflicts and organisation of plantation labourers see M. Hall and V. Stolcke, 'Greves de *colonos* na Primeira República', CEDEC, II Seminário de Relações de Trabalho e Movimentos Sociais (São Paulo, 1979) (mimeo).

49. W. Cano, *Raízes da concentração*, p. 41, Table 2. Upon their arrival immigrants would prefer to work on established plantations but once they had gathered some experience they would endeavour to move to the frontier. P. Monbeig, *Pionniers et Planteurs a S. Paulo* (Paris, 1952) p. 156. Family composition and productive capacity also influenced mobility, small families tending to be less stable (M. S. Beozzo Bassanezi 'Fazenda Santa Gertrudis'.)

50. P. Denis, *Brazil*, pp. 206–7, who also pointed out that 'The crisis has brought to light the most serious danger of the policy of subsidised immigration. Not being proprietors themselves, the Italian colonists remain imperfectly bound to the soil. They have been given a subordinate place as labourers and they will only serve as long as they are offered generous terms . . . Moreover, every planter does his utmost to retain his staff. But the colonists are in love with their independence and refuse all arrangements for more than a year' (p. 217); also F. W. Dafert, *Ueber die gegenwaertige Lage*, p. 48

51. As S. Coletti, 'Lo stato di S. Paolo e l'emigrazione italiana', *Bollettino dell'Emigrazione*, 14, Part I (1908) noted, planters occasionally tried to retain their workers by delaying the settling of accounts, thereby preventing them from finding work on another plantation as the new crops had already been started.

52. There are colourful accounts in *Fanfulla* (5 October 1900 and 20 May, 6 July and 22 October 1901) of the murder of Almeida Prado.

53. W. Dean, *Rio Claro*, pp. 181–3.

54. From 1913 onward, the annual reports of the *Patronato Agrícola* published in the *Boletim do Departamento Estadual do Trabalho* and/or in the *Relatórios* of the São Paulo Department of Agriculture usually give the numbers of rural strikes brought to the attention of these agencies, and sometimes some additional information as well as other complaints by labourers or planters but, as W. Dean, *Rio Claro*, p. 179, notes, conflicts were not necessarily reported. Dean himself lists three strikes in the late nineties on the well-run plantation Sta. Gertrudis.

55. E. Bonardelli, *Lo stato di S. Paolo*, p. 68.

56. *La Barricata* (24 May 1913).

57. *L'Emigrazione Italiana dal 1910 al 1923*, p. 284.

58. E. Bonardelli, *Lo stato di S. Paolo*, p. 68.

59. E. Bonardelli, *Lo Stato di S. Paolo*, p. 68.

60. *L'emigrazione Italiana dal 1910 al 1923*, p. 286; E. Bonardelli, *Lo stato di S. Paolo*, p. 71.

61. *Boletim do Departamento Estadual do Trabalho*, VI (24) (1917).

62. The main contenders in this polemic are W. Dean, *Rio Claro*, M. Hall, 'The Origins' and M. Hall, 'Emigrazione italiana' on the side of the critics and on that of the defenders T. H. Holloway, 'The Coffee Colono in São Paulo, Brazil: Migration and Mobility, 1880–1930, in K. Duncan and I. Rutledge (eds), *Land and Labour in Latin America* (Cambridge 1977); T. H. Holloway, *Immigrants on the Land: Coffee and Society in São Paulo* (Chapel Hill, 1980); M. Font, 'Changing Patterns in the Social Organisation of the Coffee Sector in São Paulo,

1889–1930', paper presented at a seminar on 'Society and Politics in Export Economies', CEBRAP (São Paulo, 1982); M. Font, 'Planters and State: the Pursuit of Hegemony in São Paulo, Brazil, 1889–1930', Ph.D. Dissertation (University of Michigan, 1983)). And T. W. Merrick and D. H. Graham, *Population and Economic Development* who offer the most optimistic interpretation of all.

63. W. Dean, *Rio Claro*, p. 190; C. F. de Lacerda, *Estudo da Meiação*, p. 37, warned in 1903 of massive departures.

64. Quoted by T. H. Holloway, 'The Coffee Colono', p. 321 from A. Rossi, 'Condizioni dei Coloni'. It is very difficult but politically relevant, nonetheless, to enquire into the meaning of the desire for a piece of land of their own, so often attributed to the labourers. One possible interpretation is that they sought work and economic security when they left their country and once they had experienced life on the plantations they only hoped to escape the planters' oppression. One way was to own some land.

65. T. H. Holloway, 'The Coffee Colono', pp. 299–321; W. Dean, *Rio Claro*, p. 188, suggests that in the county of Rio Claro where coffee had penetrated in the last two decades of the nineteenth century, foreign landowners at least until 1919 were mostly town merchants and professionals from the start.

66. T. M. Holloway, 'The Coffee Colono', p. 314.

67. T. H. Holloway, 'Migration and Mobility: Immigrants as Labourers and Landowners in the Coffee Zone of São Paulo Brazil, 1886–1934', Ph.D. Dissertation (University of Wisconsin, 1974) p. 434.

68. M. Font, 'Changing Patterns'.

69. M. Font, 'Changing Patterns', p. 15 used as a basis the figures given by T. H. Holloway, 'Migration and Mobility', p. 436.

70. M. Font, 'Changing Patterns'.

71. J. Brandão Sobrinho, *Apreciação da situação*, p. 24, who noted, however, that the effect the different grains had on coffee yields varied. Beans use few soil nutrients and can be grown on land that is useless for other crops whereas maize is a more demanding grain, p. 35.

72. *L'emigrazione italiana dal 1910 al 1923*, p. 283.

73. *La Barricata*, 10 and 24 May 1913; E. Bonardelli, *Lo stato di S. Paulo*.

74. W. G. McCreery and M. L. Bynum, *The Coffee Industry*, pp. 18–19. On an average coffee trees continued to produce without fertilising for about 35 years. Yields began to fall off from the 15th year onward and decreased steadily thereafter. As long as new fertile land was available, planters saw no need to invest in soil conservation methods.

75. *Boletim do Departamento Estadual do Trabalho*, 12 and 13 (1914) pp. 800–1.

76. J. Papaterra Limongi, 'O trabalho agrícola no Brasil', *Boletim do Departamento Estadual do Trabalho*, VI (24) (1917) p. 460. See also (25) (1917) pp. 646–8 where the massive move of *colonos* to new areas is noted.

77. Planters could also eradicate the oldest trees on their plantations and thus maintain average yields, using particular care in cultivation as

some seem to have done, for instance, in the area of Socorro and Jundiai; P. Monbeig, *Pionniers*, p. 171.

78. *Boletim do Departamento Estadual do Trabalho*, VI (25) (1917) pp. 650–4.
79. Contract changes were also used to cheat labourers into staying on. *L'emigrazione italiana dal 1910 al 1923*, p. 306.
80. M. Font, 'Changing Patterns', p. 38.
81. M. Font, 'Changing Patterns', pp. 9–10.
82. M. Buesco, *Evolução Económica do Brasil*, 2nd edn (Rio de Janeiro, 1974) p. 126, quoted in A. A. Kageyama, *Crise e Estrutura Agrária, A agricultura paulista na década de 30*, Master's Dissertation, Escola Superior de Agricultura 'Luiz de Queiroz (Universidade de São Paulo, 1979).
83. M. Font, 'Changing Patterns', p. 7, Table 1.
84. J. de Souza Martins, *O Cativeiro da Terra*.
85. P. Monbeig, *Novos Estudos de Geografia Humana Brasileira* (São Paulo, 1957) p. 113.
86. *Boletim do Departamento Estadual do Trabalho*, VI (25) (1917) pp. 650–4; *Boletim* X (38–9) (1921) p. 100, where the break up of large plantations is deduced from an increase in the number of properties without a corresponding rise in the number of coffee trees in some areas; cf. also P. Monbeig, *Pionniers*, p. 172.
87. P. Monbeig, *Pionniers*, pp. 183–4.
88. P. Monbeig, *Pionniers*, pp. 182–4; R. H. P. L. de Albuquerque, 'Relações de produção na cotonicultura paulista', Unicamp (Campinas, 1982) (mimeo) pp. 21–2.
89. P. Monbeig, *Pionniers*, p. 172 noted that the situation on the eve of the 1929 depression was fundamentally different from that at the beginning of the century. By the 1920s many planters abandoned the older coffee regions where yields were low in search of virgin lands. For the rate of new coffee planting see W. Cano, *Raizes da Concentração*, p. 41. Table 2; for the distribution of coffee trees among the different regions see W. G. McCreery and M. L. Bynum, *The Coffee Industry*, pp. 69–75; M. Piza, 'O trabalho na lavoura', p. 9. Coffee prices doubled in 1919. When European markets reopened, a severe frost in 1918 had damaged millions of coffee trees in São Paulo; the 1918–19 harvest was the smallest since the 1890s. Supply fell when the world was feeling a true 'hunger for coffee'. (A. de E. Taunay, *Pequena História*, p. 408). While trees were recovering planters temporarily intercropped foodstuffs and even cotton. In 1920 prices went down again but recovered in 1923 and remained high until the 1929–30 collapse. E. P. Keeler, 'Cotton versus Coffee in Brazil', *Foreign Crops and Markets*, US Dept. of Agricultural Service Division, 31 (1935) pp. 815–36. W. Cano, *Raízes da Concentração*, p. 48 shows that beans, rice, maize *and* cotton increased substantially in the period 1919–1921.
90. *Boletim do Departamento Estadual do Trabalho*, VI (24) (1917) p. 457, notes that before the First World War several proposals had been made to attract and discipline national labourers, but to no avail. During the war national workers were hired and by the 1920s there

was a steady flow of these workers into São Paulo. Several sources note that there was no shortage of labour at the time, although coffee growers' needed to be responsive to the *colonos'* demands and there was considerable labour mobility. Moreover, the crisis in the textile industry improved labour supply in agriculture. Cf. the Secretary of Agriculture's Reports of 1928 and 1929 and W. G. McCreery and M. L. Bynum, *The Coffee Industry*, pp. 22–6. The 1929 Report, p. 223 informs that native labourers tended to work as casual peons and were regarded as even less stable than the *colonos*. Cf. *Boletim do Departamento do Trabalho Agrícola*, XXI (73–4) (1932) for propaganda on the virtues of national labour.

91. National labourers came to São Paulo to a significant extent from the Northeast where droughts and the end of the rubber boom around 1910 had produced widespread misery. *Boletim do Departamento do Trabalho Agrícola* XXI (72) (1932) pp. 9–10.

92. W. G. McCreery and M. L. Bynum, *The Coffee Industry*, p. 26; M. Piza, 'O trabalho na lavoura', p. 2.

93. J. W. F. Rowe, *Brazilian Coffee*, Royal Economic Society Memorandum 35 (London 1932) p. 12.

94. *Relatório da Secretaria da Agricultura* (1929) p. 222.

95. The American Consul in Rio de Janeiro noted in 1925 that 'the coffee planters are struggling with greatly increased labour costs'. He was presumably referring to the growers in the old coffee zone; US National Archives, microfilm 519, roll 23, frames 889–90: 'Wages and Labourers on Coffee Plantations. M. Font, 'Changing Patterns, pp. 51–3 gives the evolution of wages on two plantations: the *fazenda* Santa Gertrudis in the county of Rio Claro and the *fazenda* Star of the West, based on M. S. Beozzo Bassanezi, 'Fazenda Santa Gertrudis', and T. H. Holloway, *Immigrants on the Land* respectively. Both plantations are located in what was the declining region in the 1920s and in both instances wages increased markedly in that decade.

96. J. W. F. Rowe, *Brazilian Coffee*, p. 43.

97. S. Coletti 'Lo stato di S. Paolo', p. 381; *Relatório da Secretaria de Agricultura* (1929) pp. 223–4; as A. de E. Taunay, *Pequena História*, p. 428, noted, the President of the Republic, Washington Luiz, in 1930 maintained that the coffee crisis had been solved because although coffee prices had slumped by 35 to 40 per cent, planters had cut wages by the same proportion allowing *colonos* to intercrop foodstuffs instead.

98. P. Monbeig, *Novos Estudos de Geografia Humana*, p. 116. Settlement companies often only demanded an initial down-payment upon signature of the contract. The outstanding amount was to be paid in instalments with the returns from the farmers' future crops.

99. P. Monbeig, *Novos Estudos*; J. W. F. Rowe, *Brazilian Coffee*, for a description of the regions where this occurred; A. A. Kageyama, 'Crise e Estrutura Agrária, p. 84 shows that between 1930–1 and 1931–2 the absolute number of properties owned by foreigners in São Paulo increased by over 25 per cent (from 56 540 to 70 920). The percentage of foreign-owned farms in the total number of properties remained the

same, however, and the proportion of land occupied by foreign-owned farms in the total area occupied increased only from 25.1 per cent to 26.4 per cent.

100. J. W. F. Rowe, *Brazilian Coffee*, pp. 12, 52–3. Rowe's is the best contemporary description of the crash and the earlier and subsequent price-support schemes. Rowe was a colleague of Keynes in Cambridge and a staunch defender of market intervention against its critics, the advocates of *laissez-faire*; as he argued in 1932, *laissez-faire* with regard to coffee would have resulted in a social catastrophe. It would have swept away coffee planters, bankers and coffee brokers. He was in strong disagreement with Sir Otto E. Niemeyer, a Director of the Bank of England, who also visited Brazil in 1931 and was extremely critical of what he regarded as Brazil's misplaced efforts in the form of the price-support programmes to produce goods for which there was no demand, instead of promoting other, more diversified crops: 'Report submitted to the Brazilian Government' by Sir Otto E. Niemeyer, KCG, GBE (London 1931).

101. Average export prices in domestic currency had dropped 44 per cent between 1890 and 1902–6, a decline equal to that between 1929 and 1930. The fall in average export prices in gold sterling was somewhat greater, namely 51 per cent in each period. Also, by 1929 average export prices in gold sterling were higher than those paid in 1890. W. Cano, *Raízes da concentração*, 41, Table 20.

102. 1928 had seen the largest coffee harvest ever in São Paulo amounting to 18 million bags: W. Cano, *Raízes da Concentração*, p. 41, Table 2; in 1938–9 Brazil's exportable coffee production amounted still to 23 million bags, produced predominantly in São Paulo, Brazil, *Anuário Estadístio do Café*, Coordenadoria de Estudos da Economía Cafeeira. 11 (Rio de Janeiro, December 1977) p. 53.

103. J. W. F. Rowe, *Brazilian Coffee*, p. 57.

104. C. Furtado, *The Economic Growth in Brazil*, especially Part V.

105. C. M. Peláez, 'An economic analysis'.

106. J. L. Love, *São Paulo in the Brazilian Federation*; M. L. Coelho Prado. *A Democracia Ilustrada, São Paulo, 1926–1934*. Doctoral Dissertation, (University of São Paulo). We know little about the associational structure of the agricultural sector. J. L. Love, *São Paulo in the Brazilian Federation*, pp. 219–29, shows that all associations that sprang up until the 1930s did so in response to a particular economic conjuncture which demanded concerted action. All organisations were led by powerful planters and politically relevant differences among their associates are not immediately apparent; sometimes different organisations were led by the same men. The *Sociedade Nacional de Agricultura* (National Society for Agriculture) founded in Rio de Janeiro in 1897 was followed in 1902 by the *Sociedade Paulista de Agricultura* established by powerful coffee producers and brokers to deal with the crisis and the flow of immigrants. The *Sociedade Rural Brasileira* was founded in 1919 by coffee planters, exporters and representatives of foreign meat-packing houses in the context of the

crisis in international trade produced by the First World War. And the *Liga Agrícola Brasileira* established in 1921 organised opposition against the export levy.

107. This party's programme advocated getting rid of bankers and agents, demanded a moratorium, condemned high taxes on coffee exports and appealed for the abolition of all export levies. The party was, however, defeated in the elections. M. L. Coelho Prado, *A Democracia Ilustrada*. J. L. Love *São Paulo in the Brazilian Federation*, p. 228.

108. J. L. Love, *São Paulo in the Brazilian Federation*; Antonio Prado was among the founders of the PD; beside growing coffee he was partner of the coffee export firm Prado Chaves Exportadora, banker and industrialist. D. E. Levi, *A família Prado* (São Paulo, 1977).

109. Otavio Alves de Lima, for instance, was a planter-merchant associated with coffee-export interests, Director of the daily *Folha da Manhã* through which he was the first to attack Vargas's economic policy, had been director of the Banco Noroeste in the 1920s and was President of the *Cooperativa de Cafeicultores do Estado de São Paulo*. M. L. Coelho Prado, *A Democracia Ilustrada*. The organisation that preceded the *Federação* also had a hand in the São Paulo banker, Whitaker's, resignation as first Finance Minister of the Provisional government when it accused him, as well as the newly founded National Coffee Council, of being out to destroy coffee agriculture by imposing the tax in gold instead of raising resources for price support by printing money.

110. Also in 1930 the *Associação Commercial de Santos* (ACS) (the Association of Merchants of Santos) proposed to the São Paulo Finance Secretary to exchange low-grade coffee in Santos for 'milds' and to incinerate the former. The SRB opposed this proposal making at least three alternative suggestions: (1) to ship the whole 1929 crop to Santos in order to re-establish confidence in the market, to improve the financing of coffee production and reactivate trade, (2) the partial destruction of one crop presumably exempting high-grade coffees and (3) the eradication of old coffee groves to the benefit of the new trees. M. L. Coelho Prado, *A Democracia Ilustrada*.

111. P. Prado, 'O martyrio do café' in P. Prado, *Paulística História de São Paulo* (Rio de Janeiro, 1934), p. 217.

112. *Revista da Sociedade Rural Brasileira* (RSRB) (October 1934, p.6; November 1934, p. 54 and December 1934, pp. 12–17) which reproduces a Memorandum addressed jointly to the Federal Foreign Trade Council (*Conselho Federal de Commercio Exterior*) by the SRB, the ACS, the *Centro de Comissários de Café de Santos* (CCCS) and the *Centro de Exporta dores de Café de Santos* (CECS) demanding that constraints on trading coffee below type 8 be lifted since they had neither reduced production nor improved the quality of coffee; *RSRB* (March 1935) p. 6. The demand was reiterated at an ordinary meeting of the association.

113. *RSRB* (February 1935) p. 34, (March 1935) p. 24. As some members of the association argued, although the onus of exchange confiscation

had diminished, withheld exchange still benefited those importing luxury goods.

114. *RSRB* (February 1935), they demanded the extinction of the National Coffee Department which had only disrupted the coffee market with its unfortunate interventions. The state coffee institutes were perfectly qualified to implement coffee policy, p. 29. Pp. 54–66 reproduces a speech by the São Paulo Deputy to the Federal Chamber of Deputies, Cincinato Braga, on 14 February 1935. He denounced the supertaxation of coffee planters as the 'greatest evil' because heavy levies on coffee only served to protect foreign competitors. What was required, instead, was to free coffee exports. Braga presented a bill reducing the export tax considerably, eliminating the compulsory sale of foreign exchange to the Bank of Brazil and suggesting a new tax of 3 Shillings to be applied for servicing the foreign loan obtained in 1930 for coffee defence. In 1935 one of the Directors of the National Coffee Department died and was replaced by Cesario Coimbra, the President of the São Paulo Coffee Institute and former President of the SRB. The government clearly wanted to gain the coffee sector's support, but in August of the same year, the Directors of the Department resigned, including Coimbra. A. de E. Taunay, *Pequena História*, p. 475.

115. *RSRB* (May 1935) pp. 20–5.
116. M. Palacios, *Coffee in Colombia*.
117. *RSRB* (October 1936) p. 22.
118. *RSRB* (August 1937) p. 52. See also *RSRB* (May 1937) for the reproduction of a Memorandum by the association to the State Governor demanding free trade.
119. An additional grievance at that point for São Paulo coffee planters seems to have been the more favourable shipping conditions granted coffee from other producing states. *RSRB* (April 1939) pp. 40–5.
120. *RSRB* (March 1939) Editorial; (April 1939) p. 44.
121. E. Carone, *O Estado Novo (1937–1945)* (Rio de Janeiro, 1976) p. 34.
122. The sharp decline in cotton prices beginning in 1940–1 also worsened the situation for planters who had moved into cotton growing.
123. Every coffee crisis had been followed by an International Coffee Conference, as in 1902 and 1931. The first Pan-American Coffee Conference was held in Bogotá in 1936 but failed; in 1937 a Pan-American Conference was held in Havana. Only the third Pan-American Conference produced an agreement on coffee market control. A. Delfim Netto, 'Sugestões para uma política cafeeira', in the Brazilian Coffee Institute's *Curso de Economia Cafeeira* (1962) II; Peláez has suggested that the 1940 agreement was no selfless gesture on the part of the United States to protect its American neighbours from disaster but a shrewd move to ensure Latin America's allegiance during the war. C. M. Peláez, 'The Inter-American coffee agreement and Brazilian coffee during World War II', in C. M. Peláez (ed.), *Essays on Coffee*, p. 253.
124. E. Carone, *A Estado Novo*, pp. 33–5.
125. E. Carone, *A Estado Novo*, pp. 20–1; C. M. Peláez, 'The Inter-American coffee agreement; W. Cano, *Raízes da Concentração*, p. 41 estimates the

decline in coffee trees in São Paulo between 1935 and 1942, however, at 384 million trees.
126. J. W. F. Rowe, *Brazilian Coffee*, p. 75–6.
127. *RSRB* (February 1930) p. 806.
128. UK Dept of Overseas Trade, *Economic Conditions in Brazil* (December 1932) p. 34.
129. *RSRB* (January 1931) p. 44. Planters were probably especially incensed by this criticism, which appeared in the *Diário de São Paulo*, because it came from one of their own class. The author of the article was Cicero da Silva Prado, the son of Martinho da Silva Prado who had done so much as founder of the SPI, for subsidised immigration. *RSRB* (December 1930) p. 1376; Cicero da Silva Prado proposed that a minimum wage be fixed for rural labourers because, 'a country's prosperity depended on the living standard of its inhabitants'.
130. UK Dept. of Overseas Trade, *Economic Conditions in Brazil* (December 1930) (London, 1931) p. 35.
131. W. G. McCreery and M. L. Bynum, *The Coffee Industry*, p. 26.
132. J. W. F. Rowe, *Brazilian Coffee* pp. 57, 76.
133. In 1931 out of a total 2603 legal complaints by rural labourers that reached the São Paulo Labour Department, 2121 were over delays in the payment of wages. *Boletim do Trabalho Agrícola*, 172 (1932) p. 17; *RSRB* (October 1933) p. 534; M. Piza, at a weekly meeting of the SRB stressed that coffee production was in need of new labourers because in view of low wages many *colonos* were abandoning their plantations to establish themselves on their own.
134. F. Maurette, *Some Social Aspects of Present and Future Economic Development in Brazil.*
135. In 1937–8 coffee production in São Paulo was still 14 per cent higher than in 1930–1, A. A. Kageyama, 'Crise e estrutura agrária', p. 103.
136. *RSRB* (December 1933), p. 676; in 1931 a project had been submitted to the SRB for the eradication of 400 million coffee trees against compensation in coffee by the Coffee Institute; in late 1933 a new plan was proposed for subsidised eradication by another member of the association. However, the SRB did not agree to attack the oversupply crisis at its root; not even in 1936 when foreign competition became intense was eradication accepted as solution. *RSRB* (October 1936), p. 22. In the neighbouring state of Paraná which was partly exempted from the prohibition, coffee planting had begun in the 1920s; it continued throughout the 1930s mostly on rich, red soils; by 1939 the state had about 61 million coffee trees. J. W. F. Rowe, *Brazilian Coffee*, p. 34.
137. A. A. Kageyama, 'Crise e estructura agrária', p. 109. In absolute numbers 288 834 coffee trees were abandoned between 1930–1 and 1935–6 as compared to almost 1 500 000 trees under production in the latter year; in the same period 835 458 new trees were planted. See also J. W. F. Rowe, *Brazilian Coffee*, p. 13.
138. A. A. Kageyama, 'Crise e Estructura Agrária', pp. 35–8 for a survey of these positions; P. Monbeig, *Novos Estudos*, pp. 113ff. stresses the disruptive effect of the crisis on the prevailing property structure; A. V.

Vilela and W. Suzigan, *Política do Governo e Crescimento da Economía Brasileira, 1889–1945* (Rio de Janeiro, 1973) have more recently restated this optimistic position. See also J. de Souza Martins, 'As relaçoes de classe e a produção ideológica da noção do trabalho', *Contexto*, 5 (São Paulo, 1978) p. 51, attributing the increase in smallholdings to the combined effect of fragmentation of large estates and the continued move to the frontier.

139. S. Milliet, *Roteiro do Café* (São Paulo, 1939).
140. A. Cándido, *Os Parceiros do Rio Bonito* (Rio de Janeiro, 1964).
141. S. Milliet, *Roteiro do Café*, p. 107. Milliet's analysis of the spread of smallholdings in the early 1930s was obviously inspired by his antagonism to the coffee latifundia. Milliet traces the numerical evolution of landholdings of different sizes between 1930–1 and 1935–6 but unfortunately has no figures on shifts in the area under the different categories. He classified holdings into four categories by size:

Smallholdings	up to 60.5 ha
Medium-holdings	62.9–242 ha
Large holdings	244.1–1210 ha
Latifundia	over 1210 ha

Milliet's four categories are given in *alqueires* (1 alq = 2.32 ha) D. A. Romão, 'Do auto-consumo a produção' has suggested that at least four different types of small production emerged between 1930 and 1960: sharecroppers on large estates, squatters on the frontier, smallholders on official settlement schemes and, to a lesser degree, small properties that resulted from the fragmentation of large estates due to the decline in their main activity (p. 31).

142. A. A. Kageyama, 'Crise e estructure agrária', p. 1430.
143. *RSRB* (November 1935), pp. 12–14. In a joint memorandum by the *Centro dos Comissarios de Café de Santos* (CCCS) (Centre of Santos Coffee Brokers), the SRB, the ACS and the *Centro dos Exportadores de Café de Santos* (CECS) (Centre of Santos Coffee Exporters) addressed to the National Coffee Department on 16 October 1935, these associations demanded the partial suspension of a 1930 prohibition of low-grade coffee exports arguing that this was the only quality that because of its price, could successfully compete with African and Java coffee. At no time during the 1930s did large coffee interests in the SRB voice any antagonism toward small domestic coffee producers.
144. *RSRB* (June 1930) p. 1064, and (November 1930) p. 1358.
145. J. F. Normano, *Brazil: A Study of Economic Types* (North Carolina 1935) p. 55. The UK Consular Report of December 1930 noted that 'Efforts are being made to improve the position not only in regard to the quality of the raw product and the various treating processes, but also by closing down unprofitable plantations and by putting the whole business on a really sound basis. Foremost in the general reconstruction – besides the purely technical improvement founded and supported by the planters, but in the management of which they have nothing to say, as it had in raising, harvesting, treating and

selecting the brands – is the proper financing of planting and the final disposing of the formerly not always carefully handled stores in warehouses, the entire reorganisation of the Coffee Institute, founded and supported by the planters, but in the management of which they have nothing to say, as it had passed into the hands of the government. With this change it is firmly believed that the coffee production of this state will soon regain its predominance upon the world's market'. UK Dept of Overseas Trade, *Economic Conditions in Brazil*, December 1930 (London 1931), p. 72.

146. A. A. Kageyama, 'Crise e Estrutura Agrária, p. 122; cotton production in São Paulo rose by over 2 000 per cent.

147. A. V. Vilela and W. Suzigan, *Politica do Governo*, A. A. Kageyama, 'Crise e estrutura agrária, p. 45.

148. E. P. Keeler, 'Cotton versus Coffee'. As Keeler noted, 'While labour and capital already established in the coffee industry may be expected to shift only slowly from coffee into cotton inasmuch as a coffee plantation represents an investment of around 5 years' time until the trees come into bearing, it may be expected that new capital, labour and land will be turned to cotton rather than coffee at times when cotton prices are favourable in relation to coffee prices' (p. 823).

149. S. Milliet, *Roteiro do Café*, p. 66; A. A. Kageyama, 'Crise e Estrutura agrária'; F. Maurette, *Some Social Aspects*, for a description of differing production structures of three plantations located in different regions.

150. R. H. P. L. de Albuquerque, 'Relações de produção'; D. A. Romão 'Do auto-consumo a produção'; A. A. Kageyama, 'Crise e estrutura agrária', p. 132 have all interpreted these sharecropping or small tenancy arrangements as forms of risk sharing adopted by landowners for crops of uncertain results, in the case of cotton attributed in part to the climatic vulnerability of the crop. M. R. G. Loureiro, *Capitalismo e Parceria* (Rio de Janeiro, 1977) has underlined, by contrast, the efficiency of sharecropping in reducing labour costs.

151. Rural wages are said to have risen by about 30 to 40 per cent by 1935, *RSRB* (November 1934) p. 52, (February 1935) p. 59, (March 1935) p. 29; from 1933 onward there is talk of labour scarcity in industry as well as agriculture, UK Dept of Overseas Trade, reports on *Economic Conditions in Brazil* for 1934 to 1938; F. Maurette, *Some Social Aspects*, p. 73 notes the competition for labour between coffee and cotton; see also E. P. Keeler 'Cotton versus Coffee'; a family labour system was recognised as being as advantageous for cotton as it had proved to be for coffee. In the *Boletim do Departamento Estadual do Trabalho*, XXII (1933) p. 65, it was stressed that 'it is evident that for the [yearly cultivation] the owner of the coffee grove, the cotton field, the cane field or the banana grove always prefers families of workers rather than casual labour'. It has been estimated that in 1940 there were three small tenants for each sharecropper in São Paulo. Both cultivated between 10 to 15 ha. Small tenants paid a fixed rent in advance and sharecroppers handed over a proportion of the product. Because small tenants often lacked resources of their own they operated with credit from shopkeepers. Some of the tenants had been smallholders

who preferred to cultivate better land under a tenancy arrangement. Sharecroppers were permitted intercropping of foodstuffs with cotton when soils were poor rather than increasing their share in the product. R. H. P. L. de Albuquerque, 'Relações de produção', pp. 20–8.

152. UK Dept of Overseas Trade, *Economic Conditions in Brazil*, September 1935 (London 1936) p. 41.
153. Nortz, a representative of North American coffee importers, visited São Paulo coffee regions in late 1937 and wrote: 'the large plantations are disappearing, fragmented into smallholdings . . . As in other countries, the times of great feudal lords, dominating large areas, and with an active voice in politics, are coming to an end'. But neither had coffee planters been feudal lords nor was there such widespread fragmentation and loss of political power. The President of the National Coffee Department in 1936 seemed to share this view; in his inaugural speech he emphasised the change that coffee cultivation had undergone; small properties were said to have increased enormously overtaking the latifundia. A. de E. Taunay, *Pequena História*, pp. 456, 510.
154. A. de E. Taunay, *Pequena História*, p. 502; UK Dept of Overseas Trade, *Economic Conditions in Brazil*, September 1935 (London 1936) p. 41.
155. A. A. Kageyama, 'Crise e estructura agrária', p. 130 suggests that food production in São Paulo stagnated in the period, i.e. did not accompany the 17 per cent population growth in the state in the 1930s.
156. UK Dept of Overseas Trade, *Report on Economic and Commercial Conditions in Brazil*, September 1936 (London 1937) p. 6, notes that cotton planting has not only caused an acute shortage of agricultural labour but, by occupying land formerly used for other crops had led to a shortage of grains and a corresponding rise in the cost of living.
157. *RSRB* (February 1935) p. 62.
158. E. Carone, *O Estado Novo* p. 120; UK Dept of Overseas Trade, Consular Reports on the *Economic Conditions in Brazil* (1934, 1935, 1936, 1937 and 1938) all stress labour shortages; F. Maurette, *Some Social Aspects*, notes a wage increase, competition for labour between cotton and coffee, and rural exodus.
159. Caio Prado Jr, 'Contribuição para a análise da questão agrária no Brasil', *Revista Brasiliense*, 28 (1960) pp. 181–205, for an example of the classical position on the incompatibility of cash crops for export and food crops.
160. A. Ellis Jr, *A Evolução da Economia Paulista e suas Causas* (São Paulo, 1937) pp. 453–4.
161. P. Prado, 'O martyrio do Café', p. 217.

3 The Transition: From *Colonos* to Wage Labour

1. P. Singer, 'Os novos nómades', II, *Movimento*, 18 (1975), J. F. Graziano da Silva, 'Progresso técnico e relações de trabalho na agricultura

paulista', Doctoral Dissertation, (Universidade Estadual de Campinas, 1980) pp. 162–3. For the figures on the composition of the labour force on São Paulo coffee plantations in 1958 see 'A indústria do café em São Paulo', *ASP*, VIII (3) (March 1961) p. 17.

2. Until the early 1950s sugar cane in São Paulo was also cultivated by *colonos*. A. F. Cesarino Jr, 'Os colonos paulistas e sua situação em face do estatuto da lavoura canavieira', *Trabalho e Seguro Social*, IV (1) (October 1943) describes the arrangement under which the sugar-cane *colono* worked. They were paid for the sugar-cane they delivered. All other contractual conditions were the same as in coffee, including self-provision. In the early 1940s over half of the sugar cane grown in the counties of Piracicaba and Santa Barbara was produced by *colonos*. There is little information on the way productive relations evolved on São Paulo sugar-cane plantations. O. Ianni, *A Classe Operária Vai ao Campo*, Caderno CEBRAP; 24 (São Paulo, 1976), a historical study of one sugar-cane area, Sertãozinho, lacks information on the labour process. We can only speculate. In 1968 labour needs for sugar-cane production compared with coffee were 1:4. ('A nova face da agricultura', *Coopercotia* (October 1968) p. 16) indicating a high level of mechanisation since sugar cane grown manually is even more labour-intensive than coffee. By contrast with Pernambuco, the traditional sugar-cane producing state, the topography of São Paulo is more appropriate for mechanisation of cultivation. R. Miller Paive, S. Schatten and C. F. Trench de Freitas, *Sector Agrícola do Brasil* (São Paulo, 1976) p. 170. On new sugar-cane plantations, soil was presumably already prepared with the aid of ploughs and tractors in the 1950s cane being planted in large continuous areas rather than by individual *colono* families. Labour needs for soil preparation thus diminished markedly while remaining unchanged for the harvest. Sugar-cane plantations would, therefore, increasingly hire casual wage labour for seasonal peaks, using resident workers for soil preparation and cane planting. *The Estatuto da Lavoura Canavieira* of 1943 may have played a relevant role in putting an end to the sugar-cane *colono*. J. C. Saboia, 'De senhores a trocadores de cebola', Master's Dissertation, Universidade Estedual de Campinas', (Campinas, 1978) has shown that in Cravinhos, bordering on Sertãozinho, where sugar cane and food crops replaced coffee, planters and labour contractors dated the appearance of gangs of casual wage labourers hired through a labour contractor to the 1940s. See also O. J. Thomazini Ettori, 'Mão-de-obra na agricultura paulista', *ASP, VIII* (12) (December 1961), p. 16, who noted the existence of *colonos* on sugar-cane plantations in 1955. 'Situação e perspectivas da produção café no estado de São Paulo', *ASP*, IX (4) (1962) p. 29 notes that the expansion of sugar cane in São Paulo between 1948 and 1952 was made possible also by substantial capital investment in mechanisation of the crop which came to occupy the second place in value in the state. But more research is required.

3. Reviews of existing literature on the casualisation of rural labour are: J. Gomez da Silva and V. L. G. da Silva Rodrigues, ' "O bóia-fria":

contradições de uma agricultural em tentativa de desenvolvimento', *Reforma Agrária*, V (9–10) (September/October 1975) pp. 2–44. D. Goodman and M. Redclift, 'The "bóia-fria": rural proletarianisation and urban marginality in Brazil', *International Journal of Urban and Regional Research*, I (2) (1977) pp. 348–64; W. S. Saint, 'The wages of modernization: a review of the literature on temporary labour arrangements in Brazilian agriculture', *Latin American Research Review*, 3 (1981) pp. 91–110. A series of conferences held by the São Paulo State University in Botucatú between 1975 and 1980, played an important part in the debate on the emergence of the *volante*. Cf. Universidade Estadual Paulista, *A Mão-de-Obra Volante na Agricultura* (São Paulo, 1982). D. Goodman and M. Redclife, *From Peasant to Proletarian: Capitalist Development and Agrarian Transitions* (Oxford, 1981) contains a long essay, 'Brazil: towards the intensive agricultural frontier', dealing with the emergence of casual wage labour. Most of the research focuses on the state of São Paulo. A very valuable exception is L. Sigaud, *Os Clandestinos e os Direitos, Estudo sobre Trabalhadores de Cana-de-Açucar de Pernambuco* (São Paulo, 1979).

4. S. G. Vassimon, 'Ruptura da mentalidade patriarcal', *Coopercotia* (October 1968) pp. 22–3; 'A nova face da agricultura', *Coopercotia* (October 1968) pp. 14–21; S. G. Vassimon, 'Estudo preliminar sobre o problema da mão-de-obra volante na agricultura do estado de São Paulo' (São Paulo: CERU/University of São Paulo, 1969) (mimeo); R. Miller Paiva, S. Schattan and C. F. Trench de Freitas, *Setor Agrícola do Brasil*, pp. 93–4.

5. J. F. Graziano da Silva, 'Progresso técnico e relações de trabalho na agricultura paulista'.

6. V. Caldeira Brant, 'Do colono ao bóia-fria: transformações na agricultura e constituição de mercado de trabalho na Alta Sorocabana de Assis', *Estudos CEBRAP*, 19 (São Paulo, January/March 1977) pp. 37–92.

7. P. Singer, 'Os novos nómades', p. 7.

8. M. C. D'Incão e Mello, *O Bóia-Fria: Acumulação e Miséria* (Petrópolis, 1975).

9. V. Caldeira Brant, 'Do colono ao bóia-fria' is probably the only author who makes an attempt to take into account the politics of proletarianisation and in particular landowners' reactions to the Rural Labour Statute.

10. V. Caldeira Brant, 'Do colono ao bóia-fria', p. 70.

11. 'A indústria do café em São Paulo', p. 41, attributes low mechanisation to 'the difficulty in mechanising the main tasks, especially the harvest which absorbs on average about 40 per cent of the labour. Since there is plenty of labour on the estate to ensure that the harvest is carried out in time, planters are not interested in mechanising weeding which is done during the rest of the year. In addition, the high cost of machinery compared with the low cost of labour is one of the main factors discouraging the mechanisation of coffee production'. J. F. Graziano da Silva, 'Progresso técnico', pp. 152–3, appears to share Brant's view and interprets the said incompatibility of the *colonato*

system with the use of machinery *not* as an expression of the planters' interest in the full utilisation of the *colonos'* family labour throughout the year but as caused by a general shortage of labour which prevented planters from dismissing the workers that would have been made redundant by weeding with cultivators.

12. M. C. D'Incão e Mello, *O Bóia-Fria*.
13. D. Goodman and M. Redclift, 'The "Bóia-Fria"' made this point.
14. P. Singer, 'Os novos nómades'. Other authors, however, have more recently suggested food production for the domestic market did not participate in the process of capitalisation of agricultural production which was primarily confined to cash crops for export. O. Queda, A. A. Kageyama and J. F. Graziano da Silva, *Evolução recente das culturas de arroz e feijão no Brazil* (Brasilia, Ministério da Agriculture, 1979).
15. J. F. Graziano da Silva, 'Progresso técnico', p. 168.
16. UN, ECLA, *The Economic Development of Brazil* (New York, 1956) vol. 2: Analyses and projections of economic development, pp. 4, 9. L. Sola, 'The political and ideological constraints to economic management in Brazil, 1945–1963', Doctoral Dissertation (Oxford University, 1982) p. 26.
17. The Economic Development Bank was to become the stage for the most ardent clashes between different more or less 'nationalist' conceptions of development held in Brazil. L. Sola, 'The political and ideological constraints'; UN, ECLA, *The Economic Development of Brazil*. The study of São Paulo coffee in UN, *Coffee in Latin America*, Productivity Problems and Future Prospects, II (Brazil, São Paulo) ((1) The state and prospects of production, Mexico, 1960 (hereafter UN FAO, *Coffee in Latin America* (1) and (2) A. Case study of 33 coffee farms, B. Analysis of the functions of productions, Mexico, 1960 (hereafter UN FAO, *Coffee in Latin America* (2)). Both reports were also published in São Paulo in consecutive issues of *ASP* under the general titles 'Café' no estado de São Paulo: situação e perspectivas de producção' in 1961 and 1962 and 'Estudo de 33 propiedades cafeeiras típicas do estado de São Paulo', in 1962.
18. O. Gouvêa de Bulhões, *A Margem de um Relatório* (Rio de Janeiro, 1950) p. 162.
19. Joint Brazil/United States Economic Development Commission, *The Development of Brazil*, Report by the Joint Brazil/United States Economic Development Commission (1954). P. Malan *et. al.*, *Política Económica Externa e Industrialização no Brasil (1939–1952)* (Rio de Janeiro, 1977) pp. 47–56 for a discussion of the report produced by the first Brazil/United States technical mission, called the Abbink Mission, which preceded this Commission in 1948.
20. Brazil, Comissão de Desenvolvimento Industrial, *O Problema da Altimentação no Brazil* (Rio de Janeiro, 1954), Relatório Klein and Saks. Already in 1945, Brazilian industrialists and representatives of agriculture at a meeting in Teresópolis on the state of the Brazilian economy diagnosed as one of the principal needs the expansion of food production. At a second congress of 'producing classes' held in

Araxá in 1949, the first point on the agenda was again the problem of food supply for the domestic market. *Carta Económica de Teresópolis* (1945) Conferencia das Classes Productoras do Brasil, Teresópolis (1945); Conferencia Nacional das Classes Productoras, Araxá (1949); the food-supply problem was diagnosed as follows: 'Point one concerns the supply of foodstuffs for the domestic market and more especially for the towns. It implies two problems: one is an emergency concerning the present shortage of foodstuffs, the other refers to normal supply once this period of difficulties is over... The supply problem affects the whole cycle from production to distribution to the consumer' (p. 4).

21. M. Edel, *Food Supply and Inflation in Latin America* (New York, 1969) UN ECLA, *The Economic Development of Brazil.*

22. A. A. Kageyama *et al.*, 'As transformações', pp. 39–40. This study refers to the state of São Paulo.

23. The amount of foodstuffs produced for self-provisioning presumably is not included in the aggregate figures used by the UN ECLA, *The Economic Development of Brazil*, and M. Edel, *Food Supply.*

24. W. Baer, *A Industrialização e o Desenvolvimento Económico do Brasil* (Rio de Janeiro, 1975) pp. 133–5.

25. G. Vargas, *O Governo Trabalhista do Brasil* (Rio de Janeiro, 1954) II, p. 433.

26. G. Vargas, *O Governo Trabalhista* (1954), II, p. 344. *Hispanic American Report (HAR)*, VI (5) (May 1953) p. 40. In 1953 Rio's shanty-towns accommodated a reported 340 000 people. In 1954 several instances were noted of evictions of shanty-town dwellers in Rio. Brazil, Cámara dos Deputados, *Anais* (1954) II (1–20) (April 1954).

27. E. Lodi in an interview published in *Cidade de Barbacena* (23 April 1953) under the title 'Façamos a revolução pela comida'.

28. Similar contradictions can be detected elsewhere in Vargas' speeches.

29. Bill No. 3. 406 1953. M. C. Soares D'Araújo, *O Segundo Governo Vargas*: 1951–1954: Democracia, Partidos, e Crise Política (Rio de Janeiro, 1982) pp. 94–6.

30. Message No. 124 1954 which became bill No. 4264/54 which extended the benefits of the *Consolidação das Leis do Trabalho* (CLT) passed in 1943. The renowned lawyer, Cesarino Jr, an active advisor to the *Confederação Nacional da Industria* (CNI), was very critical of this bill because of its many imprecisions. *Folha de São Paulo*, 6 April 1954. Vargas's first Labour Minister was Danton Coelho of the PTB who had resigned in protest over Vargas's conciliatory politics. Vargas nominated the lawyer, Segadas Vianna, in his place and requested him to create yet another commission to study the extension of the labour laws to agricultural workers. It drafted two bills, one regarding the legal protection of rural workers the other regulating sharecropping contracts. J. de Segadas Vianna, *O Estatuto do Trabalhador Rural e sua Aplicação* (Rio de Janeiro, 1965) p. 39. The same year, at the opening session of the Fifth Conference of American States members of the ILO in Petrópolis Vargas had declared:... it is our lively

concern to receive suggestions that will allow us to achieve more rapidly and easily that which is today our principal national and governmental goal, namely to effectively make extensive the social legislation that protects the urban proletariat, to rural workers, modify the production methods and economic relations that prevail in agriculture . . . we need to create a less unjust system of distribution of the fruits of agricultural labour and extend to the countryside a little of the hope and comfort urban workers enjoy'. J. de Segadas Vianna, *O Estatuto do Trabalhador Rural*, p. 42. The concession of the statutory minimum wage to rural workers was already debated in the early 1940s. A. P. Brasil, 'O salário mínimo na lavoura paulista'. *Legislação do Trabalho* (October 1941) for the kind of arguments used against its enforcement then.

31. G. Vargas, *O Governo Trebalhista* (1969) IV, p. 477. In 1948 approximately 100 000 ploughs and 6000 tractors were in use on the over 2 million rural properties in the country. Joint Brazil/United States Economic Development Commission, *The Development of Brazil*, p. 23. In 1954 15 000 tractors, 8726 ploughs, 5033 harvesters and 10 488 disk harrows were imported with foreign credit under the Joint Brazil/United States Commission provision of US$18 000 000 for the import of agricultural equipment. Comissão Mista Brasil/Estados Unidos para Desenvolvimento Económico, *O Programa da Comissão Mista*, Rio de Janeiro (1954); R. Miller Paiva and R. Araujo Dias, 'Recente evolução da agricultura em São Paulo', *ASP*, VII (1) (January 1960) p. 29. UK, Board of Trade, Overseas Surveys, Brazil, *Economic and Commercial Conditions in Brazil* (London, 1954) pp. 58–9 has an assessment of agricultural mechanisation in São Paulo, and notes that in the early 1950s interest among farmers was increasing partly due to shortage of labour.

32. R. Miller Paiva and R. Araújo Dias, 'Recente evolução', p. 16.

33. G.W.Smith, 'Brazilian agricultural policy, 1950–1967', in H. S. Ellis (ed.), *The Economy of Brazil* (Beverley, 1969) p. 277; imports of fertilisers which in 1963 still amounted to 77.2 per cent in terms of value of total supply, were granted very favourable treatment under the multiple exchange-rate system of 1953.

34. R. Miller Paiva and R. Araújo Dias, 'Recente evolução' p. 16; taking 1948–52 as a base, the average price index of fertilisers rose to 358 in 1959 whereas that of tractors had risen to 1187.

35. Quoted by M.V. de Mesquita Benevides, *O Governo Kubitschek, Desenvolvimento Económico e Estabilidade Política* (Rio de Janeiro, 1976) p. 210.

36. Quoted by C. Lafer, 'The planning process and the political system in Brazil: a study of Kubitschek's target plan, 1956–1961', Doctoral Dissertation (Cornell University, 1970) p. 41.

37. C. Lafer, 'The planning process', pp. 182–5.

38. C. Lafer, 'The planning process', pp. 186–7. Between 1957 and 1960 almost US$100 million were spent on importing tractors. By contrast with the rapid expansion of a domestic motor car industry, one of the most important features of Kubitschek's target plan, and the local pro-

duction of washing and sewing machines, the manufacture of farm equipment was remarkably slow in getting off the ground. Until 1955, the manufacturing of tractors was confined to the *Fábrica Nacional de Motores*. Early in 1956, it was rumoured that Brazilian and German capitals were about to establish a plant for the manufacture of a wide variety of agricultural equipment from ploughs to harvesters in the state of São Paulo. The Economist Intelligence Unit (EIU), *Quarterly Economic Review of Brazil*, 18 (May 1956) p. 6. By the middle of the year local tractor production was going ahead. Intramag was erecting a tractor plant in Taubaté, São Paulo state. At the same time another tractor plant under licence from a Hamburg firm, Karl Ritscher, was under construction in Porto Alegre. Finally, the German tractor firm, Hanomag, was also considering manufacturing in Brazil; *Quarterly Economic Review of Brazil*, 19 (August 1956). Early the following year, Massey-Harris-Ferguson of Ontario set up a Brazilian subsidiary which began with the manufacture of parts and components but would proceed to produce tractors and farm equipment as well; *Quarterly Economic Review of Brazil*, 21 (March 1957). After this initial spurt of activity, farm machinery manufacture stagnated, and only in late 1959 was a new initiative taken by the government. The motor car industry's executive group was made responsible for developing a tractor industry, now considered essential to Brazil's economic progress. Japanese, Italian, British and Brazilian industrialists showed interest and proposals from several large foreign firms were received; *Quarterly Economic Review of Brazil*, 32 (November 1959) and 33 (February 1960). Of 20 proposals 10 received governmental approval for producing light, medium and heavy, as well as cater-pillar, tractors; *Quarterly Economic Review of Brazil*, 34 (May 1960). Farmers, however, looked on these projects with misgivings. They feared cost increases if they had to substitute locally-produced tractors for imported equipment which was subsidised; *Quarterly Economic Review of Brazil*, 33 (February 1960). Not all was going ahead as planned, anyway. Massey-Ferguson shelved its project to build light tractors in conjunction with the German concern, Vermag, and Fiat ran into difficulties with the official limit set on the use of foreign com-ponents, particularly engines; *Quarterly Economic Review of Brazil*, 35 (August 1960). In 1961, there were only three firms manufacturing tractors; *Quarterly Economic Review of Brazil*, 41 (February 1962). It was not until the late 1960s, when the country had emerged from the reces-sion, that the manufacture of agricultural equipment was con-solidated in response to increasing demand stimulated by more generous agricultural credits and minimum price policies for agricultural commodities.

39.   In 1956, 95 per cent of the total nitrogen fertilisers consumed in the country had been imported; by 1960 when consumption had almost trebled, only 54 per cent were imported. The share of domestic produc-tion of phosphates in the total amount consumed rose from 25.1 per cent in 1956 to 58.8 per cent in 1960, while total consumption had increased by somewhat over 25 per cent. C. Lafer, 'The planning

process', p. 187. G.W.Smith, 'Agricultural policy, 1950–1967', in H. S. Ellis (ed.), *The Economy of Brazil*; G. E. Schuh and A. Veiga, 'A política de importação de insumos agrícolas no Brasil, 1948–1967', *ASP* XXIII (1) (1976) pp. 141–69 for a discussion of preferential treatment of fertilisers and agricultural equipment imports.

40. G. E. Schuh, *The Agricultural Development of Brazil* (New York, 1970) pp. 153–61. From a very low level, the number of tractors in Brazil increased by 69 per cent between 1954 and 1958, and in São Paulo by 74 per cent. R. Miller Paiva and R. Araujo Dias, 'Recente evolução', p. 30.

41. W. Baer, *A Industrialização*, p. 139. Between 1952 and 1956 only 4 per cent of the Economic Development Bank's total credits in national currency went to agricultural activities, the share in credits in foreign currency being even lower, namely 1.7 per cent. See also F. B. Homem de Melo, 'A política económica e o setor agrícola no período pósguerra', *Revista Brasileira de Economia*, 33 (1) (January–March 1959) p. 48 for the evolution of agricultural credit between 1951 and 1974.

42. R. Miller Paiva and R. Araújo Dias, 'Recente evolução', p. 31.

43. Brazil, Câmara dos Deputados, *Anais* (1956) XXXIII, p. 254; *Folha da Manhã* (11 October 1955). As Kubitschek stressed in an interview: 'The rural labourer needs better protection. We will bring to him the benefits of the law and the advantages that are enjoyed by urban workers and commercial employees. We will give him social justice, the guarantees of the labour laws and of social security'.

44. Quoted by T. Skidmore, *Brasil: de Getúlio a Castelo (1930–1964)* (Rio de Janeiro, 1969) p. 455, n.15.

45. T. Skidmore, *Brasil*, p. 457, n.21. The most prominent among these was Fernando Ferrari.

46. Brazil, Câmara dos Deputados, *Anais* (1955–54) I (29 December 1955) p. 267; the composition of this pressure group is yet unknown. Lobbies such as this are formally-constituted pressure groups within Congress.

47. *O Estado de São Paulo* (1 May 1956); *Folha da Manhã* (6 December 1959).

48. One of those who was most explicit in his opposition to any legal reforms of power relations in agriculture was PSD Deputy Daniel Faraco who, while President of the congressional committee for the economy, in 1956 declared: 'While I am President of this Committee no land-reform programme will pass through it'. In effect, between 1946 and 1958 a total of 213 land-reform programmes were rejected by the Chamber of Deputies. M. V. de Mesquita Benevides, *O Governo de Kubitschek* (Rio de Janeiro, 1976) p. 219. *O Estado de São Paulo* (1 May 1956).

49. R. A. Dreifuss, *A Conquista do Estado*, pp. 23–30.

50. N. H. Leff, *Economic Policy-Making and Development in Brazil 1947–1964* (New York, 1968) pp. 19–34, who has dated the coffee sector's political eclipse to the 1950s on account of the government's almost unlimited freedom of action in policy making.

51. The share of coffee in foreign exchange earnings rose from 36 per cent in 1946 to 74 per cent in 1952 and stayed at roughly 55 per cent until 1967. A Delfim Netto and C. A. de Andrade Pinto, 'The Brazilian coffee: twenty years of set-backs in the competition on the world market 1945/1965' in C. M. Peláez (ed.), *Essays*, p. 283.
52. Brazil, Câmara dos Deputados, *Anais*, (1957) X, (27 April–4 June 1957) p. 382, Deputy Oliveira Franco.
53. J. W. F. Rowe, *The World's Coffee: A Study of the Eonomics and Politics of the Coffee Industries of Certain Countries and of the International Problem* (London, 1963), p. 14. Rowe seems to have had a special flair for coffee crises. As in 1931, he was again in São Paulo in the early 1960s during the renewed over-supply crisis.
54. In 1948–9 São Paulo still produced 54.4 per cent of the country's registered coffee as compared to 10.2 per cent grown in Paraná which by 1960, however, had outranked São Paulo with 46.9 per cent compared to 27.6 per cent produced by the latter. A. M. M. McFarquhar and G. B. Aneury Evans, *Employment Creation in Primary Production in Less Developed Countries*, Development Centre Studies, Employment Series 6, OECD (Paris, 1972). 'Registered coffee' is the coffee crop minus the amount retained by coffee producers. São Paulo's and Paraná's exportable production increased between 1951–2 and 1958–9 by 41 and 67 per cent respectively. J. W. F. Rowe, *The World's Coffee*, p. 33. The annual rate of new planting rose from an average 19 million in 1934–8 to 65 million trees in 1956–8 in São Paulo. 'A indústria do café em São Paulo', *ASP*, VIII (3) (March 1961) p. 22.
55. 'Estado e tendencias da agricultura paulista', *ASP*, X, (5 and 6) (May/June 1963) p. 29.

Changes in area grown in selected crops, São Paulo 1948–1958

Crop	(%)	Crop	(%)
Coffee	+ 23	Rice	+ 10
Cotton	− 62	Beans	+ 72
Sugar cane	+ 150	Oranges	+ 350
Maize	+ 43	Manioc	+ 109

56. J. W. F. Rowe, *The World's Coffee*, p. 15.
57. In 1955 the coffee price had dropped to 57¢ per lb which was maintained until 1957. By 1961 it had fallen to 35¢ a lb F. W. F. Rowe, *The World's Coffee*, pp. 16–17.
58. P. de Oliveira Adams, 'Café e cambio', *RSRB* (November 1952) pp. 35–41 for a discussion of coffee exchange policy in the 1930s.
59. *RSRB* (November 1950), Editorial (March 1951), Editorial (June 1951).
60. A. Delfim Netto and C. A. de Andrade Pinto, 'The Brazilian coffee', P. Malan *et al.*, *Política económica externa*; P. Malan, 'Foreign exchange constrained growth in a semi-industrialised economy: aspects of the Brazilian experience (1946–1976)', Doctoral Dissertation (University of California, 1977); E. Lisboa Bacha, 'A política cafeeira do Brazil,

1952/67', in E. Lisboa Bacha, *Os mitos de uma década* (Rio de Janeiro, 1976).

61. The proportion of foreign exchange earnings from different commodities that could be exchanged on the free market varied between 15 and 50 per cent; the official rate was Cr$18.7 the dollar compared with Cr$43.3 on the free market.

62. *RSRB* (July 1953) p. 25.

63. Memorandum by the *Federação das Associações Rurais do Estado de São Paulo* (FARESP, the Federation of the Rural Associations of the State of São Paulo) addressed to the Finance Minister Aranha on 22 June 1953. A. Alves Novaes e Cruz *et al. (eds), Impasse na Democracia Brasileira 1951–1955*, Coletánea de Documentos, CPDOC, Editora da Fundação Getúlio Vargas (Rio de Janeiro, 1983) pp. 184–8.

64. SUMOC Instruction 58 (15 June 1953). SUMOC stands for the *Superintendencia de Moeda e Crédito*, the Foreign Trade Department of the Bank of Brazil.

65. P. Malan, 'Foreign exchange', p. 132.

66. *A Rural: Revista da SRB* (AR) (December 1958) p. 29 (in October 1955 the former *Revista da SRB* changed its name).

67. *RSRB* (June 1953) p. 27.

68. P. Malan, 'Foreign exchange', p. 133.

69. J. Bergson and A. Candal, 'Industrialization: Past Success and Future Problems', in H. S. Ellis (ed.), *The Economy of Brazil* p. 33.

70. In the marketing year of 1953–4 Brazil's world-market share fell to 39 per cent. A large part of this loss was absorbed by African producers. A. Delfim Netto and C. A. de Andrade Pinto, 'The Brazilian coffee', p. 290.

71. A. Boito Jr. *O Golpe de 1954: A Burguesia Contra a Populismo* (São Paulo, 1982) pp. 47–50, suggests that coffee growers, as distinct from exporters who are said to have favoured devaluation, paradoxically shared the industrial sector's opposition to free exchange, currency devaluation and free imports of manufactured goods behaving like importers of industrial inputs rather than as exporters. However, as I have shown, before 1953 coffee growers and exporters were generally against devaluation because they feared the destabilising effect on the coffee market and the drop in coffee prices. During 1953, however, while being sceptical about free exchange for coffee, growers objected above all to 'exchange confiscation'. Agricultural equipment was anyway classified as super-essential and subsidised.

72. SUMOC Instruction 109 (November 1954) raised coffee exchange to Cr$31.52 and Instruction 114 of February 1955 to Cr$37.06, A. Delfim Netto and C. A. de Andrade Pinto, 'The Brazilian Coffee', p. 290; cf. W. Baer, *A Industrialização*, p. 120, for an estimate of the compensatory effect of bonuses.

73. 'Memorial da Associação Commercial de Santos' (24 January 1955) in E. Carone, *A Quarta República* (1945–1964) (São Paulo, 1980) pp. 335–9.

74. EIU, 13 (London, February 1955) p. 5.

75. Brazil, Câmara dos Deputados, *Anais* (1957) IX (21–24 May 1957) (Rio de Janeiro, 1958) pp. 639–46.

76. In mid-1955 there had been another such attempt. Producers' organisations in São Paulo, Paraná and Minas Gerais had called a meeting in Marilia where it was decided to march on the Presidential Palace 'to make themselves heard' though nothing came of it in the generally unsettled political situation at the time. *AR* (July 1956) p. 10.

77. Brazil, Câmara dos Deputados, *Anais* (1957) XXII (22–28 August 1957) (Rio de Janeiro, 1958) pp. 671–9. UDN Deputy Herbert Levy was one of the most vocal and persistent defenders of free exchange for coffee in Congress in the 1950s and explicitly denounced the preferential treatment accorded industry to the detriment of the coffee sector. He, together with his brothers, established the coffee brokerage firm, *Escritório de Corretagem para Negociar Café na Bolsa de Valores*. However, even he had to admit in June 1957 that the authorities had probably missed their chance for a successful exchange reform that would not jeopardise foreign exchange earnings from coffee. Brazil, Câmara dos Deputados, *Anais* (1957) XI (5–13 June 1957) (Rio de Janeiro, 1958) pp. 551–2. Attacks on industry for benefiting from 'exchange confiscation' were rare. Generally, the coffee sector blamed the government for this iniquity. Possible splits between the coffee sector and industry need further investigation, in particular the important question of the extent to which coffee capital branched out into banking and industry, blurring possible conflicts of interest.

78. This was denounced by São Paulo Deputy for the PTB Batista Ramos in August 1957. Brazil, Câmara dos Deputados, *Anais* (1957) XXXI (15–21 August 1957) (Rio de Janeiro, 1958) pp. 267–76, XXII (22–28 August 1957) (Rio de Janeiro, 1958) pp. 131–8.

79. *HAR*, XI (3) (March 1958) pp. 171–4; it was rumoured that Finance Minister Alkmim had resorted to rather unorthodox methods to improve the coffee trade such as buying coffee on the New York market and condoning under-invoicing.

80. *HAR*, XI (9) (September 1958) p. 522.

81. Brazil, Câmara dos Deputados, *Anais* (1958) (7–15 October 1958) XVII, p. 517

82. *AR* (December 1958) p. 28 announced that: 'The government succeeded in stopping the producers' march, curtailing the agriculturalists' freedom through the use of the army' and denounced the measure as 'most unhappy from an economic and political point of view'. In the Chamber of Deputies the UDN condemned the use of the armed forces to put down a movement which, after all, had been organised by 'thoughtful conservative and peaceful men'. Only its leader in the Chamber, Armando Falcão, who later became Minister of Justice under General Medici, made strenuous efforts to justify the government's action with an array of legalistic constitutional arguments. The PSD felt caught between its loyalty to President Kubitschek and that to the landed interests and the PTB was expectedly critical. Brazil, Câmara dos Deputados, *Anais* (1958) XVII, XVIII (October 1958) (Rio de Janeiro 1959).

83. Câmara dos Deputados, XVIII (16–28 October 1958) p. 281. For additional information on the producers' march see also *HAR*, XI (10) (October 1958), p. 580 and *EIU*, 27 (September 1958) p. 4. N. H. Leff, *Economic Policy-Making*, p. 27, has interpreted the defeat of the march as one indication of the loss of power by the coffee sector. But it can also be argued, that the coffee planters' power was such that the movement required no less than the armed forces to be put down.

84. Rumours that coffee exports were to be encouraged through a further depreciation of the coffee exchange were followed in 1959 by two adjustments of the coffee bonus. At the same time the official price for surplus purchases was raised. EIU, 29 (March 1959) p. 1 and 31 (August 1959), pp. 3, 6; *HAR*, XII (1) (March 1959) p. 60. In the general uncertain and confused situation at least two contrasting positions crystallised among coffee producers affiliated to the SRB. Exporters and producers in the older coffee regions of São Paulo who had heeded advice to renovate their coffee groves now defended free exchange, not least because the inevitable price decline would eliminate marginal producers. Piecemeal exchange readjustments were no good because they were in no time reabsorbed by falling prices. But there were others who opposed free exchange and demanded better domestic prices without exchange readjustments instead. They were not ready for a 'price-war', presumably because lower yields and quality of coffee made them less competitive than the former. *AR* (March, July and November 1959). Exporters in the meantime denounced, ever more vehemently 'the unfortunate valorisation of 1953' for 'the trade saw itself so often with its hands tied by artificial exchange, unpredictable withholding of coffee and minimum prices . . . government interference in the coffee trade is increasing all the time' as the President of the ACS complained at a lunch offered by the President of the Brazilian Coffee Institute. *AR* (December 1959) p. 11. In July 1960 the coffee dollar was raised yet again, this time to 90 Cr$. EIU, 35 (August 1960) p. 3.

85. In September he resigned under accusations of having betrayed Brazil's independence by giving in to the demands of the IMF. *O Estado de São Paulo* (22 April 1961, 9 September 1961) and *Jornal do Brasil* (22 October 1961); SUMOC Instruction 204 (March 1961) abolished the previous exchange system.

86. EIU, 38 (May 1961) pp. 5–6; price guarantees were also established graduated according to quality and low-grade coffee stocks held by the government were to be destroyed. After further readjustments which amounted again to some sort of differential exchange rates, in 1963, the scheme was once more totally overhauled. The Brazilian Coffee Institute was henceforth to fix a guarantee price for each type and quality of coffee. The grower was obliged to sell half or more of the crop to the Institute. Any remainder up to half could be sold to exporters directly. The proportion sold to the Institute constituted the 'equilibrium quota'. If the producer also chose to sell the other half of

his crop to the Institute, the so-called 'market series' he received a better price than for the 'equilibrium series'. The export tax now consisted of the difference between the guarantee price and the actual value of the exports. As McFarquhar and Evans have estimated, the net burden of taxation on the coffee sector fluctuated around one-third of export value. A. M. M. McFarquhar and G. B. Aneury Evans, *Employment Creation in Primary Production in Less Developed Countries*, pp. 80–1.

87. *O Estado de São Paulo* (18 May 1961).
88. P. Malan *et al.*, *Politica económica externa*, p. 168.
89. W. Baer, *A Industrialização*, p. 103.
90. F. B. Homem de Mello, 'A política económica e o setor agrícola no período pósguerra', pp. 33–5; C. Lessa, 'Fifteen years of economic policy', UN ECLA, *Economic Bulletin for Latin America*, IX (2) (December 1964) p. 183; E. G. Schuh and A. Veiga, 'A política de importação de insumos agrícolas no Brasil, 1948–1967', *ASP*, XXIII (1) (1976) p. 141.
91. *Conjuntura Económica*, VI (8) (August 1959) pp. 67–73.
92. J. W. F. Rowe, *The World's Coffee*, p. 52.
93. *HAR*, XI (9) (September 1958) p. 522.
94. A. Alves Novaes e Cruz *et al.* (eds) *Impasse na Democracia*, p. 159, letter addressed by José Soares Maciel Filho to Getúlio Vargas on 14 July 1952, reproduced as Document 54.
95. UN ECLA, *Economic Survey of Latin America* (1949) p. 225. The Report by the Joint Brazil/United States Economic Development Commission, p. 23, notes that rice, wheat and sugar cane lent themselves well to mechanisation being temporary crops often grown on large farm units. Cf. also G. E. Schuh, *The Agricultural Development of Brazil*.
96. The data on weeding task-rates paid *colonos* for the tending of 1000 coffee trees per year unfortunately are scattered and incomplete. Nonetheless, they show a trend which is confirmed by the wage series for

Date	Cr$/1000 trees	Date	Cr$/1000 trees
Oct 1951	2000–3000	Nov 1955	3500–4000
Sept 1952	2400–3500	1957–58[a]	3000–4500
Sept 1953	2500–3500	Feb 1961[b]	10 000
Oct 1954	3500–5000		

Sources: *ASP* (October 1951) pp. 9–10; (September 1952) p. 11; (September 1953) p. 10; (October 1954) p. 24; (November 1955) p. 24. Between April 1954 and July 1956 when the first series of the journal ends, *ASP* contains monthly assessments of coffee cultivation, prospects and labour supply in São Paulo. The journal resumed publication in 1960.

[a] O. J. Thomazini Ettori, 'Mão-de-obra na agricultura de São Paulo', *ASP*, VIII (12) (December 1961) p. 28.

[b] *AR* (February 1961) p. 4.

resident day-labourers and harvest work. The nominal weeding task-rates in the years for which data are available were the following;

97. R Kahil, *Inflation and Economic Development in Brazil, 1946–1963* (Oxford 1973) pp. 144–54 is a monetarist critique of structuralist theses on unequal development in Brazil. In the absence of wage data Kahil bases his estimates of fluctuations in rural wages between 1947 and 1963 in São Paulo and Paraná on two kinds of data: (1) on labour demand and supply as determined by the coffee cycle and internal migration into the two states, and (2) on inferences from the changes in urban wages for unskilled workers. He concludes that during coffee expansion between 1947 and 1950 which increased labour demand while supply was inadequate, rural wages in São Paulo rose by about 30 per cent in real terms; between 1950 and 1957 as immigration increased, wages dropped by 24 per cent, whereas after 1957 they rose once more. This is not only a much more optimistic, but a radically different picture from that conveyed by the data used here. There is at least one fundamental problem with Kahil's calculations. Rural wages in the 1950s were substantially lower than those of unskilled urban workers. Moreover, the spread between the rural wage and the legal minimum wage increased markedly in the 1950s (R. Miller Paiva, S. Schattan and C. F. Trench de Freitas, *Setor Agrícola do Brasil* p. 92). The rural and urban labour markets were *not* unified. Vargas's programme to achieve unification failed because of the landowners' opposition. An extension of labour laws to agriculture would have made the redistribution of income to landowners on account of inflation more difficult. (W. Baer, 'The inflation controversy in Latin America: a survey', *Latin American Research Review*, II (2) (1966) pp. 3–25). When available, Kahil uses rural wage data for 'spade workers' (*trabalhadores de enxada*)). But such data are no good for assessing *colono* wages. The rural population of São Paulo declined from 48.1 per cent in 1948 to 30.2 per cent in 1962; after 1957–8 the rural population diminished in absolute terms. *ASP*, X (5–6) (May/June 1963) pp. 18–19. UN ECLA, *The Economic Development of Brazil*, p. 96. In May 1959 planters complained that because of very low returns many were unable to complete the coffee harvest because, since they could not offer their *colonos* better wages the labourers were abandoning the plantations for the towns, attracted by the much higher minimum wage. *A Gazeta* (18 May 1959).

98. UN, FAO, *Coffee in Latin America* (2) p. 25; the survey also revealed a lack of variation in the use and intensity of labour between coffee plantations of different sizes. Because most tasks continued to be performed with the hoe, labour intensity and productivity depended on yields rather than the reverse, p. 41.

99. *AR* (August 1952) Editorial. J. W. F. Rowe, *The World's Coffee*, p. 43. Of the total 1300 million coffee trees in existence in the state of São Paulo in 1958, only 38 per cent had been planted after 1945; 39 per cent dated from before 1929 and 22 per cent had been planted between 1930 and 1945.

100. *RSRB* (August and November 1952).
101. *AR* (March 1956) pp. 8–9.
102. *AR* (June 1957) p. 49; (July 1956) p. 8.
103. UN ECLA, *The Economic Development of Brazil*, pp. 96–7.
104. In 1958, it was estimated that 15 to 20 per cent of new plantings followed the new system. UN FAO, *Coffee in Latin America* (1) p. 6 (November 1957) p. 80.
105. *ASP*, VIII (9) (September 1961) p. 67.
106. *AR* (November 1957) p. 80.
107. *AR* (May 1959) p. 26.
108. UN ECLA, *The Economic Development of Brazil*, pp. 99–100.
109. UN FAO, *Coffee in Latin America* (1) and (2).
110. *ASP*, VIII (3) (March 1961) p. 73.
111. *ASP*, IX (2) (February 1962) pp. 8–9.
112. *ASP* VIII (9) (September 1961) pp. 54–5.
113. Intercropping among adult trees by size of holding, São Paulo – 1956–58) (percentages):

Year	Total	Family farms	Small plantations	Medium plantations	Large plantations
1956	33.7	44.3	32.6	26.3	38.0
1957	37.4	50.7	32.6	34.5	39.7
1958	39.9	68.1	34.9	39.1	39.7

Source: UN FAO, *Coffee in Latin America* (2) pp. 34–5. The extent of intercropping is probably underestimated in this sample of 33 farms since the level of organisation of these was above average.

114. Between 1958 and 1959 the average price of tractors doubled while that of chemical fertilisers increased by half. The prices for other agricultural equipment presumably behaved similarly. R. Miller Paiva and R. Araújo Dias, 'Recente evoluço', p. 16. The FAO survey estimated that with new cultivation methods production costs per hectare increased by 50–80 per cent as compared with traditional practices. The three main items that accounted for this increase were greater density of planting per hectare, soil conservation and chemical fertilising. It was thought, however, that higher yields and alternative use of freed land would compensate for this increase in costs. *ASP*, IX (2) (February 1962) pp. 6–7.
115. J. F. Graziano da Silva, 'Progresso tećnico', P. Singer, 'Os novos nómades'.
116. 'A indústria do café em São Paulo', pp. 81–4.
117. UN FAO, *Coffee in Latin America* (2) p. 5.
118. *ASP*, VIII, 9 (September 1961) p. 57.
119. Manuring required 113 man/hours as compared to 31 man/hours for chemical fertilising per thousand trees/year. *ASP* VIII (11) (November 1961) p. 67.

120. 'A indústria do café em São Paulo', pp. 28–33. On São Paulo coffee plantations on average 15.9 per cent of the area was grown in coffee which accounted for 51.6 per cent of farm income; 51.5 per cent of the area was in pastures, meat and dairy produce accounting for 22.5 per cent of farm income; 8.4 per cent of the land was occupied by workers' food plots and another 6.8 per cent by other minor crops, foremost among them sugar cane.
121. UN FAO, *Coffee in Latin America* (2) pp. 45–50, for an analysis of labour needs of crops other than coffee.
122. O. J. Thomazini Ettori, 'Mão-de-obra na agricultura de São Paulo', p. 27.
123. P. Monbeig, *Novos Estudos*, p. 190.
124. P. Monbeig, *Novos Estudos*, p. 187 noted in 1957 the tendency for some ex-*colonos* to live in town and travel to the plantations by truck daily as well as the use of '*empreitas*', i.e. contracts for specific tasks, which he relates to the introduction of technological innovations in coffee cultivation. O. J. Thomazini Ettori, 'Mão-de-obra na agricultura de São Paulo', p. 18 is the first to describe the new phenomenon of the *volante*, the casual labourer. These were day-workers living in town but working on the plantations during certain periods of the year. They were paid by day or by task and their wages were entirely monetary. They were usually hired through a labour contractor who was in charge of the gang and was called *gato*.
125. UN FAO, *Coffee in Latin America* (2) pp. 16–17; sharecroppers were more efficient in terms of labour input per 100 kg of processed coffee than *colonos*. 'A indústria do café em São Paulo', VIII (3) (March 1961) pp. 45–60.
126. *AR*, June 1953, p. 14.
127. UN FAO, *Coffee in Latin America* (1) p. 80.
128. *AR* (March 1960) p. 8.
129. *AR* (May 1960) p. 8.
130. As stocks accumulated it was rumoured that serious dissensions at the International Coffee Agreement meetings in Washington were impeding a more ample accord that included above all African producers who were constituting a growing threat to Brazil's world market share. For a discussion of the 1961 conjuncture see *HAR*, XIV (1–10) (January – October 1961).
131. L. Guarnieri, 'A experiencia brasileira de planejamento no setor cafeeiro', IFCH, UNICAMP (Campinas, 1981) (mimeo) for an excellent discussion of government planning of coffe production from 1961 onward and the achievements of GERCA.
132. A. M. McFarquhar and G. B. Aneury Evans *Employment Creation*, p. 74.
133. L. Guarnieri, 'A experiencia brasileira', p. 14.
134. A. M. M. McFarquhar and G. B. Aneury Evans, *Employment Creation*, p. 75; S. Panagides, 'Erradicação do café e diversificação da agricultura Brasileira', *Revista Brasileira de Economía* (Rio de Janeiro) 23 (1) (January/March 1969) p. 45, estimates the coffee trees uprooted outside the GERCA programme at 350 million.

135. *ASP*, IX (2) (February 1962) p. 13.
136. Governor Carvalho Pinto made this warning at a meeting with union leaders in July 1959 in São Paulo. The São Paulo journal, *O Estado de São Paulo*, which traditionally defended coffee interests, reacted sharply by calling the Governor an alarmist. At the same time it produced a survey of agricultural employment in the state to prove that unemployment in agriculture was limited. *O Estado de São Paulo* (12 and 14 August 1959). L. Guarnieri, 'A experiencia brasileira', has suggested that the GERCA programmes implicitly benefited large coffee producers since they aimed at reducing capacity by eliminating small low yielding producers to convert them into food producers. This may have been the intention but whether the schemes achieved this goal is debatable, for the greater resistance of family farms to a decline in prices as well as the small farmers' difficulties in gaining access to loans on account of the bureaucratic complications involved, made eradication in their case less likely.
137. S. Panagides, 'Erradicação do café', p. 46. Some new planting also occurred at the time mostly under new cultivation methods. A. M. McFarquhar and G. B. Aneury Evans, *Employment Creation*, p. 79 estimated an annual rate of new planting in São Paulo of 17.8 million trees between 1958 and 1962. It is unlikely that this rate increased until 1967–8. L. Guarnieri, 'A experiencia brasileira', p. 27 quotes recommendations made by GERCA for new coffee planting. Weeding was to be done with cultivators. Supplementary labour for the harvest was to be hired either in the rural areas or in town 'especially from among the women and children who produce little in industry anyway'.
138. Caio Prado Jr, 'O estatuto do trabalhador rural', *Revista Brasiliense*, 47 (May–June 1963) pp. 1–2 noted the lack of interest among left-wing and progressive political forces when the Rural Labour Statute passed through Congress.
139. *HAR*, 1 (January 1961) pp. 84–5; this was state law 5994 enacted on 30 December 1960 and implemented by decree 38 328 (14 April 1961). Expropriations were to be financed with rural territorial taxes but it was calculated that São Paulo revenues from this tax would provide only about 1000 landless peasants of the almost 1 million in the state with a small plot per year. *O Semanário* (1 February 1961). Expropriations became even more difficult in 1961 when the collection of rural territorial taxes was transferred by law to the counties, thus placing them under the control of large landowners. *Jornal do Brasil* (21 January 1962). All the Agrarian Revision Law, in fact, achieved was the expropriation of two estates, *fazenda* Santa Helena in Marilia and *fazenda* Capivari in the region of Campinas and the distribution of family farms to 212 peasants. Moreover, 'many landowners who were farming all their land would, in addition, receive a discount on their taxes even though they might be using the most primitive and unproductive methods of production. Landless persons would often be unable to meet the downpayment on the land being sold, and there was insufficient provision for agarian credit', *HAR*, 1 (January 1961).

140. J. Gomes da Silva, *A Reforma Agrária no Brasil* (Rio de Janeiro, 1971) p. 178.
141. *O Estado de São Paulo* (30 November 1960).
142. The best analysis of rural political mobilisation in the Northeast in the late 1950s and early 1960s is A. Alcántara de Camargo, 'Brésil Nord-Est; Mouvements Paysans et Crise Populiste', Doctoral Dissertation (Université de Paris, 1973). Other sources are C. Moraes, Peasant Leagues in Brazil', in R. Stavenhagen (ed.), *Agrarian and Peasant Movements in Latin America* (New York, 1970); M. E. Wilkie, 'Report on Rural Syndicates in Pernambuco', Centro Latinoamericano de Pesquisas em Ciéncias Sociais (Rio de Janeiro, 1964) (mimeo); R. E. Price, 'Rural Unionisation in Brazil', The Land Tenure Center (Madison, Wisconsin, 1964) (mimeo); D. C. Dumoulin, 'The Rural Labour Movement in Brazil', The Land Tenure Center (Madison, Wisconsin, 1965) (mimeo); S. Foreman, 'Disunity and Discontent: A Study of Peasant Political Movements in Brazil', in R. Chilcote (ed.), *Protest and Resistance in Angola and Brazil* (Berkeley, 1972); G. Hewitt, 'Brazil: The Peasant Movement in Pernambuco', in H. A. Landsberger (ed.), *Latin American Peasant Movements* (Cornell, 1969). Information on rural labour conflicts and organisation in other regions of the country before the 1964 military coup is still scant. Some data on the state of São Paulo are contained in A. Feitosa Martins, 'Algums aspectos da inquietação trabalhista no campo', *Revista Brasiliense*, XL (1962) and in T. Martins, 'Proletariado e inquietação rural', *Revista Brasiliense*, XLII (1962).
143. The choice of this form of organisation instead of unions responded to the difficulties of obtaining government recognition of unions. The Leagues could easily be registered as 'civil associations'. C. Moraes, 'Peasant Leagues in Brazil', pp. 456–7.
144. A. Alcántara de Camargo, 'Brésil Nord-Est', pp. 179 ff.
145. D. C. Dumoulin, 'The Rural Labour Movement', p. 21.
146. J. Barriguelli, Conflicto e participação no meio rural', *Anais do VIII Simpósio Nacional dos Professores Universitarios de História* (Aracajú, September 1975) p. 868.
147. *O Estado de São Paulo* (5 July 1964).
148. D. C. Dumoulin, 'The Rural Labour Movement', p. 21.
149. R. E. Price, 'Rural Unionisation', p. 57.
150. D. C. Dumoulin, 'The Rural Labour Movement', p. 23; R. E. Price, 'Rural Unionisation', p. 65.
151. C. Moraes, 'Peasant Leagues in Brazil', p. 482, note 23.
152. See R. E. Price, 'Rural Unionisation' and C. Moraes, 'Peasant Leagues in Brazil', for an over-view.
153. Government attempts to institutionalise rural unions dated back to 1903 (Decree 979) implemented by Decree 6532 (20 June 1907) according to which 'persons engaged in agricultural or rural industries of any kind may organise unions for the study, support and defence of their interests'. This law was totally ineffective for rural workers. Thirteen associations were founded under it dominated by large landowners. Decree 23611 (20 December 1933) revoked the above law and provided

for professional co-operative consortiums. Finally, Decree 7038 (November 1944) implemented by Instruction 14 (March 1945) of the Labour Ministry provided that 'all those who exercise rural activities whether employers or employees [are] permitted to form associations for purposes of study, defence and coordination of their economic and professional interests'. Only two rural labour unions were formed under the 1944 law due as much to landowners' resistance as to lack of the administrative machinery in the countryside state-controlled unions required. Large landowners do not seem to have had any bureaucratic difficulties, however, in organising their professional associations, either within or without the official institutional structure. R. E. Price 'Rural Unionisation', pp. 5ff.

154. M. Cehelsky, 'The Policy Process in Brazil: Land Reform, 1961–1969', Doctoral Dissertation (Columbia University, 1974) for an analysis of the different states' and parties' attitude to land reform as reflected in the debates in the Chamber of Deputies on the issue. The attitude of industrialists and commerce toward the issue of land reform was largely ambivalent and uninterested. They opposed the Constitutional amendment because it attacked private property and the social and economic status quo and landowners could not count on their support. Nonetheless, landowners did come together with urban employers to plan joint action against the government under the *Conselho Nacional das Classes Produtoras* (CONCLAP) – National Council of Producing Classes – the main employers confederation. Landowners were, however, actively supported by the conservative wing of the Catholic Church and by a sector of economic opinion, among whom Delfim Netto was a prominent opponent of a land reform of any kind.

155. It has been suggested that the unions preferred for official recognition by Goulart were those of Communist orientation. Rotta, the President of the Catholic right-wing Federation certainly alleged discrimination against his unions persistently until 1964. From 1962 to 1964 the São Paulo journal, *O Estado de São Paulo* seems to have been only too eager to publish Rotta's denunciations of the Goulart government. *O Estado de São Paulo* (20 September 1962; 22 September 1962; 11 November 1962; 30 November 1963).

156. C. Moraes, 'Peasant Leagues in Brazil', pp. 482–3.

157. Decree 209A (June 1962) and decree 355A (November 1962).

158. Quoted by P. Schmitter, *Interest Conflict and Political Change in Brazil* (Stanford, 1971), p. 211.

159. The organisations concerned were three Catholic Federations from the Northeast and the Catholic Federation of Rural Workers of São Paulo, whereas ULTAB had one Federation in Paraná recognised.

160. R. A. Dreifuss, *A Conquista do Estado*, pp. 394–5.

161. R. E. Price, 'Rural Unionisation', p. 65.

162. C. Moraes, 'Peasant Leagues in Brazil', pp. 491–2.

163. Estimates of union membership vary greatly. G. Hewitt, 'Brazil', p. 347 suggests that Catholic organisations had about 200 000 members as compared to 30 000 of the Peasant Leagues and 50 000 in Communist-

sponsored unions. For 1962, M. Cehelsky, 'The Policy Process in Brazil', pp. 247–8 estimates a total membership of about 550 000. This compares with an agricultural labour force (including sharecroppers and small tenants and their families) of about 6 million in 1950. According to R. E. Price, 'Rural Unionisation', p. 83, based on data from SUPRA, in December 1963 a total of 270 rural unions and 10 Federations had been recognised while another 557 unions and 33 Federations were awaiting recognition in the country as a whole. The Northeast had 92 recognised unions and 193 awaiting recognition by comparison with 61 and 60 respectively in São Paulo, 47 and 71 in Paraná, and 33 and 75 in Rio Grande do Sul.

164. The Rural Labour Statute repeated the unionisation provisions contained in the CLT of 1943 and in Decree 7038 (1944). One main principle was the requirement that rural unions be recognised, i.e. bureaucratically registered by the Labour Ministry. The right to strike was subordinated to the conciliatory powers of the labour judiciary. R. E. Price, 'Rural Unionisation'.

165. The opposition to the bill was headed by PSD Deputy for Minas Gerais Guilhermino de Oliveira. *O Estado de São Paulo* (29 June 1961).

166. The provisions on job security allowed the dismissal of a labourer after ten years of work on an estate only in cases of serious misdemeanour. If a worker was fired without just cause he either had to be readmitted or paid compensation amounting to double the sum of compensation paid upon unjust dismissal before the ten years had been completed which amounted to one monthly wage per year of employment.

167. Brazil, Câmara dos Deputados, *Anais*, VI (1961) (Rio de Janeiro, 1962) p. 88; Deputy Munhoz da Rocha of the PR; for objections along similar lines to job security and severance pay see also Câmara dos Deputados, *Anais*, XXV (1956) p. 602, XXXIII (1956) pp. 236–7.

168. Interview with landowner in São Paulo in 1977.

169. Brazil, Câmara dos Deputados, *Anais*, XI (28 June 1961) pp. 719–31. *O Estado de São Paulo* (26 July 1964); for a legal discussion of the Rural Labour Statute and its history see J. de Segadas Vianna, *O Estatuto do Trabalhador Rural*; D. W. Zibetti, *Legislação Agrária Brasileira* (São Paulo, 1968); A Campanhole, *Legislação do Trabalhador Rural e Estatuto da Terra*, (São Paulo, 1966); O. Rocha, *Manual Prático do Trabalho Rural*, (São Paulo, 1969), contains a survey of the jurisprudence that arose in 1966 and 1967 from the enforcement of the Rural Labour Statute. Time and again legal claims by sharecroppers were disputed and rejected; see also C. A. Gomes Chiarelli, *Direito do Trabalho Rural Consolidado* (São Paulo, 1975).

170. *A Gazeta* (8 May 1962).

171. Judging by the number of speeches made in the Federal Chamber of Deputies, Minas Gerais, São Paulo and Rio Grande do Sul had a consistently high level of participation in the debate over land reform in the Chamber throughout the Goulart government. Cehelsky suggests that in all three states the issue of land reform was fundamentally one

of political organisation and control. She attributes the somewhat lesser activity of São Paulo deputies by contrast with Minas Gerais and Rio Grande do Sul to the fact that São Paulo agriculture was somewhat more modern. M. Cehelsky, 'The Policy Process in Brazil', pp. 174–5.

172. *AR* (January 1962) pp. 8–9.
173. *O Estado de São Paulo* (7 July 1961).
174. *O Estado de São Paulo* (1 July 1961). Already early in 1961 coffee planters had mobilised to demand readjustments of coffee financing because of the rise in the minimum wage decreed by the government even though the legal wage was demonstrably not being observed in agriculture. *AR* (January 1961) p. 43.
175. In mid-1963 it was alleged that the introduction of the minimum wage in agriculture had produced a 100 per cent increase in rural wages in São Paulo. Brazil, Câmara dos Deputados, *Anais*, X (12–19 June 1963); R. Miller Paiva, S. Schattan and C. F. Trench de Freitas, *Setor agrícola do Brasil*, p. 92 show that between 1962 and 1965 the day-wage of a resident rural worker increased by 40 per cent in *cruzeiros* of 1969; the Rural Labour Statute allowed for a discount of 20 per cent from the minimum wage for housing and of 25 per cent for food provided by the employer in addition to establishing a lower limit of 30 per cent of the minimum wage to be paid in cash under any circumstances. J. de Segadas Vianna, *O Estatuto do Trabalhador Rural*, pp. 119–24.
176. M. V. Mesquita Benavides, *A UDN e o Udenismo. Ambiguedade do Liberalismo Brasileiro* (Rio de Janeiro, 1981) P. 195.
177. *AR* (February 1963) p. 11.
178. The minimum prices were set below those proposed by the Administrative Board and the demand that coffee prices be readjusted in accordance with currency fluctuations and changes in the minimum wage and that the Brazilian Coffee Institute pay for transport and sacking for compulsory sales was vetoed. Brazil, Câmara dos Deputados, *Anais*, C (12–19 June 1963) p. 438.
179. *Câmara dos Deputados, Anais*, X, XI (1963) for descriptions of the protest movement.
180. According to these new regulations coffee was to be purchased at the higher fixed price by the Brazilian Coffee Institute in the interior of the state from the beginning of the coffee season although the difference between this and the original price was to be deposited for 180 days on an account at the Bank of Brazil.
181. *AR* (November 1963), pp. 6–8.
182. E. Lisboa Bacha, 'A política cafeeira do Brasil, 1952/67'. L Guarnieri, 'A experiencia brasileira', p.15 shares Bacha's interpretation.
183. R. E. Price, 'Rural Unionisation', p. 54. The church-sponsored Pernambuco Federation of Rural Workers demanded that the statute be applied. When negotiations with sugar-cane growers and mill-owners broke down, a general strike of workers in the sugar-cane industry was called which ended with a promise by employers to raise wages by 80 per cent. During the strike plantation owners drew up a formal protest addressed to President Goulart which reveals the landowners'

concern with loss of power: 'The stimulus to the struggle of the classes, the incitement to strikes, often unaccompanied by any legitimate demand and the insubordination that is destroying the labour hierarchy, for the purpose of creating disharmony and rendering impossible the co-operation of those who lead and those who execute, intends to destroy the agricultural and industrial enterprises'. Quoted by R. E. Price, 'Rural Unionisation', p. 54. For a description of this strike see also G. Hewitt, 'Brazil' pp. 396–7.

184. On 1 June 1963 over 100 landowners from São Paulo and the neighbouring state of Minas Gerais met in Amparo in the interior of São Paulo to combat the 'anti-democratic and anti-Christian land-reform proposals'. A declaration was drawn up which demanded that any land reform safeguard private property from socialist, anti-Christian expropriation. Deputy Herbert Levy who had attended a similar meeting earlier in Campinas, called for the need to organise before it was too late. Present at the meeting was Plinio Correa de Oliveira, the founder of the ultra-conservative Catholic Society for the Defence of Tradition, Family and Property (TFP). He was co-author, together with four other ultra-conservative Church dignitaries (Bishops Dom Orlando Rodrigues, Dom Antonio de Castro Maier and Dom Geraldo de Proença Sigaud and Luiz Mendoça Freitas) of *Reforma Agrária – Questão de Conciencia* published in 1960, a vehement defence of private property and the preservation of traditional class distinctions, which was declared the catechism for land reform at the meeting.

185. D. C. Dumoulin, 'The Rural Labour Movement', p. 24.

186. J. C. Barriguelli, 'Conflito e participação na meio rural'. For landowners' reprisals against 'insubordinate' workers C. A. de Medina, 'Relatório: Sertãozinho e Jardinópolis – São Paulo' (1962) (mimeo) pp. 68–79.

187. *AR* (February 1963) p. 32. there is also evidence of more violent conflicts in São Paulo agriculture. C. Moraes, 'Peasant Leagues in Brazil', p. 489–90 reports a peasant uprising in Jales organised by ULTAB in 1961. In 1959 a long, drawn-out conflict had occurred in Santa Fe do Sul between sharecroppers and a large landowner who wanted to expel them from the land to establish pastures after they had planted cotton to clear the land. Also in 1961 an armed clash was reported between the state police and peasants in Pato Branco in the neighbouring state of Paraná. For a debate on the circumstances under which 800 families of sharecroppers were evicted from the land in Sante Fe do Sul, see also Brazil, Câmara dos Deputados, *Anais*, XI (24 July 1959) pp. 731–4.

188. Roberto Campos, the Planning Minister and Carlos Thompson the Minister of Agriculture drafted the Land Statute which was enacted after extensive consultation with landed interests. The key part of the bill was punitive taxation on unexploited land. Expropriation against payment in long-term bonds was retained and a Constitutional amendment passed to that effect but it was limited to very large estates and the bonds would be guaranteed against depreciation. Moreover, the political context had changed and those forces that could have

pressed for implementation of the law had been disarmed. As landowners admitted, the best part of the Land Statute was that it was not
observed. M. Cehelsky, 'The Policy Process in Brazil', p. 210. The
Land Statute also regulated length of tenure of sharecroppers but
excluded the so-called 'false sharecropping', meaning concealed
forms of wage work, and thus offered a loophole to evade the law and
increasing their legal ambiguity. By contrast, President Castelo
Branco's proposal to give the vote to illiterates, which would have
meant the incorporation of large sectors of the rural population into
an admittedly limited political process, was defeated by Congress.

189.   EIU (August 1965), p. 13.
190.   Ibid. 3 (July 1966), p. 13.
191.   T. E. Skidmore, 'Politics and economic policy in authoritarian Brazil'
       (1 July 1971) (mimeo) p. 27, also makes the point that the coffee sector
       lost its power effectively only after the 1964 military coup.
192.   This fund consisted of a monthly discount of 8 per cent from the per-
       manent workers' pay-check which was paid into an account opened in
       the worker's name. Upon unjustified dismissal he or she received the
       sum that had accumulated on the account with interest and deprecia-
       tion, plus compensation amounting to 10 per cent of the sum in
       the account.
193.   In the mid-1950s the National Economic Council had opposed
       granting job security to agricultural workers unless the manner of
       financing compensation was revised in such a way as to transfer res-
       ponsibility from the individual employer to a social security scheme.
       Brazil, Câmara dos Deputados, *Anais*, 33 (1956) p. 251. FAESP
       (Federação da Agricultura do Estado de São Paulo), São Paulo's
       official landowners' association, repeatedly demanded changes in the
       labour laws. In 1971 FAESP argued that the Rural Labour Statute con-
       stituted an obstacle to coffee renewal and that the FGTS be extended
       to agriculture, above all to raise 'labour efficiency'. 4° Congresso
       Nacional do Café, *Anais* (Vitoria, 1971) p. 391. FAESP made a similar
       appeal in 1974 in a Memorandum addressed to President Geisel,
       FAESP, 'Exposição da Federação da Agricultura do Estado de São
       Paulo sobre os problemas da economía rural paulista', dirigido ao
       Exo. Sr General E. Geisel, Presidente da República (March 1974). See
       also *O Estado de São Paulo* (3 December 1970) and *O Estado de São
       Paulo* (3 March 1971) which contains a call for settling the rural labour
       force on the estates in order to reduce casual labour and rural exodus.
       The same month, the SRB expressed its dismay over President
       Medici's project to extend social security to rural labour and stressed
       the urgent need to revise the Rural Labour Statute 'to adapt it to the
       realities of the countryside returning tranquility to it and making it
       possible for labourers to return to the estates which would allow for
       better use of their labour and would have a positive effect on produc-
       tion costs'. *O Estado de São Paulo* (31 March 1971).
194.   M. R. Medeiros, 'O FGTS no meio rural', *Movimento*, 42 (April 1976).
       Symptomatic of the contentiousness of the issue and the level of political
       control at the time, this article was suppressed by the official cen-

sorship to which all publications had to be submitted for approval before publication.

195. In 1976, the first ever collective agreement for rural workers was negotiated in São Paulo. The social problem of casual labour in agriculture which had increased after the 1975 frost persuaded the Labour Minister of the state that something needed to be done.

196. J. C. Saboia 'De senhores a trocadores', pp. 139–40 who notes that between 1963 and 1974 a total of 344 court cases over non-compliance of one or other of the provisions of the Rural Labour Statute were heard by the court of Cravinhos, a small town in the neighbourhood of Riberão Preto. Such court cases became more frequent especially after 1968 when the rural labour union of Cravinhos gained official recognition. The extent to which rural labourers will pursue their rights certainly depends also on assistance by a labour lawyer (p.191–2).

197. Brazil, Câmara dos Deputados, *Anais*, 46 (956) (5 December 1956) p. 309.

198. J. de Segadas Vianna, *O Estatuto do Trabalhador Rural*, p. 87. See article 2 and article 6 of the Statute.

199. A. Sampaio, *Contrato de Trabalho Rural, Direitos e Obrigações do Trabalhador Rural em Face da CLT e da Lei No. 5. 889 de 1973* (São Paulo, 1974) pp. 11–16, 54–7. This law did not extend the FGTS to agriculture (p. 160) C. A. Gomes Chiarelli, *Direito do Trabalho Rural*, pp. 17–22 for a discussion of the legal status of the *avulso* or temporary labourer. The number of legal exegeses of the Rural Labour Statute that appeared in the 1960s is in itself evidence of the contentiousness of the law.

200. *O Estado de São Paulo* (6 April 1972) reported that landowners were reducing their resident labour force as a result of the great number of labour disputes. Some had opted for cattle raising or mechanised soy beans and wheat production resulting in the massive dismissal of *colonos* and permanent labour in general, unemployment and the decline of local commerce as well as the proliferation of casual workers. *O Estado de São Paulo* (13 December 1972) denounced those 'devil's advocates' who were inducing the workers to take their employers to court seduced by the promise of large compensations. L. Sigaud, 'A idealização do passado', shows how rural labour unions in Pernambuco endeavoured to protect labourers on sugar-cane plantations from eviction by their employers in reprisal for the enactment of the Statute.

201. *O Estado de São Paulo* (18 June 1972) attributed the closing down of the *colonias*, the clusters of houses in which the *colonos* had lived on the estates, to the new policy of coffee eradication and the labour laws. Landowners fearing labour disputes and their effects on costs dismissed large numbers of workers who then migrated to the towns.

202. Revealingly, one lawyer advised coffee planters in the 1950s to abandon the *colonato* system and hire labour for each task separately. O. Rocha, *Manual Prático do Trabalho Rural*, p. 32; *O Estado de São Paulo* (21 May 1961). The trend in jurisprudence seems to have been to exlude family labour from contractual obligations by the employer.

Law 5889 (1973) explicitly forbade discounts from the wage for food crops produced by the labourers themselves.

203. 4° Congresso Nacional do Café. Coffee planters felt nostalgia for the good old days of the *colonato*. Some in 1972 suggested the introduction of a 'modern *colonato*' in Paraná which required only modifying the labour laws and including self-provisioning in the *colono*'s pay. *O Estado de São Paulo* (31 December 1972). Wages of resident workers and their families were lower than those of casual workers from outside the estate because the former allegedly enjoyed some fringe benefits. They needed no transport to go to work, sometimes they were allowed to grow some vegetables and raise a few chickens, but they had to pay rent and electricity. Most casual workers thought that under these conditions living on estates was undesirable.

204. In the 1960s, the negative effect coffee eradication had on food supply was already noted with alarm, for 'beans are married to coffee' (*o feijão e casadinho com o café*). Brazil, Câmara dos Deputados, *Anais*, XII (1963) (26 and 28 June, 1 and 3 July 1963) pp. 240–1. In the mid-1970s acute food supply crises were caused by the rapid great expansion of export crops such as sugar cane, soy beans and oranges and pastures. The 'beans crises' of 1973 and 1976 brought rationing and the import, for the first time, of beans. A. A. Kageyama *et. al.*, 'Diferenciación campesina y cambio tecnológico: el caso de los productores de frijol en São Paulo'. Between 1959 and 1975 the availability of rice and beans '*per capita*' in Brazil diminished, raising prices. O. Queda, A. A. Kageyama, J. F. Graziano da Silva, *Evolução Recent das Culturas de Arroz e Feijão no Brasil* (Brasilia, 1979).

205. A. Delfim Netto, 'Sugestões para uma politica cafeeira'.

206. This observation was made by an agronomist and landowner in the region of Assis in an interview with him in 1977. This man had occupied a high post in the administration of the sugar mill Nova América in the 1960s, i.e. during the strike. He knew all about labour disputes in agriculture and the effects of the Statute, but he refused to talk about the 1962 strike.

4 New Forms of Labour Exploitation and New Conflicts

1. The following analysis is based on an extended case study I carried out between 1973 and 1979 of one gang of casual wage labourers working on a large coffee plantation in the vicinity of Campinas in the state of São Paulo, supplemented by a study of labour contractors operating in the nearby town of Jaguariuna where most of the members of the gang lived, carried out by Armando Boito Jr, and less systematic information obtained on other labour gangs in the region.

2. In Chapter 5 I will come back to the mythical image workers hold of President Vargas.

3. In other regions of the state the contractor is variously called *empreitero* and *gato*.

4. As one contractor in the region of Cravinhos explained, 'in those days the *empreiteros* existed but they worked with people who had no home, *andarilhos* (vagabonds), single people. They did not work with people who had a family because the estates were full of people, those extensive *colonias*. Everybody went to town and for this reason the contractor now transports them to the estates to work'. I owe this description to José Carlos Saboia who did research on the emergence of casual wage labour among landlords and contractors in the region of Cravinhos next to the larger town of Riberão Preto, now an important sugar-cane area, in São Paulo.

5. I also owe this statement to José Carlos Saboia.

6. An example of the importance of casual wage labour is the nearby town of Itapira located in the vicinity of the largest sugar mill in the area. Stimulated by government policy offering special conditions for ethanol production, sugar cane expanded rapidly in the 1970s. At that time it was said that during the harvest approximately 100 gang trucks left the town every morning to take workers to the mill. Although legally a truck could not carry more than 35 workers, at times of great demand this number was often exceeded with considerable risk to life and limb. In Itapira many of the trucks, because they were also used for transporting cane, had no roof or side boards. Workers just sat on the platform holding on as best they could.

7. At least two of the labour contractors had on separate occasions resorted to magic to solve conflicts that had arisen at work. When at one point the contractor of the gang felt generally ill and weak, he attributed this to the doings of a former woman worker who had been dismissed and who had taken him to court. He alternated between various magical agents – Umbanda centres – and made vows to Nossa Senhora Aparecida to obtain a cure. He promised to take his gang for free on three pilgrimages to the shrine of Nossa Senhora Aparecida. Another contractor resorted to an Umbanda centre to solve a conflict that had arisen between him and the administrator of the estate where he worked with his gang.

8. *O Estado de São Paulo* (23 March 1975) p. 44.

9. II Encontro Cafeeiro Regional do Estado de São Paulo held in Campinas on 19 August 1972.

10. Internal document of the Secretaria de Relações de Trabalho of São Paulo (n.d. but presumably 1977) containing a report on labour co-operatives by the Secretary of Labour, Jorge Maluly Netto. An accord signed between the Ministry of Labour and the Department of Labour Relations of São Paulo published in the *Diario Oficial* on 12 January 1977, provided for the establishment of co-operatives of temporary labour in the following towns: Avaré, Rio Claro, Guaira, Guariba, Franca, Lins, Jaú, Santa Fé do Sul, Palmares Paulista, Andradina, Junqueirópolis and Ourinhos. For further information on the labour co-operatives and the debate that developed around them, see also 'As cooperativas dos volantes', *Opinião* (3 December 1976) p. 2; 'O Brasil – a solução do governo para o drama dos bóias-frias', *Movimento* (7 June 1976) p. 6; 'Cooperativas para bóias-frias é criticada na AL', *Folha de*

São Paulo (7 October 1977); Associação de Engenheiros Agrónomos do Estado de São Paulo, Centro Paulista de Debates Agronómicos, *Painel de Debates: Cooperativas de mão-de-mbra agrícola: solução para o bóia-fria?* (18 August 1977) (mimeo).

11. In 1979 a new attempt was made, this time in the state of Paraná, to establish rural labour cooperatives. The scheme was even more unrealistic. In order to give employment to the workers during the slack season the Ministry of Labour was to puchase land for them to produce vegetables. Still, they were to continue living in town in housing provided under an agreement between the Ministries of the Interior and of Labour. These cooperatives would also provide training to the workers as carpenters, masons and electricians and again artisan crafts were to be done. The project was received with considerable scepticism both by rural employers and rural labour unions, not least because neither the funding of the cooperatives nor their implications for the workers were at all clear. *Jornal da República* (17 November 1979).

12. In 1971, the rural labour union of Cravinhos on its own initiative experimented with direct supply of labour to plantations to eliminate the contractor and at one time operated with about 300 labourers. But after two years the scheme had to be abandoned, allegedly due to competition from independent labour contractors. Associação de Engenheiros Agrónomos do Estado de São Paulo pp. 29-34.

13. *O Estado de São Paulo* (8 July 1976). The rural labour unions of São Paulo participating in the negotiations were essentially demanding a wage increase of 50 per cent and the regularisation of the condition of casual labourers, but the Secretary of Labour of the state, Maluly Netto, centered the discussion on what he vaguely called the social problems. Official concern over the situation of casual labour was enhanced in the mid-1970s by a succession of accidents that occurred in the interior of São Paulo. Tens of casual labourers were seriously injured and some died when in at least four cases the trucks in which they travelled crashed or overturned, drawing public attention forcefully to the miserable conditions of these workers. Almost simultaneously the government extended legal protection in case of accidents at work and retirement benefits to rural workers, ironically excluding again the temporary labour contractors working with casual labour. *Jornal da República* (7 November 1975) and *O Estado de São Paulo* (21 December 1974).

14. The gang I studied was one of the four permanent gangs in the Jaguariuna region and it had been working on the same estate for about seven years. Its size varied between 30 and 50 workers depending basically on the wage paid relative to other gangs. Four-fifths of the gang were older married women and young girls, the rest men. During the first year of research, from mid-1973 to mid-1974, I spent most mornings with the gang in the field and visited the workers in their homes at the weekends. At one point the labour contractor, together with the estate administrator, attempted to expel me from the estate. At the end of 1973 the workers were paid the annual bonus for the first time. The workers attributed this to my presence and the

administration's unease about it. I managed to persuade the administration of the academic importance and innocuousness of my research. After this, the contractor was unable to forbid me to continue accompanying the gang. This certainly facilitated my contact with the workers who had been awaiting the outcome of my confrontation with curiosity and glee. Until 1979 I continued visiting the gang regularly and also contacted gangs working on other estates in the region.

15. Those who regarded themselves as *volantes* were in the minority. As one worker explained, 'we work in a gang, *volantes* are those who work a little here and a little there. We have been working here in the gang for 2 years. Those who work in a gang are *volantes* because they have no *patrão* [boss], they have a contractor. Where we work I do not know the *patrão*, I don't know who he is, I only know the administrator . . . the one who is responsible for us there is the contractor, the one who comes to get us and brings us back. He hires the gang and takes us there on the administrator's behalf. That means he is responsible, he is the one who hires us. That estate there is a company, they could register us but until today they have not done so', and another worker stated categorically, 'we are *volantes*, who have no arrangement on vacations, annual bonus. If they pay these it is out of their own will; if something happens, an accident, anything, we are exposed to anything. If we die that's it. Where should we complain; rights, we have nothing, only the day's wage'.

16. Legal claims by workers over compensation, holiday pay and the annual bonus can be settled in two ways. Either the worker pursues the case to the end which, depending on the landlord's toughness, may mean that it may reach the supreme labour court in Brasilia which may take years, or he/she may settle for an *acordo* (agreement) in the first instance, in that case receiving 65 per cent of his/her claim. The claimant must produce three unrelated witnesses who can prove that the worker has been dismissed unjustly.

17. Sr José even noted that the fact that job security had been replaced by the FGTS in industry made labour rotation easier there than in agriculture where it continued to be the landlord who had to pay compensation for time worked in cases of dismissal.

18. One worker, in fact, argued that it was the contractor who was responsible for paying sickness leave because rather than being paid a wage by the estate he withheld a commission from the workers' payroll, i.e. he profited himself at the workers' expense.

19. Only very recently has more attention been paid in the literature on the politics of accumulation in Third World countries to subtle everyday forms of resistance and struggle on the part of workers. See R. Cohen, 'Resistance and Hidden Forms of Consciousness among African Workers', in H. Johnson and H. Bernstein (eds.), *Third World Lives of Struggle* (London, 1982) and J. Breman, 'Between Accumulation and Immiseration: The Partiality of Fieldwork in Rural India', *The Journal of Peasant Studies*, 13 (1) (October 1985).

20. In Amparo, however, a town about 40 minutes away from Jaguariuna and located in a region where coffee had been replaced by cattle and

some annual crops, the large contractor who controlled all the gangs explicitly refused to work with women. He would not even do the cotton harvest because this was executed by women and children. His argument was that women were no good, that there was always one woman who was a troublemaker. Unfortunately I was unable to find out exactly what he meant by this.

21. In the sugar-cane regions, however, cane cutting which is also paid by result, is usually though not exclusively done by men. This is a job which, because it is very tough, is considered more appropriate for men.

22. See e.g. P. Fernandez, 'Las maquiladoras y las mujeras en ciudad Juárez (México): paradojas de la industrialización bajo el capitalismo integral', in M. León (ed.), *Debate sobre la Mujer en América Latina y el Caribe*, ACEP (Bogotá, 1982).

23. In one of the local factories young girls who were not registered were regularly told to hide when the inspector came to check on working conditions. The girls who went to work in the chicken-freezing plant on the outskirts of the town there expected to do an extraordinary amount of overtime without receiving the legally-established rate. A few who dared to protest were fired.

24. V. Stolcke, 'Women's labours: the naturalization of social inequality and women's subordination', in K. Young, C. Wolkowitz and R. McCullagh (eds.), *Of Marriage and the Market, Women's Subordination in International Perspective* (London, 1981).

25. Below I will discuss how workers' displacement from the estates has also affected their needs.

26. Employers are quite flexible about using their cultural images of women. In the 1960s when *colono* families were dismissed from the estates, if any compensation was paid it was only to the husband although the wife had worked as well. A more accurate way of comparing standards of work between women and men and among women themselves, would have been a systematic time-and-motion study of the different tasks. However, not only would this have been very difficult to do politically in the context of Brazil, but it would also have involved much time which I believe was more fruitfully spent by attempting to understand the women's attitude in depth. In any case, the labour contractor was never happy about my presence and would have resented such a study even more.

27. For a good discussion of the literature on attitudes and behaviour at work in industry and the conceptual problems of determining these, see R. Hyman and I. Brough, *Social Values and Industrial Relations: A Study of Fairness and Inequality* (Oxford, 1975). The authors, however, show no awareness of possible gender-specific attitudes.

28. Another younger woman pointed out the class-specific notion of work: [the doctor] for him it is work, for us it isn't. He doesn't do anything and earns a lot. 'He only asks what one feels and already earns 40cr$. We yes, we do work'.

29. Young girls were usually regarded as less responsible at work than the older, married women.

30. She eventually left the gang because the contractor did not sufficiently appreciate her special commitment. In a quarrel with a young girl who had treated her disrespectfully, the contractor refused to take her side, which she thought undermined her authority within the gang.

31. Conversely, the 'responsible' workers take it amiss when others take advantage of them by not doing their share as, for instance, when someone leaves part of her row for the worker in the next row to weed.

32. Once she refused to allow the coffee left over from her day's work to be used to top up someone else's sack because she thought the contractor might gain the impression that the other worker had exerted herself more than she had for, after all, it was her work and it was she who had scratched her arms picking it. But she was visibly self-conscious about this. A few days later she did offer coffee to her fellow workers and on several occasions helped women who were slow in finishing their task.

33. When the contractor asked Da Cida to bring a few brooms from home to sweep up the berries that had missed the tarpaulin spread under the tree, she refused; 'it is not our business to bring a broom, the estate is not ours. We have never brought a broom. This year they have become totally relaxed. They own the estate and we are supposed to cut, tie up and put a stick on the broom to sweep up the coffee that belongs to them ... we are supposed to work a lot and earn little'.

34. By allowing workers to dictate their own pace of work, piece-work did not necessarily obviate the need for supervision. Under the *colonato* system, fast and careful work were compatible because workers harvested the same trees they had tended and since coffee yields are affected by the quality of the weeding, negligence was rare.

35. Because piece-work is designed to speed up the work process without necessarily having to pay correspondingly higher wages, the amount of extra effort needed to produce a given output often far outweighs the value of any possible increase in earnings. So, to the extent that workers need to increase their levels of effort when they are paid by result, to maximise or even maintain their wage, so too do they correspondingly decrease their effort when they are paid by time.

5 Memory and Myth in the Making of Workers' Identity

1. L. F. Rainho, *Os Peões do Grande ABC* (Petrópolis, 1980) presents research among unskilled workers employed in the large industries in São Paulo before and during the organised struggle for wage readjustments in accordance with inflation in 1977 and the first large strike of 1978. These unskilled workers labelled themselves *peões* (peons). In more generic terms, they regarded themselves as *operários* or *trabalhadores* (workers). Rainho did not inquire into their perception of the social order at large, yet it seems that, like the rural workers, they conceived of themselves also as the poor pitched against the rich.

2. There is a vast literature on the so-called messianic movements in Brazil. To my knowledge, no research has, however, been done among sectors of the working class on links between secular consciousness and religious thought in Brazil.

3. T. C. Bruneau, 'The Catholic Church and the Basic Christian Communities: a case study from the Brazilian Amazon', Discussion Paper Series 7, Centre for Development-Area Studies (McGill University, Montreal, May 1983).

4. Little is known about the effect of these *novelas* on the workers' world view and their attitude to them.

5. The massive strikes in São Paulo's motorcar industry which began in 1978, like the wave of urban riots earlier in the decade of which urban transport was the main target, were rarely shown on TV.

6. Cane workers in Pernambuco perceive the hierarchy of exploitation to which they are subjected in similar terms: 'we work for three: for ourselves, for the estate and for the contractor'. L. Sigaud, 'A idealização do passado numa área de plantation', *Contrapunto*, II (2) (November 1977) p. 166.

7. R. Miller Paiva, S. Schattan and C. F. Trench de Freitas, *Setor Agrícola*, p. 92.

8. R. Miller Paiva, S. Schattan and C. F. Trench de Freitas, *Setor Agrícola*, p. 92.

9. L. Sigaud, *Os clandestinos e os direitos*.

10. Houses for rent were scarce. Rents varied according to the size and quality of the house, but the rent for a small, very modest house could amount to almost an individual month's wage.

11. J. R. Wells, 'Distribution of earnings, growth and the structure of demand in Brazil during the 1960s, *World Development*, 2 (1974).

12. The fridge cost 1900cr$, to be paid in 20 monthly instalments. At the time they were five members in the household of whom one worked outside. The monthly family income amounted to about 2500cr$. The legal minimum wage at the time (1975) was 532cr$. A TV set bought on hire purchase at about the same time cost around 3500cr$.

13. Unskilled workers in the multinational companies on the periphery of São Paulo, however, seem to experience a similar sense of inadequacy over their humble homes and poor-quality clothes. L. F. Rainho, *Os Peões do Grande ABC*, p. 165.

14. W. Baer, *The Brazilian Economy, Growth and Development* (New York, 1983) pp. 119, 141.

15. Little research has been done in Brazil on the political memories of specific social groups. The fear that Vargas inspired in the dominant class and élitist interpretations of his popular appeal to the working classes, generally attributed his populist manipulations to the ignorance of the masses precluding any serious attempts to understand the hold of the Vargas myth over the popular imagination. In an excellent study of electoral attitudes prior to the 1978 national elections in a working-class neighbourhood in the city of São Paulo, Vargas, Janio Quadros and Joao Goulart are all remembered as having favoured the poor and as a consequence having been killed or

deposed. Among the urban electorate, however, memories of Quadros and Goulart are stronger than in the countryside presumably because urban areas had more direct and sustained exposure to their electoral campaigns. But they are generally as uninterested in and sceptical about elections as the rural workers. T. Pires do Rio Caldeira, 'Para que serve o voto?' (As eleições e o cotidiano na periferia de São Paulo), B. Lamounier (ed.), *Voto de Desconfiança, Eleições e Mudança Política no Brasil, 1970-1979* (Petrópolis, 1980) pp. 81–115; L. T. Pires do Rio Caldeira, *A Política dos Outros* (São Paulo, 1984).

16. Despite extensive mobilisation and unionisation of rural workers in Pernambuco, even they conceive of the 'rights' as something Arraes gave them rather than a gain won by their own struggles. The high level of unionisation in Pernambuco, in contrast to São Paulo, has had a further consequence. Although the workers in the gang were generally denied their 'rights', most of them felt entitled to them despite never having belonged to a rural union. In Pernambuco, by contrast, sugar workers regard union membership as a necessary precondition to becoming registered workers (*fichados*) and to benefiting from and being entitled to defend their 'rights'. Because they do not enjoy the 'rights', *clandestinos* are excluded from the unions which are thought to be reserved only for the *fichados*. In Jaguariuna, workers who resorted to the courts to claim their 'rights', did so without the support of a union. For Pernambuco, see L. Sigaud, *Os clandestinos e os direitos*; L. Sigaud, 'A idealização do passado numa área de plantation', contains an analysis of the political memory of *resident* workers on sugar-cane plantations in Pernambuco. Again, most of them attribute the 'rights' to M. Arraes but many also associate them with Vargas, who left them while Arraes made them public. This connection is sometimes, though weakly, made in São Paulo between Vargas and Goulart. For a description of Miguel Arraes's career from a Pernambuco delegate to the *Instituto do Açucar e do Alcool* in the 1940s, through Deputy to the State Assembly in the 1950s for the PSD, thereafter Finance Secretary to the State Governor in 1958, then exemplary and very popular Mayor of the state capital Recife in 1959, to State Governor in 1962 when one of the central points of his programme was to find a solution to the needs of the rural and urban poor, cf. A. Alcántara de Carmargo, 'Brésil Nord-Est', pp. 350 ff.

17. In 1930 the military movement of the *Aliança Liberal* headed by Getúlio Vargas took power. The new government also introduced the secret vote and extended the franchise to women but did not grant, however, full citizenship to the 'uneducated and ignorant people'. The new electoral code of 1932 continued to exclude the illiterate from the political process. With the end of the Estado Novo in 1945 and the redemocratisation of the country, the issue of a franchise for the illiterates was raised again. During the Constituent Assembly of 1946, the political exclusion of over 20 million peasants who made up the majority of the illiterates was hotly debated. The Brazilian Communist Party, the UDN and the PSD proposed a motion to grant the vote to illiterate people, but this was, however, overruled. The law of

electoral reform passed by Congress after the 1964 military coup reiterated the exclusion of illiterates. R. Maranhão, L. Roncari and A. Mendes Jr, 'O direito do voto no Brasil', *Movimento*, 33 (16 February 1976). In 1982 illiterates were finally enfranchised, although their participation in subsequent elections has been very low.

18. If registered voters failed to fulfil their 'civic duty' they risked being fined. A survey carried out by the Catholic University of São Paulo on the occasion of the 1978 national elections showed that although the MDB had gained some credibility as the opposition party, 40 per cent of those interviewed said that they would vote only because it was compulsory. The class distribution of the sample was fairly representative. By 1978 the electoral process imposed by the military government had lost legitimacy among all sectors of the society. T. Pires do Rio Caldeira, *A Política dos Outros*, p. 113.

19. B. Lamounier (ed.), *Voto de Desconfiança*.

20. As T. do Rio Caldeira, *A Política dos Outros* shows, by 1978 the MDB had gained some credibility as the *trabalhista* party (of the workers) although politicians were regarded with positive distrust and thought to be only out to enrich themselves and scepticism about the MDB's chances of forcing its programme onto an unwilling government prevailed among the urban workers she interviewed. L. F. Rainho, *Os Peões do Grande ABC*, p. 155, has shown that unskilled industrial workers in São Paulo were far less enthusiastic about the 1978 electoral campaign than they had been in 1974. In 1974, the workers in Jaguariuna also doubted the MDB's ability to implement its policies even if it won because both parties existed by the grace of the military government:

> If the MDB wins there will be war. Because the situation is such that we cannot vote against the graúdos [big shots] there. I believe that the MDB won't do us any good either. If it were to win do you think that things can improve for the poor? Who has the greater power? ARENA! I think that the MDB depends on them. The MDB can try, but then a revolution can break out in the situation we are in. Don't you think there can be a hunger crisis? The rich are many more than the poor. Everywhere you see the rich. They won't vote against: they will belong to the ARENA. There in the neighbourhood most people vote for ARENA out of fear. People say that it is better to vote for ARENA than for MDB. But it would be a good thing if ARENA lost. Just to see. We are lost anyway.

The belief in the MDB's lack of power is substantiated by their experience with local politicians, some of whom are known to have switched to the government party in order to gain access to local finances controlled by the government. Scepticism toward the MDB appears to have declined during the late 1970s. In the November 1983 national election, the Party of the Brazilian Democratic Movement (*Partido do Movimento Democrático Brasileiro* PMDB, which replaced the MDB after the electoral reform) comprising a range of political tendencies from the centre right to the left, won the most important state legislatures.

21. This profound scepticism is present at all times. One worker exclaimed 'The government is like a pigsty. When one has got fat another one comes in. For the poor it is always the same thing.' Another worker who voted because he was registered, defaced his vote so that it would be useless. Others did not even obtain their voters' card. But casting a blank vote (*votar em branco*) was counterproductive because such votes were added to those of the majority candidate or party and thus increased the government's vote. They just couldn't win:

> I am through with elections. I've had enough. I have to work. Nobody helps a bum. I go there, draw an ugly face and don't vote for anybody. Every night they drive around with their combis but when they manage to get elected, they get the office, they couldn't care less for the poor. And it is through the poor that they get there. Elections are a game with marked cards: 'Whatever party wins, for us it is just the same. We are the last to be looked after. Even before you notice it, his time is up. The poor have no chance. They have a chance only when it is a question of getting them into office. After that, nothing!'

22. It is ironic that one worker, a very articulate man, had received his education about land reform from the landlord who clearly felt very threatened by the growing agitation in the early 1960s. The worker had, however, reinterpreted this information from his own class perspective. When I asked him whether he had ever heard of land reform he told me the following:

> Janio Quadros himself, he was said to be a communist, that he was very good. Dr Armando [the landlord] said he didn't like him. (What is communism?) If it came it would be good because there wouldn't be *vagabundos* [idlers], everybody would have to work, but there wouldn't be expoliation [*sic*] either. The workers all said that they would like it if there were such laws. Dr Armando said that clothes, dresses would be obtained by exchange, there would be no money. The shopkeepers would also have to exist. He said that with the land one would see how much one could cultivate. One would have that plot to plant, pasture for animals, he said the government would do this, divide the land so that the worker had land to cultivate. Dr Armando told me that there was a country where it was like that. Dr Armando would not like it. It was then that there was this fight, that he started dismissing all those people, the *colonos* to plant all in pasture. Oh, they were afraid that they would have to work as well. Nobody knew, they were afraid that this division would come. That country of which Dr Armando spoke, in the

end everybody would be owner, I think it would be a good thing.
People wouldn't have any money but they would have everything
to live. Now, the ones who wouldn't want to work would starve;
nowadays hardly anybody talks about this. To reach such a
point it is difficult, one would have to do what you said once.
Everybody who is poor begin a war. In the end this will happen,
the wage rises 20 per cent and prices go up 50 per cent; it is
impossible. Where will the life of the people get in this way? If
there was this business of elections, the situation would already
have exploded. Not now, there is the army, when one leaves he
finds another one. In those days the Presidents got in badly and
left badly, they only wanted to line their pockets, that's why
there was all this deposition. The time of Getúlio was good still;
one didn't see the money but the people had something . . . people
knew no rest in order not to starve. After Getúlio things already
became worse, this business of the wage appeared . . . the
generals; that is when the merchandise went up more and
more . . . there were also many people who were afraid, who said
that communism was that confusion, who feared this.

One woman asked me, when we talked about distributing the land,
whether this was communism 'as they say' and added that it would be
a good thing but 'here in this country it'll never happen. I think it does
not happen because it is very dangerous and would cause a war.'
23. Significantly, when asked about the relative strength of the rich and
the poor, those who felt most powerless, namely the women, tended to
confuse the power derived from wealth with the numerical strength of
the rich. By contrast, men were more categorical in their assertions
that, undoubtedly, there were more poor than rich.
24. As he argued, land distribution:

cannot be done because our class [sic] is very relaxed. If you say,
let's strike, kill (you can't do that) because the landowners have
the greatest power, and there is no unity. They [the workers] are
not like the landowners who organise their unity. Let's suppose,
you say that a strike will break out, that they will die or kill, who
loses most? The poor are more; there are more rich than in the
old days, the President of the Republic himself can send a
stronger power because they, the poor, are reacting against the
greater power. He will say, it would be better for the President of
the Republic to say that he will carry out a land reform, but he
will not remain there. Who will depose him? the rich! Now the
poor, our class must always lose, one man alone dominates us.
The workers' wage is no good . . . who will depose him? We will
depose him? Few people go to work in the fields from here, there
are trucks of stone masons; tell them to strike, they are capable
of killing us. If you tell a stone mason to strike, to receive a piece
of land, work with the hoe . . . we have to thank God that many
landowners give us work to get by. A worker in the field earns

40 Cr$ a day, a stone mason, how much does he earn, 100Cr$. Will he want to strike? He will hire a helper and earn at his expense . . . In Itapira there are trucks which have only 15 men, the rest are women and children, do you think they will strike, they will begin a strike on the estates? The others are well employed. Do you think that under these circumstances a worker will be solidary? It's infuriating, really infuriating. Our class is such a miserable lot, to the point that people kill each other in the end; [a leader] they will look for him and he has had it. In the old days you were stronger. The President didn't have the power he now has. Getúlio they say he was killed, Janio [Quadros] if he hadn't resigned wouldn't he have died? Now, this President of ours, doesn't he have the army behind him? If a strike breaks out in a small town he sends the cavalry and finishes it all off.

25. It is important to quote the explanation this worker offered for why he did not want to share his experience with his fellow workers. It reveals the subtle interaction between class consciousness and fear:

I won't talk because they create problems for me. If I tell them today, they will go to work with that in their heads. There are people who are unable to keep a secret, if I talk they will change what I said. I haven't even started to work again and when I'll go [to the estate] they will refuse to give me work. Today already a relative of X came to ask whether it was true that I was paid 1,500Cr$ [he won the court case]. They [the administration of the estate] asked me not to talk about it. This business is not to be told. One should only tell those who need it. Now, those others there, they are capable of telling [the contractor], tomorrow I will go to the police if you don't pay me the compensation for the time I have worked. If they talk in the right way one does not have to be afraid, but they talk wrong, they will say, it was that one there who told me to stop being a fool, they are unable to keep things to themselves. Do you think that under these conditions I can talk. They want to take it from my mouth to give it away there tomorrow. The people here are strange. If you say that you have spat they will say that you have vomited. This here is a place, a hot place. João [a fellow worker] had conscience. One talked to him and he did not give anything away. There are people, when you tell them one word they already say three or four. I do not say anything to such people. Before you are aware they already have got your name in the midst several times over.

6 The Exploitation of Family Morality

1. M. Barrett and M. McIntosh, *The Anti-Social Family* (London, 1982) pp. 129–30. An earlier, partial version of this chapter has been

published under the title 'The Exploitation of Family Morality: Labor Systems and Family Structure on São Paulo Coffee Plantations, 1850–1979' in R. T. Smith (ed.), *Kinship Ideology and Practice in Latin America* (The University of North Carolina Press, 1984).

2. For example, M. Coulson, B. Magas, H. Wainwright, 'The housewife and her labour under capitalism – a critique', *New Left Review*, 89 (1975); W. Seccomb, 'Domestic labour – a reply to critics', *New Left Review* 94 (1975); J. Gardiner, 'Women's domestic labour', *New Left Review*, 89 (1975); S. Himmelweit and S. Mohun, 'Domestic labour and capital', *Cambridge Journal of Economics*, 1 (1977); H. I. Hartmann, 'Capitalism, partriarchy and job segregation by sex', *Signs*, 1 (3) (part 2) (1976).

3. J. Humphries, 'Class struggle and the persistence of the working-class family', *Cambridge Journal of Economics*, 1 (3) (1977); H. I. Hartmann and A. R. Markusen, 'Contemporary marxist theory and practice, a feminist critique', *The Review of Radical Political Economics*, 12 (2) (1980); G Sen, 'The sexual division of labour and the subordination of women', *The Review of Radical Political Economics*, 12 (2) (1980).

4. O. Harris, 'Household as natural units', in K. Young, C. Wolkowitz and R. McCullagh (eds.), *Of Marriage and the Market: Women's Subordination in International Perspective* (London, 1981); A. Whitehead, ' "I'm hungry mum": the politics of domestic budgeting', in K. Young, C. Wolkowitz and R. McCullagh (eds.), *Of Marriage and the Market*.

5. For example, K. Young, 'Formas de apropiación y la división sexual del trabajo: un estudio de caso de Oaxaca, México', in M. León (ed.), *Debate sobre la mujer en América Latina y el Caribe*, ACEP (Bogotá, 1982); C. D. Deere and M. León, 'Producción campesina, proletarización y la división sexual del trabajo en la zona andina', in M León (ed.), *Debate sobre la mujer*; M. Roldán, 'Subordinación genérica y proletarización rural: un estudio de caso en el Noroeste de México', in M. León (ed.), *Debate sobre la mujer*.

6. Parliamentary Papers, House of Commons and House of Lords, Select Committee on the Slave Trade, 1847–48, J. B. Moore, XXII, pp. 322, 436. I am grateful to M. Manuela Carneiro da Cunha for this interesting piece of information.

7. T. Davatz, *Memórias*.

8. D. Jaguaribe Filho, *Algumas palavras sobre a emigração*, p.19.

9. L. Karrer, *Das schweizerische Auswanderungswesen und die Revision und Vollziehung des Bundesgesetz über den Geschäftsbetrieb von Auswanderungsagenturen* (Bern, 1886), p.69; C. Heusser, *Die Schweizer auf den Kolonien*, p. 14; R. A. Natsch, *Die Haltung eidgenössischer und kantonaler Behörden*, p. 176.

10. For example, M. Palacios, *Coffee in Columbia*; A. A. Kageyama *et al*, *Diferenciación campesina y cambio tecnológico*, pp. 5–6; but B. Sallum Jr, *Capitalismo e Cafeicultura*, who emphasises the surplus labour appropriated through self-provisioning.

11. J. B. do Amaral, 'Introdução do trabalho livre', p. 245.

12. C. Heusser, *Die Schweitzer auf den Kolonien*; A. L. Ozorio de Almeida, 'Parcería e tamanho da familia no Nordeste brasileiro', *Pesquisa e*

Planejamento Económico, 7. p. 2 (1977) showing that different labour systems affect family sizes.

13. P. de Turenne, 'L'immigration et la colonisation', p. 451.
14. For a similar process of differentiation among smallholders related to differential family size cf. C. D. Deere and A. de Janvry, 'Demographic and social differentiation among northern Peruvian peasants., *The Journal of Peasant Studies*, 8 (3) (1981).
15. 'Um socialista' quoted in P. S. Pinheiro and M. Hall (eds.) *A Classe operaría no Brasil*.
16. J. P. Carvalho de Moraes, *Relatório apresentado*, p. 66; BUCICA (1903) p. 73; D. Jaguaribe Filho, *Algumos palavras sobre a emigração*, pp. 19, 32.
17. A. Ramos, *O café no Brasil*, p. 120.
18. W. Dean, *Rio Claro*, p. 71.
19. C. Heusser, *Die Schweitzer auf den Kolonien*, p. 48; D. Jaguaribe Filho, *Algumas palavras sobre a emigração*, p. 32.
20. J. Papaterra Limongi, 'O trabalhador nacional', *Boletim do Departamento do Trabalho*, 5 (20) (1916).

21.   'It's about three years ago, Marcão, the stonemason, took a copy book and wrote down the names of everybody. This was given to the mayor. Nothing happened. Then, that one left and he [the "good mayor"] came in; then they wrote another list. We asked for electric light to improve the neighbourhood. Then he said that he could not do anything. Then one day a colleague of mine came and invited me to go with him to the mayor. So we went. He said: what do you think I can do for you? You have to hand this in to the company. You have to use the appropriate sheet of paper, write a proper list and ask somebody to type it. Then we thought how to do that. We bought the sheets, went out and got the names of all of them (the neighbours). We could do what we wanted and never got more than eighty names. He [the mayor] said that if there were more we could hand the list in to the company [providing electricity for the municipality]. Then we used our heads. We spent three days getting everybody who wanted light. He said that if the company wouldn't agree he would buy a transformer and if everybody agreed he would deduct [the cost] from every family per month. Then we went around trying to catch everybody here. In three nights we got over 70 people on this side and everybody on the other side. We went from house to house and got 126 people. Then I took the copy book and the sheets to my colleague, Roberto, a very educated fellow who had already worked for the government, who took the sheets to a colleague in Campinas who typed them properly. He signed and we signed and took the list to the mayor. Then the mayor took it to the company and they accepted. Then he asked who had done this and we had to tell him and he promised that 9 months from there we would have light. It took a year. On our side it took another 5 months. When he had the election meeting he apologised for having put the light up there and not down here and promised to install it here. After two more months the light appeared here.

22. Da Maria, for instance, had first allowed a neighbour to draw drinking water from her well, only to withdraw her permission later for reasons which were never quite cleaı but which were interpreted and resented as a sign of pride.

23. Because of these constant latent tensions, despite a general dislike of the police who are regarded as arbitrary and violent, on the occasion of a wedding, parents will often ask them to keep an eye on things to prevent fights. Accusations among neighbours, not always well founded, are also rife. People are particularly sensitive to being accused of appropriating something that does not belong to them, such as a chicken. There is always a fear that children may trespass when their parents are at work and there were at least two instances when neighbours resorted to the police in accusing children of theft. The parents were both incensed and deeply ashamed. Obviously, when discussing sources of social tension it is also important to consider the role played by race, especially since the population in the neighbourhood is racially very heterogeneous. Although there is an awareness that whiteness is a source of some prestige and being black or mulattoe is a social disadvantage, intermarriage is not infrequent and for the most part racial prejudice is latent rather than overt. Only when conflicts flare up are people denigrated in explicitly racial terms.

24. This same contractor's son, who had at one time driven the truck, had beaten up one of the women at work because she was his father's lover and he thought his father was giving her money. The woman went to court and the estate provided a lawyer for the contractor. The case was still running.

25. Sexual intercourse between husband and wife is one of the spheres of experience where relations of domination are asserted and played out. The women for the most part were very reluctant to speak about their sexual relations apart from occasional bawdy jokes. It seemed that it was usually the man who demanded sexual intercourse and denial on the part of the wife was grounds for a fight. Many of the older women no longer slept together with their husbands who would only occasionally exercise their conjugal rights. One woman explained a wife's duties toward her husband as follows:

> She has to take care of everything, the clothes, everything that refers to the home. The man must work to provide for the family, the wife and the children. There are men who do not like their wives to work. There are many women who do not sleep with their husbands. (Why?) I have grown unaccustomed, I don't sleep with him anymore. He left the bed, I grew unaccustomed. He comes to my bed for a little while but sleeps in his own. It is the man who abandons the bed; not women, there is no way for women to abandon the bed. It is always the husband who commands everything. That's the way it is. Women must be quiet, otherwise there are fights. When he says anything I remain quiet.

26. A few of the families grew some vegetables in the backyard. Often there was not enough good soil for that but the men also argued that they did not have the time. They were now expected to grow vegetables. Another obstacle was lack of water. The most men will do at home is fetch firewood, mend fences and see to repairs in the house. Fetching water from the river or a neighbour's well was also a woman's responsibility.

27. See, for example, H. I. Hartmann, 'The family as the locus of gender, class and political struggle: the example of housework', *Signs*, 6 (3) (1981) where she argues that housework sharing is an important source of conjugal conflict.

28. Significantly, whereas under the *colonato* system the important contribution made by the women to the family economy was recognised by their husbands and landlords were well aware of it, the jurisprudence that arose from the workers demands for compensation when they were dismissed from the estates made women's labour invisible. Only the household head was considered entitled to compensation. See, for instance, *O Estado de Sao Paulo* (21 May 1961).

29. Desertion by men of their families in situations of economic penury and the consequent spread of households composed of women and their children seems to be a typical reaction of men who feel that they have failed in their responsibilities. Cf., for example, A. Hagerman Johnson, 'The impact of market agriculture on family and household structure in nineteenth century Chile', *Hispanic American Historical Review* (1978), E. A. Kuznesof, 'Household composition and headship was related to changes in mode of production: São Paulo 1765 to 1836', *Comparative Studies in Society and History* (1980); M. Roldán, 'Subordinacíon genérica'.

30. A. Whitehead, ' "I'm hungry mum" ', seems to suggest that because they control the domestic budget, men enjoy relatively greater 'formal freedom'.

31. This is not the place to discuss at length the extent to which gender hierarchy and women's subordination persist in advanced industrial society. Indications are, however, that the case described here is not so different from the experience of women in those countries. It seems that although women have made gains in the economic sphere, their primary definition as wives and mothers continues to shape their performance on the labour market. See, for instance, the recent report published by the British government on women and employment; J. Martin and C. Roberts, *Women and Employment: A Lifetime Perspective*, HMSO (London, 1984). An equally significant experience is that of Third World women hired by the so-called runaway industries. This is an example of the way in which multinationals exploit gender roles and in so doing reinforce them and create a new segregation of labour by gender in the process of the internationalisation of the labour market. See P. Fernandez, 'Las maquiladoras y las mujeres'.

32. It must be emphasised that physical violence against women in Brazil is by no means a preserve of poor men. On the contrary, although

those in power have many ways of hiding the ugly face of their violence, there are a number of famous recent cases in which husbands and even lovers belonging to the upper classes not only beat, which is probably not unusual, but killed their women 'in defence of their honour' as this form of homicide is officially called. Cf. M. Corrêa, *Morte em Família* (Rio de Janeiro, 1983). In Jaguariuna there was at least one case recently in which a contractor had killed his wife accusing her of infidelity, although, as I was told, she had been a respectable woman and he the one who had another woman. He was still in jail.

33. In the case of one of the women, the husband had threatened to kill her for an act of infidelity although he himself had another woman on the side. The wife had entreated him not to leave her because she was a respectable woman. When he showed no signs of leaving the other woman she herself had a son by another man. Upon this her husband threatened to kill her but she went to the police who arrested the man.

34. M. C. Ferreira Albino de Oliveira, *A Produção da Vida, A Mulher nas Estrategias de Sobrevivencia da Familia Trabalhadora na Agricultura*, Doctoral Dissertation, (University of São Paulo, 1981) provides an excellent analysis of how the casualisation of rural labour in another area of São Paulo affected the workers' family and the condition of women. The findings are very similar although she takes a more optimistic view of the supportive role of the family. But, unfortunately, she analysed the experience of women as a separate category without considering that of men nor changing gender relations in any depth.

35. Characteristically, L. Stone argues that English history saw a distinct decline in interpersonal violence as instanced by the frequency of homicides from medieval to modern times interpreting this as a sign of social advance. L. Stone, 'Interpersonal violence in English society 1300-1980', *Past and Present*, 101 (November 1983).

Postscript: The Limits of Exploitation

1. A. A. Kageyama and J. Graziano da Silva, 'El desempeño de la agricultura brasileña en los anos setenta', *Economía de América Latina*, 9 (1982) pp. 90-1; for some other discussions of the recent performance of Brazilian agriculture see G. L. S. P. da Silva, 'Reflexões sobre o papel da agricultura no Brasil', *ASP*, XXXIX (I and II) (1982) pp. 1-20; F. Homem de Melo, *O Problema Alimentar no Brasil* (Rio de Janeiro, 1983).

2. F. Homem de Melo, *O Problema Alimentar*, pp. 25-6; the relatively largest amount of calories and proteins obtained from rice, beans and manioc was available per inhabitant per day in 1965. Maize supply reached a peak in 1965 and was achieved again only in 1972 and 1977.

3. J. E. Dutra de Oliveira and M. H. Silva Dutra de Oliveira (eds), '*Bóias-Frias*' – *Uma Realidade Brasileira*, Academia de Ciências de São Paulo, Publicações ACIESP, 30 (São Paulo, 1981) pp. 1–5. Precisely those workers engaged in energy-cropping suffer from severe calorie deficiencies.

4. *Folha de São Paulo* (December 27, 1982); in 1984 the sugar-mill Santa Elisa was providing 650 warm meals to its labourers. *Isto É* (4 July 1984) pp. 34–36. In July 1984, after the strikes, the Ministry of Labour included the labourers working on sugar-mills producing ethanol under the Workers' Food Programme designed to provide subsidised meals presumably to pacify the workers' exalted spirits. As one labourer declared, however, they preferred better wages to this hand-out, more so since it did not feed their families. *Folha de São Paulo* (5 August 1984).

5. It was estimated that by increasing the cane-rows cut simultaneously from five to seven, a workers' daily output declined by 22 per cent on account of the additional time needed to collect the cane cut in heaps. For the mill, however, it meant an estimated fuel saving in cane lifting and transport of 40 per cent. *Folha de São Paulo* (17 May 1984).

6. These strikes, their context and outcome are described at length in the *Folha de São Paulo* (16–20, 23, 27 and 30 May) and (1 and 2 June 1984) as well as in the *O Estado de São Paulo* (3, 6 and 7 June 1984) and in *Isto É* (23 May 1984), *Veja* (23 May 1984) and *Isto É* (4 July 1984).

7. *Folha de São Paulo* (5 August 1984); *Isto É* (4 July 1984); *Folha de São Paulo* (11 July 1984).

Bibliography

'Agricultura nello Stato di S. Paolo', *BUCICA*, II (5) (March 1903).
'A indústria do café em São Paulo', *ASP*, VIII (3) (March 1961).
'A lavoura paulista de cereais', *Revista de Commercio e Industria*, II (25) (February 1917).
Albuquerque, R. H. P. L. de, 'Relações de produção na cotonicultura paulista', IFCH, Unicamp (Campinas, 1982) (mimeo).
Alcántara de Camargo, A., 'Brésil Nord-Est; Mouvements Paysans et Crise Populiste', Doctoral Dissertation (Université de Paris, 1973).
Alves Novaes, A. and P. Cruz, *et al.* (eds) *Impasse na Democracia Brasileira 1951–1955*, Coletánea de Documentos, CPDOC, Editora da Fundação Getúlio Vargas (Rio de Janeiro, 1983).
Amaral, J. B. do Visconde de Indaiatuba, 'Introdução do trabalho livre em Campinas', in *Monografia histórica do município de Campinas* (Rio de Janeiro, 1952).
Andrade M. de, *Café*, Concepção Melodramática (em tres atos), in M. de Andrade, *Obras Completas de Mário de Andrade, Poesias Completas* (São Paulo, 1966).
'A nova face da agricultura', *Coopercotia* (October 1968).
Araújo Dias, R., 'Problemas atuais da economia cafeeira', *ASP*, XVI (1/2) (1969).
'As cooperativas dos volantes', *Opinião* (3 December 1976).
Associação de Engenheiros Agrónomos do Estado de São Paulo, Centro Paulista de Debates Agronómicos, *Painel de Debates: Cooperativas de mão-de-obra agrícola: solução para o bóia-fria?* (18 August 1977) (mimeo).
Baer, W., 'The inflation controversy in Latin America: a survey', *Latin American Research Review*, II (2) (1966).
Baer, W., *Industrialização e o Desenvolvimento Económico do Brasil* (Rio de Janeiro, 1975).
Baer, W., *The Brazilian Economy, Growth and Development* (New York, 1983).
Barrett. M. and M. McIntosh, *The Anti-Social Family* (London, 1982).
Barriguelli, J. C. 'Conflito e participação no meio rural (A greve da Usina Nova América – 1962)', *Anais do VIII Simpósio Nacional de Professores Universitarios de História* (Aracajú, September 1976).
Benevides, M. V. de Mesquita, *A UDN e o Udenismo, Ambeguedade do Liberalismo Brasileiro* (Rio de Janeiro, 1981).
Benevides, M. V. de Mesquita, *O Governo Kubitschek, Desenvolvimento Económico e Estabilidade Política* (Rio de Janeiro, 1976).
Beozzo Bassanezi, M. S., 'Fazenda Santa Gertrudis: uma abordagem quantitativa das relasões de trabalho em uma propriedade rural paulista', Doctoral Dissertation (Faculdade de Filosofia, Ciências e Letras de Rio Claro, 1973).
Bergson, J. and A. Candal, 'Industrialization: past success and future problems', in H. S. Ellis (ed), *The Economy of Brazil* (Berkeley, 1969).

Bericht des schweiz. Generalkonsuls in Rio de Janeiro an den schweiz. Bundesrath über die Auswanderung nach Brasilien', *Schweizerisches Bundesblatt*, X. Jahrgang II, 34 (24 July 1958).

Boito Jr, A., *O Golpe de 1954: A Burguesía Contra o Populismo* (São Paulo, 1982).

Bonardelli, E., *Lo stato di S. Paolo del Brasile e l'emigrazione italiana* (Turin, 1916).

Brandão Sobrinho, J., *Apreciação da situação agrícola, zootécnica, industrial e commercial em Riberão Preto* (São Paulo, 1903).

Brasil, A. P., 'O salário mínimo na lavoura paulista', *Legislação do Trabalho* (October 1941).

Brazil, *Anuário estatistico do café*. Coordenadoria de Estudos de Economía Cafeeira 11, (Rio de Janeiro, December 1977).

Brazil, Comissão de Desenvolvimento Industrial, *O Problema da Alimentação no Brazil*, Relatório Klein and Saks (Rio de Janeiro, 1954).

Breman, J. 'Between Accumulation and Immiseration: The Partiality of Fieldwork in Rural India', *The Journal of Peasant Studies*, 13 (1) (1985).

Bruneau, T. C. 'The Catholic church and the basic Christian communities: a case study from the Brazilian Amazon', Discussion Paper Series 7, Centre for Development-Area Studies (McGill University, Montreal, May 1983).

M. Buesco, *Evolução Económica do Brasil*, 2nd Edn. (Rio de Janeiro 1974).

Caio Prado Jr, 'Contribuição para a análise da questão agrária no Brasil', *Revista Brasiliense*, 28 (1960).

Caio Prado Jr, 'O estatuto do trabalhador rural', *Revista Brasiliense*, 47 (May–June 1963).

Caio Prado Jr, *A revolução brasileira* (São Paulo, 1966).

Caldeira Brant, V., 'Do colono ao bóia-fria: transformações na agricultura e constitução do mercado de trabalho na Alta Sorocabana de Assis', *Estudos CEBRAP*, 19 (São Paulo, January/March 1977).

Camargo, J. F., *Crescimento da população no estado de São Paulo e seus aspectos económicos* (São Paulo, 1952) II.

Campanhole, A., *Legislação do Trabalhador Rural e Estatuto da Terra* (São Paulo, 1966).

Cándido, A., *Os Parceiros do Rio Bonito* (Rio de Janeiro, 1964).

Cano, W., *Raízes da concentração industrial em São Paulo* (São Paulo, 1977).

Carone, E., *O Estado Novo (1937–1945)* (Rio de Janeiro, 1976).

Carone, E., *A Quarta República (1945–1964)* (São Paulo, 1980).

Carta Económica de Teresópolis, 1945, Conferencia das Classes Productoras do Brasil (Teresópolis, 1945).

Carvalho Filho, J. J. de, *Política Cafeeira do Brasil, seus Instrumentos, 1961–1971* (São Paulo, 1975).

Carvalho Franco, M. S. de, *Homens livres no ordem escravocrata* (São Paulo, 1969).

Carvalho de Moraes, J. P., *Relatório apresentado ao Ministério da Agricultura...* (Rio de Janeiro, 1870).

Castro, A., *7 ensaios sobre a economia brasileira* (Rio de Janeiro, 1971).

Cehelsky, M., 'The Policy Piuceof in Brazil: Land Reform, 1961–1969', Doctoral Dissertation (Columbia University, 1974),

Cesarino, A. F. Jr, 'Os colonos paulistas e sua situação em face du cstatnin da lavoura canavieira', *Trabalho e Seguro Social*, IV (1) (October 1943).

Cheung, S. N. S., *The Theory of Share Tenancy* (Chicago, 1969).

Coelho Prado, M. L., 'A Democracia Ilustrada', São Paulo, 1926–1934, Doctoral Dissertation (University of São Paulo, 1982).

Cohen, R., 'Resistance and Hidden Forms of Consciousness among African Workers', in H. Johnson and H. Bernstein (eds), *Third World Lives of Struggle* (London, 1982).

Coletti, S., 'Lo stato di S. Paolo e l'emigrazione italiana', *Bolletino dell' Emigrazione*, 14 (Part I) (1908).

Coletti, S., 'Lo stato di S. Paolo e l'emigrazione italiana', in Ministero degli Affari Esteri, *Emigrazione e colonie: raccolta di rapporti dei rr. agenti diplomatici e consolari*, III (Rome, 1908).

Comissão Mista Brasil/Estados Unidos para o Desenvolvimento Económico, *O Programa da Comissão Mista* (Rio de Janeiro, 1954).

Congresso Agrícola, *Coleção de documentos* (Rio de Janeiro, 1878).

4° Congresso Nacional do Café, *Anais* (Vitoria, 1971).

'Cooperativas para bóias-frias é criticada na AL', *Folha de São Paulo* (7 October 1977).

Corrêa, M., *Morte em Família* (Rio de Janeiro, 1983).

Correa de Oliveira, P., *Reforma Agrária–Questão de Conciência* (São Paulo, 1960).

Coulson, M., B. Magas, H. Wainwright, 'The housewife and her labour under capitalism – a critique', *New Left Review*, 89, (1975).

Couty, L., *Etude de biologie industrielle sur le café* (Rio de Janeiro, 1883).

Dafert, F., 'A falta de trabalhadores agrícolas em São Paulo, Agronómico de Campinos Instituto, *Relatório* (1892).

Dafert, F. W., *Ueber die gegenwaertige Lage des Kaffebaus in Brasilien* (Amsterdam, 1898).

Davatz, T., *Memórias de um colono no Brasil* (São Paulo, 1941).

Dean, W., 'Latifundia and Land Policy in Nineteenth-Century Brazil', *Hispanic American Historical Review*, LI (4) (1971).

Dean, W., *Rio Claro: a Brazilian Plantation System, 1820–1920* (Stanford University Press, 1976).

Deere, C. D. and A. de Janvry, 'Demographic and social differentiation among northern Peruvian peasants', *The Journal of Peasant Studies*, 8 (3) (1981).

Deere, C. D. and M. León, 'Producción campesina, proletarización y la división sexual del trabajo en la zona andina', in M. León (ed.), *Debate sobre la mujer en América Latina y el Caribe*, ACEP (Bogotá, 1982).

Delfim Netto, A., 'Foundations for the Analysis of Brazilian Coffee Problems', in C. M. Peláez (ed.) *Essays on Coffee and Economic Development*, Instituto Brasileiro do Café (Rio de Janeiro, 1973).

Delfim Netto, A., 'Sugestões para uma política cafeeira', in Instituto Brasileiro do Café, *Curso de Economia Cafeeira* (1962).

Delfim Netto, A. and C. A. de Andrade Pinto, 'The Brazilian coffee: twenty years of set-backs in the competition on the world market 1945/1965', in C. M. Peláez (ed.), *Essays on Coffee and Economic Development,* Instituto Brasileiro do Café (Rio de Janeiro, 1973).

Denis, P., *Brazil* (London, 1911).

D'Incão e Mello, M. C., *O Bóia-Fria: Acumulação e Miséria* (Petrópolis, 1975).

Dreifuss, R. A. *1964: A Conquista do Estado, Ação Política, Poder e Golpe de Classe* (Petrópolis, 1981).

Dumoulin, D. C., 'The rural labour movement in Brazil', The Land Tenure Center (Madison, Wisconsin, 1965) (mimeo).

Dutra de Oliveira, J. E. and M. H. Silva Dutra de Oliveira (eds), *Bóias-Frias–Uma realidade brasileira,* Academia de Ciências de São Paulo, Publicações ACIESP 30 (São Paulo, 1981).

Edel, M., *Food Supply and Inflation in Latin America* (New York, 1969).

Eisenberg, P. L., 'O homen esquecido: o trabalhador livre nacional no século XIX. Sugestões para uma pesquisa', *Anais do Museu Paulista,* XXVIII (1977–8).

Eisenberg, P. L., 'A mentalidade dos fazendeiros no Congresso Agrícola de 1878', in J. R. Amaral Lapa (ed.), *Modos de produção e realidade brasileira* (Petrópolis, 1980).

Ellis Jr, A., *A Evolução da Economía Paulista a suas Causas* (São Paulo, 1937).

Ellis, H. S. (ed.), *The Economy of Brazil* (Berkeley, 1969).

Emigrazione agricola al Brasile. Relazione della Commissione Italiana 1912 (Bologna, 1913).

'Estado e tendencias da agricultura paulista', *ASP* X (5 and 6) (May/June 1963).

Fausto, B., *A revolução de 1930* (São Paulo, 1970).

Federação da Agricultura do Estado de São Paulo, 'Exposição da Federação da Agricultura do Estado de São Paulo sobre os problemas da economía rural paulista', dirigida ao Exo. Sr General E. Geisel, Presidente da República (March 1974).

Feitosa Martins, A., 'Algums aspectos da inquietação trabalhista no campo', *Revista Brasiliense,* XL (1962).

Fernandez, P., 'Las maquiladoras y las mujeres en ciudad Juárez (México): paradojas de la industrialización bajo el capitalismo integral' in M. León (ed.), *Debate sobre la Mujer en América Latina y el Caribe,* ACEP (Bogatá, 1982).

Ferreira Albino de Oliveira, M. C., 'A Produção da vida, A mulher nas estrategias de sobrevivencia da familia trabalhadora na agricultura', Doctoral Dissertation (University of São Paulo, 1981).

Ferreira Ramos, F., *O café, contribuição para o estudo da crise* (São Paulo, 1902).

Font, M., 'Changing patterns in the social organization of the coffee sector in São Paulo, 1889–1930', paper presented at a seminar on 'Society and Politics in Export Economies', CEBRAP, São Paulo (11–13 March 1982).

Font, M., 'Planters and state: the pursuit of hegemony in São Paulo, Brazil, 1889–1930', Doctoral Dissertation (University of Michigan, 1983).

Font, M., 'Coffee planters and capitalist development in Brazil: an alternative scenario' (August 1984), (mimeo).

Foreman, S., 'Disunity and discontent: a study of peasant political movements in Brazil', in R. Chilcote (ed.), *Protest and Resistance in Angola and Brazil* (Berkeley, 1972).

Fraga, C. C., 'Resenha histórica do café no Brasil, *ASP* X (1) (January 1963).

Franzina, E., *Merica! Merica! Emigrazione e colonizazione nelle lettere dei contadini veneti in America Latina 1876–1902* (Milan, 1979).

Furtado, C., *The Economic Growth in Brazil* (Berkeley, 1963).

Gardiner, J., 'Women's domestic labour', *New Left Review*, 89 (1975).

Gomes, A., 'O problema da productividade em cafeicultura', *Revista Brasiliense*, 8 (November–December 1956).

Gomes Chiarelli, C. A., *Direito do Trabalho Rural Consolidado* (São Paulo, 1975).

Gomes da Silva, J., *A Reforma Agrária no Brasil* (Rio de Janeiro, 1971).

Gomez da Silva, J. and V. L. G. da Silva Rodrigues, ' "O bóia-fria": contradições de uma agricultura em tentativa de desenvolvimento', *Reforma Agrária*, V (9–10) (September/October 1975).

Goodman, D. and M. Redclift, 'The "bóia-fria": rural proletarianisation and urban marginality in Brazil', *International Journal of Urban and Regional Research*, I, (2) (1977).

Goodman, D. and M. Redclift, *From Peasant to Proletarian: Capitalist Development and Agrarian Transitions* (Oxford, 1981).

Gouvêa de Bulhões, O., *A Margem de um Relatório* (Rio de Janeiro, 1950).

Graziano da Silva, J. F., 'Progresso técnico e relações de trabalho na agricultura paulista', Doctoral Dissertation, (State University of Campinas, Campinas, 1980).

Graziano da Silva, J. and J. Garcia Gasques, 'Diagnóstico inicial do volante em São Paulo', in Universidade Estadual Paulista, Departamento de Economia Rural, Facultade de Ciências Agronómicas, *A Mão-de-obra volante na agricultura* (São Paulo, 1982).

Guarnieri, L., 'A experiencia brasileira de planejamento no setor cafeeiro', IFCH, Unicamp (Campinas, 1981) (mimeo).

Hagerman Johnson, A., 'The impact of market agriculture on family and household structure in nineteenth century Chile', *Hispanic American Historical Review* (1978).

Hall, M. M., 'The origins of mass immigration in Brazil, 1871–1914', Doctoral Dissertation (Colombia University, 1969).

Hall M. M., 'Emigrazione italiana a San Paolo tra 1880 e 1920', *Quaderni Storici*, 25 (1974).

Harris, O., 'Households as natural units', in K. Young, C. Wolkowitz and R. McCullagh (eds), *Of Marriage and the Market: Women's Subordination in International Perspective* (London, 1981).

Hartmann, H. I., 'Capitalism, patriarchy and job segregation by sex', *Signs*, 1 (3) (part 2) (1976).

Hartmann, H. I., 'The family as the locus of gender, class and political struggle: the example of housework', *Signs*, 6 (3) (1981).

Hartmann, H. I. and A. R. Markusen, 'Contemporary marxist theory and practice, a feminist critique', *The Review of Radical Political Economics*, 12 (2) (1980).

Haupt, H., *Relatório*, in Sociedade Internacional de Imigração, I (1867).

Heusser, C., *Die Schweizer auf den Kolonien in St. Paulo in Brasilien* (Zurich, 1857).

Hewitt, G., 'Brazil: The Peasant Movement in Pernambuco', in H. A. Landsberger (ed.), *Latin American Peasant Movements* (Cornell, 1969).

Hickman, E. 'Optimal trade policy for a country with market power: the case of Brazil's coffee', Doctoral Dissertation. (University of Illinois, Urbana, 1980).

Himmelweit, S. and S. Mohun, 'Domestic labour and capital', *Cambridge Journal of Economics*, 1 (1977).

Holloway, T. H., 'Migration and Mobility: Immigrants as Labourers and Landowners in the Coffee Zone of São Paulo, Brazil,1886–1934', Doctoral Dissertation (University of Wisconsin, 1974).

Holloway, T. H. *The Brazilian Coffee Valorisation of 1906 – Regional Politics and Economic Dependence* (Wisconsin, 1975).

Holloway, T. H., 'The coffee colono in São Paulo, Brazil: migration and mobility, 1880–1930', in K. Duncan and I. Rutledge (eds), *Land and Labour in Latin America* (Cambridge University Press, 1977).

Holloway, T. H. *Immigrants on the Land: Coffee and Society in São Paulo*, 1886–1934 (Chapel Hill, 1980).

Homen de Melo, F. B., 'A política económica e o setor agrícola no período pós-guerra', *Revista Brasileira de Economía*, 33 (1) (January/March 1959).

Homen de Melo, F. B., *O problema alimentar no Brasil* (Rio de Janeiro, 1983).

Humphries, J., 'Class struggle and the persistence of the working-class family', *Cambridge Journal of Economics*, 1 (3) (1977).

Hyman, R. and I. Brough, *Social Values and Industrial Relations: A Study of Fairness and Inequality* (Oxford, 1975).

Ianni, O. 'A classe operária vai ao campo', *Cadernos CEBRAP, 24*, (São Paulo, 1976).

Jaquaribe Filho, Domingos, *Algumas palavras sobre a emigração* (São Paulo, 1877).

Joint Brazil/United States Economic Development Commission, *The Development of Brazil*, Report by the Joint Brazil/United States Economic Development Commission (1954).

Kaerger, K., *Brasilianische Wirtschaftsbilder, Erlebnisse und Forschungen* (Berlin, 1892).

Kageyama, A. A., 'Crise e estrutura agrária na agricultura paulista na década de 30', Master's Dissertation, Escola Superior de Agricultura 'Luiz de Queiroz' (University of São Paulo, 1979).

Kageyama, A. A. *et al.*, 'As transformações na estrutura agrária paulista, 1818–1976, IFCH, Unicamp (Campinas, 1981) (mimeo).

Kageyama, A. A. *et al.*, 'Diferenciación campesina y cambio tecnológico: el caso de los productores de frijol en São Paulo', IFCH, Unicamp (Campinas, 1982) (mimeo).

Kageyama, A. A. and J. Graziano da Silva, 'El desempeño de la agricultura brasileña en los años setenta', *Economía de América Latina,* 9 (1982),

Kahil, R., *Inflation and Economic Development in Brazil,* 1946–1963 (Oxford, 1973).

Karrer, L., *Das schweizerische Auswanderungswesen und die Revision und Vollziehung des Bundesgesetz über den Geschäftsbetrieb von Auswanderungsagenturen* (Berne, 1886).

Keeler, E. P., 'Cotton versus Coffee in Brazil', *Foreign Crops and Markets,* US Dept. of Agriculture, Foreign Agricultural Service Division, 31 (1935).

Kerst, S. G., *Über brasilianische Zustände der Gegenwart, mit Bezug auf die deutsche Auswanderung nach Brasilien und das System der brasilianischen Pflanzer, den Mangel an afrikanischen Sklaven durch deutsche Proletarier zu ersetzen* (Berlin, 1853).

Kuznesof, E. A., 'Household composition and headship was related to changes in mode of production: São Paulo 1765 to 1836', *Comparative Studies in Society and History* (1980).

Lacerda, C. F. de, *A crise da lavoura. Estudo dos causas da crise do café e dos meios de combatela* (São Paulo, 1903).

Lacerda, C. F. de, *Estudo da Meiação, Parceria, etc. e das suas Vantagens* (São Paulo, 1905).

Lafer, C., 'The planning process and the political system in Brazil: a study of Kubitschek's target plan, 1956–1961', Doctoral Dissertation (Cornell University, 1970).

Laliére, A., *Le café dans l'Etat de Saint Paul, Brésil,* (Paris, 1909).

Lamounier, B. (ed.), *Voto de Desconfiança, Eleições e Mundança Política no Brasil, 1970–1979* (Petrópolis, 1980).

Lázaro Gonçalves, F. P., *Relatório apresentado á Associação Promotora de Imigração em Minas* (Juiz de Fora, 1888).

Leff, N. H., *Economic Policy-Making and Development in Brazil 1947–1964* (New York, 1968).

LeGrand, C., *Frontier Expansion and Peasant Protest in Colombia, 1830–1936* (University of New Mexico Press, 1986).

Levi, D. E., *A Família Prado* (São Paulo, 1977).

Lisboa Bacha, E., *Os Mitos de uma década* (Rio de Janeiro, 1976).

Lopes, B., 'Comércio de café através do porto de Santos (1870–1974)', in E. Carone (org.), *O Café,* Anais do II Congresso de Historia de São Paulo (São Paulo, 1975).

Loureiro, M. R. G., *Capitalismo e Parceria* (Rio de Janeiro, 1977).

Love, J. L., *São Paulo in the Brazilian Federation, 1889–1937* (Stanford University Press, 1980).

McCreery W. G. and J. L. Bynum, *The Coffee Industry in Brazil,* US Dept. of Commerce, Bureau of Foreign and Domestic Commerce, Trade Promotion Series, 92 (Washington, 1930).

McFarquhar, A. M., and G. B. Aneury Evans, *Employment Creation in Primary Production in Less Developed Countries,* Development Centre Studies, Employment Series, 6, OECD (Paris, 1972).

Machado Nunes, S., 'Colónias na provincia de S. Paulo', in Brazil, Ministério do Império, *Relatório* (1860).

Malan, P., 'Foreign exchange constrained growth in a semi-industrialised economy: aspects of the Brazilian experience (1946–1976)', Doctoral Dissertation (University of California, 1977).

Malan, P. *et al., Politica económica externa e industrialização no Brasil (1939–1952)* (Rio de Janeiro, 1977).

Maistrello, G., 'Fazendas de café – costumes (São Paulo)', in A. Ramos, O *café no Brasile no estrangeiro* (Rio de Janeiro, 1923).

Maranhão, R., L. Roncari and A. Mendes Jr, 'O direito de voto no Brasil', *Movimento*, 33 (16 February 1976).

Marchesini, G. B., *Il Brasile e le sue colonie agricole* (Rome, 1877).

Marshall, A., *Principles of Economics* (London, various edns).

Martin, J. and C. Roberts, *Women and Employment: A Lifetime Perspective*, HMSO (London, 1984).

Martinez-Alier, J., 'Peasants and labourers in Southern Spain, Cuba, and highland Peru', *The Journal of Peasant Studies,*1 (2) (1974).

Martins, T., 'Proletariado e inquietação rural', *Revista Brasiliense*, XLII (1962).

Maurette, F., *Some Social Aspects of Present and Future Economic Development in Brazil*, ILO, Studies and Reports, Series B, 25 (Geneva 1937).

Mauro, F., *História do Brasil* (São Paulo, 1974).

Medeiros, M. R., ' O FGTS no meio rural', *Movimento* 42 (April 1976).

Medina, C. A. de, 'Relatório: Sertãozinho e Jardinópolis – São Paulo' (1962) (mimeo).

Merrick, T. W. and D. H. Graham, *Population and Economic Development in Brazil, 1800 to the Present* (Baltimore, 1979).

Miller Paiva, R. and R. Araújo Dias, 'Recente evolução da agricultura em São Paulo, *ASP* VII (1) (January 1960).

Miller Paiva, R., S. Schattan and C. F. Trench de Freitas, *Setor Agrícola do Brasil* (São Paulo, 1976).

Milliet, S., *Roteiro do Café* (São Paulo, 1939).

Monbeig, P., *Pionniers et Planteurs a S. Paulo* (Paris, 1952).

Monbeig, P., *Novos estudos de geografia humana no Brasil* (São Paulo, 1957).

Moore, J. B., Parliamentary Papers, House of Commons and House of Lords, Select Committee on the Slave Trade, 1847–48, XXII, pp. 322, 436.

Moraes, C., 'Peasant leagues in Brazil', in R. Stavenhagen (ed.), *Agrarian and Peasant Movements in Latin America* (New York, 1970).

Morais Filho F. de *et al., Trabalhadores, sindicatos e política* (São Paulo, 1980).

Mosconi, F., 'Le classe sociali nel Brasile e le loro funzioni' *La Riforma Sociale*, VII (1897).

Natsch, R. A., *Die Haltung eidgenössischer und kantonaler Behörden in der Auswanderungsfrage, 1803–1874* (Zürich, 1966).

Niemeyer, Sir Otto E., 'Report submitted to the Brazilian Government' (London, 1931).

Normano, J. F., *Brazil: A Study of Economic Types* (University of North Carolina Press, 1935).

'O Brasil – a solução do governo para o drama dos bóias-frias', *Movimento* (7 June 1976).

Oliveira, F. de, 'Economía brasileira: crítica á razão dualista', *Estudos CEBRAP*, 2 (1972).

Oliveira Adams, P. de, 'Café e cambio', *RSRB* (November 1952).

Ozorio de Almeida, A. L., 'Parceria e tamanho da familia no Nordeste brasileiro', *Pesquisa e Planejamento Económico*, 7: 2 (1977).

Panagides, P., 'Erradicação do café e diversificação da agricultura brasileira', *Revista Brasileira de Economia* 23 (1) (January/March 1969).

Papaterra Limongi, J., 'O trabalhador nacional', *Boletim do Departamento do Trabalho*, 5 (20) (1916).

Papaterra Limongi, J., 'O trabalho agrícola no Brasil', *Boletim do Departamento Estadual do Trabalho*. VI (24) (1917).

Passos Guimarães, A., *Quatro séculos de latifúndio* (São Paulo, 1964).

Peláez, C. M., 'The Inter-American coffee agreement and Brazilian coffee during World War II', in C. M. Peláez (ed.), *Essays on Coffee and Economic Development*, Instituto Brasileiro do Café (Rio de Janeiro, 1973).

Peláez, C. M., 'An economic analysis of the Brazilian Coffee Support Programme: theory, policy and measurement, in C. M. Peláez (ed.), *Essays on Coffee and Economic Development*, Instituto Brasileiro do Café (Rio de Janeiro, 1973).

Peláez, C. M. (ed.), *Essays on Coffee and Economic Development*, Instituto Brasileiro do Café (Rio de Janeiro, 1973).

Pinheiro, P. S. and M. M. Hall (eds), *A Classe Operária no Brasil: documentos* (São Paulo, 1981) II.

Pires do rio Caldeira, T., 'Para que serve o voto?' (As eleições e o cotidiano na periferia de São Paulo) in B. Lamounier (ed.), *Voto de Desconfiança, Eleições e Mudança Política no Brasil, 1970–1979* (Petrópolis, 1980).

Pires do Rio Caldeira, T., *A Política dos Outros* (São Paulo, 1984).

Prado, P., 'O martyrio do café' in P. Prado, *Paulística, História de São Paulo* (Rio de Janeiro, 1934).

Prebisch, R. *The Economic Development of Latin America and its Principal Problems* (New York, 1949).

Price, R. E., 'Rural unionisation in Brazil', The Land Tenure Center (Madison, Wisconsin, 1964) (mimeo).

Queda, O., A. A. Kageyama and T. F. Graziano da Silva, *Evolução recente das culturas de arroz e feijão no Brasil* (Brasilia, 1979).

Queiroz Teles, A. de, 'La culture du caféier à São Paulo, Brésil', *L'Economiste Français*, VI (49) (7 December 1878).

Rainho, L. F., *Os Peões do Grande ABC* (Petrópolis, 1980).

Ramos, A., *O café no Brasil e no estrangeiro* (Rio de Janeiro, 1923).

Reid, J. D. Jr, 'Sharecropping as an Understandable Market Response: the Post-Bellum South', *Journal of Economic History*, 33 (1973).

'Relação das colónias existentes na provincia de São Paulo no ano de 1855', 8 March 1856, Archive of the Instituto Histórico e Geográfico Brasileiro (Rio de Janeiro, lata 71/7).

Rocha, O., *Manual Prático do Trabalho Rural* (São Paulo, 1969).

Rocha Viana, C. da, *Reformas de base e a política Nacionalista de Desenvolvimento* (Rio de Janeiro, 1980).

Roldán, M., 'Subordinación genérica y proletarización rural: un estudio de caso en el Noroeste de México', in M. Leon (ed.), *Debate sobre la mujer en América Latina y el Caribe*, ACEP (Bogotá, 1982).

Romão, D. A., 'Do auto-consumo a produção capitalista: a evolução da produção de feijao no Estado de São Paulo', Doctoral Dissertation (State University of Campinas, 1981).

Rossi, A., 'Condizioni dei coloni italiani nello stato di San Paolo', *Bollettino dell'Emigrazione*, 7 (1902).

Rowe, J. W. F., *Brazilian Coffee*, Royal Economic Society Memorandum, 35 (London 1932).

Rowe, J. W. F., *The World's Coffee: A Study of the Economics and Politics of the Coffee Industries of Certain Countries and of the International Problem* (London, 1963).

Rozwadowski, A. L., 'São Paulo', in *Emigrazione e colonie; raccolta di rapporti dei rr. agenti diplomatici e consolari* (Rome, 1893).

Saboia, J. C., 'De senhores a trocadores de cebola', Master's Dissertation (State University of Campinas, 1978).

Saint, W. S., 'The wages of modernization: a review of the literature on temporary labour arrangements in Brazilian agriculture', *Latin American Research Review*, 3 (1981).

Sallum Jr, B., *Capitalismo e Cafeicultura, Oeste Paulista: 1888-1930* (São Paulo, 1982).

Sampaio, A., *Contrato de Trabalho Rural, Direitos e Obrigações do Trabalhador Rural em Face da CLT e da Lei No. 5.889 de 1973* (São Paulo, 1974).

São Paulo, Secretaria da Agricultura, *Inquérito Agrícola sobre o Estado da Lavoura Cafeeira no Estado de S. Paulo* (São Paulo, 1904).

Schmitter, P., *Interest Conflict and Political Change in Brazil* (Stanford, 1971).

Schuh, G. E., *The Agricultural Development of Brazil* (New York, 1970).

Schuh, E. G. and A. Veiga, 'A política de importação de insumos agrícolas no Brasil, 1948-1967', *ASP*, XXIII (1) (1976).

Seccomb, W., 'Domestic labour – a reply to critics', *New Left Review*, 94 (1975).

Segadas Vianna, de J., *O Estatuto do Trabalhador Rural e sua Aplicação* (Rio de Janeiro, 1965).

Sen, G., 'The sexual division of labour and the subordination of women', *The Review of Radical Political Economics*, 12 (2) (1980).

Sendin, P. V., 'Elaboração de um índice de salários rurais para o Estado de São Paulo', *ASP*, XIV (II) (1972).

Sider, G. M., *Culture and Class in Anthropology and History – A Newfoundland Illustration* (Cambridge University Press, 1986).

Sigaud, L., 'A idealização do passado numa área de plantation', *Contrapunto*, II (2) (November 1977).

Sigaud, L., *Os clandestinos e os Direitos, Estudo sobre Trabalhadores de Cana-de-açucar de Pernambuco* (São Paulo, 1979).

Silva, A. M. da, 'Família e trabalho na cafeicultura', *Cadernos de Pesquisa*, 37 (São Paulo, 1981).

Silva, G. L. S. P. da, 'Reflexões sobre o papel da agricultura no Brasil', *ASP*, XXXIX (I and II) (1982).

Silva, S., *Expansão cafeeira e origens da indústria no Brasil* (São Paulo, 1976).

Silva, S., 'Agricultura e capitalismo no Brasil', *Contexto*, 1 (1976).

Singer, P., 'Os novos nómades', *Movimento*, 18 (1975).

Skidmore, T., *Brasil: de Getúlio a Castelo (1930–1964)* (Rio de Janeiro, 1969).

Skidmore, T. E., 'Politics and economic policy in authoritarian Brazil' (1 July 1971) (mimeo).

Skidmore, T., *Black over White, Race and Nationality in Brazilian Thought* (Oxford University Press, 1974).

Slenes, R. W., 'The demography and economics of Brazilian slavery: 1850–1888', Doctoral Dissertation (Stanford University, 1975).

Smith, G. W., 'Brazilian agricultural policy, 1950–1967', in H. S. Ellis (ed.), *The Economy of Brazil* (Berkeley, 1969).

Soares D'Araújo, M. C., *O Segundo Governo Vargas: 1951–1954: Democracia, Partidos e Crise Política* (Rio de Janeiro, 1982).

Sola, L., 'The political and ideological constraints to economic management in Brazil, 1945–1963', Doctoral Dissertation (Oxford University, 1982).

Sori, E., *L'emigrazione italiana dall' unitá alla seconda guerra mondiale* (Bologna, 1979).

Souza Martins, J. de, *A imigração e a crise do Brasil agrário* (São Paulo, 1973).

Souza Martins, J. de, 'As relações de classe e a produção ideológica da noção do trabalho', *Contexto*, 5 (1978).

Souza Martins, J. de, *O cativeiro da terra* (São Paulo, 1979).

Spindel, C. R., *Homens e máquinas na transição de uma economia cafeeira*, (Rio de Janeiro, 1980).

Stolcke, V., 'Women's labours: the naturalization of social inequality and women's subordination', in K. Young, C. Wolkowitz and R. McCullagh (eds), *Of Marriage and the Market: Women's Subordination in International Perspective* (London, 1981).

Stone, L., 'Interpersonal violence in English society 1300–1980', *Past and Present*, 101 (November 1983).

Straten-Ponthoz, Le Comte Auguste von der, *Le budget du Brésil* (Paris, 1854).

Taunay, A. de E. Z., *Pequena História do Café no Brasil*, Departamento Nacional do Café (Rio de Janeiro, 1945).

Thomazini Ettori, O. J., 'Mão-de-obra na agricultura de São Paulo', *ASP* VIII (12) (December 1961).

'Der Traum des weissen Sklaven – Brief eines italienischen Emigranten aus Brasilien', *Freibeuter*, 30 (1987).

Tschudi, J. J. von, *Viagem às Provincias de Rio de Janeiro e São Paulo* (São Paulo, 1953).

Turenne, P., 'L'immigration et la colonisation au Brésil', *Revue Britannique* (February 1879).

UN, FAO, *Coffee in Latin America, Productivity Problems and Future Prospects: II, Brazil, São Paulo* ((1) The state and prospects of production) (Mexico, 1960).

UN, FAO, *Coffee in Latin America, Productivity Problems and Future Prospects, II, Brazil, São Paulo* ((2) A. Case study of 33 coffee farms, B. Analysis of the functions of production) (Mexico, 1960).

Universidade Estadual Paulista, Departamento de Economía Rural, Facultade de Ciências Agronómicas, *A Mão-de-Obra Volante na Agricultura* (São Paulo,1982).

Valdetaro, M. J., 'Colónias de S. Paulo', in *Brazil, Relatório da Repartição Geral das Terras Públicas apresentado em 31 de março de 1858* (Rio de Janeiro, 1858).

Van Delden Laerne, C., *Brazil and Java: Report on Coffee Culture* (London, 1885).

Vangelista, C., *Le Braccia per la Fazenda, Immigranti e 'caipiras' nella formazione del mercato del lavoro paulista (1850–1930)* (Milan, 1982).

Vargas, G., *O Governo Trabalhista do Brasil* (Rio de Janeiro, 1954) 5 vols.

Vassimon, S. G., 'Ruptura da mentalidade patriarcal', *Coopercotia* (October 1968).

Vassimon, S. G., 'Estudo preliminar sobre o problema da mão-de-obra volante na agricultura do Estado de São Paulo' (São Paulo: CERU/ University of São Paulo, 1969) (mimeo).

Vergueiro, J., *Memorial acerca de colonização e cultivo de café* (Campinas, 1874).

Vilela, A. V. and W. Suzigan, *Política do Governo e Crescimento da Economía Brasileira, 1889–1945* (Rio de Janeiro, 1973).

Viotti da Costa, E., *Da senzala à colónia* (São Paulo, 1966).

Viotti da Costa, E., 'Política de terras no Brasil e nos Estados Unidos', in *Da Monarquia à República: momentos decisivos*, (São Paulo, 1977).

Viotti da Costa, E., 'Colónias de parceria na lavoura de café: primeiras experiencias', in *Da Monarquia à República: momentos decisivos* (São Paulo, 1977).

Wells, J. R. 'Distribution of earnings, growth and the structure of demand in Brazil during the 1960s', *World Development*, 2 (1) (1974).

Whitehead, A., ' "I'm hungry mum": the politics of domestic budgeting', in K. Young, C. Wolkowitz and R. McCullagh (eds), *Of Marriage and the Market: Women's Subordination in International Perspective* (London, 1981).

Wilkie, M. E., 'Report on rural syndicates in Pernambuco', Centro Latinoamericano de Pesquisas em Ciências Sociais (Rio de Janeiro, 1964) (mimeo).

Witter, J. S., 'Um estabelecimento agrícola no Estado de São Paulo nos meados do século XIX', *Revista de História*, 98 (1974).

Young, K., 'Formas de apropiación y la división sexual del trabajo: un estudio de caso de Oaxaca, México', in M. León (ed.), *Debate sobre la Mujer en América Latina y el Caribe*, ACEP (Bogotá, 1982).

Zettiry, A., de, 'I coloni italiani dello stato di S. Paolo', *La Rassegna Nationale*, LXX (1893).

Zibetti, D. W., *Legislação Agrária Brasileira* (São Paulo, 1968).

Index